In Mixed Company

Julia Roberts

In Mixed Company
Taverns and Public Life in
Upper Canada

UBCPress · Vancouver · Toronto

16 15 14 13 12 11 10 09   5 4 3 2 1

Printed in Canada with vegetable-based inks on FSC-certified ancient-forest-free paper (100% post-consumer recycled) that is processed chlorine- and acid-free.

Library and Archives Canada Cataloguing in Publication

Roberts, Julia, 1962-
  In mixed company : taverns and public life in Upper Canada / by Julia Roberts.

Includes bibliographical references and index.
ISBN 978-0-7748-1575-8 (bound)
ISBN 978-0-7748-1576-5 (pbk.)
ISBN 978-0-7748-1577-2 (e-book)

  1. Taverns (Inns) – Ontario – History. 2. Taverns (Inns) – Social aspects – Ontario – History. 3. Ontario – Social life and customs. I. Title.

TX950.59.C3R62 2009   647.94'09713   C2008-903335-3

Canadä

UBC Press gratefully acknowledges the financial support for our publishing program of the Government of Canada through the Book Publishing Industry Development Program (BPIDP), and of the Canada Council for the Arts, and the British Columbia Arts Council.

This book has been published with the help of a grant from the Canadian Federation for the Humanities and Social Sciences, through the Aid to Scholarly Publications Programme, using funds provided by the Social Sciences and Humanities Research Council of Canada.

Printed and bound in Canada by Friesens
Set in Stone by Artegraphica Design Co. Ltd.
Copy editor: Lesley Erickson
Proofreader: Stephanie VanderMeulen
Indexer: Noeline Bridge

UBC Press
The University of British Columbia
2029 West Mall
Vancouver, BC V6T 1Z2
604-822-5959 / Fax: 604-822-6083
www.ubcpress.ca

In memory of my brother,
David K. Roberts, 1964-2003
– because he liked a glass or two in company

Contents

Illustrations

Preface

The great detective Sherlock Holmes once accused his chronicler, Dr. Watson, of degrading "what should have been a course of lectures into a series of tales."[1] In this book I am most certainly guilty of the same crime. For it is built on stories – as told by tavern-goers, tavern-keepers, and tavern regulators – in which they reflect on taverns as particular types of public spaces and what everyday public life inside taverns meant to them as members of the mixed populace of early Canada. If, in the pages that follow, my penchant for stories and their tellers has come to resemble historical scholarship, this transformation is the result of intellectual, personal, and practical support from my mentors, colleagues, and friends. At the University of Toronto, Allan Greer supervised this work in its doctoral phase and continues to remain generously supportive. Ian Radforth, Jane Abray, and Sylvia Van Kirk each provided lasting contributions as did my fellow doctoral candidates, especially Jeff McNairn, Jane Harrison, Adam Crerar, and Marlene Epp. Two other institutional affiliations helped in the writing of this book. At Laurier Brantford, my experience of learning how to teach colonial history in a way that might appeal to the interdisciplinary, Contemporary Studies students who fill large classrooms has helped me shape and clarify the language in every chapter. In addition, my favourite sentence in this book (the stats sentence in Chapter 4) came from my psychologist colleague and buddy across the hall there – Judy Eaton. Now that I feel at home in the history department at the University of Waterloo and have gained a sense of place there, that too has informed the writing of this book. My thanks go to my new colleagues for their warm welcome. In addition to those people named above, several others have read various versions of various chapters: Craig Heron, Thomas Hueglin, Wendy Mitchinson, and, of course, the anonymous peer reviewers throughout the revision process. I sincerely appreciate their time.

Thanks are also due to Richard Simeon, who first introduced me to the people at UBC Press. Melissa Pitts has done everything a first-time author could hope for and gave critical help in shaping the final manuscript. Lesley Erickson did a wonderful job with my prose, and my debts to archivists are abundantly clear in the notes. Thanks also to Ann Macklem for overseeing the production process in such a smooth and author-friendly way. I am particularly grateful to the host of small town, local History Society members who responded to my queries in the early stages. Some of their clues and contributions were invaluable. I benefited enormously from the knowledge and professionalism of archivists in the following places: the Archives of Ontario, the Baldwin Room at the Toronto Reference Library, the Chatham-Kent Museum Archives, the Lambton County Archives, the McMaster University Archives, Library and Archives Canada, the Niagara Historical Society and Museum, the Stratford-Perth County Archives, the Thomas Fischer Rare Book Room, University of Toronto, the United Church Archives, and the Upper Canada Village Archives. Thanks too, to the friends and neighbours who asked the questions that friends and neighbours ask and thus prompted me to explain why a book on colonial taverns matters: the Gruber-Kellys, the Wang-Scheeles, the Winburns and siblings, Rosemary Arthurs (the local potter), Karen Rosenthal (who has since left us but once asked a question that made me rethink how historians do what they do), and Lisa Morgan.

And then there's my family: I thank my husband, Thomas Hueglin, for being just that and being good at it and also the collection of acquired kids that we have between us: grown-up Hannah with her sister Amanda; the new ex-steps; Jacob, our 'little mistake,' who at fourteen is hardly little anymore; and, of course, lovely Christian and her own small guys, Malachi and Khalil. My mum is permanently great, incredibly supportive, and likes pubs too. My father and his wife Dhora have long recognized the importance of an academic career to me. My sister, Bronwen, even mailed me boxes and boxes of primary documents that I left at home in Canada and thought I wouldn't need during a year in Germany. Finally, this book is dedicated to my brother who died in a motorcycle crash while I was revising it from a dissertation into its current form. Though David never read any of this book, he did wake me up once by phoning at nearly two in the morning to settle a bet at a loud drinking party: "What year did Newfoundland enter Confederation?" he asked. I answered his question, and his friends figured that with a PhD and all, I could be right. So he won the bet, but for what stakes I'll never know.

In Mixed Company

Introduction

Hundreds of tavern-goers and tavern-keepers people the pages of this book, shaping its analysis and suggesting its lines of enquiry. Their words invite us inside and encourage us to see for ourselves how Upper Canada's different peoples (men and women, Natives and newcomers, whites and non-whites, privileged and non-privileged, and mixtures in between) belonged in unequal and not always predictable ways to public life itself. Some American Quakers tell us how, in 1793, they "had the company of a young Shawnese chief" at Dolsen's tavern on the Thames River. "He ... had at least one thousand silver brooches stuck on a new silk hunting shirt. He behaved at table with great gentility." In 1794 three labourers "amused themselves with drinking in good fellowship" at Gouin's tavern in British-occupied Detroit. Around 1805, near Ancaster, missionary William Case saw "large companies of neighbours ... drinking, dancing &c ... When I have passed by these haunts & seen their wicked practices, I have felt the spirit of the Lord to rest on me to warn the Tavern keeper against such conduct." In 1808 the justices in Quarter Sessions in York "read the petition of Magdalen Belcour Widow, praying for leave to continue to hold under the tavern license granted her late husband ... Granted." Along the St. Lawrence in 1817, printer Charles Fothergill reached a tavern "filled with people who had been attending a funeral ... [and] offended some of them because I would not drink brandy before my dinner with them." Thomas D. Sanford of Cramahe, in 1819, "informs his friends and the public that he still keeps a public house ... where gentlemen and ladies may find good entertainment." George Brooks called into Patrick Nolan's tavern, near Gananoque, in 1820 to buy a grinding stone from the attached king's store and to get the tavern-keeper to fill "a small jug of spirits and g[i]ve it to me ... for the nourishment of the men that was to carry the stone." In 1834 "a coloured man stopped at Mr Schaeffer's tavern ... with another coloured man, his assistant," and got breakfast. "Spent an hour at the North American Hotel with William Elliot and Mr McDonnell & others.

Drank rather too freely," wrote John Prince, MPP, in Sandwich in 1837. One evening in Kingston in 1843 a government clerk "walked into town and drank gin and talked of theatricals with Mrs Armour at Belanger's" saloon. "And with reference to Leonard Long," wrote the tavern licence inspector in Uxbridge in 1852, "we believe himself & wife well and suitably adapted to keeping an inn."[1]

Taken together the words of colonial tavern-goers, tavern-keepers, and tavern inspectors run the gamut of themes addressed in *In Mixed Company*. They raise issues of racialized identity in a colonialist language of "race" that presumes a white prerogative to label and to judge. They address issues of class and class identity in a pre-industrial language that favoured occupational and cultural designations (such as "labourers" and "ladies") to signify differences in economic access. They speak to issues of gender, and they position women within public life in the context of a social structure that granted men and boys unquestioned, albeit frequently subverted, precedence there over women and girls. They emphasize the rituals and routine of alcohol consumption, its power to forge social bonds and its association with nourishment. One early voice contests the as yet rarely challenged social and cultural role of alcohol. Others nod to matters of regulation in an era that preceded the growth of the state and the ideal of self-discipline. My questions, then, about contemporary concerns such as issues of cultural membership and belonging mesh well with the preoccupations of tavern-goers and tavern-keepers in their own time. They thought about the contours of public interaction and the not unproblematic rituals that structured it in the colony's public houses, and they expressed their ideas in the language and parameters available.

Indeed, the very definition of a tavern is theirs. A tavern in the colonial context was a building that was open to the public (and, for travellers, open at all hours), licensed to sell spirituous and fermented liquor by small measure (by the glass, gill, half-pint, or pint), and had the facilities to provide food, lodging, and stabling. The tavern was almost always a family home. Colonists distinguished this understanding of the tavern from three other public drinking options: beer-houses, which emerged briefly in the nineteenth century and were licensed to sell fermented but not spirituous liquor; shops that were licensed to sell liquor by large measure (a quart or more) and sometimes purveyed it, illegally, by the glass; and unlicensed, illegal drinking houses. Some colonists indeed patronized unlicensed houses, but they did not call them taverns. Darius Doty, for instance, was explicit on the point. In his own words, in 1830 he frequented "Mr Carroll's who keeps liquor – not a tavern," somewhere in the Long Woods between London and Chatham. Taverns, in contrast, were known by the words above their doors: "licensed to sell wine and other spirituous liquors."[2]

Everybody in Upper Canadian society, even those quoted in government records, used the words *tavern, inn, public house,* and, later, *hotel* interchangeably. When a keeper in Stratford crafted an advertisement in 1855, for example, he settled on this formulation: "As there is no greater comfort than after the day's journey to arrive at a good place of rest; a house of entertainment, under the varied names of hotel, inn, and tavern fitted up ... with an attentive landlord may be certain of being a house of call."[3]

Taverns stood every six to eight miles along country roads, on prominent town corners, and among houses and shops on smaller streets. They made more of a mark on the landscape than did schools, churches, or government buildings, and they were the most accessible colonial public buildings. Licensing rules directed tavern-keepers to "at all times provide proper attendance" for travellers. The round-the-clock, seven-days-a-week right of entry they enjoyed created the assumption that taverns never closed. On Sundays, communities tolerated peaceful sociability within taverns, despite regulations against it. Barrooms closed by 10 o'clock at night, but people expected to be admitted at all hours and unhesitatingly roused tavern-keepers from their beds. There was no formal opening time. Two men arrived at Linfoot's tavern outside Toronto at "a little after 4 o'clock a.m. ... each got a glass of whiskey." Because the tavern-keeper got up early, his house was open.[4]

Because it is about the taverns of Upper Canada, this book concerns informal, or everyday, public life. It begins with a history of real spaces and objects – the tavern buildings and outbuildings, furniture, linens, and larders – that were the material settings of public life and determined its possibilities and limitations. The daily balance negotiated between the needs of tavern-keeping households and the realities of the space as a public one also shaped taverns. The simultaneity of household life and public life meant that each shaped the other in particular ways. This reveals much about taverns, to be sure. It also lets us see the relationship between "the private" and "the public" in an early colonial, pre-industrial, and pre-Victorian period and to distinguish each from the more familiar patterns of the late nineteenth century. And the uniqueness of tavern space as public space is apparent. Tracing how the aficionados of tavern culture worked to balance the centrality of drink, and drink's ritualized consumption, with their concerns for personal success, colonial development, and peaceful community relations takes us into barrooms, with their rituals, dances, and storytelling. We encounter the odd drunk, and the odd scuffle, but find groups of companions (a tavern company) more commonly characterized by good order. It was within tavern companies that the promises of social cohesion made by mutual association over drink were either kept or broken and where the terms of access to public space and public life had to be negotiated among people made unequal by what racialized identity, class status, and gender meant in a colonial context.

Because it focuses on taverns as one way of writing about wider social and cultural patterns, *In Mixed Company* revises the historiography of taverns in early Canada by bringing their history more in line with international scholarship. Once the province of amateur enthusiasts, tavern studies have recently undergone a renaissance among academic historians in western Europe, the United States, and, most recently, Canada. The new historians of the tavern examine what public houses looked like, how rural taverns differed from urban taverns, how taverns worked as the pre-eminent communication node in predominantly oral societies, and how the rituals of drink enacted among patrons bound them together and set them apart.[5]

In Mixed Company is not the first book to be written on the subject in Canada. Edwin C. Guillet published his multivolume *Pioneer Inns and Taverns,* an absorbing, well-researched treasury of tales and facts, in the 1950s. When novelist and literary critic Robertson Davies reviewed the work for *Saturday Night* magazine, he commented that the subject led author and reader "deep into the society of our country as it was."[6] And he was right. But today, because historians, like other scholars, are interested in how different people negotiated their membership in the wider public, this book takes the study of taverns in new directions. It presents taverns primarily as public spaces and asks questions about who frequented them (and who did not): How did tavern-goers interact with the space and others in it? What customs and laws governed their behaviour?

The political reformer William Lyon Mackenzie once described the crowd gathered outside Forsyth's tavern in Niagara for an 1824 election as

> an assemblage, as motley, as varied in its materials, as the four quarters of the world could afford to send together ...
>
> There were Christians and Heathens, Menonists and Tunkards, Quakers and Universalists, Presbyterians and Baptists, Roman Catholics and American Methodists; there were Frenchmen and Yankees, Irishmen and Mulattoes, Scotchmen and Indians, Englishmen, Canadians, Americans, and Negroes, Dutchmen and Germans, Welshmen and Swedes, Highlanders and Lowlanders, poetical as well as most prosaical phizes, horsemen and footmen, fiddlers and dancers, honourables and reverends, captains and colonels, beaux and belles, waggons and tilburies, coaches and chaises, gigs and carts; in short Europe, Asia, Africa and America had there each its representative among the loyal subjects and servants of our good King George.[7]

Despite differences in religion, nationality, race, class, gender, and education, Mackenzie implies that this multitude mixed gladly and shared a common sense of imperial identity. Inside the taverns, people did not always make as much room for each other. Many rubbed shoulders freely, but others tried to enforce a less heterogeneous version of public life. The most important reason for studying the taverns of Upper Canada is to learn how colonists saw their early mixed society and how they navigated its currents.

"The public" under discussion here differs conceptually from three other, more familiar constructions. It is not limited to the classic liberal sphere of politics and markets (even though activities associated with both took place in taverns); instead, the tavern public reached past it to embrace purely social forms of interaction. Nor was it a public sphere dedicated to the creation of public opinion through rational debate. Though taverns housed the associational life sustaining the public sphere, their public was often more preoccupied with personal matters or local scandals, and it placed no premium on rationality. The tavern public willingly employed "irrational," potentially messy forms of communication, such as drinking games, gossip, and, even, violence. Women and children frequented taverns, as did those individuals and groups who were not often seen as potential equals, such as blacks and First Nations. Finally, in their casual, impromptu nature, tavern companies differed from the public as it was officially represented in parades and organized fêtes. In comparison to each of these constructions, the taverns supported an *informal* public life. Drinking and singing were as important as making money and voting. Silliness existed alongside rationality. Spontaneity was as valued as planned gatherings.[8]

Yet public life in the taverns was not entirely unstructured. Cultural rituals and social rules set broad boundaries on the forms of interaction to be encouraged, merely tolerated, or resisted. Because the colony's mixed peoples were in the process of defining patterns of association, studying the tavern public captures some of the potential conflict or uncertainty in people's ordinary, everyday lives. Theirs was not a simpler world. It was one in which the terms of admission to public space and membership in public life were under negotiation.

Colonial taverns also demand study in their own right. Neither Peter De-Lottinville's now-classic study of Joe Beef's tavern in industrializing Montreal nor Robert Campbell's theoretically informed work on moral regulation in twentieth-century Vancouver beer parlours addresses a pre-industrial and largely pre-regulatory period. Craig Heron's recent book *Booze: A Distilled History* contains a measured consideration of colonial drinking practices. It persuasively situates alcohol and the colonial taverns in which alcohol was publicly consumed within the context of a fundamental ambivalence that lies at the heart of Canada's long history with booze – the contested meanings that "wets" and "drys" attached to it. Other university-based historians, particularly those who study the temperance movement, tend to be quite pessimistic in their assessments of public drinking houses. Perhaps this is because it is their *subjects'* views that come to the fore – views that placed alcohol, and its purveyors, at the root of the many social ills to which temperance advocates bore witness during a period of urbanization and economic change.[9]

Nevertheless, taverns raised concerns in their time. State officials continually worried that the seeds of sedition might take root there. Hard-working members of society worried that taverns encouraged indolence. Orderly farmers and townspeople worried about the nature of a society in which some tavern-goers caused too much of a ruckus. And many, many colonists, such as women, blacks, Indians, and the poor, had reason to worry about the welcome they might receive from tavern companies dominated by white middling males who felt they belonged together over their glasses. Taverns, then, caused individuals and groups in colonial society to confront hard questions about the nature of public association and the social role of alcohol.

A diverse group of historians who stress remarkably similar themes relating to colonists' broadly understood social goals suggest the context in which to address these questions. Despite their differences – Douglas McCalla focuses on the Upper Canadian economy, Bruce Elliot and David Gagan on migration patterns, Jeffrey McNairn on public opinion, Jane Errington on working women, Cecilia Morgan on gendered ideals, Lynne Marks on moral regulation, a host of historians on "labouring lives," and others on temperance – acknowledge the level of serious concern with which colonists regarded the world they were making. Ordinary settlers' lives centred on and revolved around rational and sensible decisions about production and the allocation of resources; their articulation of political will; land ownership; family, kin, and community networks; a common motivation to provide a secure future for the next generation; and a sense that moderation in all sorts of consumption was needed to realize their goals. In short, the historiography of colonial Canada reveals the need to interrogate the tavern's position vis-à-vis these widely shared social beliefs.[10]

Doing so means grappling with the changing meaning of alcohol, which altered the environment of the taverns in colonial Canada. The emergence of a mass temperance movement in the 1840s marked a shift in ideals. New attitudes toward alcohol defined it as being in opposition to the responsible, progressive, and improving society envisaged for Upper Canada and North America as a whole. As a quarter to a third of the Canadian population became convinced of the need to sign pledges averring their abstinence from spirituous or all liquors, the new social definition of alcohol redefined taverns as ever more problematic sites. Some closed. Some people stopped drinking. And most colonists became more thoughtful about their previously unquestioned consumption. Yet many colonists continued to throng to the taverns for drink, and some tavern-keepers made huge profits from its sale.

"The barroom was full of people all the evening," observed one early tavern-keeper. "I spent the time tending barr and charging accounts till 10 o'clock." We know very little about customary drinking behaviour in the taverns, about its customs and how these represented terms of association. Although we still clink our glasses together, still make toasts on formal and informal occasions, and have accepted a level of social responsibility for controlling excess drinking (especially when it is associated with driving or domestic violence), we give little thought to how members of a colonial society ritual-ized and controlled consumption. Despite colonists' temperance-inspired reorientation toward liquor by mid-century, in terms of numbers the taverns survived the temperance decades unscathed. There were just as many taverns relative to the population in 1850 and 1860 as there had been in 1830 (a decade well before activists succeeded in swaying significant portions of public opinion). Given that the value of moderation became increasingly central to idealized understandings of familial and moral success, the rela-tionship between moderation and the taverns begs to be studied.[11]

Tavern-goers and tavern-keepers had enough to say about their habits in enough sources to begin to approach these issues. As inmates of the most numerous social institutions in the colony, they left evidence everywhere in the historical record: in the correspondence of government administra-tors, in Legislative Assembly journals, in letters to local magistrates (who li-censed taverns until 1849), in the notes that judges made at the bench, and in wills, personal diaries, published travelogues, newspapers, and tavern-keepers' account books. Artwork commemorates them.

However, references to tavern-goers and -keepers are often fragmentary, and this can be a problem. Stories begun cannot be finished. For example, whatever happened to Mrs. T. Mary Moore, a recent widow, who wrote to the magistrates in the Western District in 1838? She wanted her dead hus-band's licence renewed in her own name and needed to have the fee reduced from over £9 a year to about £3 in order "to bring up my family in a decent manner."[12] We never find out if she got the licence or the fee reduction. But being unable to tell the outcome of Moore's story can be viewed in a positive light, for uncertainty removes us from the realm of the anecdote and pushes us to ask analytical questions of many sources at once. How many Mary Moores were there in the colony? Do government licensing records show female names? In what number? Does this change over time? How do travel-lers comment on the landladies at the taverns where they stayed? What work did they notice women doing in the public houses? What about female pa-tronage? What did diarists who regularly went to the taverns write about the women they accompanied or encountered? How did they characterize female public house sociability? How did women appear in tavern settings when judges recorded witnesses' descriptions of them in courtroom testimony?

The fragmentation of the sources, then, does not rule out addressing big issues. In this example, Mary Moore's short letter enjoins us to adopt an expansive approach to the place of women in public life.

Tavern-goers and tavern-keepers often disagreed among themselves about what was notable in public houses. This too can pose problems of interpretation. For example, there is conflicting testimony on drinking. Newspapers liked to highlight incidents of drunkenness in local taverns, while tavern-keepers' account books, with their records of routine consumption patterns, make such incidents seem atypical. In other words, contemporaries represented taverns in different ways, and they represented them differently at different times: if they told loud stories of drunken disorder, they also told quieter tales of steadiness and moderation. Records offer conflicting interpretations on many issues relating to taverns; they reflect the diversity and multiple viewpoints of those who created them and highlight the need to employ a variety of sources.

Records also suggest the number of taverns. In 1801, the first date for which such statistics are available, there were 108 taverns in the colony. Upper Canada was exactly ten years old, having been legislated into existence by the Constitutional Act of 1791, as part of the long aftermath of the American Revolution. The colony was intended as a home for Loyalists (refugees of the revolution) in all their diversity. They were predominantly white Americans and women and children rather than men, and included a small minority of blacks (both enslaved and free) and Six Nations allies. All these refugees joined, and later displaced, the original occupants of the region: culturally defined groupings of Iroquoian and Algonquian peoples. In 1801 the population of the colony was about 34,600, which meant that there was one tavern per 320 people. The relative scarcity of taverns in comparison to the British Isles, western Europe, and the longer-settled new republic of the United States to the south was due to the late colonization and low density of settlement in the region. The colony was a big place. Geographically, its borders remained unchanged for several generations. Bounded by the Ottawa River to the east, Lakes Ontario and Erie to the south, and Lake Huron to the west, Upper Canada shared borders with the United States and French Canada.

Until 1815 American Loyalists and latecomers in search of frontier land made up nearly 80 percent of the colonial population. The remainder was British – English, Scots, and Irish – with a few French Canadians, Germans, Scandinavians, Russians, Jews, and other western Europeans mixed in. The population became more British in number and tone after 1815, however, when wave after wave of immigrants from the British Isles began to arrive, reaching a peak in the 1830s. The end of the Napoleonic Wars and intensified industrialization had created economic uncertainty in Britain, and anti-American sentiment following the War of 1812 prevented American migration to Upper Canada.

Increasingly, the largest population group was the native-born children of colonial families. By the 1830s blacks constituted less than 2 percent of the population, but they did so unevenly. In some places black families lacked black neighbours, whereas in other places, such as Chatham, they could form a good third of a town's population. The colonists' farms, towns, and emerging cities steadily displaced Native peoples. Numbering about seven thousand in 1800, Native peoples constituted one-fifth of the population and enjoyed significant political and military power. By mid-century, however, they accounted for barely over 1 percent of the colony's population and fought for cultural, political, and material survival. By this time the settler population had reached nearly 1 million due to natural increase and immigration.

Denominationally, the Anglican church enjoyed the status of an established religion, replete with rights to land and civil functions, but the majority of the settler population adhered to the more scriptural faiths, Presbyterianism and Methodism in particular. Others practised Roman Catholicism.

The first governor of the colony, John Graves Simcoe, intended to make Upper Canada into the image and transcript of the British constitution, with an aristocratic, preferably English ruling class, but he confronted the levelling democratic desires of his North American citizens. The waves of British immigrants after 1815, aware of the democratizing intent of the 1832 Reform Act and early movements toward working-class organization and social reform in England, also participated in changing governance in the colony. It shifted, in starts and jerks, toward a democratic polity for white males and a handful of their non-white counterparts by 1850.

Throughout the period, Upper Canada's population remained overwhelmingly agrarian, with only 14 percent of inhabitants dwelling in the thirty-three towns and cities that had one thousand residents by 1851. The remainder of the population lived outside the towns, and about half of them laboured for wages, pursued artisanal trades, practised professions, or engaged in commerce. The other half, just over 40 percent, farmed. Among them all, many formed into charitable and voluntary associations (some of which questioned the seemingly assured place of alcohol in the colony) and founded newspapers, churches, schools, postal and transportation services, libraries, and bookshops.

Taverns grew apace from about 500 in 1825, to just over a 1000 in 1837, to 2723 in 1852, when the colony's first industrial revolution began to change the nature of social relations.[13] By concentrating on developments in Upper Canada prior to the 1850s, this study depicts a largely pre-industrial and colonial moment, but one that was lived out in a rapidly industrializing empire and continent. Colonial society in Upper Canada was marked by the simultaneous development of, or intellectual movement toward, Victorian ideas about class identity, gender, the essentialism of race, and the differences between public and private.

Not surprisingly, given the mixed and contending political, national, and religious allegiance of Upper Canada's population, its linguistic variation, and the economic and intellectual transitions taking place, the tavern public was heterogeneous. It included a "great mixture of rank and persons."[14] It always included labourers, farmers, artisans, merchants, the gentry, and later, the newly emergent middle and working classes. It included women as well as the men who dominated the space. It sometimes included Native peoples and blacks. Yet heterogeneity did not necessarily imply inclusion. The meanings of inclusion in mixed company, the social and cultural circumstances surrounding its negotiation, and the rare instances of its apparent realization are what this book about colonial taverns is about.

1
Architecture, Design, and Material Settings

If not fine, they will, as far as my experience goes,
be found clean, respectable, and moderate as respects charges.

– William Chambers, *Things as They Are in America*

Tavern-keeper James Donaldson died in Amherstburg, Upper Canada, late in 1801. To settle his affairs, the executors of Donaldson's will took an inventory of all his real estate and his personal possessions. The list they made as they walked through the rooms of his tavern, opening cupboards, measuring the barroom stocks, and poking about in the kitchen, is the best description of the goods and furnishings of an early tavern in the colony that we have. The list shows how the tavern-keeper used material things to define the space under his management, the image he projected to an occasionally discerning clientele, and the standards of service available in an ordinary early colonial tavern. Donaldson's was far from a bad house, but neither was it an uncommonly good one.

The tavern-keeper was an ex-soldier (formerly a sergeant in the King's Regiment) who made himself rich over the course of a decade in the tavern trade, first in Detroit, then across the river in the town where he ended his days. The public house in Amherstburg with its contents was worth nearly £900, and Donaldson left three other developed properties to his children, one of which was an old tavern stand in Detroit kept by his daughter, Ann Coates. Perhaps because of his humble beginnings, Donaldson collected the sort of clothing, furniture, and goods that advertised his success. With them he created a tavern environment that worked against raucous disorder. He presented himself in the very image of a prosperous landlord. Three of his thirteen waistcoats were scarlet. He had enough linen to always show a clean cuff and collar, especially because he kept a black enslaved woman, Clara, whose job it would have been to keep these at the ready. He plated his body in shiny buttons and buckles. He put silver ones on his shirts, knee breeches, and shoes, and gilt ones on his coats. He had fancy handkerchiefs, a gold watch, and a red morocco pocketbook. Donaldson did own buckskin (leather) and corduroy working clothes, but when he dressed the gentleman, he showed off his accomplishments in easily recognizable emblems of respectability.[1]

Donaldson dressed his tavern as he did his body. Symbols of material success graced his public rooms. There were silver candlesticks, mirrors, cloth-covered tables, wine glasses, and easy chairs. Patrons had plenty of cutlery and settings of Wedgwood's Queensware. Donaldson left books about for his patrons, including a copy of *Chambaud's French and English Dictionary* – always useful in the mixed-language region of the Western District – as well as *Observations on the New Testament*. He stocked tea and everything needed to consume it properly – teapots, cups and saucers, and silver sugar tongs and teaspoons. His bar held a wide array of liquor – not simply the usual rum, brandy, cider, and house-brewed spruce beer, but also Port wine (a brandy-fortified red from Oporto) and Tenerife (a white from the Canary Islands). John Askwith, a local gentleman and the notary and clerk of the District Court, regularly shared bowls of punch and sangria in Donaldson's Detroit tavern with his cronies. The landlord ladled these expensive drinks from pure silver. Never would he have tolerated the kind of unruly behaviour that would threaten his valuable possessions or undermine the attractiveness of his house to lucrative, gentlemanly drinking parties.[2]

On the other hand, Donaldson's tavern was in no sense exclusive. Askwith, for example, treated two soldiers to a pint of rum there in the summer of 1794. And the tavern-keeper made room for unrestrained conduct. His Amherstburg place was plain in many ways, like many late eighteenth-century houses and public houses. Floors, with the exception of two rush mats, were bare wood. Most windows had no curtains. Common chairs, pine benches, coarse earthenware, and cheap tin dominated in the barroom. Brass candlesticks were used instead of silver ones, but they lit the room amply. The barroom was also warm, with a stove and nine lengths of pipe, and standing in it was the most valuable item in the house – an extremely expensive eight-day clock.

We do not know anything more about Donaldson's tavern than what his possessions tell us. He left no account book, no diary, and no letters. No travellers or patrons (except Askwith) left records of the place. Still, what he owned is telling. His investments in good everyday crockery, fine silver, and rich landlord outfits carry straightforward messages of social and economic achievement. They also suggest the diverse social makeup of his tavern's clientele. Donaldson used different kinds of material goods to define different areas in his public house. Some, like those in the dining area, called for polite comportment; others, such as the barroom furnishings, granted more freedom. The landlord obviously thought it likely that his customers would include those with "cultured" tastes as well as those who had rougher pleasures in mind. Accordingly, he made room for both to spend their money inside. By placing his single most expensive piece of furniture – the £18 clock (which cost as much as his horse) – in his barroom, Donaldson shows us that no simple equation existed in his mind between roughs and rowdiness. The way he placed his goods also indicates that he expected reasonable behaviour from soldiers and gentlemen alike.

When the executors of Donaldson's will made their list of his possessions, they did more than fulfill a legal obligation: they generated a document that makes his tavern visible as a place where decisions about organizing and using interior space, forms of sociability, and how to behave in public were made. These matters reveal much about the day-to-day workings of colonial social relations. Donaldson's inventory of goods, and the issues it raises about the nature of public houses, suggests the value of systematically studying taverns as material settings.

Colonial taverns like Donaldson's balanced the sometimes conflicting demands that the public made on them. This balancing act is central to understanding the cultural relationship between taverns and the mixed colonial populace. The material settings provided by tavern-keepers enabled tavern-goers to enact cohesive rituals of mutual belonging over drink (or tea, or breakfast, or dancing). But tavern-keepers also acknowledged the powerful differences separating members of the colonial public by designing their houses to enable, even encourage, a degree of social separation. That this was desired by some, disregarded by some, and foisted on others is traced in subsequent chapters that explore how members of the taverns' mixed company responded, not at all predictably or consistently, to each other's desires for mutual accommodation or distance.

Despite their shared ambition to balance the competing and potentially conflicting claims on them, a world of difference existed in the quality of service and accommodation afforded by the colonial taverns as a whole. This was particularly so after 1830, when immigration and settlement intensified to an unprecedented scale. If some taverns had unsavoury reputations and others in the backwoods were hardly more than shacks with spare beds and a licence to sell liquor, most others, like Donaldson's, opened substantial material settings to the public. What these taverns looked like, the layouts of their rooms, how they changed across time and by location, and how it felt to be in them are the subjects of this chapter. Without a sense of the buildings, furniture, tableware, food, and drink that created the environments for public life, neither the possibilities of that life nor the limits placed on it by the tavern setting can be understood.

Although the earliest taverns in the colony responded to design cues from elsewhere, they expressed ideals about the conduct of public life in a colonial setting. What architects call "Georgian" is a design principle that invokes classical ideas about geometry, proportion, and symmetry. Georgian design came to England in architectural books published during the Italian Renaissance, notably by Andreas Palladio, and it is visible there in the work of Inigo Jones (1573-1652) and in the work of Christopher Wren and James Gibbs following the Great Fire of London in 1666. Georgian building design emphasized breadth over height through the use of strong horizontal lines. It emphasized symmetry and rhythm over the gothic exuberance in ornamentation that had come before it. It favoured brick and painted wood over ornate finishes. The style consequently lent itself to modestly scaled interpretations by the middling ranks of Georgian society. Georgian style quickly became an internationally fashionable vernacular, and it was exported to the thirteen colonies through publications such as Batty Langley's *City & Country Builder's and Workman's Treasury of Designs*. Such books made the principles of Georgian design available to farmers, propertied townspeople, and tavern-keepers, who, by the time Upper Canada was founded, preferred (if they could afford it) to build Georgian houses as a matter of course.[3]

The Georgian style, and approximations of it, made sense to people who made claim to what they saw as a wilderness. Georgian design not only conveyed prosperity and modern style, it was also uniquely suited to a colonial setting, where settlers claimed land just wrested from First Nations. Through their "ordered array of line, surface, mass and space," Georgian buildings announced permanence and expressed authority over what had been "untamed."[4]

A sketch of the King's Head Inn on Burlington Bay, which was originally drawn in 1795 by Elizabeth Gwillam Simcoe, the wife of the lieutenant-governor, illustrates the Georgian style (see Figure 1). It was one of the "government houses" that Simcoe ordered built to improve travel conditions in the colony. State-owned, the inn was leased and run for profit by the Bates family.[5] It stood as a classic example of Georgian architecture. A timber-framed, gable-roofed, two-storey structure faced in clapboards, the inn had windows that were made of twelve panes hung over twelve panes and chimneys that aligned in perfect symmetry. The main entryway in the inn's centre focused the design. Shallow pillars and a low-pitched roof formed an ornamental portico, and an elaborate fan of small windows (called lights) on top framed the door. The orderly exterior reflected the organized way space flowed in and divided the interior. Rather than an open, pre-modern hall put to multiple uses by all and sundry, the Georgian building defined space carefully.

Simcoe noted that the King's Head had eight rooms in the main house. She breakfasted in the one "to the S.E. which commands the view of the lake."[6] It may have been the public dining room where everyone else dined, but it could also have been a room specially prepared for the use of the governor and his entourage. The house also contained a barroom, kitchen, and bedchambers for household members and overnight lodgers.

Figure 1 The King's Head Inn, Burlington Bay, ca. 1795, by John Ross Robertson, from a drawing by Elizabeth Gwillam Simcoe. The tavern sign of the King's Head is clearly visible and the symmetry of this Georgian government house expresses the overwhelmingly orderly and balanced conduct of public life in tavern space.

Image taken from *The diary of Mrs. John Graves Simcoe, wife of the first lieutenant-governor of the province of Upper Canada, 1792-6; with notes and a biography by J. Ross Robertson, and two hundred and thirty-seven illustrations, including ninety reproductions of interesting sketches made by Mrs. Simcoe,* ed. John Ross Robertson (Toronto: W. Briggs, 1911), 323

A better sense of how the King's Head was used on an everyday basis comes through in the diary of Ely Playter, a prosperous settler and former tavern-keeper from York (Toronto), who stopped there in August 1805. Two of his grown-up sisters, two male friends, and a teenaged brother accompanied him. Playter described the comfort and conviviality of the place: "We got through to the government house about four o'clock p.m. where we got a good dish of tea and feed for our horses after which we concluded to stay all night, about sunset Mr Weekes came on his way from York to Niagara. – A young man a taylor by trade on his way to York afforded us some amuse-ment, being in liquor and pretending to be very polite, sung us a song &c. – We made ourselves comfortable till morn'g."[7] The journal entry captures the accessibility of the public houses to travellers, to women as well as men, and to various members of pre-industrial society. The company included Playter's own prominent Loyalist family, who farmed extensive lands around York and whose men held a number of local offices. William Weekes was an attorney and member of Parliament. And there was, as well, the inebriated artisan who knew how to poke fun at polite society.

Playter's description of the King's Head is nothing like Simcoe's, but both remarked in different ways on their satisfaction with the place. Simcoe counted the rooms and found it "a pretty plan," emphasizing ideas of design and spatial separation.[8] Playter emphasized its publicness, the place of liquor as well as tea, and his enjoyment of sociability in a mixed company. Together they suggest that a tavern worked well within a Georgian house. The customary organization of space encouraged public life in rooms specifically designed for that purpose and kept public life separate from family and household life, private interactions, and work that needed to be done.

None of this was new. Successful tavern-keepers in Britain and the older, settled parts of North America had already established the conventions of the tavern trade generations before the earliest tavern-keepers in Upper Canada hung out their signs. All agreed that the best taverns of old New York City and Philadelphia, or the upper-class coaching inns and bourgeois taverns of England, set the tone. The multi-roomed and often multi-floored buildings they inhabited, their elegant appointments, and the deluxe supplies with which they stocked their larders and their bars defined a good public house.[9]

The tavern trade in the colony did differ in one important respect from the metropolitan model: aside from the material limitations imposed by a new colonial setting, most Upper Canadian tavern-keepers spent less than five years in the trade. On average, only a third of all licensees still held a licence five years later, as measured in 1820-25 and 1832-37. Across a ten-year span, between 1827-37, only 15 percent persisted beyond five years. Both rates differ starkly from England, where two-thirds of publicans maintained their businesses for a minimum of six years. The Upper Canadian averages do hide the lifetime careers of some tavern-keepers, such as Benjamin Olcott, Peter Davy, Joseph Losee, and Daniel Ostrum in the Midland District, Michael Fox in the Western District, and a number of female tavern-keepers whose success in the trade is discussed in the final chapter. The averages also hide the careers of keeps like George Washington Post and Russell Inglis who put in long apprentices as barkeeps before opening houses of their own. Nevertheless, the colonial trade was clearly less stable than the British trade, reflecting the mobility of settlement society, an emerging economy, and a comparatively low population density.

To a certain extent the state's licensing system in Upper Canada reflected these colonial realities. It assessed tavern licence fees in different grades according to location – the more central the location the higher the fee. The maximum licensing rate in the mid-1830s was either £10 or £7 10s. (it varied by district), and the rate was reserved for public houses located on the main streets of a town. A sliding scale from there meant a location in a smaller town or a less desirable "back street" location. Taverns in town that paid only £5 annually (and in small towns £3) were very modest affairs that were awkwardly located for all but the neighbours. Rural licence fees always ranged between £3 and £5, depending on the district, and their relative affordability reflected their location, not necessarily poor standards of service, for some rural taverns were extremely comfortable. The state recognized the need for taverns in undeveloped tracts and recognized that these taverns would have fewer customers; it set low licensing rates to encourage potential tavern-keepers.[10]

Within this different trade climate, Georgian understandings of balanced design and imported metropolitan standards of comfort and service nevertheless shaped the taverns of the new northern colony, just as they inspired the common alehouse keepers in England and the keepers of country ordinaries in the United States. James Donaldson clearly had such ideals in mind when he bought silver candlesticks for his dining table and imported wine for his bar. Similarly, William Cooper, who opened a tavern in York in 1801, explicitly acknowledged his debt to conventional public-house style. He pledged to keep his tavern "as nearly on the footing of an English inn, as local circumstances" permitted.[11] He also assumed that everyone would know what he meant. Cooper called his place the Toronto Coffee House. The name drew on the cachet of the coffee houses of old commercial cities, where merchants and financiers had met for nearly two centuries to discuss markets and politics. Like them, it was licensed as a tavern. And its rooms hosted a mixture of public and private activities. A coroner's inquest met there. Men traded in land and sealed their deals with gin and water, and they met more formally to settle financial disputes with the assistance of arbitrators. York's earliest dancing assemblies organized at Cooper's. Townspeople came in for drink, and Cooper kept stocks of the "best wines, brandy, Hollands [gin], shrub, fresh lime juice, [and] London porter" on hand. They could buy cigars, pipes, and tobacco and eat oysters, red herring, and anchovies. If the tavern-keeper hired the "clean, sober woman who understands cookery well," for whom he advertised, then dining was satisfactory.[12] Cooper's tavern, drawing on long-established public house conventions, used Georgian design to offer a well-run environment. There was plenty of room for both private business and public activity (see Figure 2).

Many tavern-keepers adopted the same architectural style or, at least, accepted its implicit preference for spatial definition. The Georgian style worked well to project an image of prosperity and comfort, particularly in the practical sense that it enabled different activities to go on in the house at the same time. In the 1790s, for example, the tavern at Carrying Place on the Bay of Quinte looked almost the same as the King's Head or Cooper's, as did Stephen Fairfield's beautiful place, which still stands on Bath Road just outside Kingston, the Walker brothers' first tavern in Kingston, Chesley's tavern

Figure 2   In Cooper's tavern (front left, with the sign over the door), townspeople of all sorts found room to drink, conduct business, dance, and dine, successfully balancing public and private activities. We can see some of the mix characteristic of the colonial society that taverns housed, in the figures of the Native family making their way into town, and the British officer just outside the tavern, gazing across Toronto Bay.

Elizabeth Frances Hale, *York on Lake Ontario, Upper Canada,* 1804, watercolour, 11 x 17.5" | Library and Archives Canada, W.H. Coverdale Collection of Canadiana (Acc No. 1970-188-2092)

in Cornwall, Joseph Keeler's tavern in Cramachi (Colborne) (see Figure 3), and Cook's Tavern on the St. Lawrence. The famous print of the killing of Colonel Moodie in the Upper Canadian Rebellion of 1837 depicts John Montgomery's tavern building, which was built in Georgian style, in the background (see Figure 4). And when Sebastian Fryfogel put up a new tavern on Huron Road between Berlin (Kitchener) and Goderich in 1845, it was built according to the same plan. Not surprisingly, when architect John G. Howard designed an inn he saw no need to deviate from proven practice.[13] It is a vernacular Georgian design: a large, symmetrical two-storey house, made striking by the detailing of the main door. It included a driving shed, stable, and privies (see Figure 5).

   Most notable is the way the space inside Howard's inn echoed the order established outside (see Figure 5). It shows how important it was, as a principle of tavern design, to keep public and private space in equilibrium. The

Figure 3 The image of Keeler's tavern depicts the continuing importance of Georgian tavern design well into the settlement era and emphasizes the taverns' role in colonial transportation networks that Chapter 3 discusses.

James Pattison Cockburn, *Inn at Cramachi, Bay of Quinte,* ca. 1830, 8.5 x 11" | With permission of the Royal Ontario Museum (942.48.16) © ROM

Figure 4 Again, the tavern building is classically Georgian. The image also captures the taverns' deep engagement in the political sphere, here, during the Upper Canada Rebellion, outside rebel headquarters at Montgomery's tavern on Yonge Street, Toronto.

Adrian Sharp, *The Death of Colonel Moodie,* 1837, engraving/print | Library and Archives Canada (C-004783)

left side of the house is given over entirely to public life: it includes a public room (where the public dining table was customarily located), a barroom and bar (downstairs), and an assembly room (upstairs). The bar itself (as opposed to the barroom where people drank) was strictly a service area, used only by household members (be they family or staff), and a place for locking

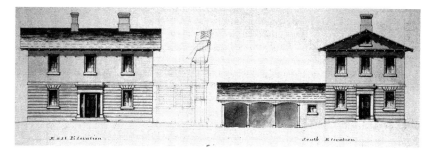

Figure 5   The architect designed tavern space to facilitate a balance between public life – in the assembly room, public room, and bar – against the claims of more private interactions in the parlour, and upstairs chambers, and against the domestic demands of the tavern-keeping household in kitchens and other workspaces.

John G. Howard, "Exterior view and floor plan of 'An Inn,'" architectural drawing | Toronto Public Library, Toronto Reference Library, Baldwin Room, John G. Howard manuscript collection (#355)

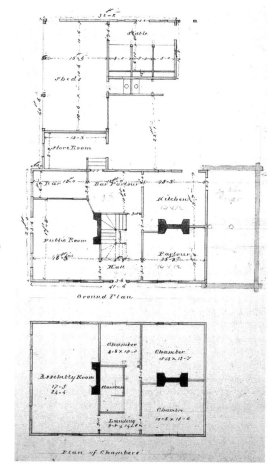

Figure 6   The reconstructed bar shows the utility, rather than the sociability, of the tavern bar circa 1850. It is a workspace, designed to facilitate liquor (and tobacco) service and safe storage, and to provide easy communication with the kitchen behind. To socialize, patrons gathered in the (woodstove-warmed) barroom at the tavern tables just glimpsed in the foreground. Suggesting the range of food and drink available are the wine glasses, matching coffee and tea cups, a cream and sugar set, as well as a vegetable serving dish on the bar shelves. The pipes are clay. The metal tongs are for picking embers out of the fire, and the other object is for chopping tobacco plugs. The Tavern Regulations – enjoining orderly conduct – are clearly posted above the bar.

Image of reconstructed colonial bar, Battle Ground Hotel Museum, Lundy's Lane, Niagara Falls, photograph by Kevin Windsor | City of Niagara Falls Museums

up the drinks when the tavern was closed. It was here that tavern-keepers stored glasses, jugs, punch bowls, sufficient stocks of liquors for anticipated short-term demand, and the ingredients (such as sugar, citrus extracts, and nutmeg) for mixed drinks. It was here that they measured, poured, and blended the drinks and kept the accounts. As in Howard's sketch, liquor in large barrels was often stored in an attached cellar.

The small portioned-off corner bar (as opposed to the modern long open counter, which was already coming into vogue in urban England and Scotland) was typical in the colony (see Figure 6). Resembling a bank or betting-house wicket, tavern bars had a grille of slats or turned posts that ran from the counter to the ceiling. This grille opened when needed (either by sliding sideways or by hooking onto a ceiling latch). Panelling ran from the floor to the countertop, and shelves hung inside for storage. Here, customers ordered drink and paid for it, or they put it on their account. Some might have a quick shot while standing there, but often the counter only extended inward, offering clients little to lean against and no foot rail, so most sat down for a leisurely drink.

The right side of the house, by way of balance, offered the potential for seclusion or exclusive association. One could remain relatively undisturbed there, especially in the parlour, the only downstairs room without direct access to the bar. As Chapters 6 and 7 show, as the century progressed this spatial feature of the taverns became increasingly important to socially privileged women called "ladies" and to "gentlemen" who were just as intent on defining themselves against the commonality.

As the architect's sketch shows, the kitchen also stood apart. Indeed, its placement so far from the public room set up a perpetual problem for women working in the house. Howard's plan shows insensitivity to the demands of domestic labour. Yet the possibility for social distancing that the kitchen enabled meant that it could be employed in contradistinction to the public rooms. For example, when several Mississauga came to Jacob Finkle's tavern in Fredricksburg in 1805, he "[told] two to go to his kitchen & get what they wanted" for supper, providing a "tin sconce & a candle which hung in the room to lite them while eating." Although we can only speculate about why the tavern-keeper ushered these First Nations men away from his public trade, the presence of a separate kitchen gave him the opportunity to do so.[14] In John Howard's design and its encapsulation of common tavern practice, rooms that enabled social separation stood alongside those that enabled public exchange. We do not know if this house was ever built; nevertheless, the architect makes an important point: a tavern, by design, gave the public access to a building of substance and grace, a space planned to balance the competing claims made on it.

In contrast to the cultural expectations encoded in Georgian architecture, the frontier taverns of the 1830s came as a terrible shock (to the sensibilities of tavern-goers accustomed to standard design). The primary characteristic of the frontier taverns was a promiscuous use of space. As immigrants flooded the backwoods of the colony, the taverns they built and encountered reflected frontier conditions. They differed in every respect from their Georgian counterparts in more settled areas. In the place of choice liquors and good dining came local whiskey and salt pork. In the place of carefully defined areas that distinguished between sociability and seclusion came primitive log-cabin interiors, where drinking, cooking, and sleeping were jumbled together. The backwoods taverns have been immortalized in the published travelogues of British gentlemen and gentlewomen. Catharine Parr Traill,

Figure 7   Nestled into a landscape under colonization, this backwoods tavern offered crucial shelter and sustenance. Yet, settlers and travellers alike complained that in the place of the balanced design of the Georgian taverns was cramped, multi-purpose space; in place of good meals and a selection of drink were frontier basics such as salt pork and whiskey. These backwoods taverns existed only as long as raw frontier conditions did, and until tavern-keepers and tavern-goers could replace them with public houses more attuned to their common understanding of good standards of accommodation.

George Russell Dartnell, *View from the Summit of the Ridge above Nicholl's Tavern, Penetanguishene Road,* 30 May 1836, watercolour and ink, 8.5 x 11" | With permission of the Royal Ontario Museum (952.87.8) © ROM

for example, went out of her way to get a look at one on the Otonabee River, near Peterborough, in the early 1830s (see Figure 7). She described it with words that emphasized coarseness and crudity and absences. The tavern was a single room "of rough unhewn logs," its ceiling was "unplastered," and the furniture, "of corresponding roughness," consisted of a "few stools, rough and unplaned, a deal table ... only held together by its ill shaped legs, [and] two or three blocks of grey granite placed beside the hearth [that] served for seats for the children." And the place was crowded with men, women, children, a calf, some pigs, and chickens. There was no separation of space, no means to offer privacy, and no ability to respond to the sensibilities of a gentlewoman.[15]

Other travellers developed the themes of promiscuity and primitiveness. Parr Traill's brother, Samuel Strickland, described a frontier tavern as having "only one apartment which answered for the treble purpose of parlour, kitchen and barroom." Another British traveller, William Pope, noted that backwoods taverns consisted of nothing more than "a miserable log building – only one apartment below and a kind of cock-loft above ... at one end of the house opposite the fireplace were ranged three or four beds into which at the proper time tumbled men, women, and children." Built into such complaints is the expectation that space be properly defined and function- ally separated. Although they provided shelter, there was nothing about backwoods taverns that met even minimum standards of public accommo- dation as they had developed in the colony. Backwoods taverns lacked cus- tomary ornamentation. There was, for instance, "no varnished clock to cleck behind the door, no pictures placed for ornament ... no broken tea cups wisely kept for show." A backwoods bedroom was "*sans* wash-hand-stand, *sans* dressing table, *sans* bureau, *sans* pot de chambre, *sans* everything." Backwoods taverns lacked customary services, like fresh water in the rooms and proper care for the horses; they lacked the sense of ease and comfort cultivated by tavern-keepers such as James Donaldson and the Bates family in the government house. Backwoods taverns lacked all provision for the conduct of meaningful public, or private, life.[16]

Of course, genteel travellers, reeling in culture shock, were at their best when they conveyed all that backwoods taverns were not. They compared these primitive houses not only to their Georgian counterparts elsewhere in the colony but also to taverns in Britain. There, the word *tavern* connoted a posh place to stop, where you could converse, drink wine, eat well, and sleep comfortably, albeit expensively. Even England's much simpler alehouses had been respectable places for nearly a century. Similarly, even though an equivalent to the backwoods taverns existed in new areas of settlement in the nineteenth-century United States, since the days of the Revolution and early Republic the rest of the public houses had been places where genuine public life cohered, where men and women began to create the contours of modern civil society in solid, well-designed buildings.[17] The same held true in British North American colonies, especially in the old cities of Halifax, Saint John, Montreal, and Quebec City. Even small Ferryland, Newfoundland, boasted the London Inn, "a very comfortable situation ... a large roomy house and genteel furniture ... had an epicure been one of the guests he could not a found fault with a single dish."[18] Miserable gin shops and very simple public houses kept by and for the poor existed on both sides of the Atlantic, but within the broad context of the trade, the frontier taverns stood out for their appalling material conditions and repellent use of space. Aside from answering a real need for shelter in the backwoods, their only saving grace was a short life. Frontiers move, as do the conditions associated with

Figure 8 The Lord Nelson tavern is the clapboard building on the corner, a minor house in a relatively central town setting that like all minor houses differed from backwoods taverns. They provided separate rooms for separate activities, solid fare, and a good selection of liquor for moderate charges. Minor houses comprised the vast majority of the more than 2,500 taverns in the colony by 1851, dotting town streets, such as this one, and rural roadways. They depended, as Chapter 7 reveals, on women's domestic labour for their success.

A.R.V. Crease, *St. George's Church Toronto, from My Dressing Room Window,* July 1851, watercolour and pencil, 20 x 26.8 cm | Toronto Public Library, Toronto Reference Library, J. Ross Robertson Collection (T 12594)

them. By the end of the 1830s, primitive public houses were a thing of the past in core population areas and along important travelling routes. They could, however, still be encountered well into the second half of the nineteenth century in newly settled areas.[19] Their existence said more about the pace of settlement and the state of economic development within a region than it did about popular ideas concerning the appropriate conduct of public life.

Indeed, travel books authored by the gentry offer an alternative depiction of colonial public houses. Alongside accounts of "higgledy-piggledy adventures ... in the backwoods" is the grudging acknowledgment that "we would scarce hold it fair (I guess) to produce a hedge alehouse or a Highland *clachan* as a fair sample of what travellers are to expect when passing through Britain."[20] More substantial and more permanent than the backwoods taverns were the very numerous minor public houses of town and country alike (see Figure 8). They constituted the vast majority of the taverns in the colony. (There were about one thousand taverns in 1837 and twenty-seven hundred in 1852.) The minor houses were diverse, yet they differed from backwoods taverns in similar ways. Their architectural layouts, the level of service available, and the material conditions inside acknowledged and continued the tradition of the Georgian taverns of the 1790s.

All minor houses had different rooms for different functions: a barroom, a dining room, and a parlour or sitting room. At a minimum, they provided three extra beds for lodgers, but not always in separate rooms. All had a stable for patrons' horses and secure storage sheds for their goods. (In fact, beginning in 1836, tavern-keepers could not get a tavern licence unless they had beds, a stable, and a lockable shed.) The minor houses served substantial "meat and potato" meals. Some did so adequately, while others excelled and earned solid reputations for their food. Because all minor houses ran primarily on the labour of the tavern-keeping household, the sense of sharing space in a family home could be pronounced, especially in the countryside.

There were some "good establishment[s] for the country,"[21] but as a rule the minor houses in town were better, in the sense that they were bigger, the level of public access more completely set the tone of the place, and they tended to employ some help, especially a barkeeper, a hosteller, and more chambermaids or maids-of-all-work. While some minor houses offered only the simplest accommodations, the more substantial ones were extremely comfortable points of call, well known to travellers and locals alike.

Their long collective history, numbers, and diversity rendered the minor houses vulnerable to competing interpretations in travellers' accounts. In what is probably the most oft-quoted passage about minor houses, Englishman John Howison wrote, "Most of the taverns in Upper Canada are indeed a burlesque on what they profess to be." His specific list of complaints included the "American" manners of tavern-keeping families (that is, assumptions of equal social standing), repetitive food, too much tea, and the scarcity of (male) hostellers, which was made worse by tavern-keeping women's reluctance to look after his horse. He even carped about the "mistress of the hotel" sending her children to the woods for herbal tea ingredients when she ran out of Chinese black.[22] Similarly, William "Tiger" Dunlop, a long-settled physician, author, and member of the provincial Parliament wrote:

> Our inns are bad: that is to say, many of them are clean and comfortable indeed enough, and the landlords almost uniformly civil and obliging, but the proverb of God sending meat and the devil cooks never was so fully illustrated as in this country ...
>
> To Dress a Beefsteak: Cut the steak about a quarter of an inch thick, wash it well in a tub of water, wringing it out from time to time after the manner of a dish clout; put a pound of fresh butter in a frying pan (hog's lard will do but butter is more esteemed) and when it boils put in the steak, turning and peppering it for about a quarter of an hour; then put it into a deep dish, and pour the oil over it until it floats and so serve it.

To Boil Green Peas: Put them in a large pot full of water, boil them until they burst. Pour off one half of the water, leaving about as much as will cover them; then add about the size of your two fists of butter, and stir the whole round with a handful of black pepper. Serve in a wash-hand basin.[23]

Doubtless there were minor houses in the colony where the food was this bad. Yet the Tiger himself remarked on their general cleanliness, comfort, and civility. Hidden in Howison's complaint about herbal tea is evidence that the tavern-keeper took the trouble to give him her idea of a proper meal. Each author undermined the intended thrust of his own passage. So these minor houses were not the London Tavern or the City Hotel in New York, but neither were 86 percent of the public houses in England or the United States.[24] Instead, the minor houses were, in general, places where tavern-goers could expect solid meals and access to well-defined rooms appointed with comfort in mind.

The staple tavern meal consisted of "wheat bread, butter, boiled potatoes, fried pork, pickles and tea." On a journey a traveller stopping at taverns along the way might well get the same meal two, even three, times a day.[25] Better-provisioned minor-house keepers routinely enlivened their tables with the addition of beefsteak, poultry, eggs and ham, cheese, pies, and cakes. None offered à la carte menus. Callers asked for breakfast or dinner or supper and ate what arrived at the table. Sometimes this could be very good and tavern-goers lavished praise on the delicacies available in some minor houses: "finely preserved plums ... in maple sugar," "delightful venison ... kept three or four weeks ... in such a fine state that it almost fell to powder under the knife," "a brace of fine fat wood ducks and fried black bass," "a fry of delicate pink fleshed trouts," "very good turkey," and "excellent stew." And sportsmen, like travellers who hunted along the way, relied on their landladies to cook up their game or fish for supper at the end of the day.[26] At a cost of between a shilling and a shilling and a half per meal, tavern-goers bought satisfying and occasionally surprisingly good fare.

Sleeping arrangements likewise ranged from the adequate to the very comfortable. Even the smallest houses provided private chambers as a matter of course, with beds "clean and plain, with cotton sheets and linsey-woolsey coverlets." Taverns run by French Canadians were favourites because each bedroom usually had its own small stove. In some districts tavern regulations required that three beds beyond those needed by the family be provided for lodgers; other districts required four. The expected scale of operations was obviously small, but since a minor house might well have only the minimum number of beds specified, the arrival of a large party, a storm, or a town crowded for a court sitting or market strained its resources. Pallets on the floor, shared rooms, and even shared beds resulted. During busy times tavern-keepers always filled their rooms singly at first. But they warned lodgers occupying double or multi-bedded rooms that they could expect company by morning. One either accepted lodging under such conditions or tried a different house. Sharing a bed was much rarer than sharing a room, but it happened. For example, in 1854 at the Clyde Inn in Toronto, which was a large and well-patronized place, the hosteller remembered "having to put two to a bed" while the Quarter Sessions convened elsewhere in town. William Long, according to the hosteller, "had to sleep with a stranger." Long remembered the incident with some distaste. He said he neither looked at nor spoke to the other man.[27]

A bed in a minor house was an uncertain commodity during peak times. But unlike in the backwoods, tavern-keepers always kept sleeping space separate from the rest. They made single rooms and single beds available unless numbers prevented it. The fact that patrons remembered sharing beds illustrates its rarity. If the best intentions were not always met, tavern-keepers nevertheless held helm. Under normal circumstances, even privileged British travellers gave the minor houses favourable assessments. For example, William Chambers generalized about them at mid-century: "If not fine, they will, as far as my experience goes, be found clean, respectable, and moderate as respects charges. On the present occasion for the accommodation of a small sitting room, warmed by a stove, tea, and beds for two persons, the charge was only four English shillings."[28]

Chambers was a satisfied customer, and it is worthwhile using tavern-keepers' estate inventories and account books to put his remarks into a more substantive context. On the one hand, surviving account books do confirm that the charges Chambers reported were typical. Whether at Abner Miles' tavern in early York, James Philips' tavern near Brockville in the late 1820s, or Thomas Robinson's tavern in Prescott in the '40s, a tavern bed cost a predictable six pence (6d.) a night. A space on the floor, perhaps on a pallet, could be had for half that (and sometimes for nothing) in some taverns. A minor-house meal, as noted, cost between a shilling (1s.) and a shilling and a half, depending on the quality, size, and location of a tavern. At Miles' tavern a meal was 1s. 6d., whereas at Philips' and Robinson's taverns it was usually 1s. 3d. One could also get a small cold repast, perhaps bread, cheese, and pickles, for 6d.[29]

Although these account book charges agree with Chambers' prices, it seems unlikely that everybody would have regarded them as "moderate." If a man made the average daily wage in the colony of between 4 and 5s. a day, then a tavern meal was quite an expensive proposition. Having a drink with it cost at least 2d. more for a glass of average whiskey, and as much as 6d. for a fancier mixed drink. However, because it cost much less to board longer term, especially in the country, many single men, as well as some women and childless couples, opted to live in taverns. In a minor house in the tiny village of Simcoe in 1849, for example, where "the fare was good and abundant," a half-pay officer, when asked how much he paid per week, said "he got his bed, three meals a-day, and his boots cleaned for 2½ dollars a-week (12s 6d sterling), and if he asked a friend to dinner it was an English shilling extra." The price of liquor, personal laundry, and keeping a horse were not included. Lodging at this rate was at least 40 percent of the average wage. Taverns in town were more expensive, as much as double in big places such as Toronto.[30] Although many people made more or less than the average, and others found themselves paying less, accommodation – whether drink, food, or shelter for the night – was hardly cheap, even in the minor houses.[31] At best, tavern accommodation was affordable for an ordinary income earner, but well beyond the reach of the poor.

Chambers' impressionistic portrayal was more accurate in other ways. What he wrote about the customary division of space in minor taverns and the respectability of their appointments is supported by the evidence from nine tavern-keepers' estate inventories: one dated 1833, seven in the 1840s, and one in 1853.[32] Though few in number and oddly clustered in the Western District, these inventories show how minor-house keepers organized their houses and appointed their rooms to make them comfortable. Brass or tin candlesticks, clocks, looking glasses, and several stoves were universal, meaning that all these minor houses were adequately lit, warm in winter, and at least minimally decorated. Some keepers distinguished themselves further by hanging framed pictures, providing fancier lighting (such as William Hall's "globe lamp" in his Sandwich tavern), covering the windows, or using better than average linens. At Cecilia Dauphin's, in East Tilbury, for example, six beds had counterpanes (decorative bedspreads), sheets, and blankets; two of the beds had hangings.

The number of beds varied. They numbered nine on average, with a maximum of eighteen at Dauphin's tavern. Both good feather beds and inexpensive straw ticks figured in the inventories, often in combination at the same house. Thirteen of Dauphin's beds were simple straw, and some of them were probably stacked and kept in readiness for a busy night because she had only nine bedsteads. Each tavern-keeper had blankets, quilts, "bed furniture," bolsters, and pillows – or "bed clothes" – but they clearly differed in quality and abundance. Although it is impossible to know how many beds were used by family members, none of the minor houses represented in these inventories seem to have had difficulty meeting minimum licensing terms for lodgers. On the contrary, they suggest that significant numbers of minor-house keepers exceeded the minimum.

Dining rooms sat between eight and twelve callers, usually on common wooden chairs and at one long, or public, table. Typically, minor houses had sets of crockery and cutlery for twelve, though Claude Gouin's house in Chatham in the '40s had knives and forks for two dozen. That all minor houses had coffee mills indicates its routine availability. Kitchens contained the frying pans, Dutch ovens, reflector (roasting) ovens, pie dishes, stone crocks, pickle jars, and tinware that testify to straightforward cookery.

Two taverns boasted expensive Windsor chairs in their parlours or sitting rooms. One of these, in Sandwich in 1844, also contained a homemade carpet, curtains, a walnut table, and a case looking glass, which were the nicest items in the place. Similarly, John Willson, in St. Thomas in 1847, accumulated nearly £10 worth of furniture and knick-knacks in what must have been his parlour. He grouped a sofa with two pillows, a rocking chair, six rush-bottom chairs, and three small tables together with a carpet, a looking glass, a wooden American clock, flower vases, candle shades, Japan trays, and pictures and a map on the walls.[33] There was also a "toy sheppardess," presumably a figurine. The array of goods in these parlours testifies to their importance. Minor-house keepers made a point of providing appropriate space for patrons who chose, or sometimes chose to avoid, the more public rooms.

Barrooms contained at least six chairs, as well as benches and assorted tables. Three taverns seem to have had a dozen or more barroom chairs, although it is not always possible to distinguish exact locations given the structure of some inventories. We do know that John Symes' barroom in his Pickering Township tavern in 1853 had six chairs, eight decanters, fifteen glasses, six small kegs, as well as stands, measures, and a small desk. Presumably, some patrons stood. Gregoire LeDuc's barroom seems to have had only two benches, an empty barrel, decanters, jugs, kegs, measures, and a scale with weights. Yet there were fourteen chairs in the house as a whole, which one could easily fetch. In the three taverns where the inventory-takers actually counted the glasses rather than jotting, for example, "1 lot tumblers," the number of glasses averaged thirteen. When tavern-goers wrote or talked about a "crowded" tavern, and especially crowded barrooms, then, they almost certainly had no more than about a dozen patrons – at most – in mind.

The inventories make it apparent that minor-house keepers paid as much attention to their beds and bed linens, the design of their parlours, and their table settings as they did to the barroom. They make it apparent that, although the scale of operations was modest, tavern-keepers worked at crafting spaces conducive to various forms of public life. Tavern-keepers with better means, time, and locations in town, such as John Willson, managed to create solid material settings, replete with markers of their relative prosperity. Others, such as Symes and LeDuc, provided the basic tools for sociability. However, there are clear limitations in looking at the public houses through the lens of tavern-keepers' estate inventories. Although the picture comes into focus on particular objects and on the layout of the house, no real sense is gained of how the tavern fit into its surrounding society.

In contrast, although we have little idea of what the minor tavern kept by James and Salomé Philips looked like, it can be firmly grounded within its community. It stood on the Sixth Concession in Bastard Township, twenty-five miles northeast of Brockville. First licensed in 1828, it was open until 1837. Although we know the tavern was on the Philipses' farm, that a fence surrounded it, and that it sat fifty yards back from the road, only the sketchiest details of the building itself are known. A frame construction, probably one and a half storeys tall, it had a barroom downstairs with a stove, a public dining room, an "inner room" with a table, a kitchen, and a "square room" for storage. There were a dozen chairs, "crockery &c," and four beds. Philips' tavern had no large room for meetings or dances. The nearest tavern that did was the Derbyshire Inn in Farmersville, ten miles away. County-wide associational or political meetings convened in the large public houses of Brockville.[34]

Situated in a rough triangle at the junction of three township roads among a constellation of shops, Philips' tavern made up a key part of the local service centre. A shoemaker, William Emerson, kept shop in a separate building on the tavern property. Across the road, Jonah and James Brown, probably relatives of Salomé, ran a mill. A blacksmith worked nearby. Philips himself also operated a tannery and a potashery, and he rented his potash kettle to neighbours. Together with his wife, Philips also kept a small general store, where he sold flour, salt, sugar, nails, seeds, and other basic goods. Many entries in Philips' account book show no tavern purchases at all; others blend tavern and store debits. Charles French, for example, who lived on the Fifth Concession with his wife and five children, stopped in for half a bushel of salt on 16 September 1829 and added a quarter pound of tea and a pint of whiskey the next day. James and Salomé did have the help of a hired barkeeper, William Faulkner, but with their store, an apple orchard, fifty acres of cleared land, cows, and two small children running about to attend, neither the tavern-keeper nor his wife could have had much time to devote to their tavern patrons' needs.[35]

Yet as far as the locals were concerned, things ran smoothly enough. Their names fill Philips' account book. His most regular customers were his closest neighbours. Edward Conly lived on the next concession, two lots over. Robert Parsons lived next door to him. And Arnold Stevens lived, like Philips, on the Sixth Concession, just over a mile away. Most customers clustered on the Fifth, Fourth, and Third Concessions, just above and within an easy ride of the public house. Short-distance travellers brought in some custom. In March 1835 William P. Loucks, Esq., for example, stopped for dinner on his way back from nearby Beverley. Patrons bought a lot of whiskey and lesser amounts of brandy and rum. The odd one took a glass of gin or a mixed drink such as sling. Though these entries are rare, Philips seems to have kept the stocks on hand. He sold tobacco and pipes. His beds cost the standard

6d. a night, while meals were 1s. 3d. Philips' tavern was in every sense a local tavern. It fit into the local economy and stood, quite literally, as a farm, a store, and a tavern among other artisanal and service shops. Philips' licence to sell drink by small measure and the unpretentious space he maintained for sociability over it clearly satisfied the needs of many in his community, according to their consistent appearance in his accounts.[36]

When colonial travellers moved away from the back concessions and into the more important arteries of transportation, and the towns themselves, they were treated to a higher level of service. W.J. Sumners' Grove Inn, thirty-five miles from York on the Dundas Road, operated according to an entirely different dynamic than Philips' tavern. Through many newspaper advertisements Sumner crafted an image of his house as the resort of the respectable, the tasteful, and the quality conscious. He promised the best liquors from Montreal marketplaces, "good fires, good wholesome provisions, good stabling, hay and oats, and clean comfortable beds." Although Sumner stopped short of making claims to fashionability, he attracted genteel travellers to his house. They described it as "well conducted, and kept by an obliging person," and wrote that it enjoyed "a great run of business," including the patronage of "fashionably attired" ladies and gentlemen. By 1834 Sumner was successful enough to move to larger premises in town, the Oakville House Hotel. Here, he put up a viewing gallery from which he claimed guests could see the spray of Niagara Falls. He decorated his parlour with prints of Parisian haute couture and European literature, such as the epic *Don Juan*. Through such means, Sumner imparted a smart, metropolitan tone to his public house. Unlike the majority of minor-house keepers, he aspired to be fashionable, the quality that set the principal houses of the colony apart from the rest.[37]

The principal public houses, often called hotels, were located in the towns, in resort areas, and (occasionally) along important travelling routes. In place of the meat and potato fare of the minor houses, the hotels distinguished themselves by offering colonial haute cuisine. In place of extra beds and shifting bedroom arrangements, hotels always offered private bedrooms and, often, private sitting rooms as well. Although the minor houses likewise maintained spatialized zones like their Georgian counterparts, the principal houses brought this to a fuller realization. Also, in addition to a landlord, landlady, and their children, principal houses had staffs to meet the needs of their guests. However, principal houses were very few in number; Rowsell's 1850 *City of Toronto and County of York Directory,* for example, listed 136 taverns and called only six of them "principal."[38] This proportion held true elsewhere. Yet the presence of principal houses made the urban and resort tavern trade qualitatively different from its rural counterpart. Principal houses offered those who could afford them a grade of accommodation not available in the countryside.

Figure 9   The Jones Hotel, in the market place circa 1856, shows the location of a principal house in the very heart of town. It shares prominent public space with the railway and City Hall. Also called hotels, the relatively few, expensive principal houses differed from the rest also in their claims to fashionability, their haute cuisine and extensive barroom stocks, guaranteed levels of privacy, and standards of service. By mid-century the best colonial hotels, such as the Rossin House in Toronto, discussed below, offered international-class accommodation.

Edwin Whitefield, *In Guelph*, ca. 1856, 8.5 x 11 inches. I With permission of the Royal Ontario Museum (955.215.2.T) © ROM

Many, from the 1790s onward, claimed the name hotel, and people accepted the term as a rough indicator of quality. Though his tongue is in his cheek, traveller John Goldie tells us that, when he stopped in Stoney Creek in 1819, he chose the one tavern "which was dignified by the title of hotel." Similarly, Claude Cartier's advertisement read: "As a good name is essential to a good tavern, he has adopted for his the title of 'The Steam Boat Hotel.'" The word *hotel*, for much of the Upper Canadian period, distinguished (or claimed to distinguish) a principal house from even the more substantial minor houses.[39]

The designation "principal house" was important. Principal taverns stood apart from the rest because of their size and their location near central public offices, shopping districts, and transportation facilities. They were the public houses at a town's major intersection, kitty-corner to cathedrals, banks, markets, and, by the mid-1850s, railway stations. In 1856 the Jones Hotel in Guelph enjoyed such a location, sitting close to City Hall, which is in the foreground (see Figure 9). Most importantly, principal houses stood apart because they offered patrons a fashionable, swanky milieu. They promised to be oases of gentility. They granted their patrons the opportunity to maintain social distance from the rest of the mixed colonial populace. As early as 1817 James Rogers targeted "Genteel Company" for his Niagara Coffee

House. His was a "large and commodious house ... near the centre of the village" that offered entertainment in a "handsome style."[40] According to Rogers, it was everything a principal house should be: spacious, well situated, elegant, and conducive to selective association. Even though there were early hotels, the development of the principal house trade hinged on the economic development of the colony. Thus, even though government houses, such as the King's Head, were comfortable and well provisioned, they were by definition not principal houses: the state built and leased them in remote newly settling areas as a service to travellers – all comers, not simply the consciously genteel – and they made no claims to fashionable life.

Sheer size was a key defining feature of principal houses. By the 1840s travellers called the principal taverns "rambling," "vast," "extensive" "monsters." Advertisements celebrated their size. The Eberts' House at Chatham boasted "three stories," "5 large sitting rooms, 25 bed rooms, bar room and other apartments." The Albion Hotel in Stratford, which had been built in 1855 to meet the railway traffic, was four brick storeys, with "40 rooms," including a "large and truly warm and comfortable bar-Room," a "large dining room," and several sitting rooms. It was near the termini of two rail lines, housed the telegraph office, and commanded "the best situation in town."[41]

Principal houses routinely advertised central or marketplace settings. The hotel at the corner of Front and Yonge Streets in Toronto in 1847 was "the best situation in Canada for a first class hotel, being opposite the principal wharves and the custom house and in the immediate vicinity of the banks and leading mercantile houses." In 1836 James McDonald's British American Hotel enjoyed a "most desirable site ... directly opposite the court house and nearly opposite St. George's church in one of the most pleasant, healthy and fashionable streets in Kingston." A site "in the very heart of a city" connected the principal public houses and their clientele to a swelling "population and political and commercial consequence."[42]

Owners of public houses also chose their location to capture the tourist trade. Forsyth's Pavilion at Niagara Falls was a "handsome frame building, of ample dimensions, three stories high, with piazzas on both sides." Its windows framed views of the falls. It enjoyed genteel patronage. Guests dressed for dinner. Porters carried the luggage. The stagecoach stopped at the door. Forsyth was personally disliked because of his attempts to monopolize business at the resort. Nevertheless, his place basked in its reputation as a "celebrated" hotel.[43]

These houses delivered service of a superior standard. This meant a "Table d'Hotel ... kept in the very best style." Meals were carefully planned, prepared, and served. There was the "finest fish and fowl," "mutton chops and lobster," and "oysters, ... salmons, sardines &c." "Choice wines" made the dining experience more satisfying; "choice liquors" were always available from the bar. And apartments of "excellence and comfort ... in regard both to parlours and bedrooms; all of which are furnished in the very best style" helped to cultivate an aura of exclusivity and good taste.[44]

Naturally, there are reasons to take some tavern-keepers' promises with a grain of salt. In Kingston, for example, in 1837, Segro Carmino advertised his Mansion House Hotel, located on "the principal and most central street," as an establishment unsurpassed throughout the colony for the excellence of its appointments. But according to a traveller who stayed there, the apartments were most notable for the view they commanded "of the pigs, dogs and chickens in the back yard; three old sleighs [and] a goodly pile of firewood." Similarly, the promised comfort of the parlour and sitting room in reality amounted to only a few "broken sofas, cracked chairs, and a fragment of dubious-looking carpet." Surely other taverns that boasted about their classy amenities and services in newspaper advertisements likewise proved to be bitter disappointments in reality.[45]

Nevertheless, the proprietors of the principal, or would-be principal, houses represented them as sites of fashionability, and, as Chapter 6 will reveal, relatively well-off colonists embraced and pursued their promise. To be the best hotel west of New York, or, if your claims were more modest, the best hotel west of Montreal – or, at the newly settling Lake Huron Shore, the best hotel west of London, Canada West – was a distinction that tavern-keepers avidly sought. They located on prominent sites, they emphasized fine cuisine over substantial fare and style as much as comfort, and they invited the "gentility" inside. And they made sure that patrons who wanted to maintain a degree of social distance could do so.

By the 1840s it was routine for the principal houses to make "private parlours and suites of rooms" available to "families and others." They set parts of their buildings, such as the whole west wing of the North American Hotel in Toronto, aside for family groups. Principal-house keepers willingly catered to the desires of "private parties." They made sure that "ladies and gentlemen" knew they could be "accommodated with well-furnished and pleasant rooms for any time they may wish to tarry." Clearly, it was possible, if you had enough money, to stay aloof from the barroom throng in the principal taverns. Although gender had much to do with the patterns of tavern patronage, by promising "families" room in the principal houses, tavern-keepers made sure they continued to court the custom of those with money, particularly the emerging colonial middle class.[46]

Certainly, the many-roomed, multi-storey houses of the 1840s and beyond were facilitated by population growth, economic development, more efficient travel, and the spread of settlement. The same impulse that caused Donaldson to create different social zones for different kinds of interaction also played a role. The principal houses were more successful at achieving the division, however, for they did more to attract parties of the gentry and the well-heeled and they abetted them in their desire to be exclusive. And to a degree, principal house prices limited access to the accommodations. For example, in 1817 a printer decided not to go to Walker's, "the head inn" in the Kingston marketplace, because of its "extravagant" charges. In 1841 a government clerk found the weekly rate of $9.00 at the Sydenham Hotel, also in Kingston, "out of sight."[47]

However, the principal taverns never quite became the havens of gentrified life that their advertisements proclaimed. Their very size worked against it. The well-advertised scale of dining and barrooms meant that they were designed to welcome far more people than the colony's small upper crust could supply. The 60 ft. x 22 ft. billiard room in the Eberts' Hotel could never have been supported by gentlemen alone. In fact, genteel patrons constantly complained about the riff-raff in public dining rooms. For example, one gentleman, employed in the government service and long accustomed to life in the colony, grumbled about the "vulgar set" eating breakfast near him at Barton Philips' National Hotel in 1840s Kingston.[48] And anybody could get a drink as cheaply in the bar of a principal tavern as anywhere else, even though better stocks were on hand for those with more to pay. Travellers and settlers tell us over and over that the barrooms of the principal taverns were always socially mixed. One observer listed tailors, barbers, strolling players, quack doctors, hackney coachmen, shoemakers, and lawyer's clerks as patrons; another noted the "large proportion of the male population of every city and town" that resorted to them and added, "it is not regarded in the slightest degree derogatory to the character for any gentleman to take refreshment" there.[49] There is no reason to think that the principal houses were really less public than the smaller taverns dotting the side streets. But with two or three storeys of relatively private space in parlours, sitting rooms, and bedchambers stacked above the barroom ceiling, the whole feel of the principal taverns was different. Not only was it feasible to remain apart from the concourse of public life in them, but many were positively invited to do so.

This impulse to separation, seen first in the Georgian taverns of the 1790s, reached its fullest material expression in the 1850s when something no longer definable as a tavern appeared on the urban landscape. The best hotel in Upper Canada was Toronto's Rossin House, which was purchased by the Rossin brothers in 1856. The Rossin House represented the height of publican splendour in the colony; it was "one of the chief architectural ornaments of the city," replete with "white pressed brick" and "substantial dressings of Ohio freestone, handsome iron pillars, cornices, and balconies." It was a massive structure of five storeys that accommodated five hundred guests in over two hundred rooms, "exclusive of reading-rooms and the principal parlours." It cost $2.50 a day to stay there (excluding wine and washing); by comparison, in the same period it cost $1.00 a day to stay at the Wellington Hotel, a comfortable principal house on the Toronto waterfront. The Rossin House had

> two private entrances ... an extensive reading room, lighted by a large and handsome glass dome ... fifteen elegantly furnished stores on the ground floor ... a long row of parlours and reception rooms, the principal of which is a ladies parlour ... a dining room 100 feet by 38, and 18 feet high adjoining which is the carving room, dish room, dessert room ... three staircases, two for the use of guests and the third for servants ... a very extensive barroom, with billiard table underneath ... a barber's shop and gentlemen's bathing room containing ten baths ... and a book and news depot where one may obtain local and European journals, or handsomely bound volumes which address alike the students of light or abstruse literature.[50]

Nobody would have referred to the Rossin House as a tavern, and its presence was part of the evolving public-house trade in the colony. Where many public houses in the 1850s remained recognizable to late eighteenth-century eyes, the Rossin House and others in its image marked a distinctly new style in public entertainment that left the pre-industrial tavern behind.

In the 1850s we glimpse, too, an early form of the historiographically well-known working-class saloon, or tavern.[51] Inside, working people drinking together in public space presaged fuller expressions of working-class collectivity. For instance, in Toronto down by the new Grand Trunk Railway line, one block west of the Toronto Grey & Bruce Railway yards and two blocks west of the Northern Railway station, Patrick Roach ran a tavern at the north corner of Tecumseth and Douro Streets. Not surprisingly, he called it the Railway Inn. Nearby workers thronged to steel and iron works and busy commercial wharves. Roach's account book survives for the years 1855 to 1859, listing regulars and less frequent callers. Some we know only from entries like the following: "Thomas the blacksmith," "Tim that boards at Cacey's," "Brock's man," "James, fare man," "the watchman," "Dave engineer," and "the man that works at Northern." Such entries nevertheless evoke the patronage of the house. Like Philips in Bastard Township, Roach enjoyed the custom of his neighbours. His place was the local for working men and working women. The majority of the men, by far, were labourers: several were railwaymen and a few were carpenters and blacksmiths. There was one (railway) clerk among them, along with a police constable and a bacon curer. They all lived within easy walking distance of the tavern. As Chapter 7 discusses, the occupations of three women in Roach's books are suggested in city directories: a dressmaker, a washerwoman, and a boarding-house keeper. They belonged to the same working population as the men who patronized Roach's. The clientele at the Railway Inn and its location in the industrializing

West End mark it as a tavern where public association over drink supported a burgeoning sense of mutual identity among workers.[52]

The Georgian taverns of the 1790s and beyond were built on the need to define, separate, and balance space. They acknowledged the importance of public life by granting full access to it, and they simultaneously validated more exclusive forms of social interaction by incorporating parlours and sitting rooms into their design. The same logic operated in the minor houses, where it was often, if not always, just as possible to indulge in robust public exchange as it was to find a quiet place to be a family, a woman, or in select company. After all, it was because of their unrelenting spatial promiscuity that elite travellers and ordinary colonists alike left one-room frontier taverns behind them as quickly as possible. There is a hint, too, that less desirable minor-house patrons (such as the Mississauga at Finkle's) were shunted away from the public trade and into rooms such as the kitchen. The principal houses distinguished themselves by the heightened degree of fashionable selectivity that they supported. There were limits to their success, to be sure, but what is most salient is that the material setting of the principal houses was structured by an impulse to balance public life with desires for a degree of social separation. The diary of one early tavern-keeper, explored in the next chapter, discloses the ways that the men and women who frequented taverns, and especially those who lived inside them, negotiated what was public space, what was private, and how what happened in between affected each.

Summary of types of taverns

2
Households and Public Life in a Tavern-Keeper's Journal

Sophia was complaining about the manner of Living in a Public House.

– [Ely] Playter diary, 4 June 1802

Ely Playter kept a tavern in York, Upper Canada, in 1801 and 1802. At night, "after all had gone to bed," he "filled up the journal of the day."[1] On pages describing the routines of work and sociability in his well-patronized house, he wrote women and household life into the history of taverns. Playter's journal allows us to see the material world of the tavern as gendered. Although it abounds with the names of men and accounts of their activities, the tavern-keeper clearly never thought of taverns as uncommonly male spaces. Without questioning the precedence men enjoyed, he depicts his public house and those he frequented as places where men and women both belonged. When Playter writes about the female members of tavern-keeping households – especially Mary Thompson, who lived at his place, and Sophia Beman, a neighbouring tavern-keeper's daughter whom he courted – he brings the hidden domestic side of the tavern into view. In the journal we see children who need tending, problems with the servants, and friends calling to visit not the bar but the parlours and sitting rooms of their tavern-keeping neighbours. In rooms that were sometimes household space and sometimes public space, "Miss T" and "Miss B" gathered with their polite acquaintances to drink tea and wine, make music and conversation, and read aloud in mixed company. They fostered forms of sociability separate from the rituals of drinking culture that played out in the barroom. By writing women and domesticity into the taverns, Ely Playter's journal gives vivid content to late pre-industrial gendered ideas about public life and household life in a setting where the two met, occasionally collided, and mutually shaped each other.

Although historians agree that taverns had both public and private (by which they mean household or domestic) dimensions and that sometimes women frequented them, more than one has confessed to an inability to address matters of gender or the relationship between the household and the public house. Evidence, for the most part, has proven to be unyielding or absent.[2] Female tavern-keepers, who are well documented in licensing records, are one exception, but even in this case historians tend to interpret the evidence in terms of women's access *to* the public rather than the household's shaping *of* the public.[3] In Europe, English medievalist Barbara Hanawalt's work on travellers' inns, early modernist B. Ann Tlusty's work on the German drink trade, and W. Scott Haine's study of Parisian wine shops during the Revolution are important exceptions.[4] Ironically, although most historians who employ new approaches to the study of taverns are well aware that the taverns were not entirely public and not entirely male, their work centres on their publicness, particularly on tavern association among men and its political implications. This is what makes Ely Playter's journal an important source. It contains rare insights into issues that have troubled, yet eluded, historians.

Only a tavern-keeper could have written this journal, but not just any tavern-keeper. What it reveals about living in a tavern household and gender relations in tavern space could only have come from Playter in the winter of 1802. At that time, he was twenty-five years old, single, and envious of married men. He paid an abundance of attention to unmarried women: "See a young woman here from the Bay of Quinty [sic], a Miss Rea & her brother come up to settle at York."[5] With his bachelor friends, lawyer Thomas Ward and government clerk Stephen Heward, who came daily to his tavern to dine, Playter frequently "sat talking," cigar in hand, "on our favourite conversations of our amours with the ladys."[6] His journal includes references to men with their wives and to his mother and sisters and the female members of his and other tavern-keeping households. Still, it is mixed-gender gatherings in tavern parlours that draw the bulk of his remarks, sometimes in extraordinary detail, because they held out the promise of courtship and because of the pleasure he took in mixed company.

Naturally, much of what Playter wrote about the gender dynamics of tavern space had much to do with the quirks of his personality and intellect. The journal opens on St. Valentine's Day, 14 February 1802, which was a Sunday. Aside from a quick note that the "house was clear of company," today's reader has no sense of being in a tavern as we understand them. "Miss T asked me for a book. [I] gave her the *Adventures of Versorand* and we read [till] past 9 o'clock, she in the book I lent her & I in M[onsieur] Zimmermann's *Influence of Solitude on the Mind & the Heart*."[7] The entry illustrates the domesticity of the tavern household on a quiet day. It also positions the tavern-keeper in a particular relationship to both public life and household life.

The book that made its way to Playter's York tavern centred on the tension between "the enjoyments of society" and "the tranquillity of solitude" (which included an idyllically conceived domestic circle). It argued that only by finding a balance between them could human beings attain "true felicity."[8] The resonance these themes evoked in Playter explains much of what he has to tell us about taverns. He wrote about public life and household life because they coexisted and interacted at his house and also, as his reading material suggests, because he invested each with significance in the pursuit of a meaningful human existence.

In 1801, York, located on the northwest shore of Lake Ontario near the gateway to the Toronto Passage long used by Native and French traders, was "just emerging from the woods but bid[ding] fair to be a flourishing town."[9] Founded in 1793 as the naval arsenal and temporary capital of the new British colony of Upper Canada, the town itself extended a mile and a half along the lakefront above Toronto Bay. The garrison was another mile to the west, separated from the town by its reserve. Yonge Street ran north through an emerging agricultural hinterland, passing through settlements of Germans from Genesee County, New York, at Markham, French Royalists at Vaughan, and Pennsylvania Quakers at Gwillimbury, which sat at the mouth of the Holland River, thirty-six miles distant. Dundas Road went west to Head of the Lake (Hamilton), where it connected with routes to Newark, Niagara, and Detroit. Danforth Road enabled travel east to Kingston, a village on the St. Lawrence River. In the town itself, settlement was clustered in ten compact blocks at the harbour and called Old Town. It then straggled westward through New Town. A few public buildings and the residences of the governing and merchant elite claimed the waterfront. The households of lesser merchants, artisans, and labourers were located farther back from the water.[10]

When Playter kept his tavern, there were perhaps seventy-five to one hundred houses (contemporary counts vary) in York.[11] Three hundred and twenty people lived within the town, and another 429 lived in the surrounding townships of Etobicoke, York, and Scarborough.[12] In addition, the garrison housed between 235 and 246 soldiers and officers.[13] Being the capital, York had Parliament, courts, and administrative offices. It was a commercial centre as well as a port, and it was an important entryway to the colony. As such, it also had a constant floating population of travellers and temporary sojourners, which is unaccounted for in population estimates. "The town looks quite throng," Playter noted in May, "a number of strange gentlemen walking the street."[14] Because of York's compound political, military, and commercial identity, men and families with high status and education had an unusually strong social presence for a new colonial town.[15] York may have been more a raw walking village than a classic pre-industrial walking city, but its settlers experienced a surprising heterogeneity in their day-to-day, face-to-face encounters in public spaces. The governing class was British and Loyalist, but the people were diverse, comprising Loyalists and recently arrived Americans, English, Scots, Irish, French, and Germans. They practised, sometimes eclectically, a variety of religions. It was a multiracial population that was mostly white but included both free and enslaved blacks and the Mississauga who maintained a presence in and about the town.[16]

Playter's tavern stood on the corner of King and Caroline Streets in the Old Town, within sight and sound of Elisha Beman's tavern. When Playter sat at his writing table he could look out and see Sophia Beman "often at her window (which was in view from mine)." His house had two storeys and at least seven rooms. Like others, it maintained a division of space. There was the barroom, which was always kept warm, that included an enclosed lockable bar and a place for "charging accounts." The parlour had another fireplace, a card table, and enough light for reading, writing, and needlework after dark. An upstairs room (or rooms) was open to customers seeking separation from the rest of the company in the house. "Messrs. Shivers and Joshua Cozens," for example, "dined upstairs and drank plentifully of whisky." Ely's own room had a door that fastened, and it must have been on the ground floor because late-night callers banged on the window to wake him up. There was a "south chamber" for lodgers, a kitchen where we glimpse a black woman named Elizabeth (Betty) Johnson at her work, and a "sellar" for "storing away my empty casks." In addition there was a public dining table and beds enough for the numerous people who slept there each night.[17] Playter maintained the principle of balanced use that lies at the core of good design, demarcating household space from public space without making rigid boundaries between them.

Conviviality spilled throughout the tavern, with the house "in the evening full of noisy company singing in two or three different rooms at once."[18] And liquor, both spirituous and fermented, flowed freely. Belonging integrally to the amusements of the bar, alcohol was also employed in parlour gatherings. By offering flexible spaces that allowed relative seclusion or full public engagement, depending on the wishes of the company in the house, Playter, like many other tavern-keepers, encouraged members of a diverse public to seek their particular entertainments at his tavern. The domestic areas, where servants and household members laboured, supported this public world of sociability.

And the tavern public at Playter's, as in most taverns where drink-sellers welcomed the custom of all comers to make a good profit, was heterogeneous. Playter names "Mr Proctor and another man from the Quaker settlement" and "two American soldiers" as barroom patrons, and he notes that when "two familys of Dunkards" called for lodging, they "staid in the kitchin with their children."[19] Maybe religion was their motive and the kitchen offered shelter from the more worldly environment of the tavern's public rooms. If so, the material possibilities provided by balanced design allowed for real social distance. In the house generally, Playter depicts men trading furs, refers to lake schooner captains Kendrick and Sillich, and makes it clear that, along with the many settlers and substantial farmers who predominated among his patrons, there were merchants and their clerks, government clerks, lawyers and physicians (Thomas Stoyells was both), the sheriff of the Home District, Alexander Macdonnell, and his brother Angus, who was the treasurer of the Law Society. Several of these men held local office and commissions in the militia.[20] A 1796 account book for the house indicates that shoemakers, joiners, sawyers, blacksmiths, masons, millers, British military officers and soldiers from the garrison were patrons of the bar.[21] Seven of the more substantial men who charged their drinks in 1796 appear again, by name, as patrons in Playter's journal.[22] But we only know of the continuing patronage of blacksmith John Hunter through the intervening years because of the trouble he caused: "It [was] 12 oclock before I got to bed & just after J. Hunter knocked at the door ... & plead[ed] some time for me to get up and let him have a pt. rum but I answered him very determined that I would not."[23]

Apart from Quakers and the Dunkard family, Playter does not disclose his patrons' religion. But his clientele represented the denominational range characteristic of the colony itself. For example, Ward and Heward each belonged to the Church of England, Stoyells was a prominent Methodist, and the Macdonnel brothers were Roman Catholic. Patrons also included families and individuals that Playter identified as Dutch, German, French, and American, as well as those known to be Irish, English, and Scottish. The clientele was overwhelmingly white, but Peter Long, enumerated as a black man in the town's list of inhabitants, frequented the house when it was under Miles' sole management, as did "Molat, Negro."[24] In Playter's time Betty Johnson, "the Blackwoman," worked within the tavern, probably as a servant but maybe as an enslaved woman, although the family's Quakerism suggests that the latter was unlikely. Lester Stuard (who was black) played the fiddle for customers and told long tales.[25] And although the journal reveals no patronage by the local Mississauga, in one entry a (white) man came in accompanied by an "Indian."[26] The shifting ways in which racialized identity affected the membership of blacks and Natives in tavern sociability claim a separate chapter. As Playter wrote, his tavern was indeed filled with "all kinds of people."[27]

To this already mixed patronage, Playter's journal adds women, and his observations reveal the power of gendered norms to affect tavern customs and patterns of use. The colonial society that Playter inhabited empowered men politically, legally, and economically at the expense of women. The tavern-keeper's journal reveals that – without at all disrupting common notions of the hierarchical relations between the sexes – Playter recognized tavern space as mixed-gender space. His journal exposes the ways men and

women shared and sometimes contested space, and how gendered understandings of their relative places in household life and public life mediated
the terms of their access to those spaces. It reveals how gender-shared space
did not translate into gender-equal space. The pre-industrial tavern, as Playter
renders it, was a space in which male precedence shaped the parameters of
women's worlds.

Colonial public houses fell within women's ambit. Playter writes of a "lady
guest" at his tavern, a Mrs. Carpenter. He has already disclosed that "Miss
Rea" was there with her brother, as were the women mentioned in brief descriptions like, "A Dutchman and his family staid all night," the "two familys
of Dunkards" above, "a family by the name of Charles Hatters," and "my
bed taken up by a man and his wife."[28] In addition to the references to
women included in these phrases, Playter named forty-three different women
in the eight months he kept tavern. He placed well over half (twenty-seven)
of them inside taverns: fourteen lived there as members of tavern-keeping
households, fifteen called in as tavern patrons, and six of them were travellers. Five of the women, Playter's mother among them, called regularly at
taverns to visit family and friends. The numbers do not add up because the
categories overlap. Bettsey Miles, for example, who was old enough to get
married in December 1802, lived at Playter's tavern whenever her parents
were in town, called for drink at Yonge Street taverns in male company, and
regularly popped in and out of Beman's to see Sophia.[29] Neither Playter's
house nor Beman's or McDougall's taverns – or any tavern to which Playter
called while travelling – were ever clear of women. Still, ritual and custom
imposed careful controls on women's freedom of movement, as callers and
patrons, within these public spaces.

Customarily, women went to taverns with men. Married women usually
went with their husbands or grown sons. Sometimes these were quick calls
for refreshment, as when Playter and Bettsey Miles "rode pretty fast" down
Yonge Street, "called at Everson's Tavern & got something to drink after
which we rode on more fast." Or when Playter, Bettsey Miles, her fiancé
John Arnold, her sister Lucy, Stephen Heward, and one of Playter's sisters
"all stopped at the tavern and drank some sling." Sometimes these stops
were longer and often occurred in the context of a day spent in town. At
Playter's, "Mr & Mrs Stoyells ... came in and staid [to] dinner."[30]

The common pursuit of public house sociability in mixed company is most
apparent in Playter's journal. "[T]he ladys and Mr. S[tephen] H[eward] were"
waiting when Playter and several male friends returned to Gilbert's tavern
from a charivari, and all "set some time talking" throughout the long summer evening.[31] "There was Mr. Taylor, Miss Tid & Mr. Gilbert" at Wilson's,
wrote Playter, "& after we drank some whiskey we all started on together ...
Taylor & Miss Tid were to get married tonight."[32] In 1805 a party of men and

women related by familial, marriage, and household ties, some married and others not, went on a sightseeing excursion from York to Niagara Falls. They stayed away for several days and called and lodged at numerous taverns along the way:

> We had a pleasant ride, called at the sign of the horse and got something to drink – had a pleasant and satisfying view of the falls, returned to the first tavern and fed our horses, drank some brandy and water. A Mr. Laughton fell in company with us[;] he was on horseback but having to leave his horse desired to ride with us to Niagara. We called at a second tavern by request of the stranger and drank some wine – he being a young man I in a joke got him to set between Hannah and Miss S[wazey] which I was afterwards sorry for as he had drank too much his behaviour was some annoyance to them.

Playter's inclusive language indicates that women were integrated into the pleasure-seeking group's tavern going – everybody stopped three times for "something to drink," for "brandy and water," and for "wine." Despite the gender-specific joking, the presence of women posed no perceivable barrier to traditional drinking practices. Women joined casually in drink and public sociability; however, whereas men frequently drank and socialized among themselves, women experienced tavern going mostly in the context of close male companionship.[33]

When Playter stopped with a friend in 1805 at his old stand, renamed Stoyells' Tavern, he "drank 5 pints of wine – Andrew Thompson & wife were there & rec'd money for land sold to J. Kennedy. E. Payson was also there and helped us drink wine &c."[34] It is the phrase – "Andrew Thompson & wife" – in this last sentence that embodies women's relationship to public houses: their presence, while quite customary, was understood as parenthetical to and dependent on male company. Although women often made tavern calls early in the century and their presence expressed a desire for public sociability over drink – and although the evidence of mutual tavern going by married couples is valuable because it competes effectively with the presumption of an exclusively male presence – women did not, as a rule, go to taverns alone. Women in Upper Canada went to taverns as members of their households. This was a pattern of public-house patronage closely akin to that of early modern Germany, where women likewise accompanied husbands to taverns but rarely went without them. In one sense, then, tavern companies tolerated only a carefully defined female presence in public rooms, one that imaged women within their households.[35]

Paradoxically, women's occupation of public space in taverns also reveals the flexibility of a pre-industrial understanding of women's household status, as compared to later (Victorian) norms. We have known for a long time that the pre-industrial household contained many public elements, such as production for the market; the presence of non-family members as boarders, apprentices, or servants; and a vulnerability to moral regulation by the church, state, and community. In recent historical writing, the penetration of the pre-industrial public by households and the informal associations of their members, especially women, has become a complementary theme.[36] Taverns – the most public of all households – offer a unique perspective on this relationship because they are a setting where the household and public intersected by definition.

Playter understood women as embedded in household relationships, as domestic beings who were subject to the authority of men. In his journal, female access to public drinking and the networks of relations it underpinned depended on male gatekeepers. Yet no one challenged women's presence in the taverns' public rooms if they were properly accompanied, which lent female comportment within these spaces a remarkable degree of freedom. There was a party of American women at Fralick's Tavern on the Kingston Road in 1817, for instance, that so shocked a journal-keeping gentleman that he devoted a copious entry to them. "Indelicacy," wrote Charles Fothergill, "prevails":

> Obliged to take tea with divers Yankees of no agreeable cast – many of them coming up country to settle – the kind of freedoms of manners amounting to downright impertinence & great mixture of rank & persons ... is extremely disagreeable to an Englishman ... decent & even pretty girls hawking & spitting abt the room, occasionally scratching & rubbing themselves & lounging in attitudes in their chairs in a way that in Britain wd be unpardonable & throwing out more than broad hints occasionally about the sexual intercourse.[37]

Leaving aside the diarist's dismay, it is apparent that in the company of male kin – those disagreeable and "divers Yankees" – these women felt free to take their ease at the inn. Their experiences were nothing like the women of Paris who were challenged and treated to sexual insults if they entered wine shops in this period. Rather the opposite, in fact. As was the case in England, where alehouses became respectable places patronized by (sexually and economically) respectable women in the late eighteenth century, and Hallowell, Maine, where "no taboo" restricted female access to mixed-public-house gatherings, so in Upper Canada, women's presence in taverns was easily reconciled with existing patterns of daily life.[38] In household company women occupied a legitimate place in community life and its forms of public sociability. Settlers in Upper Canada understood women's domain in ways akin to early modern Britons and republican Americans; they regarded drinking houses as part of women's space and regulated them accordingly.[39]

We also have to add taverns to the list of spaces that men and women shared because women were literally at home, and therefore at work, in them. Married couples, living with their children, ran almost all taverns. Playter's single status is an anomaly, but Miles' wife, Mercy, and their daughter, Bettsey, came to the house frequently. Their regular presence testifies to their work in the tavern household. Although Playter fails to pay much attention to women's domestic labour, he does hint at its content in his journal. It was Mercy who noticed that the servant, Betty Johnson, had fallen ill, and she took turns with Bettsey, Miss T., and Playter as they "whatched her" over several nights.[40] Miss T. "doctor[ed]" Playter's "sore thumb."[41] And Playter once noted, "The ladys soon prepared supper." Women's working presence is evident in Playter's description of the way that meals always materialized at appropriate hours, in the fact that Playter "had [his] room emptyd and cleaned," and in his sudden note that "John Playter" had to call "for [Playter's] foul linnens to wash" after Mercy Miles had left the house. Clearly she, Bettsey, and Betty Johnson performed a multitude of domestic tasks.[42] After Playter gave up tavern keeping, "Moore ... with his family" took over, followed by "Mr Clark & his wife."[43] Women's household work – managing servants, nursing, cooking and serving, cleaning, and laundering – translated well into tavern-keeping work and enabled the trade in crucial ways. Chapter 7 takes up this topic at length, positioning it in the tavern trade of the mid-nineteenth century, where public and private held new meanings for tavern households, especially their female members.

Mary Thompson – Miss T. – also lived at Playter's tavern. She was the daughter of a substantial farm family from Scarborough Township. Her father, Archibald, was a master stonemason and a Justice of the Peace from 1806. Nothing about the way she is presented in the journal suggests less than respectable young womanhood. Playter never explains why Thompson lived in the tavern rather than on her family's farm, and only once does he describe her at work: "I seated myself by the parlour fire & finished my letters to Mr & Mrs Rogers, it was one o'clock in the morning before I retired to bed. Miss T sat at her work till I had finished writing."[44] Playter's brief reference to what was probably needlework combines with other, equally cursory sources to suggest that Thompson may have pursued a textile trade in York, working for the families of the governing elite. Thompson was certainly not a servant in the tavern; she socialized in the same circles as the tavern-keeper and came and went as she pleased.[45] Playter locates her almost exclusively in the parlour, usually in the context of polite household sociability.

Household life in the taverns affected the ambience and the conduct of public life. When Playter and a companion called by mistake at Miller's out in the countryside, "thinking they kept tavern, we staid all night. Lucy told Mr. Mercer they did not keep tavern & he apologised for the liberty we took."[46] Expecting to encounter a familial tavern environment (which is revealed in Playter's use of the pronoun "they,") there was nothing about the place to signal the group's entry into domesticity rather than public space. The two were often, if not interchangeable, indistinguishable. Tavern-keepers' wives and daughters naturally joined companies of callers: "Called at Mr Post's [tavern] had a game of whist with Mr P and Mr Hunt, the latter left us & Miss Post took his seat, we sung some songs, staid til 9." At Captain Wilson's tavern, outside York, "the old lady amused me with her observations on our York young ladys."[47] The very domesticity of taverns meant that children were always about, needing love and attention, and also helping with the patrons. At Bates' tavern (on a trip east of York) Playter and his mother "took breakfast with Mrs Bates & her two daughters very fine young girls."[48] At Beman's tavern, perhaps because Elisha was a recent widower, the need to care for baby Eli was highly visible. Playter enjoyed "tending [his] favourite little boy" there. Playter's description of "Mrs Clinger appearing with the little boy" reveals a rare glimpse into local networks of childcare, which were needed as much in tavern households as elsewhere.[49] Barbara Hanawalt's critical insight that members of the medieval London public shared "domestic and primarily female space" in taverns translates surprisingly well into the context of Playter's colonial York.[50] A parallel understanding that household life intersected with public life in taverns is implicit throughout Playter's journal, particularly in his entries describing the mistake at the Millers' and baby Eli at Beman's tavern.

Indeed, household life, with its attendant hubbub, spilled into putative public space. At Playter's, the sound of "Miss Bettsey and Mary ... romping & making a great noise" pervaded the tavern after "the company retired to bed." Occasionally, the "Black woman made some disturbance as she usually did when she got too much to drink."[51] In fact, only once did the inmates of the house come to the attention of the authorities, and that was because of a violent incident that occurred in household space and household life – not public space and public life. The incident that Playter describes as "a great disturbance [that] took place between Betty & Sagar in the kitchin – as he had struck her down with a pair of shoes and she got a summons from Mr Willcocks to prosecute him but the boat was of[f] with him before she got him apprehended," appears in the minutes of the Court of General Quarter Sessions as follows: "Elizabeth Johnson, a Black woman called upon her recognisance, to prosecute a certain Jacob Segar, for an assault & battery. She does not appear."[52] At no other time did a disorderly incident in the house erupt into the public domain. None of the company in any of Playter's rooms that day, or the night Bettsey and Mary romped, could have overlooked the presence of the tavern household or its noisy female members.

Household life in these moments overwhelmed public life; each was the permanent context for the other.

Having experienced the domestic, household nature of tavern space, early nineteenth-century women and men would rightly scoff at historical characterizations of public houses as settings that, by definition, discouraged female access.[53] The very casualness with which Playter's female relatives and acquaintances entered taverns stands in contrast. Playter's Quaker mother called at his tavern for a visit whenever she was down from the farm: "Mother was in town, call'd on me a short time, went to Beman's to tea."[54] His sisters did the same.[55] Mary Thompson entertained her father, Archibald, in the parlour.[56] And Mary and Sophia visited back and forth between their two tavern homes: "Miss T ... had been at high romps with Sophia."[57]

Nothing about the open-to-the-public nature of their homes worked to exclude the women of tavern-keeping households from local networks of female friendship and association: "See Miss Beman, the Miss Jarvises, and Miss Robinson on their way home as they had been visiting."[58] Similarly, when Playter saw "Mrs Beman as [he] pass'd the door," he "gave [his] sisters' compliments to her as they had requested in their letter"; he facilitated female networks through conventional politeness.[59] And in their taverns these women crafted a female space for sociability into which they also welcomed men.[60] "Miss T, Miss B, and Miss S[wazy] just returned from a walk"; they spent the afternoon together in Beman's before Playter "went over to see the ladys ... staid some time."[61] "Miss N. McDougall call'd" there several days later, "and sat some time with us."[62] In August, Playter "[h]eard Miss Robinson & Miss Beman singing Psalm tunes in the evening" from the tavern across the road.

The fact that it is male eyes, ears, and words that reveal this female world of sociability poses no interpretative stumbling block. Rather, it affirms the publicness of the female world of sociability. English historians have dated the emergence of household withdrawing rooms (or parlours) in public houses to the 1830s, presenting their emergence as evidence of a shared middle-class need to remove the private sphere of familial relations from the intrusions of a wider, coarser world.[63] In Playter's and Beman's taverns, the parlours adopted by women as feminized zones of social interaction predate this process by decades, suggesting that a different dynamic was at work in the creation of female space. Far from inuring themselves within private space, the women of tavern-keeping households created an alternative public space, one that enabled them to pursue alternative forms of public sociability.[64] Women valued a separate female public life of mutual association. This alternative public space was enabled by the common architectural arrangements of colonial taverns, which were always built with distance from the rhythms and practices of the bar in mind, for example, through the routine provision of parlours and private sitting rooms. The women of tavern-keeping households embraced the specificity of their experience. They enjoyed each other's company in their tavern homes. In coming and going freely, in congregating in tavern parlours, and in disturbing the house when they drank or romped, women resisted attempts to construct the public house as anything but a space in which they felt they belonged.[65]

Yet the realities of gendered power in pre-industrial society and the fact that female-centred sociability took place in a household location, and therefore under the patriarchal authority of men, worked against women's authority over the space. The best example is Sophia Beman's courtship story. She and Ely Playter conducted their romantic exchanges largely in what was not, as it turned out, her parlour but her father's. They began seeing each other regularly in the middle of March. By 20 July "some occurrences that had taken place in the afternoon while I was with Miss B appeared to me again in my dreams in the night with a portended lecture that I expected from Mr Beman." It took nearly a month, but "I received a letter from Mr Beman concerning my [?] conduct to his daughter." Playter "immediately concluded" that "some busy person had been meddling and infused those thoughts in his head." Before the end of August, Playter "had made Mr Beman a promise not to give him further room for his jealousy." Playter acknowledged and accepted the authority that Elisha Beman wielded over his household and his daughter's doings. If it were not for the fact that Sophia continued to receive Ely in her father's absences – Playter discloses that as Beman "entered one door I came out at the other" – it would seem plausible that she, fifteen at most, had asked her father to intervene with this man, who was eleven years her senior.[66] As Playter presents the evidence, though, and considering that they married in 1806, it appears that prying eyes in a busy household and its patriarch's authority sharply contained Sophia's autonomous control over her space in her family's tavern.[67]

Nevertheless, Mary Thompson, Sophia Beman, and their circle of female friends and relatives used their parlours just as members of the provincial respectability – a term referencing both economic solidity and socio-cultural adherence to moral norms – customarily did, as sites for genteel exchanges among a select company of women, or men and women both. Echoing the glittering assemblies of the gentlefolk of Georgian England and republican America, where men and women flocked to specialized rooms in public buildings to dance, sup, play at cards, and converse among themselves, parlour gatherings at Playter's and Beman's taverns sustained a sense of exclusive identity.[68]

We know tavern design incorporated the presumption that self-selected groups would seek space apart from the barroom throng. While their ability to do so never went uncontested, the opportunity to withdraw was the preserve of the relatively privileged members of York society.[69] The claimed domains of tavern space "inscribed class and cultural hierarchy across the common landscape."[70] The respectability, like the gentry or upper classes, used parlour sociability to sustain a cultural identity based on polite conversation, mannerly deportment, musicality, and practised literacy, and each activity found its fullest meaning when men and women enacted it together. Expressions of civilized masculinity and femininity benefited from the other's presence as foils.[71] By articulating the rituals of gentility, women shared in the creation of a "genteel public culture," a style of public life that emphasized social distance and the possession of social authority.[72] Mary Thompson and Sophia Beman used their parlours as privileged women did everywhere – as sites for female public life that fashioned and displayed an elite (or elite-inspired) cultural identity.

Playter's detailed reconstruction of an extended evening in the parlour at Beman's tavern in 1803 brings the themes of this discussion to life:

> Went over to Mr Beman's where mother and Mrs. Ward went to spend the night. As we [Playter and Ward] entered the parlour we perceived the ladys. Mrs and Miss B[eman], Miss R[obinson], and the above, Mr C. Willcocks, Mr Ridout, Mr J. Small Jnr., and Mr Pudney. Mr Willcocks was amusing the ladys with the flute, Mr Small soon left us, Mr W[illcocks] soon after. Mrs Beman called on Mr W[ard] for a song to which he complied. I sung the 2nd Mr Pudney the 3rd and Miss Sally Robinson the last. Mr Ridout then left us. The young ladys went to writing. Mr Dean, Mr Pudney and me went upstairs, Mr W[ard] soon joined us, and we sat a long time. A Mr Eaton came in a law[y]er from the States, called for more brandy as we had been drinking and made a great deal of mirth till past 12 o'c.[73]

The company in Beman's parlour defined itself through select membership – the men and women shared position and prosperity. Elisha Beman, who was an established merchant as well as a tavern-keeper, owned at least two thousand acres of land, filled several local offices, and held a commission as a Justice of the Peace for the Home District. Nine months earlier he married Esther Sayre Robinson, the widow of a Loyalist member of the governing elite. (Her son, John Beverley Robinson, who was then eleven years old, would become attorney general, solicitor general, and chief justice, and his name still reigns in Canadian historiography as a symbol of pre-Reform, hierarchical Upper Canada.) The Bemans belonged securely among locally prominent families and the company in their parlour shared their social position. Ridout and Willcocks each enjoyed family ties to the economic and political elite, as did John Robert Small, who, like Ward, was a practising lawyer. Much less is known about Joseph Pudney, but both he and Erastus Dean, who worked as Beman's clerk, lived at Beman's tavern in 1802. The "ladys" included Playter's mother, his sister Mary, who wed Thomas Ward in January, Esther Beman, her daughter Sally Robinson, and her new step-daughter Sophia Beman, Playter's love.[74] Gathered together for polite sociability under Sophia and her stepmother's patronage, members of York's professional, merchant, and office-holding families distinguished themselves through their social affinities.

When the "young ladys went to writing," they demonstrated another aspect of the group's discriminating membership – its common possession and mutual enjoyment of literacy. Literacy rates, as measured by the ability to sign one's name, stood very high in York, as they did in North America as a whole in 1800. They approached 90 percent among men and probably 80 percent among women. However, only a small minority participated in written culture to such a degree that they would consider writing as natural a form of communication as speech. Members of this minority could be found daily in Playter's and Beman's parlours, brought together partly by their desire to share literate culture and its expression among themselves. Those townspeople who were still bound by oral culture knew enough to seek out the literate at the tavern: "Wrote a letter for A. Davison to go to his former lover in Ireland. Shew[ed] it to Miss T in the evening." Playter studded his journal with accounts of reading aloud in company, writing, exchanging letters, drawing up notes, taking pleasure in shared composition, and bandying silly jests: "Chloe's now married & looks on men no more / Why then 'tis plane for what she looked before." In his own parlour, Playter "spent the evening writing for the amusement of J[ames] Miles and Miss T. I gave them the perusal of some scraps on various subjects, some extracts, and some of my own composition." Playter refers to a wide range of reading material, and his entries show that he spent a significant amount of time reflecting on and preserving it. Although it is likely true that little "serious reading" took place in barrooms given the "good deal of conviviality" that occurred within, polite conviviality and literary expression entwined quite naturally in tavern parlours among household members and their guests. Just as American gentlemen modelled their sociability on forms derived from literature, sometimes in tavern settings Playter's circle emphasized shared literacy as a tool of mutual pleasure. Both instances highlight literacy's power in privileged cultural formation.[75]

When Playter and Ward entered the parlour, they entered a space that has been defined in private homes as a "third social sphere," distinct from the public of the street and the inner rooms of the private house. This third sphere supported the "refinement" of Euro-American society in the second half of the eighteenth century, when many middling-rank consumers gentrified their homes and their habits of sociability. In Beman's tavern and in Playter's, the parlour played a similar mediating role; it provided the exclusive stage on which genteel tavern-goers and female household members enacted the rituals of genteel public life. The material culture of colonial parlours fixed them as spaces for polite social intercourse. Although common drinks such as grog were consumed within parlours, both Playter and Beman stocked the brandies, wines, and punches that were preferred by their genteel companions: "Call'd for a glass of punch & walked into the parlour with Sophia, sat till we drank our punch." Both tavern-keepers also placed tea tables in their parlours, where their patrons and companions gathered about to take tea. Sometimes they ritualized the act further by extending invitations. Sophia "asked me into the parlour for tea," wrote Playter in August.[76]

Musical instruments and sheet music provided a means of practised diversion, inviting performance and informed appreciation. Playter owned and played a flute, and he annotated his music and wrote songs. He wrote that Mr. Willcocks' ability to "amus[e] the ladys" with his flute was "universally considered as an elegant accomplishment." The company's customary use of sheet music links polite amusement to preparation and practice. Playter noted, "I set singing with Miss Beman till bedtime; she had borrowed a musick book of me & I was teaching her till late." Polite society identified their secular music as "parlour tunes"; by doing so, they explicitly fused music to the pursuit of genteel ritual within the crafted space of the parlour.[77]

A mannerly code of conduct set the pattern for parlour sociability in the tavern household as much as it did in the private household. Playter's journal entries signify adherence to unstated rules of deportment. He emphasizes the same rituals of invitation, conversation, song, and tea time etiquette that structured parlour gatherings in private homes. For Playter, as for parlour denizens everywhere, such conventions served to separate the genteel from the common. Within York itself, for example, Anne Murray Powell, the wife of the chief justice, wielded a rigid standard of etiquette as a weapon in ongoing battles for social position within the small circle of York's governing elite. Parlours, no less than ballrooms and dining rooms, were sites for determining just who belonged and who did not. Powell's "sense of propriety" valued proper behaviour both as a means to identify the select and as an index to moral worth. Similarly, when local lawyer and physician William Warren Baldwin wrote to his friend the attorney general to decry the table manners of an associate, he too affirmed the social value of proper conduct. To put aside one's knife in favour of a piece of bread was "outlandish" and "coxcombical." It was an "impudence" that filled him with disgust. Moreover, it was probably "some damned French ... fashion." And Playter's customer Alexander Mcdonnell kept a diary in which he chronicled tea drinking, dining, and conversation. He too could be either an acidic judge of other's poor conduct or an appreciative observer of their polish.[78] Playter and his friends were far from alone, then, in adhering to a code of conduct in their parlour exchanges. As for others, such rules served to affirm a sense of being among the select.

Playter's use of titles and surnames for people with whom he enjoyed daily contact implies more than an adherence to formality; it was a defence against the heterogeneity that surrounded him. His construction of the exchange between Mrs. Beman and Mr. Ward as a formal "call" for song and the gentleman's complaisant response, indeed the assumption that gentlemen stood willing to amuse ladies in social gatherings, highlights the prominent role granted to women, due to their sensibility, within polite society and the rules of sociability. The fact that patrons numbered songs suggests that parlour culture manifested a predictable rhythm. Although they deployed music, books, and tea rather than grog and a willingness to box with a companion, the women of tavern-keeping households participated in a culture no less ritualized and no less public than that of their male counterparts. From the perspective of Playter's journal, women may have disavowed close association with the throng who filled their houses daily, yet they enacted an alternative vision of public life and association. They marked out feminine zones in their tavern households to which they, and the genteel culture that reserved room for them, belonged.

The distinction that Playter draws in his reconstruction of the evening at Beman's between the mixed-gender companionship of the parlour and the male sociability of brandy and mirth "upstairs" points to a disjunction in behaviour between women and men. By revealing the freedom that men enjoyed to move between parlour culture and drinking culture (even though the latter was still defined by select company), Playter's diary suggests the limits of women's ability to control their domain. For example, after Ward and Heward spent a long evening of excess in male company at Playter's, they breached the parlour, where Mary Thompson sat, and "exposed the effects the wine had on them." Thompson made light of it, and "laughed much at me this morning on our high bout," but the threat of incursion was a permanent one for these women conducting gentility within earshot of a busy barroom.[79]

Tavern interiors gave spatial expression and support to desires for social distance and cultural difference; by doing so, they supported women's (and men's) desire to map genteel sociability onto the public that surrounded them. The parlour was an alternative public space that was female-initiated and -enabled; its select companionship and mutual enactment of specialized cultural rituals stood in direct contrast to the openness and potential disorder of barroom association. The parlour's claim on the tavern's public space sought to perform a function similar to the bourgeois ritual of promenades on the "promiscuous" streets of nineteenth-century New York City, by which participants and onlookers "together ... mapped an elite public-within-the-public."[80]

Although a similar attempt to map an elite public took place in tavern parlours and upstairs withdrawing rooms in Upper Canada, the balance of power could be uncertain. Even though selective association and distance from the barroom throng were important to the parlour's habitués, there is no indication that Playter (or Beman) ever turned non-genteel patrons away. Thus, the devotees of politeness in York were as likely to scuttle for cover as they were to exercise the prerogatives of social prominence in their claims on tavern space. "The house," wrote Playter of Beman's tavern on Militia Day in June, "was full of all kinds of people, and we shut ourselves up in the upper room." Sophia, Mary, Ely, and a "Mr Canby from Queenston," claimed a space for themselves behind closed doors where Canby sang two songs. But it is by no means clear that the group's ability to occupy the upper room as an exclusive zone actually expressed a significant degree of social or cultural authority. When the desire for selectivity collided against publicness, as it did on Militia Day in York, the public of "all kinds of people" dominated tavern space.

That night Playter wrote, "Sophia was complaining about the manner of living in a public house," and he could only sympathize that "it was certainly very disagreeable for her."[81] Sophia spoke from a position of cultural privilege that valued polite discourse and practised diversions over the rituals of drinking culture. Yet she enacted polite sociability only at the mercy of the barroom company. She spoke as a (very) young woman whose claim to a feminine domain in her tavern household depended ultimately on the acquiescence of men: her father, the gentlemen with whom she associated, and the throng who filled her father's bar. As Sophia's complaint to Ely suggested, the tavern setting exaggerated not only the limitations that were placed on the precedence of the privileged in colonial society but also the much deeper limits that were placed on female authority in the eighteenth and early nineteenth centuries. Within these limits, it was the mixture of women and men and household space and public space that defined the pre-industrial colonial taverns of Playter's York. Without challenging the gendered hierarchy, Playter's journal places taverns firmly within the pre-industrial social landscape. Like streets, churches, squares, markets, and commons, taverns were spaces where both women and men belonged.

3
Public Houses as Colonial Public Space

At Haw's tavern I said, "I wish I could swear my oath over again."

– Trial of William Townsend, alias Robt. J. McHenry, 1854

The ideal of balanced use was at the core of tavern design in Upper Canada. The household dimension of the public that Ely Playter depicted in his journal was inherent to that ideal; so too was its counterweight: public life in public space. Public space was, and is, both real and conceptual. Real places, like squares, piazzas, and parks, are designed by planners today to facilitate access and encounters among diverse segments of populations. The modern design ideal is profoundly democratic in what it envisages as the social goal of public space. Historians have taken up the idea of democratic access and have used it to assess the patterns of use in real spaces such as Central Park in nineteenth-century New York. The certainty that good public space enhances citizenship for all members of a mixed society is implicit in their work.[1]

Conceptually, or philosophically, approaches to public space are frequently embedded in the politics of post-modernism and anti-colonialism, seeing in public space a site rife with the possibilities for (and failures of) meaningful, multiple, cultural exchange.[2] Frequently, critical analyses point to the limitations of public space in practice. Feminists delineate gendered restraints on democratic access, offering insights into the barriers placed around women's participation in public life and public space, both historically and in the present. Modern anti-racism advocates (some of whom are the same feminists), like their nineteenth-century counterparts, focus on the extent to which public space and public life advanced the interests of racially and gender privileged groups at the expense of others.[3]

These critical perspectives can enrich our understanding of tavern space as public space in early Canada, and I employ them in subsequent chapters.

In this chapter, I establish the tavern's bona fides as public space in a manner that may be less attentive to the issue of difference than is desirable. Although I am well aware of the importance of difference to this book's preoccupation with the sharp qualifications that changing "identity politics" placed on social membership and cultural belonging in public spaces, such as colonial taverns, I largely set it aside in this chapter. While the sources available to me show how important taverns were as public space – as meeting halls, markets, mustering points, churches, courts, polls, theatres, community centres, and so on – they tend to be less revealing about who actually came to occupy them. In other words, when we approach taverns as "public in the more pedestrian, colloquial, but critical way – in their openness and accessibility to the people," we tend not to know who those people were.[4]

We know, for example, from a traveller's journal, that about forty colonists, both men and women, crowded into a country tavern near St. Thomas in 1835 to see a show put on by a "travelling mountebank" who ate fire and tumbled.[5] It is evident that this tavern functioned on this occasion as a festival site, as a public space open to many. But the source offers no insight into the nature of the multitude's terms of association. The tavern-goers were mixed by gender, but did that mean that men and women came together as families, independently, or both? Was the crowd otherwise mixed? For example, did blacks and Natives or Reformers and Tories rub shoulders? Did chambermaids and farmers jostle against gentlefolk for a good view? The newspaper advertisements, published travelogues, and court records, on which my analysis rests, include information that is as opaque as the story about the mountebank. Consequently, I focus on the ways that the taverns *were* public, how they were indispensable for transportation, the economy, politics, and community life. Their very publicness, for all its potential exclusions, explains the taverns' resilience in the decades when the meanings of tavern going seemed to be changing.

A new generation of Upper Canadians was forced by an evolving social and cultural debate to question the easy acceptance of alcohol and the customary integration of drink into the rhythm and rituals of everyday life that had characterized tavern going in Ely Playter's generation. In the 1840s and 1850s the temperance movement achieved enormous success in transforming drinking habits across North America. The movement was inspired initially by "dry" voices from the United States, scriptural religiosity, and the demands of an economy just beginning to rapidly urbanize and industrialize. Temperance activists inspired a mass movement in these decades; half a million British North Americans (a significant minority of the population) were moved to pledge moderation in or abstinence from the consumption of alcohol. Sobriety, and the self-disciplined individual it subsumed, came to be a crucial component of respectability and prosperity. Taverns and their keeps were entirely complicit in the drink trade, and they threatened the ideal of progress that was at the centre of Christian-inspired temperance activism for social salvation.[6] The *Canada Temperance Advocate,* in an article entitled "Death Among Tavern Keepers," made the link between abstinence and salvation explicit when it beseeched tavern-keepers and -goers to "reflect upon the possibility of being called direct from the barroom to the judgement."[7] I do not question the earnestness of the reorientation toward drink that temperance inspired, but this chapter makes the point that taverns were not that affected by the movement. Numbers tell part of the story. Because the state derived revenue from tavern licences, it kept good records of the number issued each year. Civil servants tallied the information submitted by license inspectors in the districts and published the totals in the annual *Journals* of the Legislative Assembly. From 1801, when the first statistics become available, to 1852, when the temperance movement was in full swing, the number of taverns increased from 108 to 2,723 (see Table 1).

The tavern to population ratio in Upper Canada was low in comparison to the ratios for US cities and western Europe, where tavern to population ratios were approximately 1 per 200. In Upper Canada they averaged well over 1 per 300 for the first three-quarters of the nineteenth century, in part because the colony's population was largely rural and agrarian. It is also notable that this ratio did not decline until well after Confederation.[8] Although temperance advocates swayed many Upper Canadians to their cause, there were as many taverns relative to the population in 1874 (1/334) as there had been in 1802 (1/320). The explanation for this phenomenon tells us much about the identity of taverns as public spaces that enabled public life.

Like members of any society that tolerated public drinking places in their midst, Upper Canadians invested taverns with positive meanings and valued them often for pragmatic, utilitarian reasons as much as for the support they lent to sociability. Taverns enabled transportation, especially on the roadways, and this role was not deeply altered by the completion of railway lines in the mid-1850s, since most taverns were embedded in local rather than long-distance transportation networks. Taverns extended the sphere of economic activity by encouraging patrons to transact business, set up shop, and practice their professions on the premises, though public houses were more likely to fulfill this role in the 1790s than they were in the 1850s. Taverns housed political expression, overwhelmingly civil but sometimes violently conducted; and they housed community life by making room for activities that bound neighbours and friends together or in which they aired their disputes. Tavern space worked as public space well beyond the mid-1850s, even though temperance-related issues and a range of alternative venues, which were made available through economic development (such as community halls), changed the constellation of groups seeking them out. Still, well after the middle of the century, rural taverns fulfilled many early-century functions long displaced from their urban counterparts.

Table 1

Ratio of Upper Canadian taverns to population, by year

Year*	Population	Taverns	Ratio per capita
1801	34,600	108	1/320
1820	109,740	428	1/256
1825	154,381	476	1/324
1827	177,174	588	1/301
1832-33	295,863	931	1/317
1837	400,286	1,009	1/397
1839	409,048	1,114	1/367
1840	437,681	1,446	1/303
1842	487,000	1,084†	1/449
1843	521,090	1,611	1/323
1845	596,596	1,970	1/303
1846	638,357	2,096	1/305
1847	675,067	2,218	1/304
1849	776,691	2,367	1/328
1850	885,364	2,523	1/351
1852	952,004	2,723	1/350
1874	1,600,000	4,793	1/334

* Public accounts do not survive for the years 1802-19, 1821-24, 1826, and 1828-31. This record ended in 1853 when tavern-licensing revenue reverted (temporarily) to the municipalities.

† Surely the 1842 number is incorrect. For example, the Eastern District, which reported only 10 taverns in 1842, reported 65 taverns in 1841 and 70 in 1843. The Home District likewise reported 184 taverns in 1842, 294 in 1841, and 323 in 1843.

Sources: Population figures are based on McCalla, *Planting the Province,* Appendix B, Table 1.1, 249; Armstrong, *Handbook of Upper Canadian Chronology,* Table 3, 275. Data for tavern numbers is from Fraser, ed., *Eleventh Report of the Bureau of Archives for the Province of Ontario,* 749-50, 752-53, 757-78, 774-75; Fraser, ed., *Tenth Report,* 293-97; and Upper Canada, House of Assembly, *Appendix to the Journal of the Legislative Assembly of Upper Canada* (1825, 2nd sess., 9th Parl., Public Accounts (PA) no. 9 – the licences issued after October are missing; 1827, 4th sess., 9th Parl., PA no. 12; 1832-33, 3rd sess., 11th Parl., PA no. 10 and 4th sess., 11th Parl., PA no. 10; 1837, 3rd sess., 13th Parl., PA no. 14 and 4th sess., 13th Parl., PA no. 5); *Appendix to the Journal of the Legislative Assembly of the Province of Canada* (1839 and 1840, vol. 1, 1st sess., 1st Parl., App. B, PA no. 4; 1842, vol. 3, 3rd sess., 1st Parl., App. A, PA no. 3; 1843, vol. 4, 1st sess., 2nd Parl., App. A, PA no. 3; 1845, vol. 5, 2nd sess., 2nd Parl., App. C, PA nos. 3 and 5; 1846, vol. 6, 3rd sess., 2nd Parl., App. A, PA nos. 3 and 30; 1847, vol. 8, 2nd sess., 3rd Parl., App. A, PA nos. 3 and 34; 1849, vol. 9, 3rd sess., 3rd Parl., App. C, PA nos. 3 and 24; 1850, vol. 10, 4th sess., 3rd Parl., App. B, PA nos. 3 and 28; 1852, vol. 13, 1st sess., 5th Parl., App. B, nos. 3 and 22); and Drummond, *Progress Without Planning,* 294, 292-99.

The colony's first governor, John Graves Simcoe, made the tavern's role in transportation explicit in one of his first official acts. He ordered the military to build government houses (state-owned, but privately leased and run taverns) in order "to facilitate communication."[9] Simcoe understood it was essential for the public good to set Crown land aside to pay for "the expenses of ... building *inns* or posts necessary for communication."[10] He drew on centuries of British practice, whereby urban and provincial inns promoted efficient transportation and supported commercial exchanges between long-distance traders and merchants. In the thirteen colonies and the United States, legislators likewise deemed taverns so fundamental to transportation that any tavern-keeper who refused admission to a traveller risked his or her licence. In Upper Canada, Justices of the Peace first began to frame tavern regulations in 1818; they immediately assured free access to the public by requiring "that every innkeeper shall at all times provide proper attendance, particularly for travellers, horses, baggage &c."[11]

The diary of Crown Lands agent Harry Jones, who travelled by stagecoach on government business in January 1837, testifies to the importance of the roadway and tavern travel network.

Friday 20th: Walked down to the stage office and back ... Breakfasted ... told it was at Cotter's [New British Coffee House] walked down there ... Supposed it had gone off without me – Swore – a false alarm for it soon made its appearance and called at Perry's [boarding house] ... Started & tolerably fair day – picked up Young, Street, Dr Hamilton of Queenston and Thos. Horatio Taylor – Stopped at the Credit – saw Mosier formerly one of the st[eam] b[oa]t captains on Lake Ontario – the man is dreadfully changed, looks grog-stricken. Talked to Street abt the Hamilton & Port Sarnia rail-road and to Dr Hamilton on matters & things ... Reached Hamilton before dark and took up my quarter's at Burley's [Tavern] – drank tea, took two or three horns, smoked a segar – laughed at Stevenson the stage proprietor, who was on a spree, most particularly drunk and went to bed in a dirty room.

Saturday 21st: Found on coming down that the Brantford Stage had been off for more than an hour – very pleasant – swore immensely and then smoked a segar ... Read a whole file of New York papers (the *Spirit of the Times*) ... Major Holcroft came up in the stage from Toronto – engaged with him in making a series of chemical experiments with the view of determining how little warm water was necessary to the manufacture of port wine negus – Took my seat in the stage and went to bed.

Sunday 22nd: Called up at 6 o'clock and of course kept waiting until near 8. Major Holcroft very impatient, comforted himself with a little rum and milk. – Made a very slow passage to Ancaster ... Breakfasted and admired the Misses Rousseau vastly – Got rid of the Major and enlisted an old woman ... All the tavern keepers on this road rejoice in the name Odell – Dined ... saw nothing wonderful save a parcel of cream coloured girls without the slightest tinge of red about them and lots of pious Christians in every stage of bluism at every tavern ... Oh! By Jove! I had nearly forgotten the bride we met at Burford's whose affections were so much divided between her new but very ugly husband and a glass of hot stuff – Faith! she stuck to the tumbler like grim death. Proceeded at a fine pace and reached Martin's tavern

(Oxford) early in the evening, where we found we were to remain until morning, which mightily irritated a Yankee fellow passenger who like all his countrymen was in a hurry.

Monday 23rd: Started at 4 am and reached London by 11 [am] ... quarreled with the stage driver who wanted to force breakfast down our throats before daybreak ... Found on our arrival that the Chatham Stage had left – Yankee ... offered to give me $25000 if a railroad or anything else west went through Canada direct. – Saw young Steers ... who told me that his sister wished to go to Chatham and would be glad to avail herself of my protection; assented of course – Went to a nigger's opposite Gregory's who most invitingly offers "comfort in shaving," in large gilt capitals ... listened to a fine display of the prowess of the London amateur band ... – Walked back, had a long confab with my lawyer namesake Stewart Jones who has I am told reformed and went to bed.

Tuesday 24th: Got up at 2½. Received my lady-companion in all due form from her brother. Picked up VanNorman of Long Point a decided Radical at Delaware. Breakfasted at Miller's [Tavern]. Got out to ease nature at Nash's [Tavern] – Stage went off during the operation and obliged to run half a mile with my breeches ... Stopped a few minutes at Aubrey's [Tavern] and arrived at Chatham before dark – took leave of my companion with great politeness and again took up my quarters at Freeman's. Found everyone well ... drank tea and sundry horns and went to bed.[12]

Over four days and a distance of 180 miles (288 kilometres), which were bracketed by taverns at each end, Jones' stagecoach called at twelve other taverns along the way. Delays and frustrations aside, the tavern-stagecoach combination followed a certain logic. In the absence of railways, land transportation was fuelled by muscle power and moved at a rate of approximately three to four miles per hour, stopping roughly every three and a half hours. When the timing worked it made sense for humans and horses alike. (By 1850, when surfaced roads became more common, some travellers noted horse-drawn speeds of up to 10 miles per hour.)[13]

Travellers went to taverns to pay the fare, book a seat (just as the diarist did before bed at W.D. Dutton's Brantford Cottage), and set out. The colony's first regular stage route, between Newark and Chippewa, began operations in 1801. It was owned by two tavern-keepers, Joshua Fairbanks at one end and Thomas Hind at the other. In 1820 travellers in Kingston who wanted to go to York called first at the public house of Daniel Brown, "opposite the marketplace," to make reservations. Going the other way, the tavern-keeper at Jordan's Inn, York, organized the details. In 1851 the City Hotel in Hamilton was the stage house and general booking office for the web of routes that intersected and connected in that city. Taverns were the stations of their day, functioning as points of embarkation, transfer, and terminus. Some taverns on lakeshores or riverbanks integrated their services with steamboat travel. The Eberts brothers in Chatham, for example, ran the Royal Exchange Hotel opposite the wharf in the 1840s, owned the steamboat *Brothers*, which docked there and plied up and down the Thames, and operated a line of stages offering connections to the east. Taverns were also the rent-a-car agencies of their day. Horses, carriages, and even drivers were hired out. Tavern-keepers ran two of Hamilton's livery stables in 1851, and Toronto was served by the Lovejoy House Hotel and Livery Stables and the Wellington Hotel Livery Stables. While Kingston had Mink's Telegraph House Hotel, General Stage House, and Livery Stables, Prescott had Gilman's Commercial Hotel, Stage House, and Livery Stables. At Tesimond's small tavern in the Western District, a traveller "procured a horse, a regular bog trotter glorying in the name of Jerry."[14]

The completion of railroads connecting Montreal, Toronto, Hamilton, Niagara Falls, London, and Windsor by 1856 eliminated the significance of key stage routes and houses. But the taverns remained valuable, especially to local travellers and, to a lesser extent, to steam and rail passengers. The majority of travellers on the roads had never used stagecoaches in the first place because they were expensive and had limited space for luggage and goods. Most travellers drove their own horses or oxen, wagons or sleighs. They too relied on the taverns. "The little snow that had fell," wrote an early York tavern-keeper, for instance, "brought people to town from the country and it looked quite lively. We had four or five sleys in the yard that stayed all night." At mid-century it was no less common than it had been at the beginning of the settlement era for tavern-keepers to include, with the price of lodging and "for the use of travellers," "good stabling and [a] lock-up barn or driving house for the safe keeping of horses, cattle, carriages and waggons."[15] Not only did tavern regulations require that tavern-keepers do so, but also advertisements suggest that it made good economic sense. Most, if not all, tavern-keepers appended remarks about the good quality of their stables. George Carside, for example, who kept the Neptune Inn on New Street in York boasted that "farmers and others with teams will find every necessary convenience in stopping at his house."[16] For steamboat and rail travellers, taverns included the essential services of baggage handling and transportation between the wharf or station and the hotel in the price of lodging. Railways reinforced established patterns of urban growth, enabling a handful of principal taverns to benefit from the accelerated pace of travel. Principal tavern-keepers and others built purposely for the new trade, giving birth to the "monster hotels" that emerged in the 1850s.

Jones' stage trip also reveals the extent to which tavern-based travel brought colonists into public space. He catalogued a series of encounters that pushed him, perforce, into mixed public life, where he offered his perspective on racialized and gendered "others." There was the black barber who kept shop across from Gregory's tavern; the "cream coloured" women who were, apparently, non-Native; and a bride who became, perhaps, the subject of sexual innuendo. In Jones' description of the escort granted a young woman, there was a display of male precedence and the masculine assumption of belonging in public space. In Jones' travelogue, then, there is an implicit assertion of this colonial, white, privileged male's own sense of identity as he chanced on the less white, less privileged, and female members of his society and inscribed their images in language that emphasized "otherness" and difference.

More positively, taverns also provided opportunities for engagement with public space as travellers read the newspaper, mixed in the public room, or listened to a London band. Jones noted the radical politics of an acquaintance and defined himself against an American. He enjoyed some vulgarity – he laughed at a drunk and at himself for getting caught with his trousers around his ankles on the public street – and he found the opportunity to play, to spend an evening in company refining the recipe for port wine negus. In short, tavern-based travel engaged travellers in civic, political, and social activities in public space.

Classic definitions of "the public," as opposed to "the private," invoke the market economy: even though economic activity – or participation in the free market – is pursued for individual gain, classical theorists believe it belongs conceptually in the public sphere. Part of what made the taverns public space was their support of economic activity of all sorts. At the beginning of the nineteenth century auctioneers and sheriffs (whose job included seizing convicted debtors' goods and selling them to satisfy the debt) almost always held their sales at taverns. After a court sided with his creditors in 1801, Nathan Raymond, for example, suffered the sale of all his "goods and chattels, lands and tenements" by the sheriff at Hamilton's hotel in Niagara. More commonly, merchants, colonists, and land agents used the taverns as auction settings. In York, a billiard table, a calèche and harness, and assorted household furniture sold by auction at Hind's Hotel in 1797, as did an assortment of clothing at Stoyells' Tavern in 1807. As York and other early towns such as Niagara and Kingston grew and developed economically, these kinds of sales moved out of the taverns and into specialized buildings – courthouses for the sheriff's sales and commercial salesrooms for the auctions. By 1840 advertisements for tavern auctions were rare in any town in the colony. But in rural and newly settling areas taverns retained their function as the normal venue for even court-ordered sales. In 1854, for example, when a Court of Chancery suit resulted in the sale of an established farm and house, the auction took place at Irish's Tavern, County of Victoria. With the court itself in Toronto and county institutions in Peterborough, locals lacked convenient access to suitable government buildings. Irish's Tavern stood in as the closest alternative because it was conveniently located and endowed with the requisite public character.[17]

Unless the evidence is simply lacking, it appears that Upper Canadian taverns were unusual in the sense that they did not develop specialized associations with particular trades or markets. Matthew Dolsen's tavern on the Thames River did have an agricultural market in the late 1790s. Farmers brought in their produce for sale and bought goods, including liquor, in return. A. Ogden, T. White, and M. Richeson each did so, for example, and, while they were there, they each breakfasted, took a drink, or treated a companion. The racialized and gendered lines that Jones drew so clearly in his diary are smudged in this context, for Native men and women participated in tavern-based economic activity at Dolsen's. Many carried accounts that show sales of fur, corn, and maple sugar and purchases of household necessities, wine, and liquor. They too drank and dined inside the tavern. (A fuller picture of First Nations' relations with taverns is developed in Chapter 5.) More generally, sales of apples, grain, peas, and beef from local farmers appear in the books of other tavern-keepers, such as Abner Miles in early York, James Philips in Bastard Township in the late 1820s and 1830s, and Thomas Robinson at Prescott in the 1840s. A "grain merchant" set up shop at the Wellington Hotel in Toronto in 1851.[18] But this was small potatoes in comparison to the economic activity of taverns in early-nineteenth-century England, where much of the country's trade in hops, agricultural seed, corn, and malt took place at specific urban inns, as it had for centuries. In the principal market town of Preston, Lancashire, for example, the Castle Inn, the Boar's Head, the King's Head, the White Horse, and the George all provided corn houses for traders' grain and specialized rooms for their exchanges.[19] Tavern-based produce markets in Upper Canada, by contrast, were small-scale, hit-and-miss affairs.

The more informal activity of individuals making deals between or among themselves figured more prominently in Upper Canadian taverns. It is certain that a man sold a cow and a calf at Simpson's tavern in Galt in 1833 and that a woman bought a dress in a Toronto tavern in 1848. We know also that tavern-keepers facilitated transactions among their patrons because of the records they kept in their account books. Evidently tavern-goers found these sites conducive to personal economic exchanges. John B. Coles assumed that this was the primary function of a public house. When he opened the Queenston Hotel in 1824, he invited "gentlemen of the neighborhood" to come inside, receive attentive service, and transact business. Cooper's Coffee House and Beman's tavern in York served a similar function. When Ely Playter and Mr. Terry settled a land deal in 1802, they went to both places to finalize the arrangements and, ultimately, share a drink of gin before they parted ways. Matthew Dolsen also supplied basic banking services. He used his books to show debts paid by and to third parties, discounted bills of exchange, and honoured drafts. Like Abner Miles and James Philips, he also lent amounts of cash to their regular customers. Obviously, the absence of formal banking institutions played a role, but the practice extended well beyond a practical need for it. Banks existed in the 1840s and '50s, when Prescott tavern-keeper Thomas Robinson recorded regular cash loans on his books and patrons used his tavern to negotiate and settle mutual accounts. In 1843 Robinson recorded an ominous-sounding arrangement made by five men that involved insurance premiums and the purchase of a plough, a coffin, and a horse and wagon. Similarly, in 1848 peddler Patrick McBride and several colleagues met, as usual, at McBrien's tavern in Toronto. As a companion who owed McBride money later put it: McBride was "leaving his wife and wanted all ye money he could get. He urged me to borrow money of McBrien and to settle ye bill he owed him and I said I would – McBrien assented." A bank had no relevance to such an exchange: in an established mid-nineteenth-century urbanizing economy, it was the tavern that could facilitate small transactions among friends and associates.[20]

However, the evidence for economic activity is fragmentary. The other sites of economic exchange – both formal, like commercial salesrooms or general stores, and informal, like the waiting line at the mill – are so numerous that it is difficult to reach firm conclusions about the role and importance of taverns. In opening their doors to peddlers and deal-making neighbours, the taverns certainly extended the sphere of economic activity – they literally gave it more room to operate. But it would be impossible to determine what proportion of the colony's economic development was carried out as tavern-based transactions. It is clear that *formal* business activity left the taverns with the advent of specialized commercial facilities. John B. Coles' 1824 advertisement reflected common knowledge that the taverns were the natural places "to transact business"; by 1854, however, taverns had lost their primacy in this regard, except for personal exchanges among acquaintances. In St. Catharines, the central hotel stressed its suitability to businessmen through its location in the heart of town and its easy access to the railway, telegraph, and postal offices. It did not claim dedication to the needs of business itself.[21]

Still, a profusion of services continued to operate in tavern space. Many colonists who had little immediate interest in a drink passed through the taverns' doors on any given day. Early in the nineteenth century, physicians, such as Dr. J. Glennon at Marion's in York and Dr. Tolmon at Dexter's in Vaughan, undertook consultations in tavern chambers. By the 1840s, under the pressures of professionalization, tavern-based practices were a thing of the past. Lawyers, who had likewise "enter[ed] into public bar-rooms" to conduct legal business, increasingly turned to the Law Society's own building when they were away from their offices. Dentists, however, continued to travel from town to town, where they set up practice in taverns. As late as 1844, for example, Mr. C. Kahn announced that he had taken over the dental "office lately occupied by Dr Bowker at Daley's Hotel" in Kingston. And an assortment of hairdressers, shoemakers, watchmakers, jewellers, portrait painters, dancing instructors, fencing masters, and music professors all attempted, with varying degrees of permanence, to make a living from inside the tavern premises.[22]

Business meetings regularly convened there. Whether they were stockholders of the Bank of Upper Canada, the Farmers' Store House Company, or the Fire Insurance Company, or investors in the Grand River Navigation Company or the Desjardin Canal Company, shareholders and directors found tavern space practical because their own enterprises, often fledgling or transitory, lacked their own facilities. The fact that they chose to meet in a tavern rather than a private home is telling. The tavern provided a space free of the obligations of host and guest; it placed all parties and individuals on the same level playing field. In newly settling areas taverns made it possible for meeting organizers to select central locations that would make travel distances similar for all, and they gave scope to the desire to mix business with pleasure. For example, in 1836 John Prince, who was a magistrate, militia colonel, and member of the provincial Parliament, attended the "great rail meeting" at Gardiner's tavern in the Longwoods in the Western District. "I was afterwards made one of the directors and was subsequently made president! All went off well, met several friends and got rather tipsy."[23]

Colonists attended auctions, called at the rooms of shoemakers and jewellers to purchase their wares, visited the travelling dentist, and set up joint stock companies in the taverns. They did this much more frequently in the 1820s than they did in the 1840s as taverns steadily lost their prominence as public sites for formal economic activity. Stakeholders preferred specialized, purpose-built premises once these became available. And as financial prudence and fiscal responsibility came to be firmly tied to sober conduct and sober surroundings, the temperance movement no doubt played a significant role in this shift. As fragmentary as the evidence is for less formal one-on-one exchanges, it does appear that colonists continued to go to taverns to make deals among themselves, settle debts, and get small cash advances on account well into the 1850s.

Colonists also used tavern space to gain access to civic functions and associations. At township meetings in taverns, locals drafted bylaws, assessed the population for the census, and collected taxes. Miles and Playter's tavern in early York housed not only the annual township meeting but also the township rules and regulations. When Mr. Ross needed to see the bylaw on fence building, he called at the tavern. He also "sat some time & drank some grog telling me some of his old stories." At police board meetings in taverns, councillors maintained public order by balancing the books, licensing market vendors and others, and punishing bylaw offences with fines and imprisonment. In Hamilton in the late 1830s the police board sat at John Bradley's tavern; he, in turn, represented Ward 4. Here, in tavern space, the locally prominent sat in judgment over those such as "Daniel Tolliver, a black man," who was fined for keeping "a notorious house at a late hour of the nite." District school trustees were appointed to office in tavern space and candidates were selected to stand for municipal and provincial offices. At O'Neil's tavern in Toronto in 1854 Henry Josh Smith went to help "choos[e] a candidate for a ward election. A chairman was appointed. There was a good deal of talk." There was, in the end, also a short scuffle over the issue.[24]

In newly settling areas that lacked church buildings, religious congregations convened in taverns. The Methodists who met at the Toronto Coffee House in 1804 contemplated a long sermon on Genesis 2:17: "For in the day that thou eatest thereof [from the Tree of Knowledge] thou shalt surely die." In 1809 at a tavern forty miles from Sandwich, where missionary William Case "was called upon to preach that evening," things initially appeared less promising. As Case approached the door, "a man [was] cursing the priest ... and when I came in I found him half drunk, casting up a dollar for more whiskey." Nevertheless, he wrote, "they used me with kindness."[25]

In districts that lacked courthouses, courts likewise sat in taverns. In comparison to their much-studied British counterparts, we know very little about the "majesty" or theatricality of early Canadian courts. But the tavern environment undoubtedly made the courtroom less austere, more familiar. Late in the 1790s at Loucks' tavern, for example, the "gentlemen of the cortroom," the justices, and the "gentlemen of the Grand Jury" all dined, drank, and breakfasted in common company; the justices then presided over the Quarter Sessions in a separate tavern room.

Coroners' inquests also met in taverns. In 1846 in Toronto, which was then a city no longer short on public buildings, the coroner held an inquest "on the body of one William Alexander, a coloured man" at the Green Bush Inn. In short, taverns met civic needs by permitting (in return for the charge of a room and profits on drinks and food) public claims on their interior spaces.[26]

Long before public opinion and the legitimacy of the popular political will became acknowledged forces in Upper Canadian public life, taverns stood as arenas of free political expression. So clear was the link between the public houses and politics that the *Niagara Spectator* noted in 1816 that its only source for political news was "what we hear in bar-rooms and in the public streets." Patrons felt free to express themselves within taverns. During the War of 1812, for example, some patrons voiced seditious, openly pro-American sentiments. Alfred Barrett, the keeper of a respectable York tavern, was overheard to "drink a toast, 'success to the American fleet,'" in company with two others at Dye's tavern in Markham. David Hill's conversation with a yeoman, Robert Laquey, at Holden's Inn made the latter suspect him "to be a person very disaffected with the British government." And it was not as if these men found themselves in like-minded company: we know about these statements because someone turned these men in. Far from being resorts of the disaffected, wartime taverns housed a politically mixed company.[27]

Patrons likewise aired diverse views in peace-time tavern gatherings. Robert Gourlay was an early critic of the colonial administration, a fly in the ointment to those who thought the Tory regime, with its aristocratic overtones, was working satisfactorily. In 1817 he held a series of "township meetings" in which settlers articulated their concerns about the state of the colony's development and what they saw as barriers to their own success. Taverns housed the majority of these proto-subversive gatherings, partly as a matter of practicality, for they had the meeting space and accessible locations. Gourlay and his supporters also knew tavern space to be appropriate for critical political gatherings. That was the case elsewhere. As historian David Conroy has convincingly shown, for example, the spread of revolutionary ideals and will relied on communication in the taverns of colonial Massachusetts. In Paris, as W. Scott Haine writes, "the idea of the *sansculottes* emerged" from café and wine shop gatherings.[28]

That they housed political dissent is not to suggest that the taverns were in the hands of a radical or alternative minority. On the contrary, many taverns easily accommodated a diversity of opinion. One settler recalled "listening to the [electioneering] speeches, which were delivered from a small balcony before the window of the tavern" in the 1840s. "The crowd stood patiently in the snow to hear them." At Robinson's tavern in Prescott, locals expressed their differing politics through a bet. The keep "bet a keg of oysters with T. Fraser Esq., that Mr Patrick Clark gets 50 votes over Dr Jessup. John McMurray, witness." Given the multiplicity of political events they hosted, it makes little sense to identify taverns exclusively with reformist thought and action. Freeman's tavern in the Western District provided the civic space for a reception honouring Lieutenant-Governor Francis Bond Head in 1836. Local residents shook his hand, read an address, and generally conducted themselves as loyal citizens. The fact that two-thirds of the gentlemen present were "obliged to balance themselves against the wall in order to maintain an upright position" detracted somewhat from the image. A thoroughly masculine construction of the public is also apparent on this occasion.

In the summer of 1841 inhabitants gathered at Chatham's British American Hotel "for the purpose of ... erecting a monument to the memory of Tecumseh, the late Indian warrior, who consecrated his honour and patriotism, and sacrificed his life in defense of the British flag." In this case, the tavern's openness to civic association enabled participants, as they came together as citizens in common, to articulate a colonial sense of identity and acknowledge the heroism of a Shawnee ally. Moderates, engaged citizens, and even the violently Tory, anti-Reform Constitutional Society made as much use of tavern space, then, as did radicals. The Constitutional Society, for example, met at the British Coffee House in Toronto in 1836. It was "rather a humbugging, a few miserable speeches" only, but the existence of this meeting helps to make the point that early Canadians articulated conservative as well as alternative visions of politics in tavern space.[29]

It is somewhat surprising, then, that taverns have been presented as chaotic sites of anti-democratic activity. In his history of the Canadas, for example, J.M.S. Careless writes that during elections "nearby inns at times were battle headquarters, centres of vote-buying, mob-hiring, and the 'treating' evil, where the simple citizen might be plied into fuddled acquiescence or fired into battle lust."[30] His qualifications get lost in the pile of words that associate the taverns with wickedness and iniquity.

It is true that taverns "at times" worked as Careless describes them. In the late 1830s and '40s, for example, Coleraine's tavern in Toronto was the acknowledged centre of Orange Tory popular politics. A street riot ricocheted in and out of it during the municipal election of 1841. A commission of inquiry investigated the violence, and those who testified consistently singled out Coleraine's as "a notorious partisan's house," "an Orange Lodge district house ... *an open house during the election for Sherwood and Munro's friends,*" "a *famous place of rendezvous* for that class of persons."[31] The tavern's notorious reputation suggests that such a strong political association was most unusual. Coleraine's was atypical and problematic precisely because it had such a rigid political identity. These statements imply that taverns and tavern-keepers in Toronto tended to keep more open houses and more open minds.

Yet the excessively democratic potential of tavern gatherings raised concerns among officials. When the Rebellions of 1837 reminded administrators of the potential for sedition within the colony, executive councillors sent around a letter advising judges and magistrates of the need to regulate taverns properly. "Several of the tavern keepers in different parts of the province," the letter read, "are openly disaffected ... and allowing their houses to be made places of resort by persons disaffected and evidently for seditious and treasonable purposes." As was the case in the history of the American and French revolutions, there was some basis for administrators' fears. Near Toronto, rebel Samuel Lount addressed his followers "in a revolutionary style" at Hewitt's inn, while his co-conspirator, Silas Fletcher, "served out whiskey ... bidding them keep up their spirits."[32]

But the executive councillors knew that the majority of tavern-keepers and their patrons were loyal. They asked local authorities to ensure only that a licence holder be "a good subject," "a loyal man – attached to the British Constitution," and not anti-Reform. In Sandwich William Hall was undeniably one of these. He proclaimed himself and his public house loyal in printed verse:

> With flashing swords and arms to guard,
> Roast beef and British beer,
> We'll drink and sing, long live the Queen!
> We're ready to defend her
> 'Gainst Yankee Patriots and Brigands
> To whom we'll ne'er surrender!

And when Harry Jones took his gun and his coat and headed east for Toronto to fight for his queen in 1837, he stopped for a night in London, finding "every bar room full of politicians, the greater part of who if not radically inclined, showed no great attachment to the other side – I heard from no single individual anything like a warm expression of loyalty ... Took up my quarters at O'Neil's [Hotel] which appeared to be the headquarters of the tories and was on the whole tolerably quiet."[33] These barroom politicians voiced broad sympathy for a Reform agenda but distanced themselves from rebellious initiatives. Tories too made themselves at home in tavern space. For all their fame as sites where progressives articulated alternative visions of the polis during the Rebellions of 1837, taverns actually housed diversity.

As discussed above, taverns stood as public spaces where political opinion was freely expressed. However, the fact that specific taverns could become associated with specific political perspectives reveals a great deal about the conduct of politics and political exchange and, ultimately, the workings of democracy in early Canada. In his tightly focused examination of Toronto politics and taverns in the 1840s, historian Gregory Kealey uses evidence from the *Report* of the commissioners who investigated the election riot surrounding Coleraine's tavern in 1841 to demonstrate that, in the immediate aftermath of the rebellion, members of the conservative Orange Tory Corporation (city council) that governed the city licensed only tavern-keepers who agreed with their politics.[34] To do so, they strategically allowed the number of licensed taverns to expand and gained control over votes in the process. Kealey's argument, like Careless', suggests that taverns played an anti-democratic role. By rewarding friends and punishing enemies, the Corporation gained influential political supporters. "Friends" voted Tory, obtained tavern licences, and encouraged their patrons to do likewise.

However, Kealey's evidence that the taverns "expanded" under Orange Tory control is not strong. It is based on the statement of one (Reform) alderman who claimed there were only 36 licensed taverns in 1836, when his party was in charge of licensing, compared to 119 taverns five years later, when the Tories were in charge. But even the incomplete listings in the *City of Toronto Commercial Directory* list at least eighty-three taverns in 1836.[35] Also, for all that it tried, the Corporation had very limited success in licensing only Tory Orange tavern-keepers. Five tavern-keepers testified to the intimidation tactics used against them by Orangemen prior to the election, including demands that they run open houses and vote the right way. One tavern-keeper, John Lindsay, clearly lost his license for refusing to do so. Another, Arthur Clifton, did not apply for renewal. And another, John Power, claimed he did not apply: "From the part I took in the last election I am sure the Corporation will not grant me a renewal." But Power did, actually, obtain a licence. All prospective tavern-keepers were most vulnerable to refusal when they applied for a licence. When James Kearney applied for his first license in 1841 his politics became the subject of intense scrutiny. Having "interested himself" in the wrong side, Kearney's application was eventually turned down. Finally, when Peter Harkin applied for a new license he did not legally qualify for it because he lacked sufficient accommodations for travellers. In return for Harkin's support, the Corporation promised him a licence anyway. When Harkin decided to vote for the opposition, the Corporation prosecuted him for selling liquor without a licence. Harkin had changed his mind "on the grounds that all his neighbours voted the other way – that he was dependent on the good will of his neighbours and wished to vote with them." To Harkin's mind, tavern-keepers exerted no influence on patrons' politics – it worked the other way around. Of the five tavern-keepers who appeared before the commission, only one was denied a routine license renewal. The others either did not apply or were in unusually vulnerable positions. Without denying that the Corporation attempted to entrench its power through patronage, the evidence reveals severe limitations on its ability to do so.[36]

The *City of Toronto Poll Book* provides further evidence of the Corporation's limited power. It lists by name and occupation the voters in the same election that sparked the riot and the commissioners' investigation.[37] In this pre-secret ballot era, it also showed how they voted. Of the sixty-seven men who were identified as tavern-keepers, twenty-one voted Reform and forty-six voted for the Corporation. Of the twenty-one men who classified as Reform, four actually split their votes, giving one vote to a Reformer and one to the Corporation. According to the same John Lindsay who lost his licence, this practice was fine with the Corporation. He said, "Just before the election, Davis, the city inspector called at my house and told me 'if I would either not vote at all or split my vote'" the Corporation would still pay for an open house.

It is worthy of note that a high proportion of tavern-keepers (roughly a third) voted Reform during an era when licensing was controlled by Orange Tories. It is even worthier to note who still had a licence a year later. According to the list of the inspector of licences, James McDonnell, just over 76 percent of the Reform voters obtained licence renewals for 1842. (When the four who split their votes are excluded, the figure drops to 57 percent.) Of those who voted for the Corporation, 59 percent had a licence the next year. By 1843, 52 percent of those who voted for Reform still had licences, as did 48 percent of those who voted for the Corporation.[38] The similarity between the figures is striking. Regardless of whether the Corporation was willing to exploit its patronage powers over vulnerable applicants, it did not organize a successful campaign against Reform-minded tavern-keepers. Despite the Corporation's stranglehold on licensing, tavern-keepers voted as they liked, and very few suffered any consequences.

Regardless of whether the setting was Toronto in the 1840s, a barroom during the War of 1812, or London in the midst of the Rebellions of 1837, taverns functioned as public spaces where Upper Canadians could articulate a range of political opinions. A tavern or a tavern-keeper might support a seditious company, might reinforce an existing authority, or might be open to favours in return for political support. More often, however, taverns and their keepers hosted everyday political exchanges among companions. When Harry Jones walked to the Blue Bell, a tavern just north of Toronto in 1840, for example, he did so with two fellow government employees. They drank, and they talked politics. One of the men denounced the moderate Reform policies of Robert Baldwin, while another planned to support him.[39] Far from being undemocratic in tenor, taverns worked as good public space that encouraged contact among colonists with diverse opinions and the articulation of opinion in the face of competing perspectives.

In this sense, taverns housed important elements of the burgeoning public sphere. Historians have debated the extent and timing of the public sphere's emergence in many settings. Jeffrey McNairn's discussion of the rise of deliberative democracy and the increasing legitimacy of the force of public opinion as the primary political engine in Upper Canada shows that the public sphere actually functioned in the colony's many taverns.[40] Taverns did not create the public sphere, but given the extent to which the sphere relied on free association and the free exchange of opinions, they did offer a supportive public setting. It can also be argued that taverns were *involved* in the creation of the public sphere because its emergence depended on the circulation of a free press and the open debate of ideas in voluntary association. Tavern-keepers routinely subscribed to newspapers and made them available to patrons. They were not the only sites to do so. Commercial newsrooms in particular made a wide array of papers and journals available to subscribers for a small annual fee. Nevertheless, in 1826 five of the ten newest subscribers to William Lyon Mackenzie's *Colonial Advocate* were tavern-keepers. In Prescott, tavern-keeper Thomas Robinson subscribed to both the *British Whig* and the *Patriot,* which had competing political perspectives. Other public house keepers distributed papers for local subscribers. A minor house, such as the one that Englishwoman and settler Susanna Moodie found herself in, whiling away a long day in Cobourg in the 1830s, might have only the local papers, which were "soon exhausted." But at more substantial houses, patrons usually found the "newspapers from England, Ireland, and Scotland ... laid on the table for [their] amusement" or an "extensive bar and reading room" well stocked with the "principal periodical publications of the day."[41]

Although some historians have quite reasonably suggested that a tavern was hardly the ideal setting for reading and reflection, it appears that a good deal of both took place. When a traveller named Morleigh reached a Chatham barroom in about 1840, he borrowed a "well-thumbed newspaper" and commented that the "barroom of the American" in Detroit was the only place to see a newspaper "for five minutes." Newspaper reading was very much a part of the tavern-going experience, as was the discussion and debate it inspired. Moreover, it was within the confines of the barroom that the printed word might become available to many who would not otherwise encounter it. Public notices were posted, read, and commented on at taverns. Sometimes they were read aloud. For example, when he was offered free drink at Freeman's tavern before an election in 1849, Patrick Flanagan, who could not read, heard a political handbill read aloud to him in company "with the number there." (His phrasing suggests that others who lacked reading skills gathered about too.) The barroom and its company facilitated Flanagan (and his company's) participation in the formal workings of the public sphere. It put tavern-goers in touch with issues under debate and the electoral process itself. In so doing, the tavern supported a more fully realized – because it was more participatory – version of the public sphere.[42]

The taverns' support of the public sphere is evident in the place they gave to voluntary associations. These were organizations of individuals who came together for mutual purposes, whether as Freemasons, as members of literary or artistic societies, as temperance activists, as fellow horticulturalists, or as members of the Mechanics' Institute, to name but a few prominent examples. Agricultural societies resorted to the public houses for meetings throughout the period. There is a notice, for instance, in the *Upper Canada Gazette* of 1807 informing York members that a meeting "will be holden at Moore's Hotel on Tuesday the 13th instant at two o'clock." The Kent Agricultural Society likewise published a notice for a meeting at the Royal Exchange Hotel, Chatham, in 1843. And John Ross Robertson's *History of Freemasonry* names many taverns as Masonic halls early in the nineteenth century. The Masons typically rented a tavern room for a year; only they could use the room, which was decorated and arranged according to Masonic ritual. Similarly, the Hibernian Society convened at Mrs. Patrick's Inn in Kingston in 1820. In April 1832 the "magistrates and gentry" of Cobourg met at Stiles Inn, where "resolutions were passed expressing the intention of those present to form a relief society." That same year, the Malahide and Yarmouth Committees of Vigilance met at Burbee's Inn. Three years later an assembly of Masons and stonecutters convened at Carnerous' Inn in Cornwall "to condemn" attempts to reduce their earnings. Finally, from its inception in the eighteenth century, the Orange Lodge gathered in rented tavern quarters, which were decorated, like the Masons', with the emblems of their association.[43]

By the mid-nineteenth century, however, voluntary associations began to withdraw from tavern space. In 1859 leaders of the Masons imbibing the temperance message banned Masonic tavern gatherings. Other voluntary associations followed suit, either because they agreed with temperance idealism or because they had obtained their own purpose-built halls. The taverns' legacy as public space supportive of participation in the public sphere should not be downplayed, however. Throughout the Upper Canadian period taverns housed associational meetings dedicated to the expansion of knowledge, rational debate, and the growth of informed public opinion. In this regard, as was the case in their openness to diverse political expressions, taverns worked in support of the democratic process and its fuller realization.

Historians often overlook the relationships between neighbours, friends, and strangers that took place outside the household in their analyses of the public. This is because, in comparison to the public sphere of published press debates and voluntary association activity, community-based relationships were informal and unorganized. These relations tended to be documented only in a context of community tension. It is apparent from the available evidence, though, that tavern space was very much community space. It was in the public houses on his circuit that missionary William Case first saw those "large companies of neighbours and others convene" in the opening years of the nineteenth century. A generation later, organizers still placarded the woods with notices for tavern dances, and local "settlers, young and old, male and female, flock[ed] to the place of rendezvous." A marriage party in "two sleighs fastened together and drawn by four horses," led by a "small brass band," arrived at a tavern in Niagara in 1849, "pleasure bent."[44] These events facilitated patrons' sense of mutual belonging in local networks of neighbourliness and affiliation.

Colonists also used the taverns in a more intentional way, as places to define their community relationships. There was room within to accommodate friction, to make private issues public matters. In taverns patrons found the potential to make the personal the political, to bring community attention on one's self or one's family. This is a fundamental characteristic of a functioning public space. Only when women and men enjoy access to forums where they can air individual concerns can they see themselves as active members of society.[45]

Upper Canadians acknowledged that taverns were informal courts of public opinion. They were places where one went to say something in public to have it heard and noted. For example, a witness at a murder trial in 1854 wanted to change his testimony publicly because he had made a mistake about an accused man. He did this in court, but only after he made a public declaration in a tavern. He emphasized the earnestness of his courtroom testimony by stressing that "at Haw's tavern I said 'I wish I could swear my oath over again.'" Similarly, Louis Fluete regarded an aspersion cast on his friend's honesty as very serious indeed because it "was said in a public house." Luke Teeple and Enock Moore were at Francis Beaupré's tavern in London in 1830 during a sitting of the Court of Requests. In the barroom where "both were drinking" in company, Moore spoke "in heat, shaking his fist" to accuse Teeple of a theft in town. Teeple called him a "poor wretch" and a liar and then "took his hat and went away." The power of Moore's barroom words, which tavern-keeper Beaupré had heard "often before," "satisfied" Beaupré that Teeple "had stolen that money." Moore used Beaupré's barroom to create a public opinion favourable to his own construction of local events. Teeple, responding to the seriousness of such publicly aired words, sued him for slander and won.[46]

The process of using taverns as informal courts of public opinion was neither benign nor particularly rational. It was based on gossip and slanderous public accusations that could explode into violence. Nevertheless, the tavern provided a forum in which issues of an intrinsically personal nature – one's respectability, reputation, and honour – could be publicized before neighbours or strangers alike. The taverns enabled the transformation of the personal into the political.

From 1793, when the lieutenant-governor built taverns "to facilitate communication," to the 1850s and beyond, taverns extended the sphere of economic activity, enabled transportation, and housed political expression and community gatherings in Upper Canadian society. Although taverns declined in importance as public spaces in some of these areas as businesses and voluntary associations relocated to purpose-built buildings and as railways supplanted stage houses on long-distance routes, taverns in general retained important functions. Travellers, colonists, tradespeople, and a miscellany of travelling dentists, physicians, theatre troops, and wax museums still utilized tavern space, both in public rooms and rented chambers, well after the mid-nineteenth century. Groups continued to gather in taverns to write petitions, organize local improvements, or elect representatives. And communities acknowledged taverns as courts of public opinion, where individuals vented matters of local reputation. The residents of Upper Canada had many more public spaces to choose from at mid-century then they had had in the 1790s, but taverns remained a popular option, as the steadiness of their numbers demonstrates.

Despite the many attractions of a temperance movement that espoused a progressive, disciplined vision of colonial society, those who chose sobriety, like those who did not, had equally compelling reasons to visit the taverns in their neighbourhoods and during their travels. Colonists, surely including some temperance advocates among them, invested the taverns with positive meanings and functions even as they came to question the social role of alcohol and re-evaluate its place within their daily lives. Whether one went to a tavern as a member of a voluntary association, as an elector, or as an individual seeking to defend his (or her) good name in an informal court of public opinion, one recognized the taverns as valuable public spaces.

This is not to suggest that drink had nothing to do with the tavern's attraction. Contemporaries described Stevenson, the stage proprietor, on a "spree," and Major Holcroft and Harry Jones experimented with the manufacture of port wine negus during a stagecoach journey. Farmers Ogden, White, and Richeson sold their corn to Matthew Dolsen and took a drink in his tavern, and Ely Playter and Mr. Terry sealed their business in 1803 with gin. The peddlers at McBrien's drank beer while negotiating personal business, and John Prince got "rather tipsy" at the great rail meeting at Gardiner's. Seditious toasts were proposed to the "success of the American fleet," and drunken gentlemen propped themselves against the wall at a governor's reception at Freeman's, where Patrick Flanagan got free liquor on the eve of an election. When Luke Teeple and Enock Moore, who had business before the court, sat in Beaupré's barroom, "both were drinking." Clearly, the culture of drink played a fundamental role in tavern going. By lubricating discourse, sustaining everyday sociability, and symbolizing the nature of interpersonal contacts, alcohol facilitated the public expression of colonial social relations. Sometimes the results were controversial.

4
Regulation and Ritual in Everyday Public Life

He shall keep and maintain good order and rule and shall suffer no drunkenness, or any other disorders or unlawful games to be used in house.

     – Daniel McGuinn's tavern licence, 1790s

One may speak of an impulse to sociability in man. To be sure, it is for the sake of special needs and interests that men unite in economic associations or blood fraternities, in cult societies or robber bands. But, above and beyond their special content, all the associations are accompanied by a feeling for, and a satisfaction in, the very fact that one is associated with others and that the solitariness of the individual is resolved into togetherness, a union with others.

     – Georg Simmel, 1910

This human impulse for sociability centred tavern culture and gave it purpose; it made tavern going an expression of public life every bit as much as the less esoteric connections tavern going also enabled (to the economy, transport, politics, and community). The sociable use of public space in taverns shows colonists dissolving their "solitariness" into "togetherness." As spaces designed forthrightly in the unalloyed service of informal public life, there is no mystery to the taverns' attractions, no need to find complex reasons to explain the public's disposition to go there.[1] The desire to associate with others underpinned the site-specific drinking customs and group activities – whether dances or card games or cockfights – that played out in the taverns' public rooms, and it explained much about violence when it erupted. Taverns were full of the cultural rituals that facilitated making and maintaining social bonds, and they were full of the symbolism that represented these bonds. Simultaneously, taverns were full of contrary possibilities, for celebration of "special interests" might come at the expense of inclusive association. Forms of disorder (the favourite colonial code word for drunkenness and/or violence) might undermine the very cohesiveness that people and groups sought through tavern association. Colonists acknowledged and responded to these inherent contradictions by regulating the taverns' public life, both formally, through law, and informally, through custom.

Colonists expressed an overwhelming preference for what they called "good order." When Daniel McGuinn, for instance, entered into a £10 recognizance with his king to keep tavern in Cataraqui (Kingston) in the 1790s, he swore "that he shall keep and maintain good order and rule and shall suffer no drunkenness, or any other disorders or unlawfull games to be used in house."[2] Although the laws that pertained to public houses in Upper Canada changed in their specifics by the mid-1850s, the desire to maintain order remained a constant. For example, in 1794 new applicants to keep tavern had to get a declaration from a minister, a town warden, or four "respectable" householders who attested to the fact that he or she was of "good fame, sober life and conversation." By 1850 potential tavern-keepers needed declarations from either two magistrates or ten householders, two of which had to be willing to pledge £50 for the tavern-keeper's good behaviour. The role of inspectors likewise changed. Provisions for them were first made in 1803, when their duties amounted to administering magistrates' licensing recommendations, collecting fees, submitting lists of license holders, and investigating complaints. By 1840 inspectors examined licensed houses twice a year, and licence renewals were dependent on their assessments.[3] This is not to say that tavern regulations at all times and places fully described tavern happenings. Yet even the president and secretary of the Chatham Temperance Society bore witness in 1841 that, even though *un*licensed houses "are the sinks of iniquity ... the licensed houses in this town are generally conducted in a manner creditable to the proprietors."[4]

Maintaining good order meant balancing the potentially conflicting claims made by mixed companies on the informal public space of the taverns. Cultural practices, especially those associated with drink, that the taverns made uniquely available, forged bonds of camaraderie, community, and a sense of mutual belonging. But because tavern sociability granted feelings of membership, its enactment in public rooms could become contested on any number of grounds. The drinking customs, singsongs, and barroom sport that bound tavern-goers together worked for some only because they excluded others.

John Beverley Robinson knew all of this. He was the scion of an elite Loyalist family, an influential and conservative Tory politician, and he was appointed as the colony's chief justice in 1829. Robinson also became a tavern-keeper's stepson at the age of eleven, when his mother, Esther Sayre Robinson, married Elisha Beman (Ely Playter's neighbour and Sophia's father) and moved her family into his tavern. Young "Jack B.," as the neighbour called him, did some of his growing up in Beman's prosperous and well-conducted public house. Its orderly rhythms and the sociability it housed were part of his childhood. Perhaps that was why, forty years later, Robinson penned a remarkable description of tavern sociability.[5] His text richly conveys the ambiguity of the tavern's public space: it describes the good order and fellowship that overwhelmingly characterized tavern association; at the same time, it acknowledges the tavern's contrary vulnerability to conflict and flashes of violence. Robinson depicts the tavern as a unique kind of public space, where tavern-goers used ritual and custom to forge social bonds among themselves.

"There had been a wedding," he writes, "in the family of a Mr English, an inn keeper in Hamilton, and the friends and relations of the parties had been making themselves merry for two or three days in succession at different inns in the town, but committing no censurable excess. – On the evening of the 10th Feb[ruary 1843] this party were at Foster's inn, in the town, where they were singing and enjoying themselves harmlessly." It was a small barroom full of people. The wedding company was noisy; some were "talking together and others singing," and "most of the party had been drinking freely." There was "no rioting or quarrelling ... nothing said or done in ill humour by any of them."

Then Hugh McCulloch came in, looking for his brother-in-law. Everybody in town knew that McCulloch was "of weak mind, easily disturbed, so that people were in the habit of teasing and trifling with him." No sooner did he walk into the barroom than the bride's brother began "to amuse himself and the company at his expense." He started "by indulging in that kind of sport which people in the barroom of an inn constantly indulge in without any idea of its leading to disastrous consequences. He pulled [McCulloch's] cap off his head and then handed it to him, saying, 'Here's your cap, Sir.'" In the crowded conditions the short scuffle that ensued "excited little attention," and things seemed to be well under control when an "older person in company" and the tavern-keeper, "for fear it might grow into a quarrel," pulled young English behind the bar. But English jumped the bar counter, confronted McCulloch, and "almost immediately cried out, 'I am stabbed.' He did not survive more than ten or twelve minutes."

Robinson described the customary sociability housed in Foster's tavern and its violent betrayal. It was, as he put it, an "inhuman" outcome, one that defrauded tavern going of the meanings conferred upon it by the impulse to human sociability. (The events leading to English's death provide a dismal comment, too, on the way this community treated its atypical members, those to whom "Providence had not given ... sense enough.") We see, through Robinson's eyes, that in taverns colonists customarily drank freely and peacefully, sang, conversed, and celebrated. In this instance, they celebrated a wedding and the bride, along with her mother, was part of the tavern company. We see evidence of the company's capacity for self-regulation in the keep and company's willingness to intervene when a scuffle first broke out. Yet, Robinson's negatively phrased constructions – "harmlessly," "no censurable excess," "no rioting or quarrelling," "nothing ... done in ill humour" – allude to his sense that their opposites (harm, excess, riots, quarrels, ill humour) haunted tavern sociability as ever-present possibilities. If the odds were stacked in favour of good order, as Robinson explicitly illustrated, fears of its disruption nevertheless marked approaches to tavern association.

"Tavern company," or simply "the company," was a rather odd expression that colonists used frequently. It meant people assembled together for companionship and good fellowship. It could be a large, ill-defined group – simply a "house full of company." Or it could mean a more closely linked group that kept company in pursuit of common pleasure. Green Macdonald and his companions had this more restrictive sense in mind when they told a new arrival who had disturbed their sing-along at Kent's Inn that "he would not be allowed to interrupt the company."[6] The phrase "tavern company" invoked the idea of a social world linked to the tavern, with its members bound together by practices of sociability that were unique to the setting.

Tavern-goers perpetually sang together. "As usual," wrote one tavern-keeper, "the house was ... full of noisy company singing in two or three rooms at once." At Perry's, John Wallington led the barroom in rounds of "God Save the King" and ordered "hats off at the chorus of his song." At Goodwin's tavern in Kingston in 1841 two young lawyers sang together "from dinner 'till tea.'"[7] Song united drinking companions by creating a sense of shared conviviality.

Dancing performed a similar function. With "company a'dancing and Lester playing the fiddle," Moore's tavern rocked early York. "Some itinerant Italian organists ... played lively tunes in the bar" of a tavern near Forty Mile Creek while soldiers "danced jigs." Patrons who had assembled in a backwoods stage house for a show "fell to dancing" when a fiddler took up his bow. And a country traveller "found a fiddler at Burwell's and danced French fours and 8 reels until midnight."[8] Music and dance created the company in these instances; it created the comradeship and good fellowship that the word *company* implies.

Tavern dance could be put to explicitly cohesive purposes. Professional men, merchants, civil and military officers, and members of the provincial Parliament, with women of similar social rank, for example, liked to celebrate their exclusivity by organizing balls at the principal public houses. A gentleman who attended one such ball described the process: "Subscription balls are very prevalent. For this purpose every respectable tavern ... is always provided with an extensive ballroom. Stewards ... send tickets to the different subscribers, give orders for the accommodations, attend to suitable decorations of the house and collect the amount of subscriptions for which the proprietor of the hotel always considers them accountable. A gentleman's subscription is generally about five dollars: the ladies never pay anything. For this sum you are entitled to bring with you a partner and servant."[9] The description reeks of group privilege celebrated in style, and it depicts the principal taverns in ways that conform to patterns observed in Chapter 1, patterns that will be glimpsed again in some colonists' quest to define a separate gentrified identity for themselves.

Storytelling, which had a natural home in the barroom, created group identification of a different sort. It allowed listeners common entry, as audience, into funny, fascinating, or awe-inspiring tales. It also existed as a form of social currency that accrued at least temporary status on the teller. For example, the lone survivor of a steamer wreck on Lake Erie in 1840 became, in the barroom, "a sort of lion, in his way, and told his 'thrice-told tale' of all the perils and dangers he had escaped."[10] The elements of audience and performance likewise characterized tavern-goers' conversations. For example, at the Exchange in Detroit (which colonists from Windsor and area treated as one of their local taverns) the barroom company "smoked and listened to an animated theological discussion between a christian and a free thinking Yankee which though blasphemous was very amusing."[11] This was not a private conversation, it was a public exchange conducted, in part, for the appreciation of other tavern-goers. There was social power to be had with a witty turn of phrase or a well-placed joke. Verbal jousting for the sake of self-aggrandizement sometimes took the form of putting down outsiders. We witnessed this when John English took "soft" Hugh McCulloch's cap and invited him to take it back. English expected a laugh from the company for his ritualized cleverness and because he had an enhanced sense of his own membership among them.

Tavern-goers, such as the "boisterous crowd who were gambling and drinking around a large table" in a country tavern in the Western District in 1809, also convened over cards and betting. When Ely Playter called at Hamilton's to meet some friends, they "agreed for a rubber at whist" and "played a long time for beer." "Gentlemen," observed a colonist in 1824, "are in the habit of assembling in parties at taverns where they gamble pretty highly." At a tavern near Niagara in 1837, James Stevenson "said he would bet he had the heaviest watch in the room. Jesse Fletcher said he would bet a dollar on it." In 1841 at Fairfield's tavern outside Kingston, "Galt and Kelly

[were] playing écarté very furiously for immense sums – ... and not too sober – what they won or lost remained a mystery particularly to themselves." At Robinson's, in Prescott, tavern-goers bet treats on a boat race in 1846.[12]

The trouble with all this gambling activity was that it was illegal. In Upper Canada almost all games played for money stakes in taverns were unlawful.[13] And tavern-keepers' licences from the 1790s onward barred them from permitting "unlawfull games to be used in the house."[14] (One could get a separate licence for billiards.) It is debatable how seriously tavern-keepers took these rules. Daniel Haskell lost his licence over gaming, though the circumstances are suspicious, at least as he told it. According to Haskell, Rufus Pooler came to his Niagara tavern in 1825 "and spoke to some of his intention of gambling." Haskell "took their cards ... showed them where to sleep ... went to bed and after about 2 or 3 hours of sleep awoke and heard some talking in the barroom ... found they had a new supply of implements for their sport – immediately showed them their beds again which was the end of their naughtiness." In this version, Pooler turned Haskell in to the authorities out of spite, and Haskell was successfully prosecuted.[15]

Other evidence reveals that tavern-keepers were tolerant of gambling, when it was conducted reasonably. In fact, taverns were regarded if not exactly as bastions of respectability in this regard then at least as institutions under appropriate control. For example, when the mayor of Toronto, William Lyon Mackenzie, wrote in 1834 of "the haunts of the worthless and dissipated" that "afforded place and room for gambling & vice in its blackest shapes," which, if not checked, would leave Toronto with "little to boast in point of manners over New Orleans,"[16] he was referring to *un*licensed, illegal drinking houses in "obscure parts of the city," *not* to taverns, which were licensed by definition. Mackenzie argued that licensed facilities were orderly precisely because they stood open and accessible to public view and regulation. That the public eye often winked at orderly transgressions of the gaming ban is apparent. Indeed, those who united in an illegal hand of cards for money stakes joined together in tavern ritual that was conducive to mutuality.

Sport brought men and women, as participants and fans, to the taverns. Lamb's, which was a principal hotel in Toronto, kept a racquet court for its genteel guests. It was once used by the Prince of Wales.[17] The Union Cricket Club likewise used Robinson's tavern at Prescott as its clubhouse, and the tavern-keeper's fields hosted matches. In August 1845 Robinson received payment from the Port Wellington Club, "on account of expenses of their match game of cricket." His house supported their celebrations; after one game, the players and their supporters drank "2 gallons of beer" and "20 glasses" of other liquor.[18]

Men wrestled and boxed in taverns as well. At Playter's, before "a barroom full of people, A. Galloway and a McBride [were] wrestling – the latter strained his leg and that ended the matter." At Waugh's, Cooper and another regular "wrestled in play"; they "often wrestled together, but not in anger." There was a thin line between roughhousing and real conflict. For instance, Playter disclosed that, in February 1802, "We had a high caper with J. Thorn who being in liquor and getting offended at Orton would box him. Orton humouring the joke in great earnest made the company very merry and all subsided very well in a short time." In June, he also notes that "we had some trouble with two American soldiers ... they had a great drunken bout & got quarrelling in the barroom – with some difficulty we got them parted and put to bed." In the boxing match between Thorn and Orton – which actually did not amount to much in the end – the tavern-keeper's anxiety (like Robinson's) that all might not "subside well" is palpable. It is also evident that Orton was willing to co-operate in maintaining good order by "humouring" the inebriated Thorn, while tavern-goers actively co-operated with Playter to quell the disorder caused by the soldiers.[19] Though roughhousing raised the spectre of disruption to good order and potential property damage, it had more in common with storytelling than it did with real violence. Roughhousing was generally an orderly form of social display, one that showcased, before the assembled public, masculine traits that were admired, such as strength, skill, and agility. Prowess could bring social rewards to the fighter.

Bloodsport, such as cock- and dogfighting, enjoyed centuries-old links to the taverns of England, where it tended to be associated with particular venues.[20] Although it was subject to increasing condemnation, bloodsport was legal until 1835. In Upper Canada some taverns continued the tradition. For example, in 1830 a group of about twenty Irishmen usually seen about the wharf and the canal gathered at Fraser's tavern in the Midland District ostensibly for a dogfight, though they denied knowing anything about it. David Clendenning claimed to have "never heard of a dog fight," while McGuire insisted "there was no cockfight or dogfight that he knew of." However, his denial suggests that cockfights were a tavern phenomenon in the colony, just as they were in the Old Country.[21] The social composition of this group – Irish canallers – suggests that bloodsport was the property of the labouring ranks, although we do not know the social class of all those who attended.

There is no evidence of bearbaiting in Upper Canadian taverns, even though it was associated with the public houses of Great Britain. Bearbaiting took place in a theatre-like outdoor setting, a pit designed specially for the purpose, usually in tavern yards. The bear was chained to a stake, sometimes declawed, and set on by trained dogs. The fight continued until either the bear or the dogs were killed. Bearbaiting attracted a very mixed crowd in England, ranging from labourers to members of the aristocracy. Although there is no evidence that this "sport" took place in Upper Canada, some tavern-keepers kept bears captive in barrooms. Joe Beef, a tavern-keeper in industrializing Montreal, is the best-known example, and his tavern suggests a link between animal amusements and a specifically working-class clientele. Yet, in 1830s Toronto, it was the British Coffee House, which was patronized as much by the gentry and members of the provincial Parliament as by farmers and local residents, that housed the bear that "with the black squirrel and turtle was very well."[22] There is no hint that these bears were intended for baiting, but Upper Canadians certainly had few qualms about blooding animals for sport. For example, in about 1824 the tavern-keepers at Niagara Falls, in a bid "to attract customers and amuse the public," came together to buy an old schooner, into which they herded "a number of wild animals on board, two bears, some foxes, and a buffalo, cats, dogs, geese, &c." They then conducted the schooner "to the head of the rapids and then left [it] to be carried down by the current." Nine thousand spectators lined the sides of the river. [23]

Horse racing was likewise popular. At Gilbert's tavern in Niagara in 1805 "there was great bantering on horse racing toward the evening," a mile and a half sprint between two horses, and a barroom so crowded that the tavern-keeper asked for help behind the bar. Although the sport was one of the "principal amusements" of the gentry, and advertisements for horse races at James Wilson's Hotel, also in Niagara, targeted "sportsmen" and called them "gentlemen," it is unlikely that any exclusivity was maintained; the very publicness of the taverns worked against it. Nor were there ever enough "gentlemen" in early Niagara to fill Gilbert's tavern to capacity. Indeed, as late as 1876, when a developing class structure was part of social relations in the region, a small-town horse race attracted a very mixed crowd to a tavern. The "bar-room swarmed," the stairs "were blocked with people," and the "sitting room was full of lads and lasses looking out."[24]

The assortment of events and organized amusements that tavern-keepers hosted defies categorization. In 1820s Kingston, Moore's Coffee House hosted a circus in its yard. A Mr. Rowley gave "an entertainment ... at Mrs Darley's Inn consisting of slack wire performance, tumbling &c." At York a "grand caravan of living animals," such as tigers, lions, a camel, a llama, and a leopard, was exhibited at Howard's Steamboat Hotel. Travellers and tavern-goers could also listen to the "grand musics machine from Germany." Forty people came to a mountebank's show at a tavern near St. Thomas (see Chapter 3), and psuedo-science attracted crowds at other taverns. O'Neil's, a London stage house, hosted "a lecture on astronomy" that included a magic lantern show and concluded with the audience participating in comic songs. "The house, in consequence, was in an uproar." "Siamese twin brothers" were displayed at Allen's Steam Boat Hotel in Sandwich in 1834, while wax likenesses of co-joined twins could be viewed at a backwoods tavern. Colonists and travellers could view wax models of the heroes of the Scottish Highlands in a small tavern on the shores of Lake Huron, while in 1831 a "Yankee show" in a tavern on the road to Ancaster celebrated "the glorious victory over the British at New Orleans." At least one British traveller called the show a "public insult." The theatre at the City Hotel in Toronto staged *Hunter of the Alps* and *Perfection* in 1840. According to a lawyer who attended, there was "very tolerable acting by an English Company." In 1854 a music and dance show, in which a white man in blackface "played the tambourine and danced," toured the Niagara Peninsula. The show stopped at Ben Diffin's tavern in Pelham, at O'Stronger's in Bayham, and at Walden's and John Latimore's in Caledonia. John Kelsey (who drove a threshing machine) said that when the show stopped at Clark's in Canboro "my boys were very anxious to go."[25]

The crowd watching the horse race from the windows of a small-town tavern, the forty people at the mountebank's show, the "uproar" at O'Neil's, and the eagerness of the Kelsey boys to see the minstrel show all attest to the substantial audiences that professional players and travelling exhibits brought to taverns. Although we do not know if tavern-keepers took a cut of the proceeds, they certainly made a great deal of money selling drink to the crowds. More importantly, the crowds themselves affirm the presumption of publicness that characterized tavern space. Seemingly, anyone with the price of a drink or a ticket to the show could get in and stay for a time.

There was a difference, to be sure, between the large, and to us largely anonymous, crowds gathered for public entertainments and those smaller groups of acquaintances who engaged in everyday tavern sociability. Yet both groups reveal something about the nature of tavern association. Men and women were members of the crowd on a least one occasion (likely all occasions), and they represented different degrees of economic privilege. Although the response to racialized identities is hidden from view, the blackface minstrel show suggests the contestation over racialized representation that was taking place in the colony. Blackface was an immensely popular form of entertainment, but it was one to which black colonists objected. In Toronto in the 1840s, for example, the black community thrice petitioned city council to censor such performances "as what they call Jim Crow and other Negro characters."[26] But the size of the crowds in attendance suggests the potential for diverse members of a mixed society to come together in common purpose. Tavern space worked much as the planners and theorists of public space envisage it: space that is accessible to and makes possible mutual exchange among many. Among smaller groups, taverns encouraged affinity through the rituals of song, gaming, and even rough play. These customs forged the bonds that made a companionable group, and the sense of belonging that was generated could result in individuals resisting intrusions by interlopers, as happened to Green Macdonald at Kent's tavern.

Rituals associated with drink had a special relevance to the creation of tavern companies. Drink was as much symbol as substance. When tavern-goers "treated" they bought drink for each other at the bar. The gift of a glass or the share of a gill (4 oz., or a quarter pint) of liquor carried a value that far exceeded its financial worth: it made, in the words of anthropologist Marcel Mauss, "the obligation of worthy return imperative."[27] This could be a return in kind (buying another round) or a return of a more interpersonal nature (an afternoon's shared conviviality or, perhaps, a mutual pledge of good will at the beginning of a working or courting relationship). The treat's power lay in its ability to create social bonds. Drink emerges as a symbol, not the purpose, of sociability, and it was capable of carrying many meanings – "a drop mixed with a friend, a reconciliation draught with an enemy, a squib with an old acquaintance, or a bowl of congratulation, condolence &c."[28]

Social bonding did not always imply equality, however. As one travelling cynic wrote, patrons "will pay for the liquor which their companions or even total strangers have drunk at a tavern, that they may prove their wealth and receive applause for their selfish generosity."[29] A pre-eminent sociologist puts it only slightly differently, noting that social exchanges function not only "to establish bonds of friendship" but also "to establish superordination over others."[30] Similarly, when a master or mistress treated a servant to drink, there was no expectation of a return in kind or of extended sociability; rather, the unequal exchange confirmed the hierarchical relationship.[31]

Treating facilitated financial transactions. It marked the completion of successful negotiations, as when Ely Playter was "busy all day drawing some writings from Smith to Mealey ... had them signed, executed, went with the parties & drank some whiskey at McDougall's [tavern]." Alcohol accompanied the bargaining process. For example, in 1835 Samuel Williams and Mrs. Stroebeck "were treating" in a tavern with a peddler who "spread his goods." Treating was so prevalent that in the 1850s a gentleman settler, J. Dunbar Moodie, once uneasily remarked that "strangers are almost inevitably drawn into it in the course of business."[32]

As Moodie implied, avoiding a treat was a difficult matter because the public ritual was so loaded with the symbolism of mutuality and inclusion. When Charles Fothergill, a printer and naturalist, stopped at Baker's Inn in Osnabruck in 1817, for example, he "found the house filled with people who had been attending a funeral upon the strength of which they were getting jovial, much as in Scotland & Ireland." By rejecting their subsequent offer of a treat, Fothergill "offended some ... because I would not drink brandy before my dinner with them." Fothergill's response reflected mistrust and disengagement rather than the reciprocity and mutuality inherent in the treating ritual.[33] Feelings were ruffled because in refusing the treat,

Fothergill refused the company's friendship and intercourse, its invitation to join the group.

For tavern-goers, the potency of treating was its ability to foster this sense of group membership and mutuality. James King and his fellow soldiers Bertrand Garland and Michael Murry were drinking together at the Rob Roy tavern in Toronto in 1838, "when the bugle sounded," which meant they were to head back to barracks. Garland and Murry instead invited King to go to "another tavern to be treated." They went to Dagin's and drank. The treat unified the threesome in a common lark: defying military authority by staying out after the bugler sounded tattoo. When they saw the military guard coming on his rounds, the three men left the public room; before he passed back, "they returned, got another glass and left – the back way."[34] In treating, tavern-goers found a flexible symbol that expressed the ideal of reciprocity and mutual association in both business and personal matters. Treating was a cultural mechanism by which people negotiated inclusion in groups borne of the mercurial good will of the moment and of sustained membership in long-standing networks of association.

Historians of the working-class who write about the industrial era find deep significance in this old pre-industrial rite. They argue that the treat, because it carried meanings of equality and solidarity, stood for anti-capitalist values. It came to imply "resistance to individualism as well as acquisitiveness" among workers who articulated more communal goals.[35] While this argument underestimates the role that the treat played in support of those very negotiations that led to "privatistic" gain – for example, Ely Playter's treat-lubricated real estate deals – it does allude to the resilience and adaptability of meaningful cultural rituals. Whereas Upper Canadian soldiers once used the treat to celebrate their common daring, workers in industrializing societies used it to celebrate a sense of distinct cultural identity, one in which the old mutuality of treating found new meaning.

Anna Clark's work on the early-nineteenth-century British working class reminds us, too, of the gendered implications of the treating ritual. We can glimpse Mrs. Strobeck engaged in the ritual. Roach's tavern account book in 1850s Toronto and others likewise hint at the possibility of female participation in treating, as is explored in Chapter 7. But treating was a ritual redolent of the sociability of the barroom, a public space we know that women tended to avoid except when in the company of close male companions and family. Treating consequently underlined male freedom of access to public space, and to the resources needed to purchase rounds of drink within it. B. Anne Tlusty's work on early modern German inns singles out control over the purse as both actual and symbolic male power. Through the treat, men in Upper Canada enacted their social precedence; even among other men, they employed its ritual in ways that prioritized their "allegiance to the homosocial world" of the tavern, sometimes at the (literal) expense of wives and households. The treat's power to bind men together through a common sense of masculinity also enhanced their social power to exclude "others," including women.[36]

None of this suggests that drink was unappreciated as a substance. People called at taverns to satisfy a thirst for liquor. Harry Jones, who (along with his diary) is the subject of Chapter 6, stated it plainly: "A desire for grog obliged us to stop" at Smith's inn. Jones' call at Smith's tavern was typical of the thousands of calls he made at taverns in his lifetime: he called in, took a drink or two, and went on his way. There is no reason to assume that the vast majority of colonists were any different. Jones' diary for 1837, for instance, records 224 tavern calls, only 11 of which mention inebriation, ranging from tavern-goers who were "rather tipsy," to those who were "decidedly blue," to those who were "drunk."[37] As a regular tavern-goer Jones knew what he was talking about, and from his perspective, taverns were sites of controlled drinking, not excess. Although this point seems obvious, historians rarely make it. Wanting a drink and going to a tavern to get one was a qualitatively different act than drinking to the point of drunkenness. We know rather more about the latter in colonial society because of historians' explorations of the temperance movement. Consequently, what we know about contemporary attitudes toward drink and drunkenness is confined to attitudes espoused in temperance literature. Even less is known about customary drinking behaviour in taverns.

Tavern-goers, together with tavern-keepers, regulated their own behaviour. Drinking was controlled in tavern spaces. Licensing regulations that represented good order as an ideal to be maintained found few detractors among tavern companies, even if their behaviour sometimes overstepped its bounds. A now classic sociological statement, MacAndrew and Edgerton's *Drunken Comportment* argues that differing world cultures permit individuals under the influence of alcohol to engage in a wide range of behaviours that reveal the degree and type of social disruption tolerated by that culture and society. Thus, if violence is permitted to drunks in a given society, violence has a recognized, if contested, social role in that society. If violence against women is permitted among male drunks, then violence against women by men in general has a tolerated social place. In other words, studying drunken comportment can reveal much about cultures and societies. Still, colonial patrons and keeps alike were well aware of the dangers of liquor. They had a nuanced understanding of the effects of alcohol. They recognized its potentially problematic effects on emotions, sensorimotor skills, and psychological inhibitions against moral transgressions. They understood that different people reacted differently to drink. In response, tavern-goers co-operated with each other and with tavern-keepers to keep the use of alcohol within community norms.

Tavern-goers monitored each other's drinking and paid attention to their own. James King knew he had taken "about 4 glasses" with his soldier friends at the Rob Roy. Harry Jones' tavern consumption throughout the 1830s and '40s ranged from a "glass of grog" to "sundry horns" in company. At Frigg's tavern in York in 1832 George Cooper and George Underhill "had two glasses each" and "had taken a glass of gin earlier." Later, at Waugh's tavern, Underhill claimed he drank nothing. Cooper, however, claimed that Underhill "drank 4 glasses of gin at Waugh's before he went away." Thomas Gilbert, though, saw both Underhill and Cooper "drink together at Frigg's – 6 or 5 glasses." He himself, of course, had only "a glass or two." William Mitchell also "drank 2 or 3 glasses that evening."[38]

Tavern-goers were perfectly sober after "a glass or two." Those who became involved in legal conflict, such as Cooper and Underhill, often counterposed their own restraint against the other's excess. The point is not whether tavern-goers actually took only a couple of glasses; it is that, by claiming restraint, they held it up as a laudable virtue. For the inmates of pre-industrial colonial taverns, drunkenness was a negative charge to level against a companion.

The quantity of alcohol consumed in colonial society is notoriously difficult to estimate. Consumption statistics found in histories of temperance activism are, as Jan Noel notes, "based on a good deal of guesswork." The reasons are numerous. The statistics rely on the accuracy of state records that quantified imports and local production, and these records do not reveal what the alcohol content of the product was, although we do know that it varied widely and unpredictably. Indeed, it is not always clear whether one is counting barrels of wine, beer, and spirituous liquor or dealing with estimates of pure alcohol. And it is not possible to account for home-based production (for example, the spruce beer that James Donaldson brewed in his tavern). Finally, these already problematic quantities can only be applied to the total population, which means that estimates do not accurately take into account the (presumably negligible) consumption of toddlers and children (who made up nearly half of colonial populations) and the above average drinking habits of those who consumed to excess. However, these statistics do appear to document decreasing levels of consumption in North America between 1830 and 1860. In both Canada and the United States annual per capita consumption of spirits rose from 2.5 gallons in 1791 to a peak of 5 gallons in the 1820s. This consumption pattern paralleled developments in Paris, England, and Germany. By the 1830s, annual consumption rates dropped back to an average of about three gallons per capita.[39]

On accepting that these are the only numbers we have to work with (and that they have been mustered to prove the success of the temperance movement), it is tempting to apply them to colonial taverns, where drink, as a substance, played such a significant social role. At its height in the 1820s the best estimates place annual consumption at five gallons per person. This does not translate into anything like heavy drinking. Five gallons is 640 fluid ounces, which, when divided by the days in the year, amounts to 1.7 ounces per day. Peak per capita annual consumption in the 1820s was much closer to one modern-day shot (1.25 oz.) a day than two.

If we rule out children as potential drinkers and assume (perhaps incorrectly) that women drank half as much as men, then we should come closer to adult male consumption averages. The equation is as follows: Five gallons is equal to the amount that each group (children, women, and men) consumed, multiplied by the percentage of the population they constituted. In other words: $5 = (0 \times 0.5) + (x \times 0.25) + (2x \times 0.25)$, where x is the amount women consumed, and $2x$ is the amount men consumed. Therefore, $5 = 0.25x + 0.5x$, $5 = 0.75x$, $5/.75 = x$, and $6.67 = x$. Thus, hypothetically, women consumed 6.67 gallons and men consumed 13.33 gallons annually. In terms of daily consumption this works out for women to just over a glass a day (2.3 oz.) and for men to slightly more than a gill (4.7 oz.).[40]

Douglas McCalla has tested the truth of "consumption stories" about Upper Canadians by analyzing the purchasing patterns of customers in the account books of general stores. McCalla carefully notes the limitations of his sources, but he demonstrates that they indicate that none of the customers bought anything close to the amount of liquor that is disclosed in the tales. The single largest purchase in 1829 was 45 quarts (11.25 gallons, or a daily consumption of 4 oz.). Other consumption stories suggest similar amounts. For instance, in about 1780 merchant John Askin instructed the captain of the *Mackinac* that "it seemed best to give Macdonald and the Indian each a quarter of a pint [4 oz.] of rum per day while on the voyage, and half that quantity to Pomp [an enslaved black man]. The whole will not amount to much and will be an incentive to good work besides keeping them from helping themselves to the cargo." A gill, then, was considered plentiful enough to prevent pilfering. A letter dated 1813 regarding "supplies to the militia on duty at Ganonoque" instructed the commander there that "some liquor will be sent down ... that a daily allowance of a quart among six men [5.3 oz. per man] may be issued." British soldiers in the colony received a gill a day rum ration. In 1837 John Prince made a notation in the margin of his diary that stated: "The 2 Pereaus came [to work] at 5s per day and two glasses of whiskey." (Customarily, a glass was two ounces.) In sum, all of the available evidence – best estimates, a hypothetical consideration of what these estimates said about daily drinking habits, an economic historian's calculations based on accounts rendered, and colonists' depictions of routine daily rations – suggests that the consumption of a gill of liquor a day was commonplace in Upper Canada and must have served as a benchmark against which to measure "excess" consumption.[41]

Average rates of consumption for the 1820s certainly do not indicate a drunken populace. Tavern-goers' patterns of attendance and travellers observations reveal a pattern of daily drinking that worked in favour of sobriety. We saw two men in Chapter 1 who called in at Linfoot's tavern before sunrise; each man "got a glass of whiskey" because the tavern-keeper was up early. It was more customary to take bitters, a gin-based compound liquor that settled the stomach and stimulated the appetite, before breakfast. In either case, drinking started early and continued throughout the day as a normal accompaniment to meals, as a physical stimulant to labour (recall the men who called out at Nolan's for "nourishment" to help them carry a grinding stone), and as a leisure activity. Colonists drank small interspersed amounts of liquor throughout the day: "Whenever they pass the bar they either sit down and smoke or indulge in potation ... all day long they drink at brandy, gin, or whiskey, taking, however, a wine glass at a time, which they mix in a tumbler with a little sugar and water." When an adult male's metabolism of alcohol (one ounce per hour) is taken into consideration, daily drinking patterns such as these meant average colonial male alcohol consumption did not necessarily induce intoxication.[42] Though Upper Canadian men may have been drinking all the time, they were mostly sober.

In contrast, Upper Canadians recognized drunkenness as a dubious condition that differed qualitatively from drinking. Colonial drinkers and their communities knew that too much alcohol affected people's ability to think clearly. John Ward, for example, articulated the link between drink and mental acuity when he argued, "Perhaps he was then [in liquor] but not much – was quite sensible." Upper Canadians likewise knew that alcohol affected sensorimotor capabilities. Abner C. Ellis, for example, said that even though John David Askin and Robert Elliot "had been drinking" in Hall's tavern, he "did not consider" the latter "drunk, though he had evidently been drinking. He could walk very well." At Woon's in Oshawa, James Wilson "was not sober – could walk," while Robert Wilson "was drunk, but could walk." Similarly, David Trare's brother-in-law used to get "pretty merry at a bee, but he could always make his way home." If these statements suggest that "drunk" meant dead drunk, they nevertheless testify to a contemporary concern with alcohol's power. Colonial drinkers weighed alcohol's attraction and symbolic value against a concern for its effects.[43]

Because of the injunction to keep good order, tavern-keepers had an investment in containing drink and drinkers. Drunkenness was a form of disorder. With their families in the same building, their licences potentially on the line, and their profits coming most reliably from patrons who were steady members of the community, tavern-keepers endorsed moderation in their own taverns. William Sebach, for example, who kept tavern on the Mitchell road in the 1840s, paid heed to the strength of the liquor he served. He knew that Isaac Macdonald was "perfectly sober" when he arrived at about 4:30 in the afternoon. "He took a glass of beer then and another in the evening." "The beer was not strong enough to make him drunk." When Robert Wilson "came in drunk" to Woon's barroom and "wanted liquor, Woon would not give him any, ordered him off." In Uxbridge the licence inspectors, "on examining into the matter ... could not find evidence" that tavern-keeper Henry Vanzant sold "liquor to persons who are in the habit of drinking to the injury of their families." And when a brawl erupted at Waugh's tavern in Toronto, it was the barkeep who came in for the severest criticism from several patrons because he "gave all drink that wanted it." Rather than facilitating order, they charged, the tavern-keeper facilitated its breakdown by abdicating his responsibility to the company. No doubt some, like the barkeep at Waugh's, failed in this regard, but both law and company expected controlled access to liquor in taverns.[44]

Yet patrons sometimes had too much drink. If they were strangers, or alone, a tavern-keeper might let them sleep it off on the floor. A patron at Murray Presentier's tavern, for example, "was very drunk in the evening" and laid down in the barroom "for the night." At Arnett's tavern in Toronto, "the bar keeper put [a patron] to bed. He was pretty merry." More often, because so many taverns served locals, members of the tavern-goer's personal network came to the drinker's aid. When Adam Stull got drunk at Milton's tavern in Niagara, his companion, Thomas Donaldson, prepared to take him home. However, when Donaldson went "to the barn for his horses," another man, Thomas Dowling, "came to Milton's to take Stull home." While the relationship between the parties is unknown, some form of neighbourhood communication summoned Dowling to the tavern to look after Stull. Similarly, Robert Wilson's brother "came and took him away from Woon's"; he had previously been summoned to Roach's tavern, where, again, "his brother came and ordered him off." Drunks, in other words, got looked after, but in different ways. Someone who took too much drink on occasion and needed a ride home got one. Yet colonists were not so likely to gladly suffer those they called "habitual drunkards," people we would characterize as alcoholics. Drunkards were refused drink (for their own and their family's good), ordered to leave, or hauled unceremoniously away by a family member. Upper Canada may have been a drinking society by modern standards, but it was one in which the members had a wary respect for alcohol's potential dangers.

When the Province of Canada passed the Dunkin Act in 1864, legislators officially recognized the social damage habitual drunkards could wreak on families and communities. The Act permitted spouses, family members, employers, and other authority figures to petition to have individuals "in the habit of drinking ... to excess" placed on a list of those interdicted from (that is, refused service in) specific taverns. Yet there are hints that municipalities had already responded to similar concerns. Jacob Byron, a tavern-keeper in the village of Whitby, for instance, received a stern, legalistic letter about Norman G. Ham, Esq., "a person addicted to drinking," in 1852. The letter warned Byron that if he gave or sold spirituous liquors or "suffered" Ham to drink at his tavern, "contrary to the clause of Bylaw no 34 of the Township of Whitby," "I shall enforce the penalty therein contained against you." The letter was signed "J.V. Ham." The letter and the bylaw suggest a community-level response, and the community's best efforts to prevent further harm, to the plight of families affected by habitual drunkards.[45]

That tavern-goers took care to separate their own drinking behaviour from the state of intoxication called drunkenness signals that being drunk was taboo. As James King put it, he "was not drunk," he "had been drinking," when he called at the Rob Roy. Similarly, Thomas Gilbert "was not drunk at Waugh's," he "had been drinking." And at Mourhale's near Cornwall, old Patrick O'Connor was "not very tipsy," he "had been drinking." When Luke Teeple and Enock Moore (whom we have already encountered) waited for their turn before the Court of Requests at Beaupré's in London, they "attended the greater part of the day" and "both were drinking"; however, "neither party was drunk." No one claimed drunkenness as a positive state of being. While it might flow from drinking, drunkenness was not inevitable, intended, or particularly desirable. When barroom companions counted the glasses they each consumed, when they expected the keep to stop serving drunks, when they looked after those who drank too much, and when they dodged accusations of drunkenness, their behaviour testified to their belief that drinking was best done in moderation.[46]

However, none of this suggests that colonists saw the occasional drinking spree as problematic. In fact, occasional drunkenness was widely tolerated. Harry Jones, for instance, "laughed at Stevenson" who was "on a spree and most particularly drunk" (see Chapter 3). But to be tolerable, drunkenness had to be episodic and, more importantly, timed so it did not interfere with an individual's work or familial responsibilities. Everyone knew that Peter McDonald spent time at George Kent's tavern. But as a local merchant and magistrate he had important obligations to fulfill. Although his barroom companions had "seen him occasionally under the influence of liquor," they "always found him ready to attend to business." The level of toleration granted to "binge drinking" stemmed from its long history and deep integration into celebratory rituals, festival occasions, and the sense of release working men marked together through heavy consumption at the completion of arduous jobs. In the cases of Stevenson and McDonald, this generalized indulgence seems to have extended to tavern-going individuals who were responding to more personal desires. The indulgence remained grounded, nevertheless, in the expectation that these men resume their responsibilities. In this regard, responses to spree drinking differed from responses to habitual drunkenness, and, although these responses suggest that notions of acceptable consumption had wide parameters in colonial society, they also draw attention to the fact that Upper Canadians held concepts of moderation and good order as the ideal.[47]

Tavern-goers and neighbours criticized specific aspects of drunken comportment. Robert Elliot of Sandwich, who was "funny but not quarrelsome," when in liquor, raised few concerns. In contrast, Jane Wright of the Midland District was "crazed" when drunk, and her behaviour was described as "very bad." Cooper, who frequented Waugh's and Frigg's taverns in Toronto, was "a very foolish man when tipsy – is abusive then." Robert Wilson of Oshawa was "a drinking man, a regular nuisance," and "quarrelsome when in liquor." Michael Clancy of Sarnia, though a "respectable" man, "gets high sometimes and then is troublesome." Clearly, there were dangerous drunks who were well known to their communities. That tavern-goers and -keepers met their quarrelsomeness and troublesomeness with concern testifies to the intense value they placed on orderly association. These drunks were disorderly by definition. They met with social disapprobation because their drinking behaviour resisted community norms that favoured moderation. No one regarded taverns as ineluctably chaotic; no one saw them as predisposed to disorder. Colonists expected peaceful association in the taverns, as they did in the community as a whole. Those who threatened the orderly nature of public association by their abuse of drink were branded as nasty characters.[48]

The place of drink in colonial taverns and society was a complex one. It carried a weight of symbolic meaning. The extension of an offer to drink, and its acceptance, represented mutuality and implied reciprocity. To treat together symbolized association between the parties. This could be understood lightly, as in the example of three soldiers drinking together beyond tattoo, or more deeply, as a pledge of formal good will in the midst of a relationship. It was a cultural routine, a normal accompaniment to business transactions. Beyond its symbolic value, drink, in taverns as elsewhere, earned respect as a potentially dangerous substance. Drunkenness meant something very different than drinking. Colonists defined the term *drunkenness* in social terms. Drunkenness affected a person's ability to behave in a sensible manner and "attend to business"; it threatened the drunk's personal safety and made it necessary for companions or family to retrieve him or her from the tavern. Most problematically, it caused disturbances to peaceful relations in the tavern and the community. In each case, drunkenness was defined in anti-social terms. The drinking culture of the taverns, especially the use of the treat as a symbol of social exchange, did not blind colonial participants to liquor's potentially disruptive power over the very social ties they hoped to create. On the contrary, customary practices contained the effects of liquor and controlled its potential to do harm. Much of the concern to regulate consumption had to do with the link between drink and violence, for violence was a fundamental breach of the good order sought in these public spaces.

Yet there is no question that colonial social relations included a high level of tolerance for violence. There is also no question that some of this violence erupted, by both accident and design, in the taverns. Historians Kevin Wamsley and Robert Kossuth found many examples of men in Upper Canada going out to the taverns to look for trouble, seeking out fights so that they could prove their manliness. Historical analyses of early Virginia, pre-Revolutionary Paris, and New York City on the cusp of industrialization revealed the same behaviour, suggesting that there is a kind of timeless link between taverns, violence, and men being men.[49] In short, public drinking houses have been written about (particularly fluently by Rhys Isaac) as if they were the strutting grounds for competing roosters intent on establishing and validating their masculinity.[50] This approach limits our sense of what constitutes colonial masculinities. The prominence of violence as a theme in tavern historiography also calls major arguments of this book into question. If men routinely went to taverns to fight, how could taverns have been accessible sites, open to multiple public uses?

That some men sometimes found fighting a seductive way to showcase their masculinity in a public setting is apparent, and historian Thomas Brennan's insight that the reasons men had for fighting can tell us a great deal about their social values is useful for explaining their behaviour.[51] The insight encourages historians to place historical eruptions of violence into the wider social and cultural context of community and familial relations. By doing so, we expand the notion of colonial masculinity by making visible what men valued highly enough to come to blows over in the public setting of the tavern. Also, we know that families lived in taverns, that women came to visit or take punch with friends, that children ran about and people danced, sang, conversed, treated, traded, attended court, voted, and caught the stage; we have to suspect that all of this could not have happened against a background of smashing glass and scuffling. In fact, just as self-regulation and cultural ritual inscribed norms and defined what was excessive in public drinking behaviour, it also managed the potential for violence in the conduct of public sociability.

Nobody wanted a quarrel. Indeed, tavern companions deployed customs that worked against violent eruptions, and failing that, they limited the potential for harm. By the very act of creating a code of conduct to govern violence, tavern-goers legitimated it as a means of social negotiation. They employed a popular code of honour, in principle, that resembled that of gentleman duellists (or contemporary hockey players) settling scores.[52] In the taverns, conformity to the code governing violence generally meant fighting fairly and only after due provocation. Like the upper class with their swords or pistols, the form of the exchange was as valuable as its outcome. Honour and reputation were on the line. Despite the legitimacy that the code granted to violence, a concern to limit the potential harm that could come to persons, social relations, and property was implicit within its formal patterning.

The tavern itself – the building, the house, and the home of the keeping family – was off limits as a site of violence. Michael Moran, for instance, at McBrien's tavern, said that "he would not fight in a decent man's house." More to the point, the keep himself said, "I would allow no one to quarrel in my place ... I forbid it." Job Perry prohibited fighting at his Western District tavern, while Richard Woon similarly "told Robert W. he had better go out – I forbid fighting in ye house ... They went out." William Curney, who witnessed the incident, agreed: "Woon's forbids fights."[53] Licensing concerns and the obvious potential for property damage figured prominently in tavern-keepers' decisions. Fighting was a serious assault on good order, and a complaint could either land a tavern-keeper in front of the magistrate or hamper the ability to renew his or her licence. For both reasons tavern-keepers enforced the "no fighting in the house" rule. And as a rule, patrons obeyed it.

Strong words always preceded violence and worked to legitimize it before it erupted. When "words passed about fighting," or when "there were no blows struck, but hard language," the dispute could escalate. At O'Neil's tavern, during a meeting to choose an electoral candidate, patron Henry Meredith recalled that "he heard Wilson getting up to speak." Wilson "denied something O'Neil had said, then they bandied the lie and lean one to another." The two men made mutual warnings of intent to transform the argument into a physical fight, which they then took outside. This was one way of demonstrating a fair fight: it showed that both parties wanted to engage in blows, that the use of force was justified, expected, and mutually provoked. Richard Woon, for example, made a note of the obligatory exchange of threats and insults between the two Wilsons who fought in his yard. "Robert W said 'you black bugger you struck me once before and now I am ready to lick you' – *or to that effect*." Here, the keep emphasized the form of the exchange rather than its content, implying that strong words were a recognized and necessary step in the initiation of violence. [54]

A man's behaviour with his coat could also symbolize his readiness to fight. At Carroll's drinking house, Justus Willcocks remembered that two men "pulled their coats off to fight," though the keeper, Mrs. Carroll, was only certain that "Harder had his coat off – forgets whether Ward [did] or not." Tavern-keeper Woon likewise told James Wilson, who had taken off his coat to fight, "to put on his coat and he did so."[55]

Tavern companions monitored violence closely. At O'Neil's, the scuffle "lasted only two or three minutes," and, because observers "did not think it very serious," no one intervened. In contrast, events escalated dangerously at Perry's tavern in Blandford. John Wallington had been drinking. His "affairs were bad," and because several patrons made Wallington angry by refusing to join in the chorus of his song, he attacked them with a "hammer end whip." The tavern-keeper promptly maintained good order. He "prohibited fighting – took the whip ... [and] broke it." When Wallington stuck a pistol into the keep's face and "said he was a dead man ... he was instantly saved by others."[56]

The incident at Perry's was an extreme example; nevertheless, it illustrates keep and company actively co-operating to regulate violence in tavern space. It was also not the only time that things got out of hand. For example, there was a classic brawl at John Waugh's York tavern the day after Christmas in 1831:

> Cooper came in, caught hold of Underhill, hauled him down by the stove – Underhill had not spoken to him – there were 6 or 8 persons there in the barroom about 9 or 10 at night. When Underhill got up Cooper seized again and they both fell together ... Cooper swept the tumblers and glasses off the bar and smashed them, can't say how many. Two were with Cooper and they all there behaved ill ... Cooper struck Underhill – gave him a black eye ... he seemed as if he had been drinking ... Cooper commenced the affray ... the barroom was thrown into great confusion – saw Cooper and others striking at the barrkeeper in the bar. Waugh was not at home.[57]

Despite its made-for-the-movies quality, the most remarkable aspect of this tavern brawl was its singularity. When Cooper came in, "noisy and bluesy," and caught hold of Underhill, he caused chaos at Waugh's. Men got "shoved off" a railing, and barkeep Mahlon Blaken "came out of the bar and struck Cooper two over the shoulder with the poker." "Gilbert struck the stove pipe" and knocked it down, which must have filled the place with smoke. Far from accepting the brawl as the normal run of business, the tavern-goers were taken by surprise. Thomas Kanrington, who lived downstairs, came running when he heard the "great noise." The barkeep, who thought it a "scandalous scene," sent for Matthews, the constable. Matthews said that when he got there the "house was in an uproar."

Not one member of the tavern company anticipated the evening's outcome. Their words and actions imply that an explosion of violence was anything but commonplace in the barroom. Nor did the company condone it. Instead, members lined up to testify against Cooper at his criminal trial for assault and for tavern-keeper Waugh in his civil suit for damages. Because the violence appeared unprovoked, it broke all conventions. In fact, it became known during the trial that Cooper and Underhill had spent most of the day together, and their conflict, fuelled by a disputed amount of gin, escalated during supper time. Underhill's version of the story presented before the court pulled on popular expectations that violence should be both provoked and forewarned. He proclaimed, with wide, innocent eyes, that Cooper simply attacked him, without even speaking. In Cooper's version of the story, Underhill started it all. And there must have been some truth to Cooper's claim, because one witness praised him for initially refusing to hit Underhill: "It is only old George Underhill," Cooper apparently said, "[I] would not touch him." The point is not that the two men tailored the truth to suit their needs, but that by doing so they invoked cultural norms. The testimony about who threw the first punch and whether it was provoked, emphasized that there had to be a reason to fight. One had to give clear warning, and starting a fight – flinging hard words, taking off one's coat, making the first clinch – placed the onus on the who started the fight for the outcome. The praise that Cooper received for his restraint was an acknowledgement that control was highly valued. Although these incidents affirm male precedence in this public space, there is no sense that manliness itself was on the line, that individual men needed to affirm it by trouncing an adversary. Everyone wanted to restore good order, and they went about it in various ways. Nothing like acceptance, never mind endorsement, of freewheeling violence can be assumed.

Despite their preference for good order, tavern companions meant to ensure a fair fight through the regulation of violence. They did not really question the use of violence, when properly conducted, as a legitimate means of social negotiation. For example, tavern-keeper Richard Woon "told Robert Wilson to go off" because "James would kill him." James did just that. But, given that James did not start the fight (Robert said he "was going to whip" him), that he was reluctant to fight (James put his coat back on), and that Robert had a reputation for being "quarrelsome when in liquor," each man in the barroom that day was willing to testify in James' defence. James' deadly beating of Robert earned the company's sanction because it was appropriately patterned.[58]

The rules guiding violence in taverns did nothing, then, to call its social value into question. Taverns served as venues for formal, semi-planned, violent confrontations precisely because of their stature as public space. One incident at the Lambton Hotel, for example, involved Michael Clancy and William Chambers who were doing business together in a joint lumbering venture. Both were "respectable men." Chambers sued Clancy for failing to live up to the terms of a deal, and he spread damaging rumours about Clancy's financial affairs. When Chambers walked into the Lambton Hotel, Clancy "came up ... said he had been waiting for me a long time and seized me by the throat, several people tried to take him off ... then he was taken away." Instances like this one broke all the rules of tavern violence. The two men scuffled in the house, no warning was given, no chance to accept the challenge was offered, and no coats were taken off. Chambers simply arrived, and before he knew it Clancy was on him, yelling that he would have his "heart's blood." Naturally, the company intervened promptly. Having been accused publicly of shady business dealings, and with rumours of ruin swirling about his head, Clancy chose the Lambton Hotel's bar as the most appropriate site to defend his local reputation. His behaviour was similar to that of the men who verbally defended their respectability before the tavern's informal court of public opinion (see Chapter 3). Reputation, or respectability, was part personal, part "public persona," making its defence in the tavern's public space a natural choice. In a society where violence enjoyed status as a legitimate tool of social negotiation, its use in a public setting could render it even more powerful.[59]

These brawling incidents demonstrate that if for men and masculinity violence proved who was the "best man" and "defined for men their self-identity and their self-perception of manliness,"[60] it did so in ways that revealed men's social connectedness, not their "competitive," ultimately atomistic individuality. These tavern-going men protected and defended their place in the social network through violence. They worried about how they fit into their communities and what their families and neighbours thought of them. Michael Clancy's tavern fighting was more than an act of rugged self-assertion: when he defended his good name he fought for continued local acknowledgement as a "respectable man." He used violence to assert the value of social ties as constituent aspects of his masculinity.[61] He used violence to stay well-connected to his community.

Clancy's declaration at the Lambton Hotel that he would have William Chambers' "heart's blood," John Wallington's pistol waving in Perry's barroom, and the Boxing Day brawl at Waugh's tavern are compelling images. Yet these fights erupted within a complex of social expectations and cultural practices that worked against them. Similarly, although tavern-goers welcomed drink as a valuable symbol and a desirable substance, they, along with the wider public, regarded drunkenness, particularly habitual drunkenness, as a social taboo. The odd spree was fine. But local censure of those who were "quarrelsome" when in liquor shows that contemporaries connected drink with unnecessary expressions of violence. Violence had a role to play in social negotiation, but it had to be appropriately patterned and seen as justified in order to achieve popular sanction. The web of customary regulation surrounding tavern going testifies to the willingness of all concerned to maintain good order. On entering the bar or other public rooms, tavern-goers expected to find people drinking in moderation. They did not anticipate getting into a barroom brawl.

All of this made the more esoteric value of tavern going, the sense of belonging it created, however fleetingly, more realizable. Tavern companies formed, sometimes for the hour, sometimes as continuing associations among regulars, to make its members feel they were a part of informal public life. When they bought drink for each other, joined together "a'dancing," or associated in common as an audience, tavern-goers participated in tavern-based rituals that encouraged social bonding. In the taverns, colonists made social groups of various sizes and intensities. That these groups celebrated specific aspects of identity by resisting intrusion by others becomes apparent in what follows. The often fragmented and divisive use of tavern space that resulted was a problematic outcome, one that reveals the tensions of a mixed colonial public and the strains these tensions placed on the generally orderly nature of the taverns that stood open to heterogeneous use.

5
Race and Space

On our arrival yesterday many Indians were in town and a few of them stayed about the taverns pretty late in the evening. Some of them, as well as the blacks and whites, drank quite freely; and I heard this morning that a fracas occurred in our landlord's barroom among the heterogenous assemblage there. Having retired early I knew nothing of it. The blame was thrown on the "negroes" by the bar-keeper who was a "Yankee" of "high pressure" prejudice, but it did not amount to much; and to-day very few Indians or blacks are to be seen in the public places.

– Benjamin Lundy, The Diary of Benjamin Lundy

This tavern story about a Saturday night on the town in Brantford in 1832 addresses racialized relations in a tavern barroom, links these relations to public space ("places"), and graphically illustrates how the social mutuality promised by tavern association could be betrayed in practice. In the story, tavern-goers who engaged in heterogenous sociability are juxtaposed with the "high pressure prejudice" of a Yankee barkeep. The incident challenges us to understand what these moments of multiracial public life meant in a society permeated by racialized thought and practice.[1] There is a strange contradiction between white settlers' marginalization of black and First Nations peoples and the sometimes easy accommodation that was afforded them in public houses. Although some settlers illegally, and sometimes violently, refused to accommodate people of colour, tavern stories complicate historical interpretations that focus on conflict. Without questioning these analyses, or the evidence supporting them, tavern stories suggest that something else was going on. Colonial taverns were simultaneously public spaces where people chose to relax racial boundaries and public spaces where they chose to enforce them. Taverns were sites where the cultural rituals of drink and "barroom sport," to borrow John Beverley Robinson's phrase, crafted a sense of mutual belonging. Because they granted this sense of membership, taverns could become contested space in racialized as in other ways.

We know that "Indianness," "blackness," and "whiteness" mattered in the making of Upper Canada. The themes of segregation, marginalization, and dispossession are common to black and Native historiography. Yet they are only a part of the history of racialized relations in taverns, because in taverns, the parallel societies of white settlers and racialized others also met.[2] Ties of good fellowship in taverns sometimes stretched to encompass a racially inclusive idea; sometimes they snapped shut to protect the whiteness of informal public life. Because race mattered in contradictory ways in Upper Canada, it is important to ask how its unpredictability "became embodied in discrete acts with real consequences" for real people.[3]

Contemporaries noticed Natives in and around taverns. In 1802 Ely Playter in York noted that "Mr. J.D. Cozens ... came about 2 o'clock with his Indian. I gave him the south chamber for his apartment." The possessive pronoun *his* casts the Native person as a dependant, and it is unclear where he or she actually lodged. In 1817, in contrast, it is very clear that an Anishinabe man, travelling a distance with naturalist and publisher Charles Fothergill, slept outside the tavern where Fothergill stopped. "Carried my Indian to Ganonoque [sic] – gave him rum his soul and body's delight laid him by a woodfire ... He promised to bring me venison in the morning."[4] The man (again referred to with a possessive pronoun) was literally on the "physical margins of the new settler society."[5] Conversely, in a tavern on the Talbot Road in 1821, Englishman John Howison "found a mixed assemblage of persons seated around the fire ... several Scotch Highlanders ... three Indians in full hunting costume; and a couple of New England Americans with some children belonging to the house." Expounding on the characteristics of each, Howison decided "[t]he Indians possessed a sort of negative superiority ... being exalted by those virtues that generally belong to the savage. Though untutored they were not in a state of debasement."[6] As he met Natives and thought, however conventionally, about racialized identities, Howison provided evidence of a mixed tavern public.

Tavern stories can inform discussions about First Nations' relations with newcomers. They say nothing about the internal dynamics of Aboriginal communities as they "remade" themselves in the new socio-cultural environment that structured Native-white relations after the War of 1812.[7] In 1800 about seven thousand Native people lived in the colony; the number then fluctuated periodically to between ten and eleven thousand, ranging from between a fifth and a third of the total population. The actual number of Native people remained steady, but the Native portion of the population fell sharply with the spread of white settlement until by mid-century it accounted for barely over 1 percent of the colony's population.[8] Native people increasingly lost land, their political and military status declined, and challenges to Native self-government intensified. Christianization spread, even if Native people embraced it for strategic reasons.[9] Until the Indian Act of 1857 made Native people both non-citizens and legal minors, their status was subject to conflicting interpretations. First Nations regarded themselves as sovereign, an understanding that was embedded in the Royal Proclamation of 1763 and confirmed by their autonomy on reserves.[10] Native men who owned land off-reserve could vote. Theoretically, Native peoples enjoyed equal standing before the courts. But self-governance and legal equality were contradicted and constrained by the Indian Department on the reserves and by a legal system that failed to acknowledge Native title to reserve land or resources.[11] As a result Native peoples stood on unequal legal and constitutional ground with white settlers. Everyday interactions between Natives and newcomers may not have been directly affected by these developments, but understanding how groups fared relative to each other can tell us much about how they perceived each other, especially how the whites who dominated public space perceived the Native people who entered it.

The image of the drunken Indian informed white perceptions. Already a stereotype by the nineteenth century, it reflected, on the one hand, the fact that some Native people engaged in excessive drinking and, on the other, settlers' uneasiness about Indians and their place in society.[12] This anxiety found expression in the 1835 Act to Prevent the Sale of Spirituous Liquors to Indians. The Act extended a long history of regulation that began in the thirteen colonies and New France by barring white settlers from any exchange of spirits with First Nations peoples.[13] The legislation consequently affected Native people's relationship with tavern sociability solely on the basis of their race. It emphasized Native people's place on the margins of public life by delegitimizing their participation in one of its everyday locales. The legislation also assumed that everyone could tell who an "Indian" was. For example, when a tavern-keeper in Delaware (southwest of London) was hauled before the magistrates in 1841 on charges of selling liquor to a party of Tuscarora, he claimed that, "as they were dressed like ourselves, and spoke good English, he never thought of refusing them." To a country tavern-keeper, Western clothing and the English language signalled an identity separate from Indianness; his understanding of racialized identity was flexible, cultural, and more sophisticated than the rigid legal definition of "Indian" that got him into trouble.[14]

Taverns did not usually support Native-centred sociability. Rather, First Nations treated taverns as useful sites to conduct relationships, including political matters, economic exchanges, and moments of interracial companionship, with Anglo-Americans. In 1793 Lenape (Delaware), Wyandot, and Shawnee delegates used Matthew Dolsen's "comfortable and easy" tavern in British-occupied Detroit for political meetings with Quaker peace emis-saries.[15] The Northwest Indian Confederation, which the delegates repre-sented, was at war with the United States over the Ohio country. As part of a peace process both sides met in Indian country, near Detroit. At the request of the Confederation, six Quakers participated in the negotiations. They travelled west, lodged at Dolsen's, and opened discussions. "We had a visit today from several Shawnese," wrote Quaker Jacob Lindley. "One of them was a middle-aged man, the most solid countenanced I had seen amongst them. We spoke to him by an interpreter, and let him know who we were, and what our views were in coming ... With which he appeared pleased, and said he heartily wished we might get through with the work of peace ... After drinking a glass or two of wine he wished us well and departed."[16] We know that the treat could affirm hierarchical relationships (for instance, when masters or mistresses treated servants) as well as mutual ones (when the ac-ceptance of drink required a reciprocal response, either in kind or, as was the case in this Quaker-Shawnee interaction, in a return of compliments). Both parties accepted the symbolism inherent in the glass of wine and used it to represent their mutual good intent in the upcoming negotiations.

The Western dinner ritual likewise facilitated communication between Native and newcomer. The Quakers dined at Dolsen's with an "Indian of the Delaware tribe," who "talked a little English," and shared political intel-ligence.[17] Those at ease with European dining etiquette communicated within Westernized cultural codes and projected themselves as cultivated individuals within these terms: "We came to our lodgings, and dined with two Wyandot chiefs who behaved with decency at table, equal to any of us, handled their knife and fork well, [ate] moderately and drank two glasses of wine, and through the whole conducted with a decorum that would do honour to hundreds of white people." The rituals of mannered sociability over food and wine worked well as tools of communication. Using the tavern, particu-larly its dining table, as a "contact zone" of intercultural communication,[18] the Wyandot delegates made their stature as "civilized" men apparent with prompts the Quakers understood. Their participation in Anglo-American tavern culture facilitated the reception of their political message.

At the same time, the adoption of Western cultural ritual symbolized the power imbalance between the two groups. The fact that this kind of exchange occurred does not mean that taverns served as a *middle ground* in the way historian Richard White developed the term. The middle ground, as defined by White, housed intercultural communication between groups of relatively equal power; the only method of communication was creative misunder-standing. At Dolsen's, in contrast, European languages and cultural codes held sway. As ethnohistorian Bruce Trigger has illustrated, the provenance of the rituals used in political and economic interaction between Natives and newcomers revealed the relative power of each. The exclusive use at

Dolsen's of non-Native cultural forms represented Anglo-American dominance of the space.[19] It suggests, in fact, that from a Lenape or Wyandot or
Shawnee perspective, tavern space may not have appeared to be all that
public, structured as it was by the dominance of newcomers' cultural
ritual.

More commonly, Native men and women used taverns to make economic
exchanges. Tavern-keepers bought fresh fish and game from First Nations
neighbours. In 1805 "a number of [Mississauga] Indians returning from
Kingston after receiving their annual presents ... stops at Finkle who keeps
a tavern and asked him for whiskey in exchange for ducks, which he gave
them." In 1833, a Native man "brought in" a "very fine" muskie to the
keeper of a Kingston tavern. There is no note of payment in this case, but
some observers in general thought tavern-keepers exploited Native suppliers.
In 1817 Fothergill saw a tavern-keeper buy "a brace of partridges from these
people for a single glass of rum," which was certainly an unfair exchange
by any standard. But the glass of rum may have been a treat, with the actual
value of the exchange entered on the books, as was normal at Dolsen's tavern
(discussed below).[20] In 1831 at Wheeler's tavern on Talbot Street, "an Indian
from a neighbouring camp came in with two 'hams' [haunches] of venison
and a deer skin ... The tavernkeeper gave him one pint of whiskey for each
ham and two pints for the skin only." The going price in a tavern for a pint
of whiskey was a shilling to a shilling and a half, depending on quality of
the whiskey. The hunter had killed two deer that day and forty in the season
(to 20 December). The hunter received spirits worth four to six shillings for
his portion of the kill; on the tavern-keeper's scales of measurement, the liquor was equivalent to a male labourer's daily earning, which suggests a fair
economic value for the hunter's work.[21]

Matthew Dolsen's tavern account book chronicles an earlier, ongoing
economic relationship with Native neighbours, including Lenape, on the
Thames River.[22] Dolsen ran his tavern as part of a mercantile complex with
a general store, a wharf, a boat for upriver trade, and a sawmill. Native names
are unmistakable among the entries in his ledger: David Indian; Amos Indian;
Simon Indian; Samuel M. Indian; Leonard Indian; Joacum Indian; Nicholas
Indian and his wife; Ludewick Indian and his wife; Tobias Indian and his
mother and mother-in-law; Bettsey Indian woman; and others. Dolsen's
account book is very clear about racial identity and depicts the mixed company in his house. It documents fair standards of exchange between the
tavern-keeper and Native peoples and shows a balanced use of tavern space
that is far removed from the image of the drunken Indian.

"Ludwick M. Indian" and "Tobias Indian" came into Dolsen's in October
1798. Dolsen debited their accounts for assorted goods and a breakfast and
supper each, and he charged them prices consistent with what he charged
non-Native customers. In May 1799 "John Dolsen, Indian" made numerous

purchases. He also sold furs, (maple?) sugar, and corn, for which Dolsen credited his account £89 2s., entering all amounts as cash. Dolsen later resold the corn at a 10 percent markup, and made, on average, a 29 percent profit on the furs.[23] The tavern-keeper merchant made a good, but fair, profit.

Some Native people purchased liquor at Dolsen's tavern. "John Dolsen, Indian," bought nearly fifteen quarts of wine, in different measures, and half a pint of whiskey. Tobias purchased half a pint of rum and took a gill with his breakfast. "Amos Indian" and "Simon Indian" bought a quart and a gallon of rum, respectively, and "Anthony Indian" included four gills, a pint, and a decanter of rum, in addition to a glass taken at the tavern, with his list of supplies. "Betsy M. Waman" bought some wine.[24] It is only the mention of Anthony's glass, "David Indian's" shilling of rum, and Tobias' gill that indicate in-house consumption. In general, the amounts purchased by Dolsen's Native customers suggest off-site consumption. And unless they paid for drink with cash (in which case the transaction would not appear in the accounts), no Native people drank as regularly in the tavern as their non-Native counterparts. The Lenape, and presumably other local Native people, came to sell corn, sugar, and pelts, to buy needed goods that included liquor, but their sociability took place elsewhere.

Within the context of colonial drinking patterns, neither the amounts of liquor taken away by Dolsen's Native customers nor their in-house consumption are remarkable. Many people purchased liquor by the gallon or the quart because it was cheaper to buy in bulk and opted for more expensive sociability over glasses or gills, as they desired. Because taking a gill of liquor meshed comfortably with contemporary notions of moderation, and because anybody who had had only a couple of drinks was reckoned sober, a drinking Indian at Dolsen's was far from being the image of a drunken Indian. Historians participating in and contributing to a growing body of literature have remarked that the role of alcohol in First Nations societies seems a particularly important theme for historical inquiry. Tavern stories, like the ones in Dolsen's account book and the Quakers' records, say nothing about alcohol's place in First Nations cultures. They do hint that Native tavern-goers oriented themselves within contemporary notions of acceptable drinking behaviour while in the public houses.[25]

Tavern sociability enabled moments of cross-cultural and interracial association. Traveller Patrick Campbell and Captain Thomas, a wealthy Native fur trader, passed an evening together at the Kingston Coffee House in 1791. Campbell wrote:

> I sent him my compliments, and if agreeable made offer to join him; his answer was that he would be happy at it. After I joined him he asked me very politely what I would choose to drink; I answered whatever was agreeable to him. He then called for a small bowl of punch, of which he took but

very little, excused himself by saying he had dined in a private family, and drank too freely after dinner. We slept in the same room. He was a tall handsome man, extremely well dressed in the English fashion, and had nothing particular about him but a string of small silver buckles hung down on his breast, fastened to his long lank black hair, from each side of his head. He spoke French fluently but not English enough to enable us to converse freely in that language; however he understood it better than he could speak, and enough to make me enjoy his company very much."[26]

Like the delegates who dined with the Quakers at Dolsen's – and an earlier seventeenth-century precursor, a "prosperous Connecticut Indian, known as King George, [who] lived 'after the English mode' and treated his guests 'with a glass of good wine,'" Captain Thomas used tavern-going rituals for cross-cultural communication. Campbell responded by accepting the cues offered by Captain Thomas' facility with languages, manners, clothing, and moderation, and he took pains to construct his companion as a gentleman before the reading public. The Quakers likewise translated, perhaps misrepresented, Native people's display into Anglo-American ideals of status. At Dolsen's the Quakers "were also visited by ... some Shawnee women, one a widow, who, because of her situation, had taken off her bobs, jewels and trinkets, with which the others shone with splendour ... I have no doubt to an amount that would have clothed them in silk and velvet." Such encounters between the privileged members of Native and non-Native societies continued to be a possibility in public houses at least until the 1830s. Mary Gapper O'Brien, an English gentlewoman who farmed near Thornhill, recorded the disappointment she had experienced in a York tavern when "the necessity of watching my baby also prevented my dining with [Joseph Thayendanegea] Brant, the Indian chief, who is staying at the inn where we stopped." The missed meeting suggests the tavern's value as a public site where race could be understood as culture, where an "Indian," in the eyes of Anglo-Americans, could have a number of alternative identities: political leader, successful trader, and gentleman (or lady). All were distant from the images of the noble savage, the doomed race, or the drunken Indian. By fashioning themselves in terms settler society could comprehend, these intercultural brokers managed to elude the racialized barriers that separated Native and non-Native societies. They demonstrated the possibilities of public space as sites where variety and difference met; as sites that accommodated intercultural communication.[27]

None of this suggests that race did not matter to Upper Canadians. Despite moments of heterogenous sociability, no one, Native or non-Native, set aside race as an important gauge of difference. Even in mixed sites where taverngoers knew each other well, complex identities could be distilled into a single racial element in the right circumstances. In Sarnia, Francis Levare, who was "part French" and "part Indian," patronized Campbell's tavern and James Taylor's tavern, which was across the road.[28] In 1852 he took a night's lodging at Taylor's and "came into the barroom" about midnight to join a sailor and his companion. According to the tavern-keeper, Levare, unprovoked, took a kitchen knife from the sailor, "and first thing I knew cut me in the shoulder." Taylor had known Levare for two years as a farmer who also "doctored" the locals on occasion, and he "had no reason to doubt his friendly disposition." Nor had Levare been drinking, as far as anyone knew. Taylor mentioned Levare's mixed blood, and acknowledged that he had integrated into settler society.[29] Yet it was Levare's Native side that took precedence when Taylor prosecuted him, almost hesitantly, for the assault. Given Levare's lengthy acquaintance with the tavern-keeper, his community involvement, and his bicultural identity, Taylor had to search for a reason to explain the stabbing and hovered around Levare's Indianness. Although Taylor initially identified Levare as "part French," he shifted his emphasis over the course of his story: Levare is "quiet – well behaved as any Indian – He does not go much with ye Indians. – Has a farm next to Wywanash [who] is chief." While this is hardly a clear-cut statement, it suggests that Taylor brooded aloud about Levare's (part-) Indian identity being a possible motivation for the attack. Perhaps Taylor thought about the connections between Aboriginal people and the "primitive," or "untameable," that pervaded nineteenth-century popular culture.[30] Regardless, he constructed a familiar acquaintance in racialized terms to explain a violent encounter.

Although the evidence is fragmentary, it is apparent that Native-white association was part of everyday life in Upper Canada, especially in public spaces like taverns. Native peoples used these sites for political negotiation, economic exchange, and mutual sociability with privileged whites and settlers. But the taverns belonged to the colonists; they welcomed only those Native patrons who accommodated themselves to the Anglo-American languages and rituals that governed interaction within them. Taverns were public in their openness to many comers, but they did not facilitate cultural exchange as a back-and-forth process between racialized groups. Rather, they reinforced the dominance of non-Native ways within informal public life.

This dominance extended over the other racialized "other" in Upper Canada, the colony's black population. Blacks constituted less than 2 percent of the total population. Of predominantly free origin, they settled in every county and city, but most lived in places that were over 97 percent white. In notable exceptions, like Chatham and Raleigh Township, blacks made up about a third of all residents.[31] Slavery, which persisted until 1834, affected fewer and fewer people.[32] Because the majority of the black population was free, everyday acts of racialized antagonism had a greater impact on the experience of blacks in Upper Canada than did slavery. Blacks in the colony realized only a very constrained freedom. Being black meant having unequal access to land and occupation. It meant segregated schools, churches, and voluntary associations. In York, authorities refused to sell prime real estate to a prominent black man, Robert Franklin. In the common schools of West Flamborough, "old Canadian families [were] unwilling to allow their children to sit promiscuously with Negroes and Mulattos." And when the regional government of the Western District stated in 1849 that "[n]o white man will ever act with them [blacks] in any public capacity" because "no sheriff in this province would dare to summon coloured men to do jury duty," it described the power of whites to define the racialized contours of the public sphere.[33] Much of the formal public literally remained off limits to blacks. But did these barriers apply to informal sites of public interaction such as taverns?

In the summer of 1836 the Sandwich *Canadian Emigrant* published a series of editorials about local blacks and their use of public space. One editorial related the following incident: "It seems that two Negroes entered a tavern and without permission began playing dominoes, their deportment it is said was exceedingly impudent and provoking. Mr. Maisonville [the tavern-keeper] ordered them instantly to leave the room which they did but at the same time threatening revenge. It seems they returned again and were playing in the parlour adjoining the bar-room abusing gentlemen who were its occupants. This annoyed Mr. M. and with a *strong horsewhip, he soon convinced them of their error and ejected them from the premises.*"[34] The event and its treatment in the press graphically illustrate how much racialized identity could matter in public houses. The editorial presumed that black men, unique among tavern-goers, needed permission to play dominoes, and it betrayed an expectation that blacks deport themselves deferentially toward (white) "gentlemen" within tavern space. It also revealed that blacks were vulnerable to violence.

The *Emigrant,* in fact, used this incident at the Canada Hotel to articulate a conception of the tavern as a space that was both masculine and white:

A couple of ruffianly Negroes rush into a parlour where gentlemen are conversing – they seize upon a table and commence their game – the gentlemen expostulate – the Negroes answer them with imprecations, and defy them to expel them. – This was after they had been once ejected from the premises ... There are few Britons who think that the colour of the skin is an index of the heart. But there never was one true Briton – one son of merry old England, taught to allow his rights to be trampled on by others – and trampled on too by such a degraded set of beings! As an Englishman ... there are no insults so long remembered, few that enter so deep in a man's soul as those directed at the undeniable rights which each Briton exercises over his home.[35]

Two processes are visible in the newspaper: the construction of whiteness in opposition to blackness and the recasting of a public house into a private place, rightly defended. In part, these developments stemmed from the Black men's preference for parlour rather than barroom sociability. The hotel parlour emerges as a site for civilized conversation among the civilized, a role that was understood as being part of the architectural design of Georgian taverns since the 1790s and consonant with actual patterns of use since at least Ely Playter's day. The gentlemanly conversation that was interrupted by the "ruffianly Negroes," readers are informed, concerned the fineness of the champagne and matters of politics and capital investments; it was, moreover, a debate that enabled "all man's best feelings to possess him." The editorial clearly drew on the ideal of the "public man" that was current from the 1830s in the colonial press and cast the men at the Canada Hotel as his prototype. Rather than presenting the men as making a narrow, racist, and ultimately self-interested claim to public space through their attack on the black men, the authors present the white men, and Maisonville with his whip, as public-spirited defenders of the British Constitution and the "undeniable rights" of Englishmen, as men who work for the good of all. Because this racially charged exchange took place in the parlour, the author associated it with "home." The tavern parlour was a space that was sometimes private and sometimes public; it welcomed women and mixed gender sociability among the relatively privileged, those who had an inclination toward the mannerly, moderate comportment that the finer material appointments of the rooms encouraged. Because the parlour supported group mutuality among the culturally and economically privileged, association in it was also about race. The "Negroes," who are described in the *Emigrant's* discursive representation with language that emphasizes violence, irrationality, and inhumanity, are the very antithesis of parlour culture. They become, ultimately, a "degraded set of beings," incapable of civilized association with truly public, albeit parlour bound, men.

Nevertheless, a measure of anxiety crept into the editor's defence of the two white men's behaviour. He backed away from his analogy to an Englishman's home, noting that, "as the riot happened in a tavern," "there is more allowance to be made" for the black men. His concession can be attributed to the context of the editorial itself. It was written in response to a stinging article in the *Upper Canada Albion* that was highly critical of the *Emigrant's* first report on the Canada Hotel incident because of its blindness to the role that racialized antagonism played in the events and its support of Maisonville. As the debate testifies, the racialized identity of public space was contested. A deeply rooted racialized antagonism, represented by the white men at the Canada Hotel and by the *Emigrant* as their public defender, confronted an equally deep-rooted belief in "the spirit of the British Constitution," which was invoked by the *Albion* in the phrase "by which every man who breathes British air is a free man."[36]

The incident at the Canada Hotel was not an isolated one.[37] Black activist Peter Gallego told a similar story in 1841. Lodging at the Mansion House in London, he took supper in the dining room with "my friend Mr. Luis, a coloured man," and received attentive service from the barkeep. But when tavern-keeper Joseph Hewitt arrived at breakfast, he called Gallego a "nigger" and threw him, with the assistance of other tavern-goers, "out into the street." Gallego literally flew headlong from comfortable circumstances into a dangerous, racially charged atmosphere. "[D]irty little acts of race" like these fundamentally compromised the exercise of black citizenship.[38]

But if race relations in taverns, and public space generally, were as clear-cut as Hewitt's attack and Maisonville's horsewhip implied, why did two black men take seats at the tavern? Why did they resist, "with imprecations," when whites objected? Why did Peter Gallego expect (wrongly as it turned out) "redress for this abusive treatment"?[39] In a sense, these men's actions foreshadowed the activism of US activist Rosa Parks. The men used individual acts of "black protest and resistance to racism" to challenge white dominance of public space.[40] Blacks worked to realize the promise of full social integration that was implicit in constitutional equality.[41] These tavern stories reveal blacks claiming an authentic space in the colony. They translated the ideals of abolitionists and anti-racism advocates into the real content and real struggles of everyday life.

Perhaps these particular men were surprised at the need for resistance to do so, because at times a mixed public was a reality in all kinds of Upper Canadian taverns. Many black tavern-goers enjoyed parallel experiences of tolerant accommodation. In the 1790s, for instance, Peter Long stopped in for rum at Abner Miles' substantial tavern in York. A man identified only as "Molat, Negro" also called there for pints. At Dolsen's, in 1798, "J. Jackman, Negro" bought rum by the quart and took a gill in the house. In both cases, the tavern-keepers reveal the importance that was attached to non-white racialized categories. Whereas these tavern-keepers put "mason," or "widow," beside the names of white patrons, they understood blacks in racialized terms when they sought entertainment among a white clientele.[42] And James Burtch kept a small public house in the Niagara District, where two black men, Jacobs and Burke, treated together with Charles Mahon in 1854.[43] In 1834, "a coloured man named Thompson ... stopped at Mr. Schaeffer's tavern" on Lake St. Clair and took breakfast "with another coloured man, his assistant." Schaeffer's was a comfortable country tavern, a customary point of call for travellers. In a Brantford tavern in 1843, Henry Van Patton, who was also black, drank with old, white Daniel Green. That same year, Abraham Rex and William Murdoch, both black, celebrated Emancipation Day in

Sandwich and spent the night at LeDuc's tavern, which was frequented by white soldiers from the garrison.

Though revealing of the complexities of colonial racialized relations, LeDuc's was a materially simple place. At his death, assessors valued Gregoire LeDuc's holdings at £35 16s. 3d., which placed him among the poorest tax-payers in the colony. The tavern had two storeys, three rooms and a passage, a working yard, and stables. The furnishings provided for the basics of so-ciability. There were chairs and benches enough for twenty people, at least three tables, and plenty of crockery; the parlour boasted a looking glass, white curtains, and a homemade carpet. The tavern's two box stoves and a cooking stove were in keeping with the reputation that French-Canadian taverns enjoyed for warmth in the winter. There were two or more bedrooms and four old feather beds upstairs.[44] After their celebration, during which the two men had "drunk a little," Abraham Rex shared one of LeDuc's beds with William Murdoch. Neither man woke up until after ten the next mor-ning. It is difficult to assign all the occupants of the house that night to the identified beds. Obviously Charlotte and Gregoire LeDuc shared one, and Rex and Murdoch accounted for another. Moses Mechie was there, as were unnumbered "people downstairs" and the LeDuc children.[45]

The LeDucs clearly ran a well-patronized establishment. They made their living from tavern keeping and had done so for many years because Gregoire was subject to "the lameness and infirmity which ha[d] rendered him unfit for hard labour." The LeDucs paid the highest annual licence fee for Western District tavern-keepers, £7 10s., a rate that was determined by their central location and a significant sum.[46] Their success shows that their tavern invited the patronage of an identifiable clientele, one that chose to spend its scarce resources within the tavern.

In January 1841, however, the magistrates refused to renew LeDuc's licence. In his written response, which was written by someone else, Gregoire LeDuc seemed unaware of the specific complaints against him but was sure that they were connected to the conduct of soldiers in his barroom:

> Nor does he know what he has been accused of ... unless it be as he is told that his proximity to the barracks has given cause of offense ... and he thinks it hard that he should be deprived of his living because the troops may by any chance though seldom and only in individual cases become irregular and sometimes not be controlled in a propensity for drink which your pe-titioner cannot prevent – when they may be inclined to indulge in that way which when that is the case will be done in one place as well as another.[47]

That the soldiers felt free to indulge themselves in LeDuc's barroom is evident in their irregular conduct. It was this same sense of assurance that Rex and Murdoch shared that morning, when Murdoch, coming down the stairs, casually invited Rex to resume drinking. Rex declined the invitation but there is every indication of ease in their comportment in a racially mixed public setting.

Perhaps it is not surprising that a place like LeDuc's raised concerns among those who defined themselves, and their own emerging middle class, as the community norm. To them, LeDuc's epitomized the "low tavern" of reformist discourse, and the problem, from this perspective, was that "low people" went there. Many blacks and whites agreed on this issue. Mary Ann Shadd Cary, the black editor of Chatham's *Provincial Freeman,* aligned her newspaper with Reform. In July 1856, responding to criticism about blacks being seen drunk around town, Shadd Cary advocated a law against intemperance for everyone: "Who patronize[s] the saloons, taverns &c in this place? Indians and coloured men only?" Her question attested to the racial mix of local tavern companies, and it revealed the distance between people like her who supported temperance within a range of reformist impulses and those like Murdoch and Rex who employed tavern sociability in ways that would have been familiar to inhabitants of early York (see Chapter 2).[48] The mixed company at LeDuc's shared the experience of being economically and socially marginalized. For them, it made more sense to treat in the tavern than to husband too-scarce resources. It is doubtful that their patronage was "either colour-blind or without internal frictions."[49] Nevertheless, the tavern emerges as a space that bridged racialized divides in this time and place and among a specific class of people.

More surprising than the denial of LeDuc's licence was the fact that he got it back. Although his petition seemed ill-designed to gain supporters or to prove he kept an orderly house, the licence inspector reported in April 1842 that "LeDuc has conducted the house for which he obtained license last year to the satisfaction" of existing standards.[50]

The shards of evidence that survive that depict blacks engaged in tavern sociability reveal the mixed messages that surrounded their participation in public life. It is clear, in the Canada Hotel incident, that racialized constructions of identity made violent opposition to black access a reality. At the same time, many taverns housed a racially mixed clientele. The problem was, there was no way of knowing if a liminal moment of interracial border crossing was in the offing or if barricades were about to be thrown up to vigorously defend the whiteness of public life. Without warning, race could, and did, become the crucial element that defined experience.

James Ferinson called at William Wright's St. Catharines tavern in 1841 "and wanted a quart of whiskey." He was a black man, a private in the 67th Regiment, and his history illustrates the dangerous ambiguity of public space for blacks. Wright "had not the whiskey, and pointed out Dolsen's house about half-way to Stinson's." While it is unclear if Ferinson ever got his whiskey, he certainly never drank it. Ferinson was later found dead. In the words of bystander Dugald James Murray: "Going towards Stinson's Inn, saw a black man followed by a parcel of boys hellewing after him." Nelson Sheppard "heard someone say in Stinson's that they had knocked one Darkey off his horse and wondered where the d–n Negro was." The company at Stinson's had gathered on Saturday night, "perhaps 10 o'c," to make a charivari of a "servant girl who was to marry the Black man."[51] Enraged by the rumour of interracial marriage, the company at Stinson's seized Ferinson as he made his way to the tavern. One of them told a neighbour concerned about the noise that "they had run down one damn nigger but he was not the right one."[52] Like Irish-American working-class "b'hoys" in nineteenth-century New York City, who used specific taverns to enforce the whiteness (and maleness) of public space, Stinson's brutal crowd built its collective identity around the violent exclusion of others.[53]

Such explosions of group violence were defining moments in the discordant history of identity politics in early Canada.[54] In colonial taverns, group violence targeted not only racialized difference, which was of primary concern to the Stinson's crowd, but also national and denominational differences. The line between each could be fuzzy because it was a time when being Irish or French (identities we would term as ethnic) was thought of as a racialized identity much the same as being black or Aboriginal. Group violence expressed simmering social tensions among, or between, groups, and perversely bolstered strong, mutual, intragroup identities.

In Upper Canada, "otherness" could mean many things. Indeed, it is not always easy to sort out how concerns about otherness marred tavern sociability. For example, it was perhaps nationalistic identity that was at the root of an affray at Fraser's tavern in the Midland District in 1830. "A party" of about twenty came from the canal and gathered at Fraser's. One man, Patrick Killete, decided to go over to McGuire's tavern, which was located on the opposite side of the street, and he made enough noise that McGuire had him thrown out. His companions witnessed the incident from Fraser's, and William O'Brien rallied them with the cry: "Let's go down and see fair play." The party burst into McGuire's, assaulted the tavern-keeper and the company, and trashed the place. When the case came to court, one witness identified O'Brien as the man who had been "swearing in Irish." Another had "heard ye Irish round at McGuire's place."[55] Even in the context of historical analyses that have firmly linked Irish canallers and violence, the significance of this information is unclear.[56] Whether this group's collective sense of identity was based on Irishness, as observers implied, or on the excitement of the moment, it was affirmed through tavern violence committed in the name of one of their number.

It was certainly tensions between Catholics and Protestants that fuelled two other tavern disturbances. In 1841, the Coleraine tavern in Toronto (as we know from the discussion in Chapter 3) was at the centre of an election

riot, where Tory Orangemen inside the tavern clashed with Reform supporters outside. Armed men stood at the windows; while some fired guns, others
threw rocks at the Reform crowd below.[57] The Coleraine incident was a
caricature of the group violence that was linked to specific taverns and rooted
in political and/or denominational conflicts. Yet a similar incident happened
in 1845 in Stratford, where there had also been an election. Daly, who was
described by participants as "the Catholic candidate," was defeated. "Some
of the Protestants" went to Jackson's Hotel to drink. "While there several of
the Catholics came into the room and endeavoured to commence a fight.
... They were very outrageous in the barroom and ... struck some of their
own party for endeavouring to keep them quiet."[58] A full-scale fight on the
street followed.

English and Scotch settlers and Canadian and Americans likewise confronted each other and came to blows. Daniel Springer kept tavern in Lobo
in 1821. He was also a magistrate and had raised local feeling to a fever pitch
by unjustly linking the Scots to a recent hog theft. The violent clash at
Springer's "was near ending in a general fight ... [which] left much angry
feeling."[59] A major fracas also erupted at Dyer's tavern in St. Catharines on
4 July 1833. Luther Dyer was an American, and when a "few youngsters"
shot off a fowling gun near his hotel, local magistrates accused them of
celebrating American Independence Day and confiscated their guns. In response, several American mechanics who had witnessed the incident spent
the day "discharging firearms somewhat frequently," while the magistrates
officiously tried to stop them. Tensions built throughout the day and came
to a head at nightfall, when "a little difficulty occurred in the bar-room between two individuals, aggravated by both parties." When two fireballs
(candlewicks that were rolled into a ball, moistened with turpentine, and
ignited) were "thrown from the rear of a house adjoining Mr Dyer's," "a
shout echoed through the mob, as if from a leader, and like well trained
blood hounds, all were on the hunt." A pro-British group vandalized Dyer's
while magistrates and constables watched from the opposite side of the
street. Dyer's American background is the only apparent explanation for the
actions of the mob that attacked his hotel, supported by the "nods and
winks" of local authority.[60]

The Coleraine tavern riot, the street brawl that began in the barroom of
Jackson's tavern, events at Springer's, and the attack on Dyer's each resulted
as much from steadily escalating tensions in the community as they did from
the involvement of the taverns. It is notable that the taverns figured differently in each incident, suggesting that tavern violence could play a uniquely
supportive but varied role as groups used violence in the construction and
contestation of identity. For instance, Coleraine's was a "notorious house,"
a Tory stronghold, entirely complicit in the violence that erupted. It stood
as an exception to the rule that taverns encouraged free public expression.

In comparison, Jackson's tavern in Stratford appears to have been a site where both Catholics and Protestants expected to go to drink: "Some of their own," after all, worked hard to keep order in the barroom. It is important, too, to distinguish group violence from the individual scuffles and disputes that broke out in barrooms (see Chapter 4). Rioting, by definition, broke through all social controls, placing it beyond the power of the self-regulation characteristic of tavern companies.

Without denying the power of places such as Coleraine's, it is important to point out that the taverns more commonly supported amicable relations between Catholic and Protestant, Green and Orange. A compelling example is Thomas Robinson's tavern in Prescott. Because Robinson kept a good set of books and a census survives for the town, the nationality and religion of his regular patrons are known. A picture of routinely mixed and peaceful interaction emerges. His regulars were predominantly Protestant (mostly Anglican, but also Presbyterian and Methodist). But a significant minority, well over a third, were Catholic. Almost half Robinson's patrons were Irish, about a fifth each were English and Canadian, and there were a few Scots and Americans.[61] Catholic and Protestant, Green and Orange, must have expected to meet each other at Robinson's. Yet, despite the fact that the region itself divided infamously between Orange and Green, there is no hint in court documents or newspapers that factiousness disrupted sociability at Robinson's. So, while incidences of gross violence in the name of group identity are compelling and reveal wide divisions in society, they need to be weighed carefully against the quieter, less accessible evidence of routine and amicable patronage in shared public spaces such as taverns.

The taverns are part of the history of violently conducted colonial identity politics, and a tavern's occasional openness to violently confrontational groups as they drank and girded themselves for battle is an important aspect of its history. Taverns, like streets, were public spaces where deep cultural and long-standing community tensions, fed by the events of the day, could explode. Taverns sustained, supported, and affirmed group identities by offering space and the public sociability that encouraged a sense of belonging. That this sense of belonging was sometimes violently defended and asserted against others testifies to the tensions endemic in early mixed colonial society.

In the context of nineteenth-century North America, blacks, like First Nations, were particularly "other." For them, encounters in public contained contrary possibilities. There was always a simmering potential for racialized violence, which differentiated black experience from white. There was also opportunity for the mixed sociability glimpsed in several taverns. Ambiguity, flux, and even an uncertain openness to blacks in public space characterized racialized relations in the colony, as elsewhere. When "those at the bottom of society" joined together in nineteenth-century American cities to create "color bars," they did so by attacking "public places known for mixing of the races," including a Philadelphia tavern with an interracial clientele. When some whites worshiped in black-led and black-centred congregations in late eighteenth-century Nova Scotia, the mixed crowds incurred assaults. Clearly, while some whites associated without racialized barriers, many others helped to erect them. Robin Winks' evaluation of this phenomenon in his pioneering study *Blacks in Canada* seems right: "[R]acial barriers shifted, gave way, and stood firm without consistency, predictability, or even credibility." But what did it all mean – this inconsistency and flux – for black public space? Michael Wayne has asked whether "race mattered more than class, gender, religious affiliation or nationality" to nineteenth-century blacks "in defining who they were or in determining their place in Canadian society." If we understand place literally, as the act of finding room in public spaces like taverns, it seems certain that race mattered more than anything else in its *potential* for defining the terms of access and inclusion. From the perspective of blacks in Upper Canada, public space was fickle and polymorphic. Easy accommodation within a mixed crowd, or the casual expectation of it based on experience, could be hideously transformed by the arrival, or arousal, of those who consciously defined themselves as white.[62]

In response, some blacks created separate places for sociability. Nero Lyons of Amherstburg petitioned for the reinstatement of his tavern licence in 1840. "With regard to there being one tavern already kept by a coloured man in the place, yr. humble petitioner wishes their forbearance to state that it is attended principally by Europeans so that the Coloured population of this town and vicinity have not a publick house that they can resort to." The desire for separate spaces for blacks probably testifies to their desire to express black cultural identity. Those seeking black-centred sociability participated in "a positive sense of group difference" that embraced the specificity of their lives and, perhaps, implied resistance to white people's dominance of public space. (As we will see, Victorian ladies adopted similar patterns of self-assertion in tavern space at mid-century.) It is also likely that Lyons wanted a safe space, set apart from threats of expulsion, harassment, and violence by white tavern companions and tavern-keepers. Unfortunately, we know almost nothing about black tavern-keepers or the companies in their houses. In the Buxton settlement in 1852 a (black) traveller described West's as "[t]he best country tavern in Kent." Given the location, its keeper was probably black. Brown's 1846-47 *Toronto City and Home District Directory* identified three black tavern-keepers by putting the word *coloured* after their names. Among them was James Mink, proprietor of the Mansion House Hotel. He is something of a folk figure in popular histories of Toronto and Kingston and the subject of a 1996 CBS Sunday Night Movie "The Captive Heart: The James Mink Story." Mink's was not the black-centred tavern that

Nero Lyons sought in his petition; it was a principal establishment that catered primarily to travellers. No evidence has been found to support a discussion of the tavern's role in the formation of black communities. It makes sense to think that, along with churches, schools, and voluntary associations, black-centred taverns also sustained local networks of sociability and support.[63]

Blacks also worked in taverns as entertainers and service staff. We have seen that at least one tavern-keeper, James Donaldson, held slaves. Clara and Pompey laboured in his Amherstburg public house in the 1790s. We know too that at Playter's, Elizabeth "Betty" Johnson, "the Black woman," worked as a servant or was enslaved. Traveller William Pope danced at a tavern to the fiddle of a black musician "who scraped away in good style" and complained about "the smallness of his pay which amounted to one dollar, a sum by no means adequate to his hard work." At Wheeler's tavern on the Talbot Road near Ingersoll, "a black man came forward and danced and offered for a few pence, to run at a door and butt it with his bare head like a ram." A steadier income came with jobs on the wait staff at large hotels. Traveller James Alexander commented on the "good attendance of coloured waiters" in a St. Catharines hotel, and A.W.H. Rose noted at the Clifton in Niagara Falls that "the waiters at this hotel are chiefly men of colour, very civil well-conducted persons." Also at Niagara, the celebrated Pavilion House provided porters: "two men of colour were met carrying trunks to the ferry, who brought ours on their return." In 1856 the dining-room waiters at Sword's first-class hotel in Toronto were "all negroes." The better houses reinforced the preferred racial hierarchy in public space. When they were confined to service roles and embedded in master-servant relationships, blacks in taverns raised no concerns. However, when blacks asserted their right to access the public rooms and public sociability, they brought forth articulations of white precedence.[64]

Tavern stories, like the one about the Indians, as well as the blacks and whites, who all drank quite freely in a Brantford barroom in 1832, are narratives about the complicated and inconsistent ways that racialized identities mattered in public space. Despite white Upper Canadians' attempt to marginalize First Nations and blacks, tavern sociability at times welcomed racialized others. For Native peoples, the taverns sustained a variety of exchanges that included political negotiations, economic relationships, and instances of mutual sociability, especially between late eighteenth-century Native and non-Native elites and, later, between bicultural reserve Natives and their settler neighbours. The taverns also stood as one more site of intercultural contact in which Anglo-American custom and culture was privileged. For blacks, instances of racially motivated violence in taverns and the denial of access to some taverns rebutted the simultaneous experience of mixed sociability that they experienced in others. The unpredictability of these spaces for blacks reflected the volatile issues surrounding their place in colonial society. It is true that the taverns' "ties of good fellowship" sometimes encompassed a racially inclusive idea. But in the end, race affected public life in ways that worked against the heterogeneity glimpsed in the tavern story about a Brantford Saturday night. Class too could work in opposition to inclusive publicity, particularly when the economically privileged claimed tavern space to express culturally exclusive public identities.

6
Harry Jones, his Cronies, and the Haunts of Respectable Men

Went to the billiard [room] but finding it full of sundry disreputable looking persons didn't play.

– Harry Jones, 5 February 1842

Harry Jones was never much of a drinking man, but he spent a lot of his privileged life inside the colony's principal taverns and hotels. In them, he and his cronies fashioned a warm male world of sociability. They used the public houses in exclusive ways, as supports for the cultural expression and mutual enactment of a gentlemanly social identity. Until recently, when historians sorted out the sites of nineteenth-century public sociability, they lodged respectable culture in the churches and the voluntary associations and rough culture in the taverns.[1] The journal that Jones kept for half a century (from 1831 to 1883) complicates this tidy division of public space and culture, for it presents a version of tavern history that lacks labouring people, violence, or even drunks, and it presents a version of "white, male, and middle-class" history that includes taverns as integral parts of everyday life.

There is a painting by Harriet Clench hanging in the Art Gallery of Ontario that could almost be of Jones and his cronies. Entitled *A Country Tavern Near Cobourg* (1849) it depicts a civilized scene (see Figure 10). The settled town is across the bay. Steamers are busy in the port, and church steeples puncture the sky. Well-crafted Windsor chairs, tasselled window curtains, a birdcage, and cultivated plants signal the comfort of the house. The woman at work, carrying a tray of drink to patrons, is respectably dressed and fashionably coiffed. Even though the focus in this chapter is masculine sociability, she stands as a visible reminder that taverns were never wholly male spaces. The three tavern-goers are gentlemen, gathered about the table in their well-cut coats and summer trousers, coloured waistcoats, and starched collars and neckties. Bottles and half-full glasses, one raised as if to toast, show the place of drink in the men's call. Clench's canvas depicts the tavern in harmony

Figure 10 Clench, Harriet (Canadian, ?-1892) *A Country Tavern near Cobourg,*
Canada West 1849, oil on canvas, 29.5 x 37.2 cm | © Art Gallery of Ontario,
purchased with assistance from Wintario, 1980

with colonial society. Tavern going coexists with the economic progress
symbolized by the vessels in the port, with a profusion of spires, and with
respectable men and women. Her image dovetails perfectly with Harry Jones'
journal.[2]

Some entries from Jones' journal deserve to be quoted in full. And though
he has often been cited in the preceding pages, here Jones' entries give a
sense of the document itself. They permit Jones to introduce his friends and
his taverns in his own words. And they depict the rhythms of tavern sociability within lives dominated by the demands of the office, the professions,
and political ambitions. The first entry was made in Toronto (then the capital), where Jones worked as a clerk in the Office of the Surveyor General.
The others are from Kingston, the new capital as of July 1841 and the location of the public offices.

March 1840, 1st, Sunday: Aft. walked up to the Blue bell [tavern] ... met Thornhill and Galt, the latter a little "corned" and very violent against Robert Baldwin who Thornhill thinks it most prudent, I imagine, to support at the next election.

July 1841, 20th, Tuesday: ... Evening walked out with Galt & Spragge who had called – drank sherry cobblers at Belanger's [Victoria Saloon] – met Sullivan there & had a confab with him.

November 1842, 11th, Friday: Newsroom. Halifax mail arrived but the news contained in the papers [it] brought was known before its arrival. – Office – ... Making out and copying descriptions ... Took a walk with Hector after office hours – After dinner walked into town – met Kelly at Belanger's and half promised to accompany him to the Theatre ... – Went to Stewart's [tavern] instead, played a couple of games of billiards, drank a glass of grog with Dr. Stewart and returned home by 11.[3]

As they made their way along the streets of colonial towns, from the office to the newsroom to the tavern, in their frock coats and top hats, Jones and his companions would not have been confused with the "rough" of early Canada. Most made their livings within the government offices and land offices. William Spragge was the chief clerk in Jones' office; Thomas Hector ranked second behind him.[4] Bob Kelly was a clerk at the Board of Works.[5] Some had active political lives. Richard Hull Thornhill was a Tory alderman in Toronto in the 1830s.[6] Robert Baldwin Sullivan had been mayor there, and as both the commissioner of Crown lands and the surveyor general he was Jones' boss until June 1841. Sullivan was also a member of the Legislative Council and president of the Executive Council in 1841-42.[7] Dr. Stewart was a practising physician, whose medical advice Jones sought on occasion. He was probably Dr. John Stewart, the man who founded and edited the *Argus* newspaper in 1846 and obtained a chair of medicine at Queen's University in Kingston.[8] Thomas Galt was Jones' closest companion. The second son of John Galt, Scottish novelist and Canada Company colonizer, Thomas had recently left his position as a clerk in the Office of the Attorney General and "joined [William] Draper as a student at law." Called to the Bar in 1845, he entered private practice in Toronto, was named Queen's Counsel in 1858, and in 1869 won an appointment to the bench in the Court of Common Pleas, where he became chief justice in 1887. He was made Knight Bachelor in 1888.[9] Jones and his cronies were clearly gentlemen. They belonged within a broad group variously called the "colonial élite," the "emerging bourgeoisie," "Victorian Ontario's urban middle class," and the "pre-industrial middle class." It was a group known, at the time and since, as "the respectability."[10]

Not that Jones ever thought of himself as middle-class. His language blended eighteenth-century concepts of rank with a nineteenth-century awareness of occupation. He referred to "circumstances or rank," to "the class of equal rank in England," and to "almost everyone of respectability." He introduced men to his journal with reference to their work: a "young lawyer," an "MPP," an "officer of the 32nd," or "Mr. Killalee, a civil engineer and very quiet gentlemanlike man." Women were "ladylike" and "respectable." He described a busy day on the streets of Kingston by its social contrasts: "Soldiers, gentlemen & would be gentlemen, sailors & loafers, ladies & whores, quiet farmers & their wives." None of these words related to class but rather to cultural and occupational identities. Yet it makes analytic sense to call Jones middle-class, in part because it locates him in his society by using a readily understood phrase, and in part because middle-class is what he became over the course of a working life that extended into the industrial era. Moreover, Jones recognized his social distance from the bottom (from the "lower ranks," "disreputable persons," "blackguards," and "loafers") and from the top (from the "big bugs" and the "nobocracy"). He sneered at farmers and freeholders, the "free and independent electors" who made Cartier's, a country tavern, "a perfect hell in the evening." These were not sophisticated terms, and they remained entangled with the languages of gentility and morality, but in using them Jones revealed his awareness of his location as a gentleman within the broad, pre-industrial middle – within "the respectability," to use his phrase.[11]

The word *respectability* carried a double meaning. It referred, with some vagueness, to a socio-economic status based on household independence and at least modest prosperity. It also referred to the moral qualities associated with that status, especially seriousness of purpose, self-restraint, and a sense of responsibility to family and society. To the limited extent that taverns and the respectability have crossed paths in Canadian history, each has emerged as the antithesis of the other, with the taverns representing all that was dangerous to the work ethic and financial prudence, to sobriety and orderliness, and to the family itself. This interpretation of the taverns prevailed in the colony's temperance movement and in, for example, regulations that prohibited apprentices and student teachers from haunting taverns.[12] Of course, many respectable people went to taverns; they had to in order to access the range of public services described in Chapter 3. Marcus Child, who was a teetotaller, merchant, and politician, for example, lived at Kingston's Royal Pavilion while he attended sessions of the House of Assembly in 1843. Walter and Frank Shanley, professional civil engineers (but not teetotallers), frequented the Ten tavern in Port Robinson and Ellah's Hotel in Toronto.[13] Like Clench's painting, these glimpses of gentlemanly patronage suggest that Jones' and his cronies' lives and behaviours are illustrative of wider socio-cultural trends and patterns.

Born in England in 1809, Jones grew up in a country house in Devonshire as the eldest child of a gentry family.[14] The extent of his education is unknown, but chance meetings with former fellows from Shaw's School in Hamilton indicate he received some formal schooling. Each day, he read avidly and critically, with wide-ranging tastes for biographies, histories, novels, and literary journals, as well as the British, American, and local newspapers. Jones subscribed to the newsroom wherever he lived but otherwise was not much of a joiner. He did enter the Orange Order in Toronto at the behest of a friend, but he attended only a couple of meetings. He also seems to have belonged to the (anti-Reform) British Constitutional Society, but he made no sustained commitment. Politically and socially, Jones was a conservative; he feared the potential for anarchy in 1830s republicanism, but within the local political scene, he was as critical of Tories as he was of Reformers. From 1835 he was a Justice of the Peace in the Western District, where he owned land and a small house. He had an eye for a "splendid room" and well-proportioned architecture. He belonged to the Church of England and attended service regularly, but he also attended Catholic Mass if asked. He drank tea and sang in the family parlours of married friends. He collected prints. He owned a thermometer and recorded daily temperatures. He fished, hunted game birds, and dabbled in amateur ornithology and taxidermy. These characteristics were hallmarks of a privileged, gentlemanly life.[15]

Jones was also a gentleman of reduced circumstances. Like countless other gentry immigrants – such as Susanna Moodie, Catharine Parr Traill, and the Shanley brothers – Jones lacked money. Unlike them, his family had come to Upper Canada not to better themselves but, rather bizarrely, to better others through socialism. Jones became haplessly caught up in the process. During the 1820s Henry Jones Sr., Jones' father, committed himself and extensive capital to realizing the utopian socialist ideals of Robert Owen. In 1829 the Jones family and a group of about fifty people, mostly Scottish artisanal families, founded a communal settlement named Maxwell on the shores of Lake Huron, near Port Sarnia. It failed within five years, but the Jones family remained, in genteel poverty, in the colony. Jones quickly found it necessary to earn a living. Being related by marriage to Lieutenant-Governor John Colborne helped; Jones received an appointment as Crown lands agent for the Western District in 1833.[16] Based in Chatham, with quarters in Freeman's tavern, the travel required by the job brought Jones into frequent contact with the minor country taverns of the district. There are abundant journal entries about "chattering with sweet Miss Mary," the tavern-keeper's daughter at Lawson's Tavern, "breakfasting at Gardiner's and dining at Nichol's," or getting "a little screwy as Kyffin calls it on brandy" at Brown's Inn.[17] The journal chronicles his social interactions with the rest of the lakeshore gentry in homes and taverns alike. However, Jones lost his job in the summer of 1838, when, in his father's words, "[a]fter having rendered some acknowledged good service ... he had, on the abolition of the Crown Lands Office, to come in at the fag end of the clerks in the Surveyor General's Establishment."[18] He remained there until retirement, advancing through the ranks to senior patent clerk by 1861.[19]

The clerkship paid £170 annually, which was substantial if compared to the wages of even highly skilled artisans but paltry when compared to the salaries of the head clerk in Jones' office (who made £300 per annum) or the professional incomes of many of his friends.[20] Jones' salary was "one of those nice little bachelor incomes which allow a man to get his three square meals a day and do a certain amount of huntin', shootin', and fishin', but ... he [was] in no sense a matrimonial prize."[21] Indeed, Jones' income barred marriage: "dreadfully in love with Mrs. Primrose's daughter Miss Black, not rich enough to make a decided fool of myself – Alfred Stow of Toronto on the same tack; he being fairly enough off will get the lady."[22] But Jones did have enough money to spend on the necessities of life: his tailor; books, journals, and newsroom subscriptions; good wine, good dinners, and cigars and billiards. And through his tavern going with like-minded cronies, Jones used the public houses to support his gentlemanly habits.

Jones preferred the principal taverns, those material settings of public life defined by their aspirations to fashionability. Of the ninety-eight taverns that operated in Kingston in 1841, eight should likely be counted as principal houses.[23] Foremost among them was Joseph Daley's British American Hotel, which was "situated in the most central part of the town, immediately in front of the court house." It had facilities that could accommodate the balls given by the officers of the garrison and the farewell fête for two hundred that was hosted in the breakfast room by Governor General Charles Metcalfe. Lord Durham stayed at the British American; so too did Charles Dickens and his wife. Francis Hincks, the inspector general, lived there with his family.[24] David Botsford's Sydenham Hotel, Alex Smith's Royal Pavilion, John Belanger's Victoria Saloon, Barton Philips' National, Thomas Bamford's City Hotel, the Lambton House, and Mr. William Parker's New Hotel and Spa at the Caledonia Springs all offered, or promised, the superior creature comforts that made them principal houses.[25] Yet there is difficulty and little purpose in drawing hard and fast lines between these eight public houses and substantial taverns such as William Goodwin's or W.L. Stewart's, which were known as comfortable, well-known points of call. While Jones and his cronies relished the fashionable material settings available in the principal houses, they patronized the substantial minor houses regularly. Both spaces allowed them to stage their social rituals of dining, drinking, and billiard playing among a restricted circle.

When Jones arrived in Kingston in 1841, he coveted the style of life promised by the aesthetics of the Sydenham Hotel. He wrote appreciatively of its
size, its beautiful stonework, and its orientation to the landscape. "[V]ery
desirous to get quarters there,"[26] Jones could picture himself ascending the
three flights of stairs to the entrance, which had colonnaded wings on both
sides, and entering a resplendent setting that put symbolic, as well as actual,
distance between its inmates and the rest of the town.[27] "[B]ut, at $9 a week"
it "was out of sight." He settled for Philips' National as a more affordable
($6 weekly) and still acceptable second best. Jones' fellow boarders were
"Galt, who has already been a year with me at Toronto, Brough a partner of
the Attorney-General, here as counsel in the contested election ... and Roblin,
the M.P.P. for Prince Edward."[28]

One would not know from the way Jones writes that the National was a
public house. It emerges as almost private, as a closed world that was restricted
to those men who filled professional offices, sat as members of the Legislative Assembly, or, like Jones, held positions as "servants of the House."[29]
Marcus Child similarly described his sojourn at the Pavilion in letters home,
emphasizing the "select" company at the public table, its "pollished" deportment, and its composition: "merchants, bankers, lawyers and gentlemen
farmers."[30] The principal houses insulated their patrons from the social mix
characteristic of urban centres.

Although Kingston thrived on its combined status as capital, citadel, and
commercial entrepôt and its boosters imagined it pulsing to a rhythm set
by swelling wealth, upper-class British officers, high politics, and the vice-
regal pomp that accompanied the resident governors general, the city had
other sides and facets. There was the "respectable" Kingston of established
freeholders, artisans, small merchants, and their families. They read the
newspapers, went to church, educated their children, and came together in
voluntary associations. Some among them accused the garrison's regular
soldiers of defiling the streets and commons, trailing violence and prostitution in their wake. They thought there were too many taverns and too much
drink. They fretted about the "pauperism" and "vice" of the surrounding
suburbs of Barriefield, the French Village, and Lot 24 (Stuartsville) and
understood these areas as "chiefly inhabited by working-classes." Many
townspeople began to regard the institutions for coping with poverty, crime,
and morality as insufficient. Swirling all about them was "migrant" Kingston.
In 1840 alone twelve thousand immigrants passed through town. They
added to a population already mixed by nationality (Irish, English, Scot, and
American), religion, race (Kingston had a few Black residents, two tavern-
keepers being among them), and class.[31]

When Jones emphasized the gentlemanly identities of his tavern cronies,
he emphasized the absence of this mixed public. By constructing public
houses as "un-public" places, he acknowledged that the respectability's need

for social separation impelled tavern-keepers to carefully balance rooms that offered public engagement with those that offered relative seclusion. Tavern-keepers supplied the material wants of the denizens of parlour culture. They attended to the myriad ways that the polite, or the privileged, or, more troublingly, the self-consciously white (or Scottish, or Roman Catholic, for instance) sought to define themselves from others. It was for people such as Jones and his cronies that principal taverns had parlours, finer, costlier liquor stocks and wine, and tables d'hôte with the best ingredients the colonial market could provide. It was for them that principal taverns had long addressed themselves to the material and cultural needs of gentlemen, and, as the next chapter takes up, ladies too.

In Jones' journal the National Hotel emerges as a world of intense social contact among gentlemen. Although women and labouring "others" were present, the hotel is depicted as a bourgeois version of the masculine homosocial culture that historian Adele Perry has identified, in part, in the wayside taverns of colonial British Columbia. The centrality of strong male ties is the same, as is the immersion in male connectedness, but there are no depictions of or allusions to same-sex sexual relationships.[32] For example, Jones, along with Thomas Galt, received almost daily social calls from twenty-six different men throughout July. He had a "long discussion [about election laws] with James Small who had called," "[p]layed whist in the evening with Hitchings, Galt and James Small," and joined "Grant Powell at tea." Small was a lawyer, the member for the third riding of York, who became solicitor general for Canada West in 1842.[33] Powell worked in the civil secretary's office; his grandfather had been a chief justice in the colony.[34] Edward Hitchings was a "young Chancery lawyer."[35] Other callers included "Stuart, a nephew of Sir James, and Dobbs, a young lawyer, [who] dined with us." "Herrick arrived from Toronto and dined with us." "Aylwin, Dunlop, Small and Hincks came in the evening. – Played whist." In addition to the professionals specified, Herrick was a physician with whom Jones had consulted and socialized in Toronto.[36] Thomas Cushing Aylwin was a lawyer, the member of provincial Parliament for Portneuf, and solicitor general for Canada East. Identifying him as "the notorious M.P.P. from Quebec," Jones remarked on his eloquence and cleverness.[37] William "Tiger" Dunlop was a physician and prolific author; he had been associated with Galt's father in the early days of the Canada Company. Jones knew him as an old Western District tavern acquaintance. Dunlop was in Kingston as the member for Huron County.[38] Initially introduced to the journal as "the editor of the *Examiner* – a regular radical party," Francis Hincks was the member for Oxford and an executive councillor; in 1851 he became co-premier of the United Canadas.[39] Jones' company can be fleshed out with one more entry from his journal: "Returned to dinner, Joe Woods and Yule, a Lower Canada M.P.P. called in the afternoon and Woods and Dr. Stewart in the evening – with the former we had a long confab all about his election, his dismissal from the magistracy, Western District politics and Western district gossip until very late." Joe Woods too was an old tavern companion and a fellow Justice of the Peace from Jones' early days in the colony; he had recently been elected as the independent member for Kent County.[40] Through its focus on whist parties, dinners, teas, and political conversation among men, some of whom were well on their way to "becoming prominent,"[41] the journal recreates the aura of exclusivity that surrounded life at Philips' National Hotel.

Daily rituals of sociability affirmed the affinities among these men. Jones' journal is full of the companionability of mealtime: "[Went to] the Sydenham Hotel where I had promised to dine with Hyndman and Dr. Dunlop," "went to Church – returned [to Philips'] with James Henderson to tea," "met Woods and his brother Robert ... [went] to Belanger's to eat," "took a whim into my noodle and dined at Stewart's [tavern] ... Had a long confab with Dr. Stewart on mesmerism during my dinner."[42] Mealtime sociability included organized events: "The game supper for which I was to stand treat had been ordered to be ready at the billiard rooms at 10o'clk ... Our party at the saloon consisted of Dr. Stewart, Hitchings, Brough, McKenzie, Galt and myself – the snipe were good and the wine not bad ... not until past 3 did I get off – very much out of sorts ... partly because the affair cost me $8 which I could ill afford."[43] There is little, in Jones' churlishness, of the open-handed generosity and easy hospitality that ideal hosts projected, and perhaps the Kingston cronies staged such assaults on each other's pocketbooks as a kind of practical joke among the relatively well off.

Still, "much depended on dinner." Gatherings to share food and drink had a serious social purpose. They invoked ancient connotations of mutuality inherent in breaking bread together. More immediately, they echoed the supper parties staged by contemporary English and American elites and the busy dinner party circuit of Kingston's private homes, in which Jones, his companions, and their wives and families all participated.[44] In a public-house setting, the meaning of dining changed to the extent that the message of mutuality was heavily gendered as male, but it remained firmly within pre-industrial class boundaries. Onlookers recognized Jones' clique in the taverns as "a class of colonists chiefly from among the middle classes of home society, who ... too frequently and readily seek, among a restricted circle, the gratification of the over-social board." Though it is disparaging, this passage captures the same quality of exclusivity that is prevalent in Jones' journal.[45]

The material culture of the public houses enabled gentlemanly wining and dining. The best description of a dining room in this period is of the one in John and Harriet Linfoot's tavern on Yonge Street, four miles north of Toronto. It was a large and prosperous house that, coincidentally, was known to Jones from his Toronto sojourn.[46] Linfoot took over the tavern from John Montgomery just days before William Lyon Mackenzie's rebels occupied it as headquarters for the Upper Canadian Rebellion. Because Lieutenant-Governor Francis Bond Head ordered it burned to the ground, an inventory of the tavern's appointments survives in the claim for losses that Linfoot submitted.[47]

The furnishings, crockery, and provisions suggest that tavern-keepers in more modest establishments than the Sydenham or the National likewise found it important to craft welcoming dining areas, the material settings in which Jones and his cronies conducted their rituals of (masculine) middle-class wining and dining. At Linfoot's, tavern-goers sat at a walnut table on twelve matching hair-bottom chairs in a room that likely had ten walnut-framed pictures. They dined by the light of five pairs of brass candlesticks on inexpensive plates and with an array of tureens, pitchers, and serving dishes all matched in blue. The larder contained fresh fowl, dried meat, fish, fruit, preserves, butter, lard, cheese, apples, potatoes, barley, tea, and coffee. There were various wines, brandies, and beers, ten gallons of "best" rum and gin, and the sugar and spices needed for punch, toddies, shrub, or sangaree. The presence of table cloths, castor sets (for seasonings, sugar, vinegar, and oil), knives and forks, teacups with saucers, and teapots and coffeepots, as well as expensive glass plates, wineglasses, and "cut" glass tumblers and decanters underlines the attention that the tavern-keepers gave to the presentation of meals. As does the cost of the appointments: their value indicates that they were, or were on par with, domestically produced goods that were "handsomely and substantially" finished.[48]

The items in the inventory were not expendable furnishings designed for a rough tavern crowd. Nor do they imply that Linfoot refused rougher patrons (recall that James Donaldson, in Chapter 1, put his expensive clock in his soldier-patronized barroom). While John and Harriet provided a setting conducive to polite dining, they needed the patronage of all comers to make a profit.[49] Less consciously respectable or less consciously polite sorts took their ease in the barroom, and when they dined, they imparted their own tone to meals at the public table. Without the hospitality and atmosphere of material solidity projected by dining rooms such as Linfoot's, or the gloss of fashionability added in the principal houses, much of the value of dinner would have simply been lost to Jones and his cronies: "Walked to Kingston Mills with Herrick, Thornhill, Steers, Hitchings, Galt & Kelly, rambled about – tried to fish – dined in a miserable attempt at dinner in a dirty tavern."[50] The cultural messages conveyed in tavern dining rooms by tablecloths, cut glass, and the like were important. They spoke to an expectation of mannerly deportment and an assumption that the meal would satisfy more human needs than mere hunger.

Manners mattered to Jones' idea of sociability. To him, "Americans" who bolted their meals, "ignorance displayed ... in the way of ... serving dinner," or a "vulgar set" of table companions diminished the dining experience.[51]

Even though much of what Jones and his companions were doing was not very different from what the farmers and artisans who made up the majority of tavern patrons were doing – they all ate, drank, and made conversation – it is apparent from Jones' journal that he and his companions nevertheless interpreted their tavern going as an exclusive activity, even once basic requirements like nice furniture and dishes, good food and liquor, and an absence of vulgarity were met. Dining affirmed their friendship and their social distance from those who had no idea about the proper pace, presentation, or conduct of a meal. There is no evidence that the gentlemen who gathered together in colonial taverns to dine were engaged in a pre-industrial version of "slumming."

Money obviously played a role in these men's self-construction. The snipe dinner for six was an unusually expensive event. But even everyday dinners with each man paying for his own meal carried a cost, especially when a good dinner demanded good wine. All tavern-keepers charged food and liquor separately. Dinner typically cost 1s. 6d. and a glass of "not bad" wine ran to 5d. Buying by the bottle, unlike ordering distilled liquor by larger measure in a tavern, was not much cheaper. If Jones regularly had two glasses with his meal, an amount he often noted, then he spent £1 6s. a month, which was almost 10 percent of his income, on wine alone. Add to this his calls at Belanger's for a gin and water, a glass of grog at Stewart's, or a coffee "at Julien's (a new coffee house man)" and the price of tavern drink climbs higher.[52] It could become prohibitively expensive. At Philips' National, Jones and Galt received their "month's account for board and lodging" at the end of July 1841. It was "found to amount to £10 each" (instead of the anticipated £6 each) and they called it "the fatal bill." Wine seems to have been the main culprit. The men gave notice immediately, and prior to leaving "found a very grand dinner prepared on the strength of our departure *with wine free, gratis, for nothing,*" a phrasing that strongly suggests that the cost of wine, never included in the price of lodging, was chiefly responsible for the size of the tavern bill. From this point on, Jones lived with Galt in a succession of lodgings, including Goodwin's tavern, and continued his daily rounds: "My days were employed at the office ... and my evenings in walks to town and visits to the billiard and news rooms."[53]

Billiards was hardly an inexpensive taste either. When the Kingston *Chronicle and Gazette* ran its first advertisement for a licensed billiard table at the British American Saloon (which was also licensed as a tavern), Jones had already been there the night before: "Stewart called after dinner and accompanied Galt, Kelly, & myself to a billiard room just opened by a Black man by the name of Smith ... played a game with Bob Kelly & lost it for which I had to pay the moderate sum of 1/6 [1 s. 6d.] ... almost glad to find that my old rage for billiards had in great measure worn off."[54] But it had not. The journal contains almost daily references to playing at the billiard room, to games and monies mostly lost but sometimes won, and occasional notes about playing "despite a strong resolution to the contrary." Jones' gaming raised troubling issues. In one of the most self-conscious passages in his journal, he wrote, "The passion for gambling is almost inexplicable – for my own part I have no great desire to win and yet I enter with eagerness into the spirit of it for the sake of the excitement produced by the fear of losing."[55] His references to rage and passion are clear signals that gambling challenged the very idea of gentlemanly self-restraint and self-possession; his attraction to it was unsettling.

On the other hand, Jones' drinking never worried him. He deplored public drunkenness among the lower ranks and habitual drunkenness in his own circle, particularly if it interfered with business. He valued moderation and consistently noted his own consumption as taking "a horn," or "a glass," or "a glass or two," which brought him tidily in line with the colonial standards noted in the last chapter. When he made the occasional frank admission to his own drunkenness, the entries are free of the angst he attached to his fetish for billiards (which attests to his shared sense, also discussed in the last chapter, that the occasional indulgence was fine). While it is clear that each man tolerated the odd "spree" by the others, for Jones, as for many of the men with whom he shared a convivial glass, tavern going equated with moderation in drink.

Jones and his companions' expensive tastes created a mutual sense of conviviality and cohesion. Their group was select and exclusive. They may not have thought of themselves as creating a class, but they certainly knew they were sustaining a distinctive, gentlemanly identity and celebrating their degrees of separation from the rest of society, including the rest of the respectability. Farmers, artisans, and shopkeepers do not grace the pages of Jones' journal as sociable companions.[56] Privileged by relatively high incomes, the possession of abundant leisure, and an appreciation for manners and informed conversation, Jones and his friends gathered in taverns and hotels to wine and dine in exclusive company.

But how did they manage it? How did they claim quasi-private spaces for themselves within the public space of the tavern? The sense of exclusivity in Jones' journal flies in the face of the arguments already raised about dominance of mixed company in public space, and in the face of travellers' testimony about tavern tables crowded with all manner of persons. Patrick Shirreff, a gentleman traveller from England, had published a typical complaint a few years earlier that "[his] waggoner breakfasted and dined at the public table, in company with two gentlemanly looking persons, lately from England, without any explanation from the landlord." He then damned the social mix and table culture characteristic of colonial taverns with this faint praise: "This was the second time drivers had appeared at table since reaching the American shore, and I did not experience inconvenience of any kind on either occasion from their presence ... A meal in the United States and Canada is simply a feeding and not in any degree a conversational meeting; and ability to pay is therefore considered the standard of admission to public tables." Shirreff implied that another "standard of admission," one that permitted his idea of meaningful social intercourse, existed at home.

Yet conversational meetings – the "confab[ulation]s" mentioned in Jones' journal – were precisely what he and the boys enjoyed over their dinners. And while their taverns – Stewart's, Daley's, and Belanger's – emerge as the preserves of gentlemanly men, there is no evidence to suggest that these sites discriminated against certain comers. Indeed, Jones is explicit on several occasions that he patronized barrooms, the most public of the rooms in the public houses: "Hawke called, accompanied him to Daley's where we sat in the bar room and gossiped on politics and various other matters." Although we know that tavern-keepers, Belanger among them, introduced separate apartments for "select family groups" in the 1840s, largely to encourage the patronage of women, even Daley's British American, the premier house in Kingston, advertised the quality of the table d'hôte rather than the separateness of the dining facilities. It was, in other words, a reportedly very expensive but nevertheless public table. In Marcus Child's account the table d'hôte at the Royal Pavilion is notable *because* of its select, polite company.[57] The pursuit of separation, then, was rife with contradiction. Sheer cost filtered out the full public to be sure, but no sense of true exclusivity could be won without a willing engagement in its creation.

Jones sometimes complained about the difficulty he experienced when he tried to preserve an appropriate degree of social distance in the public houses. Crowds routinely gave him headaches. A brief stay at Goodwin's tavern ended because "the want of a sitting room of our own" made it "insuperable ... I cannot endure a constant crowd." Smell was another problem: "Went to a boat raffle at a very dirty tavern in our magnificent village [Barriefield, a suburb of Kingston] where I endured for an hour the pleasing odour emitted by a concourse of our sweet smelling citizens. Lost $2 1/4 dollars and didn't win the boat."[58]

Because Jones was a man who cared rather too deeply about circulating among a restricted circle, the sharp disjunction he draws in his journal between the patrons of a "dirty" village tavern and the cronies he met at Daley's in the marketplace and at the other principal houses must be treated with respect. Clearly the facilities at the principal houses allowed for a degree of social separation and social filtering. Yet, even Stewart's, the men's regular haunt for supper parties and billiards, could be problematic: "Went to the billiard [room] but finding it full of sundry disreputable looking persons didn't play." Jones beat a strategic retreat rather than suffer too-close contact with those outside the respectability.[59]

In fact, the role of wishful thinking, or imagination, should not be downplayed in Jones' portrayal of taverns. It becomes gradually apparent on reading the journal that the image he created of Philips' National Hotel while he lived there was, at least in part, fiction. Much later his journal gives an entirely different sense of the place:

> October 1842, 31st Monday: ... took up my quarters at Philip's which I found blessed with the presence of the actors and actresses belonging to the strolling party now in town in addition to the usual number of haubucks, yankees &c. which haunt this most fashionable hotel.

Not only irony but also women have crept into the account, as they had on other occasions. For example, Jones called on Sarah Cockburn at Daley's Hotel. She was a widow, the proprietor of the Ladies Seminary on Market Street in Toronto. Cockburn told him that she had been tempted by the cheapness of the passage to tour the Kingston Penitentiary. One evening Jones likewise "walked into town and drank gin and water and talked of theatricals with Mrs. Armour at Belanger's" (a meeting we glimpsed in the introduction). Kingston's public houses in the 1840s made some room for women, much as those in Ely Playter's York had. Yet Jones' world differed from that earlier era. The pace and depth of settlement and economic development had accelerated, replacing the walking villages of Playter's era with a real sense of urban life. New ideas about racial and gendered identities emphasized the respective, restricted locations of blacks, First Nations, and women in mid-nineteenth-century Canadian society, especially in relation to public life. Clearly the tavern world that Jones and his cronies made in the colonial capital did not, as a rule, include women, just as it did not include people of colour.[60]

Jones' desire, which he expressed in July 1841, to focus on privileged men to the complete exclusion of "haubucks," "yankees," and women, discloses the role that the substantial public houses played in Jones' life. His social position was made ambiguous because of his poor salary. Yet his background and family connections meant Jones belonged well within the circles of prominent men. Within groups of social equals he could affirm his gentlemanliness, his superiority to the "disreputable" persons so disconcertingly present in the pre-industrial taverns, and his maleness among men, even though he was too poor to marry. The taverns played the same role in the life of Thomas Galt, who was in the same embarrassing financial position as Jones. It was he who decided that they could not afford the National; but each man could afford regular access to the principal public houses and the style of life that landlords like Philips, Belanger, and Daley made available. They also relied on the keepers of good minor houses to meet the basic minimums gentlemen needed to dine together – hence their disappointment at encountering "miserable" conditions in a country tavern. Resort to the taverns enabled Jones to remain a gentleman of leisure in the hours when he did not have to be a government clerk.

Because it has so often been remarked that the tavern functioned as a poor man's club that nurtured association and mutuality among labourers and artisans, it is worth emphasizing that relatively privileged men like Jones also used taverns as surrogate gentlemen's clubs. It was the closest they could come to emulating the private, leisurely, members-only spaces that rich Londoners and New Yorkers enjoyed in the same period. Clubbing in a colonial Canadian tavern, though, often meant wishing away the roughs as well as the respectable working people and the women who were also there. Nevertheless, when Jones and the boys clubbed in the taverns, they socialized with an (informally) vetted membership that was limited to the gentlemanly and professional strata of the respectability.

What relationship did Jones and his cronies have with the rest of the respectability? Were they seen as respectable men in the moral sense of the word? Certainly they played fast and loose with the values of thrift, sobriety, and seriousness of purpose that underpinned respectability. Their problematic lifestyle was recognized in the colonial press and pulpit. Fulminations that the arrival of the capital at Kingston had brought with it an "extraordinary growth of vice of all sorts" provoked a defensive response in Jones' journal. "The truth is I imagine," he commented about a particularly harrowing sermon, "the old inhabitants were such a stupid set, that even some of the harmless gaiety which the newcomers indulge in appears to them perfectly horrible – vice in all its naked deformity!" Similarly, when Hitchings, the Chancery lawyer, was drowned in a boating accident in the fall of 1842, the sermon preached next Sunday implied a certain profligacy about his way of life: "Hector afterwards found great fault [with the funeral sermon], alleging that the reference to be drawn from it was that Hitchings had been a very dissolute character. I couldn't see this myself. The preacher pointed to the suddenness of death in this case and warned all to be prepared for it – the dissipated by turning from the evil of their ways." The very image of Jones and his companions – "young rakes" drinking wine "within the walls of the tavern, in the context of an all-male group" – stood as a symbol of danger to middle-class domesticity, to the economic independence that underpinned it, and to the ideal of responsible and informed public manhood.[61]

There may have been a kernel of truth in these fears. Although Jones' highest accolade to a man's character was his display of "gentlemanliness," he also celebrated an ideal of masculinity specific to the demands of tavern sociability: "Very much amused by an officer of the 32nd named Campbell[,] a genius who cuts all manner of capers, perpetrates innumerable witticisms, and plays billiards as well as anyone in N[or]th America."[62] In his envy of the officer's skills and general social éclat, Jones extolled a type of man that was very different from the successful "masculine achiever," – the domesticated, hard-working, "Christian gentleman" – and from the ideal masculine type envisaged by middle-class women who needed husbands they could trust emotionally and financially.[63] Just as his ideal tavern crony operated in opposition to prescribed roles for respectable men, Jones' concern about his "passion" for billiards, his censure of excessive drink, and his sensitivity to charges of dissoluteness were an acknowledgement that societal fears about a tavern-going lifestyle were not without foundation.

But it was never the case, as Susanna Moodie claimed in the 1850s, that "[p]rofessional gentlemen are not ashamed of being seen issuing from the bar-room of a tavern early in the morning or of being caught reeling home from the same sink of inequity late at night."[64] On the contrary, Jones, for one, was quite ashamed and only too well aware of the contradictions between his lifestyle and that presented in discussions of appropriate behaviour. Jones was still celebrating the New Year on 2 January 1843, for instance, when he made social calls at various homes to see "the ladies of the family"; he then proceeded to the billiard room in male company. He "got home very much fatigued and with great difficulty through the snow – almost feared [he] should have dropped down and been found in the morning as warning to gentlemen who keep late hours and break the rules of the temperance society."[65] Jones and his journal suggest that the rake remained present among a middle class that was in the process of constructing masculinity in opposition to everything the lifestyle represented.

Jones also hints at his own orientation to temperance discourse as a tavern-going, bourgeois, Anglican male. The tensions between "wets" and "drys" that provided the dynamism for associational activities and governmental policies concerning alcohol had a personal dimension, too. They divided families over the issue of drink and caused individuals to reflect, sometimes in conflicting ways, on their own consumption.[66] As his journal reveals, Jones and his cronies embodied this tension within their own thinking about their tavern-going lifestyle and its imbrication with drink. Jones recorded a multi-layered response to what was obviously his general familiarity with temperance ideals, perhaps as a means of negotiating his own behaviours and beliefs in relation to them. On the one hand, he could be rudely dismissive of old friends newly won over and active in the temperance movement: "My old schoolfellow Count called. He is an accountant at Montreal, secretary of the Temperance Society ... very tall and like all these violent temperance men, very thin." There is a caricature at work here, a stereotype of asceticism, and it reads as a dismissal of the activist's claim to decide (and, later, regulate) social conduct for others. But the entry also hints that temperance need not be "violent," and that other versions circulating in the colony, which focused on moderation rather than abstinence, were more amenable to Jones' understanding of the social and cultural role of alcohol. On the other hand, he could also be equally dismissive of problem drinkers: "Saw Mosier ... the man is dreadfully changed – looks grog-stricken."[67] Jones' dismissal of the man's behaviour suggests a willingness to interrogate "grog" from a critical perspective. Although Jones maintained a lifestyle that seemingly contradicted its central tenets, in his journal he grudgingly provides evidence of the power of temperance activism to shape individual thinking about consumption. The layered response to temperance Jones recorded is something historians rarely see. This response betrays self-awareness, an awareness of (changing) social context and a cultural position that is ambivalently at odds with the new social construction of drink that characterized the 1840s and beyond. In the end, Jones sided with the "wets," so that "if we did not get decidedly drunk, [we] would at least have done very little credit to the bricklaying branch of the Ebenezer temperance society had we belonged to that august body."[68]

After all, Jones and his cronies successfully integrated tavern going into their responsible middle-class lives. In a sense, by complicating our understanding of its masculine expressions, the men's experiences call into question what middle-class behaviour actually was.[69] Jones held a salaried government position and garnered steady promotions. He participated, through extensive correspondence and worry, in Jones family matters. He feared that he would be unable to marry and did remain a bachelor until the age of fifty, when he wed Harriet Robinson Hall, a forty-three-year old spinster who was the sister of a military friend and tavern companion.[70] He led a social life that extended beyond the tavern to parlour teas and suppers with women and families in their homes. He regularly attended Anglican services. He made daily recourse to the newsroom for European and colonial current events. For Jones, tavern going was not antithetical to a middle-class way of life, it was an important means of engaging in some of its cultural rituals, such as dinners, informed conversation, and the maintenance of distance from "disreputable" persons. He knew, too, that tavern going was not an entirely unproblematic way of satisfying these cultural needs.

When Thomas Galt, Richard Hull Thornhill, or Henry John Jones called into the principal public houses or the substantial country taverns near Kingston, they were not just any Tom, Dick, or Harry looking for amusement. The men cared about being a select company. They cared about their social position and about maintaining an appropriate, if somewhat flexible, degree of social distance – it was fine, for instance, to go to a "dirty" tavern if one had a chance to win a boat in a raffle. Jones and his cronies also show the range of behaviour that was open to respectable men – and the gendered freedom that men enjoyed to play with the boundaries of social mores without threatening their places in society. Accusations of dissoluteness and dissipation were clear enough, they stung, and they represented real temptations. But if they were the only costs of transgressing loudly advertised moral precepts, they could be easily borne.[71] At the same time, some tavern-keepers' abilities to meet this group's penchant for exclusivity in the company they kept and the material setting they required for wining and dining in style indicate that tavern advertisements had some truth to them. If we accept contemporary understandings of places like Belanger's, Daley's, or even Philips' National – as places that were as good as a colonial tavern or hotel could be – then colonial taverns were a natural setting for the pre-industrial middle class. Once there, members of the middle class sometimes used wishful thinking to make the space a truly exclusive one, imagining away the rest of the public within. Harry Jones and his journal illustrate how the taverns and tavern going supported mutuality and group identification among the respectability as much as they ever did among "the rough."

If Jones was able to reconcile his respectability and his tavern sociability, can the same be said of the women who exist in the margins of his and other tavern-going narratives? There was Mary Lawson who lived and worked in her parents' tavern in the Western District and Harriet Linfoot who worked in a tavern just outside York that was licensed to her husband. Harriet Clench represented a woman at work in her painting of a tavern scene, and the British American at one point housed the wives of Charles Dickens and the inspector general, Francis Hincks. While Mrs. Armour was at Belanger's and Sarah Cockburn at Daley's, unnumbered actresses of the "strolling party" were known to frequent the National. The next chapter introduces many more ladies and working women to tavern space, where each in her own way negotiated a respectable place in public space and coped with the stringent new gender norms of the middle of the nineteenth century.

7
Public Life for Women in the Era of Separate Spheres

Private rooms fitted up for the convenience of ladies.

– *Canadian Emigrant,* 26 September 1834

When colonial women thought about the meaning of respectability in their own lives, or considered playing around with its dictates, gender added a layer of complexity that was absent from the similar musings of men. At the cusp of private and public, where personal character was publicly enacted and publicly judged, respectability, in its outward manifestations, was a code of behaviour – a conventionality encoded by dress, manners, and deportment – no less for women than for the frock-coated and top-hatted gentlemen who inhabited Harry Jones' world. As one traveller explained when he met "an English lady with her two small children ... without any other attendant" on the stagecoach and in the taverns where they called: "she *appeared* very genteel and respectable."[1] This woman's version of respectability was gentility. She was a "lady" and knew how to be recognized as such. Black women, Native women, and working women employed variant versions of feminine respectability, which, for all of them, worked as a readable code – one that simultaneously enabled women's activities in public space and public life even as it curtailed the meanings of those activities.

Like the English lady, many colonial women boarded public stagecoaches (and steamboats and trains), where they encountered promiscuous company. Unlike her, not all claimed gentility through deportment. As Harry Jones cattily observed outside Brantford while on his way by stage to Chatham: "Detained a short time at Putnam's for a couple of Ladies – who turned out to be two chambermaids belonging to the inn. They were amusing enough, however, and certainly if dress could make Ladies they belonged to a high class. Though descended on one side from the aboriginals, one of them particularly was a very pretty girl."[2] Their status as working women and their apparent Native parentage meant these two women did not pass as ladies in the colonial public. It seems more likely that they used public display in dress to claim a distinctive respectability – one that did not preclude taking pleasure in fashion – using it to attract the attention they clearly received and to assert pride in wages well earned and well spent, just as historians know young working women did elsewhere.[3] The chambermaids' version of dress serves notice that respectability was open to differing cultural interpretations and to varying deployments by different women. Shirley Yee has eloquently argued that this was equally so for black working women (who were often formerly enslaved). Mrs. John Little, for example, took great pride in her "bushwacking" skills, the hard, physical labour of turning a forest into a farm. At the same time, Little situated herself as a respectable woman, one who commanded a polite public reception: "The best of the merchants and clerks pay me as much attention as though I were a white woman: I am as politely accosted as any woman would wish to be."[4] Differences in deportment and economic access (often encoded by dress) and the privileges of whiteness, which were acknowledged by Little, signalled important social differences among colonial women when they were out in public.

There is a myth that the examples of the English lady, the chambermaids, and Mrs. Little help put to rest: that men and women lived in separate spheres for much of the nineteenth century. By mid-century a developing set of ideas – called by some the doctrine (or ideology) of separate spheres, by others the cult of true womanhood, and by others the cult of domesticity – certainly shaped gendered norms in Upper Canada, as elsewhere, in ways that seemingly worked against the easy accommodation into public sociability that Sophia Beman, Bettsey Miles, and Mary Thompson experienced in Ely Playter's day. The ideology of separate spheres defined maleness and femaleness as essential, timeless, morally-laden, innately different renderings of what it meant to be human. It imaged an ideal of social relations that divided and privileged the male public over the female private sphere.[5] Early historians confused prescription with reality to such a degree that the notion of separate spheres has taken on an actual, corporeal reality. For instance, current Canadian history textbooks for an undergraduate readership, in their reviews of the literature, include phrases such as "women withdrew into the privacy of the home," were "restricted essentially to the private sphere of the home and family," and were "relegated to the private sphere of domesticity."[6] Within this historiographical context it is virtually impossible to elucidate the activities of women in public (or in public houses!) because historians have been focused on their absence.

For at least fifteen years, perhaps more in the field of labour history, a list of reasons for historians' growing ambivalence about the concept of separate spheres has grown: its suggestion of rigid boundaries rather than intertwined realms; its inability to describe working-class, black, and Native women's experience; and its related tendency to universalize and naturalize what was, in reality, particularistic experience. Newer, persuasive scholarship sharpens the attack. For instance, American historian Julie Roy Jeffrey has shown that the idea of separate spheres was, in its own time, a conservative construction of gender, one among many, contested by many. For instance, the abolitionist (anti-slavery) women and men that Jeffrey studied viewed women who were critical, activist, and not deferential to the powers that be as the embodiment of true womanhood. Literary historian Sarah Wilson concurs that gender ideals were subject to debate and presents Herman Melville, the author of *Moby Dick* (1851), as a prime example of a subversive vis-à-vis separate spheres. Critical of the ideology's exclusion of the masculine from the domestic, Melville combined the two in a fictive liminal male space that emancipated male experience. Laura McCall and Donald Yacavone bluntly dismiss separate spheres as interpretive fiction, as stereotypes constructed by historians, and they point out that patriarchy and male privilege hardly require rigid gender separation. Carole Lasser characterizes separate spheres as an obstacle to historical understanding. Lasser notes that the "'anomalies' ... appear more often than the model we have been trained to see," and she stresses instead the need for historians to encompass the "plurality of womanhoods" in their work.[7]

The evidence for colonial taverns makes two seemingly paradoxical points in regard to the still-reigning paradigm of separate spheres and its critical reinterpreters. It supports a reading of separate spheres as being real enough to influence architecture at mid-century – through the introduction of ladies' parlours and ladies' waiting rooms in hotels, principal houses, and substantial minor houses – and real enough, then, to influence actual patterns of female behaviour in public. For instance, in 1854 Purdy's Saloon and Eating House in central Toronto promised a "distinct entrance for parties of ladies and gentlemen," which invited mixed patronage but separated it from the presumably male-only congress that existed beyond other doors.[8] This situation differed from the assumption of mixed access that prevailed at Playter's tavern in early York, but it also differs significantly from the assumption of female absence that permeates separate spheres discourse. Separate spheres, as a theory, did not work very well when applied to the reality of colonial taverns and women's experiences in them. Women's many activities in the public space of the tavern – not only as patrons in places like Purdy's but also as tavern-keepers' wives and daughters, widows who were licensed to keep in their own right, and travellers, drinkers, and members of local community networks – make drawing spatial boundaries between daily gendered experience untenable. It may well be that the tavern public simply differed from other public spaces, pointing as much to a plurality of publics as to a plurality of womanhoods, but it may also be that the separate spheres paradigm cannot be used to analyze the meanings of women's activities in *any* public space at mid-century, because it theorizes women out of it.

In many ways looking through the gendered prism of women's mid-nineteenth-century experience enables us to revisit prominent themes in this book from a slightly different angle of vision. We know, for instance, that the vast majority of colonial taverns were carefully designed and crafted sites that were comfortably furnished by the standards of the time with well-stocked larders and bars and able to balance the claims of many user groups. I configure women as one of those groups, though most often their patronage was not in single-sex clusters but in mixed couples, families, and travelling parties. Yet, if taverns are recognized as materially welcoming sites (replete with parlours and dining rooms), women's presence within seems less conceptually jarring than it might otherwise be in an era of separate spheres and within a historiographical tradition that has been dominated by the separate spheres paradigm. Thus, there are parallels between women's experiences and those of gentleman such as Harry Jones and his cronies who were able to live out masculine middle-class rituals of consumption within taverns. Moreover, even as the meaning of household life was theoretically transformed by separate spheres ideology, rendering it into something of a rarefied, privatized zone of domesticity, taverns remained family homes. There was ample opportunity for female patrons to find what has been called a female "space at the bar." For example, at Dow's tavern in the early 1830s one settler remembered that his "mother and sister conversed with" the tavern-keeper's "wife about the hardships, trials, and sufferings, of life here in the west," while his father chatted with the men.[9] And women's labour crucially supported all the sociable, public spaces within the tavern, regardless of the gendered dimensions of their use, as did the two chambermaids from Putnam's Inn in their daily working lives. Although the phrase "tavern-keeping was a female trade" reads as a historiographical oddity given our notions of mid-century gender roles, based on the evidence of women's work I make that case for the minor houses.[10] I align female gender with the racialized and classed aspects of social identity that were taken up in the last two chapters, delineating the not always consistent ways in which being female affected membership in everyday, informal public life. I begin by re-considering the public function of the tavern as a centre of community life from the perspective of one woman's engagement in its construction, particularly her willingness to defend her honour and respectability in the tavern's public forum.

.Hope Shewman was a hard-working farm woman, not a lady, and her consciousness of herself as a respectable member of the old Loyalist community of Hay Bay (just west of Kingston) emerged in the convoluted events that locals called the goose scrape.[11] The expression referred to a five-year series of court cases that stemmed from a dispute over the ownership of a flock of geese. It all started in 1848 when Loisanne Shewman drove off a flock from the home of Hope Shewman, her neighbour and sister-in-law. Hope, claiming the geese as her own, came and drove the geese back. Because married women could not sue for or own property, the Shewman women's husbands each brought the other's wife up on charges. Magistrate Hearn, himself a member of the Hay Bay community, found Hope guilty of "picking, stealing, and marking William Shewman's geese." On the way back from court, just outside Kingston, the Shewmans and Hearn stopped at Clark's Tavern. Hope went to "the sitting room." In the public room, her husband confronted the magistrate, saying in the presence of several persons, "You have not done justice." Hearn replied, "I would not have my wife, a woman, lay under the same scandal as [your] wife for £500." Martin Barnhart, who was present, said, "We all knew they were talking about the goose scrape." It was Hearn's words, "spoken publicly" in Clark's Tavern, that continued to fester. Three years later, in 1851, as the Hay Bay community assembled close to home at Chartres' tavern for an Agricultural Society meeting, the goose scrape still dominated the informal agenda. By then the dispute had ceased to be about birds and was instead about Hope Shewman's reputation. The goose scrape was a scandal. Other people's children "twitted" the Shewman kids, saying "goosey, goosey" to them as they made their way to school or ran errands. When Hearn took it on himself, once again, to say that Hope had stolen those geese, she, as her husband had, used a public setting to defend her name and reputation. Hope was loudly indignant. According to several who were present, she "commenced talking" in self-vindication. Feminist literary scholars Barbara Bardes and Suzanne Gosset have observed the following about fictional heroines who spoke up for themselves: "By speaking ... a woman was claiming her place as a subject rather than object, as self rather than other."[12] Historians, in contrast, would likely interpret the evidence to present Shewman behaving as an engaged social agent, one who was active in the public beyond her household but also in its defence, one who employed the tavern as others did, as a forum to negotiate local respectability. By doing so, she expressed the same desires as those men who came to blows over their local good names and, interestingly, the same sense of entitlement to make "the personal the political." There were no public and private spheres in Shewman's day-to-day life. Her vocal presence in the tavern means she was neither located in some isolated domestic realm nor even out of the public in any straightforward sense; rather the two meshed inextricably for Shewman, belying separate spheres discourse. Complications with her traditional economic role in her household – specifically, managing the poultry yard – brought her before the court and before the tavern-based court of community opinion that demanded of her a public, performative presence, which she delivered.

But Hope Shewman also stayed in the sitting room at Clark's while the rest of her party gathered at the bar. It seems unlikely, though it is possible, that Hope felt impelled to do so by solidifying gender norms. After a horrible day in court she was probably looking more for a comfortable chair and time out than a private sphere. Yet from the 1830s on, and as the tavern-keeping trade developed in the colony, many keeps began to emphasize their provision of separate facilities for ladies. William Kanous, for example, kept a principal tavern, the Union Hotel, on the busy border between Canada and the United States at Sandwich (Windsor). Kanous renovated in 1834, and a new advertisement assured potential patrons that they would find the "new and commodious" barroom completely unconnected to the dining and sitting rooms; he emphasized the addition of "private rooms fitted up for the convenience of ladies waiting" for travel connections.[13] That some ladies were anxious for such gendered separations is suggested by the story told by a British officer, in 1849, about reaching a tavern a day's travel from Hamilton:

> An old and dry Yankee attendant amused us; he was as civil as the rest of the people of the house, but on the ladies objecting to his proposal to light the fire in their room in the morning (as he stood with his slouched glazed hat and loosely-fitting jacket ... at their door, lantern in hand, to ask if they wanted any more help from him) he replied, "Well! I guess the little girl will make the fire for ye, if ye be afeard of the old man; but ye're safe enough here, I tell ye."[14]

Travelling ladies, by mid-century, demanded class- and gender-specific services when they frequented the public houses. These services were successfully negotiated, inasmuch as the limited resources of a minor house in the country could provide. This suggests the power that the class-specific needs of ladies (or pre-industrial middle-class women) had in order to make a mark on tavern space and lay claim to it in material ways. Sometimes this claim was temporary. For example, when a mixed and "numerous company" of gentlefolk at a busy wayside tavern was confronted with "only two beds ... both in the same room," they created male and female zones by hanging "horse blankets and buffalo robes" as separators. In less-crowded taverns, the ladies in a genteel travelling party typically occupied "the best bedroom of the house," as was the case in the officer's story when the men "stretched themselves on 'shakedowns' before the fire." In the more substantial public houses, such as Purdy's Saloon with its special entrance, or Kanous' Union Hotel, permanent architectural arrangements predominated as a means of attracting genteel (moneyed) female patronage. These ladies shaped tavern space in literal, material ways.[15]

The provision of distinct entrances, parlours, waiting rooms, and services for travelling ladies did, then, support a spatial imaging of the nineteenth-century public that looks very much like separate spheres. We can see the constraining nature of separate spheres, the way it indeed divided public space into predominantly male and much smaller female portions. Yet there is a suggestion, too, of the transformative potential in separate spheres in the way the private virtues associated with women – as were encoded in respectability – could be used to breach public space and enter public life. This is a literal rendering of the arguments historians have long made about women's entrance into the public *sphere* via charitable works, voluntary association activity, and, later, emancipatory activism. Whether constraint or transformation is emphasized, separate spheres was something real in the lives of ladies, which demanded negotiation in public and made their public experiences more limited by the dictates of conservative gender ideology than those of working women like Hope Shewman.

The routine provision of ladies' rooms emphasizes segregation and ladies' location apart from the (real) public. Because we do not have a woman's diary comparable to those of Ely Playter and Harry Jones, one that depicts life in the ladies' parlour, prescriptive literature can provide insights into how things were supposed to work for ladies in the parlour and in public houses in general. The plethora of etiquette and behaviour guides that flooded marketplaces and bookstalls constituted one of the most conservative bodies of colonial literature. The guides presented taverns and hotels differently for women than they did for men, although it is worth stressing that they nevertheless represented women, in their incarnations as ladies, in these public places. For instance, *Miss Leslie's Behaviour Book: A Guide and Manual for Ladies,* an American publication that first appeared in 1853 and was popular in the colony, contained a whole chapter on deportment at a hotel.[16] The author assured her readers "that a lady evidently respectable, plainly dressed, and behaving properly may travel very well without a gentleman," and followed this with much advice on how to achieve this evident respectability. "If a lady ... wishes to be treated with respect, her own deportment must in all things be quiet, modest, and retiring." Respectable ladies were to eschew white kid gloves, makeup, and salted fish. "Do not," Miss Leslie advised, "travel in white kid gloves. Respectable women never do." And "avoid saying anything to women" who do so, especially if they are also "in showy attire, with painted faces," or with "a profusion of long curls about [the] neck ... a meretricious expression of eye." Moreover, "[l]adies no longer eat salt-fish at a public-table. The odour of it now is considered extremely ungenteel." Cultural historian John Kasson is correct to emphasize that these etiquette guides promoted the fragility of feminine respectability. They not so subtly made women responsible for the outcome of public encounters, especially with men. The sometimes silly rules drew a direct link from feminine respectability to personal deportment to the right of being "politely accosted," as Mrs. Little put it, and they represented women's limited freedom of movement in public relative to men's: it was women's fault if they were impolitely accosted or worse. Yet Miss Leslie does give ladies much practical advice on travel baggage, how to get a spark out of your eye on the train, how to talk to waiters and chambermaids, how to find the sights and fashionable stores in unfamiliar cities, and, even, when to drink wine with gentlemen in hotels. By doing so, she and her fellow etiquette guide writers facilitated women's possession of public space without challenging the sense that men's needs took precedence: "If you borrow a file of newspapers from the reading-room, get done with them as soon as you can, lest they should be wanted there by the gentlemen." However, according to Miss Leslie, this should hardly be necessary, because "in most hotels, there are books belonging to the establishment, lying on a table in the ladies' parlour." Feminine respectability, while onerous to maintain and representative of the constraints that hedged in female public activity, enabled women's participation in public life. Respectability was a code that opened doors, even if they were sometimes merely the doors to the ladies' parlour.[17]

Inside the ladies' parlour, ladies ruled. The space was theirs and theirs alone: "If a lady is so inconsiderate or selfish as to violate the rules ... by inviting her husband or lover to take a seat ... there is no impropriety in sending the chambermaid to remind him that he must leave the room." In a sense, this was the separate spheres version of the parlour sociability experienced by Sophia Beman in early York, albeit a version that "implicitly marked the rest" of the public space "as off-limits to respectable women."[18] Patterns of use inside the taverns and hotels could differ sharply by gender. At the tony Cataract House on the American side at Niagara Falls, for instance, female tourists in the 1840s claimed one of the viewing galleries as their own. When a male patron ventured out "upon the balcony, which the ladies seem[ed] to appropriate for their own use," he was met by their objections as the words "*exclusion* and *intrusion*" reached his ears. In 1840, the governor general, Charles Poulett Thompson, Lord Sydenham, complained of a corresponding balcony at the Clifton House, on the Canadian side: "There is not a young lady in the hotel who does not walk up and down staring into the window of the room ... every morning whilst I am going through all the processes of my toilet" (see Figure 11). By claiming the balcony, ladies crafted a female-centred zone of sociability that put a positive value on female difference and celebrated it in a public, gender-limited setting. It was a respectable female public (even if the governor general had his doubts). Similarly, at Chartres' tavern in Hay Bay women colonized the kitchen during the annual mustering of the militia. The kitchen was not the exclusive company of the Cataract House balcony, for a male overnight lodger recorded his pleasure in joining a female kitchen party: "Drank tea and talked to the

Figure 11   The 1838 sketch shows the balconies that Governor General Sydenham, among others, acknowledged as female public space. In such areas apart from the bar, women engaged in their own gender-specific patterns of tavern and hotel going.

John Richard Coke Smyth, *Clifton House, Niagara Falls,* 1838, 8.5 x 11" | With permission of the Royal Ontario Museum (950.114.47) © ROM

women who mustered strong in the kitchen and almost all seemed blessed with babies." Male patrons otherwise dominated barrooms and other public rooms, where they resisted the impositions of women and their babies. Parlours, balconies, and kitchens became female public space that gave room to female public life. Conservative ideologues may well have viewed these female publics as private by definition. Women, for their part, probably did not construct their public sociability in opposition to the private. Yet our understanding of the colonial public is expanded to include women – be they ladies on a hotel balcony or militia wives in a country tavern – and their public-house sociability within its compass.[19]

Indeed, one of the most powerful conceptual implications of the separate spheres paradigm is the idea that space, beyond that which was clearly defined private, became by definition "exclusively male anti-domestic space."[20] This sensibility marks historians' characterizations of mid-nineteenth-century Canadian taverns. They have been described as male-only worlds "of male association and privilege" that offered "escape from the confinement of the family," as male establishments where a "male subculture flourished" and an "absence of women" set the tone.[21] We are accustomed to this interpretation, and it makes inherent sense, and much about Harry Jones and his cronies can be read in support of it. And Chapter 4, about customary pastimes and drink as a symbol that maintained and represented social bonds, is likewise about men and their creation of mutual belonging. But what we are missing in this forthright association of tavern space with male space is the rest of the story: the gendered mix that always surrounded and enabled privileged expressions of masculine togetherness.

Susanna Moodie, of *Roughing It in the Bush* fame, commandeered the space in front of the only fire at a wayside tavern so that she could warm up a toddler. At Sebach's tavern, on the way to Goderich, a "Mrs R and her little daughter Susan ... formed part of [the] company." At a tavern near Port Stanley a mother struggled to keep her children clean and made them sleep outside to avoid the "nasty beds." Mary Anne Prince waited for her husband, John, a member of provincial Parliament, at Harrington's tavern in the Niagara District, where he found her "well." Innkeeper Elizabeth Jordan, on the Niagara Peninsula, had "Mrs. Jane Fleming boarding," and Mrs. Grant boarded at Diffin's tavern nearby. Gentlewoman Mary Reid Strickland, accompanied by a servant and carrying a babe in arms, walked the Huron Road toward Stratford. Six miles from Fryfogle's tavern, a stranger "politely" offered to take the baby for her and then took off with the child so quickly that she lost sight of him. When Strickland, who feared the worst, reached the tavern, "there sat the man with the baby on his knee." She observed that "he hoped she would give him the price of a quart of whiskey for his trouble, for the child was main heavy, God bless her."[22]

Strickland extended the man the treat in response, a gesture that ended her obligation and, therefore, engaged the lady in the cultural rituals of drink and the meanings they carried. Strickland's behaviour does not mesh well with depictions of women's experience in Canadian historiography, where women join temperance societies, haul husbands home from the tavern, or imbibe in drink sometimes at home in shameful secrecy or in raucous disorder on the streets.[23] The evidence from the colonial taverns agrees with these narratives in some ways. For example, in 1855 Susan Raynor's husband had "been constantly about" Mrs. Mellon's tavern "in a state of intoxication since she took the tavern." When Raynor went there to get him, "the door was shut in my face," so she "went up along the pathway" to the other door, but Mellon came to it, "slapped her leg and said 'kiss that' ... She told me she had got a good deal of his pension and would get more ... She made use of very indecent language that I wanted drenching out and that a man would not lie with me for a reason I knew." It is not clear if Raynor's husband came home that day, but Mellon later agreed not to "harbour or cherish [him] about her house."[24] There can hardly be a clearer enactment of the male right to drink at the expense of wives' wishes and household economies, nor of the way that that gender-specific privilege represented male control of the family purse.[25] While the details of this incident agree in some powerful ways with the specifics of established narratives, evidence pertaining to colonial taverns also provides another, alternative set of stories about women's relationships with public drinking that affirms women's gain from drink's social rituals but remains attentive to the terms of their differing relationships with everyday public life. For instance, Mr. and Mrs. Cruden drank together at a tavern in Burford Township in 1839, and Mr. and Mrs. Peter Stover sat drinking together in the barroom at Sheldon's, near Kingston, in March 1842. The couples enjoyed mutual sociability in public space, in an earlier form of behaviour that we recognize from Ely Playter's York tavern that the advent of a spatially restrictive gender ideology did nothing to alter. As women continued to pursue tavern sociability in the context of close male companionship, they also, by treating with their husbands, casually affirmed the social and marital bonds between them. Women participated in the rituals of public drink and the meanings that it carried.[26]

There is anecdotal evidence that tavern-going women also bought drink on their own account. For instance, in 1847 a church acquaintance who saw Mrs. Hillas "go to a tavern and call for a glass of liquor and drink it," brought Hillas' behaviour to the attention of their mutual congregationalists. There is also evidence in tavern-keepers' books. At James Philips' tavern north of Gananoque, "Matilda" laid a barroom bet for half a pint of whiskey. At Montgomery's on the Dundas Road in Etobicoke, Mrs. Grahme charged "4 glases" of whiskey and Mrs. Campbell charged "4 Glas Beer" in February 1838. At Robinson's tavern in Prescott, "Sarah" charged half a pint of beer in 1844, and both Mrs. Welsh and Mrs. Wilson, a widow, were on the books. Welsh came in for a gill of brandy twice in the fall of 1847. And she also called in for a pint of beer. These entries are a clear indication that Welsh drank in the house, for the measure is too small to bother carrying away. What is less clear is whether she drank in the barroom. Widow Wilson lodged at Robinson's for two and a half weeks starting 31 October 1847. On her first day she charged a glass of whiskey, a glass of brandy, and several pints of beer. She then stuck to beer and her tally on the last day of her stay was fifty-six pints, an average of three pints a day. Treating others accounted for part of the total. Wilson bought a pint of beer for a girl that first day, and she bought another for Mary Wilson on the 2 November. And whatever business brought the widow to this central tavern in the first place may well have involved meetings and treating with others. If so, Wilson used the tavern the same way female artisans and merchants did in England during the same period. It is entirely possible that Wilson and her companions drank outside the barroom; given what we know of female patterns of use in tavern space – their preference for (or relegation to) feminine zones of sociability in parlours, balconies, or kitchens – it is likely. As historian Madelon Powers has observed of working-class women's saloon drinking after 1890, "their aim was sociability, not social equality; and their stepping out did not include stepping into bar areas where they were not welcome." (Powers also notes men's corresponding alacrity to vacate the more comfortable parlour when women arrived.) For the Widow Wilson, tavern drinking was an integral part of the daily routine. In the tavern's public space, she got her name put on the books and ran a liquor tab, at least some of which was consumed by women who participated in the treating ritual.[27]

At Patrick Roach's Railway Inn in the 1850s, working women found a way to integrate public sociability over drink, very likely among themselves, within the rhythms set by their daily labours. This is the same Toronto tavern that was introduced in Chapter 1 as an example of an early working-class saloon, patronized mostly by waged workers, especially from the railroads, and tradesmen. Roach kept a small store in combination with his tavern, and it is the purchasing patterns in his accounts that suggest tavern time could entwine with labouring time for women too. Mrs. Scott, for example, had a pint of beer when she came in for laundry soap and starch, and Mrs. Cane purchased a large loaf of bread and two glasses of liquor. Mrs. Hardin also bought a loaf, as well as some blacking (to polish the stove, pots, or boots), and used the opportunity to take a glass of liquor. Mrs. Hayden stopped for a pint of beer when she called in for a pound of barley, and Mrs. Mathes had a glass when she came in for vinegar. Something more redolent of real down time is indicated in Mrs. McDonald's purchase on New Year's Day of half a pint of whiskey with a stick of tobacco. It is tempting to see in these accounts moments of freedom and independence – moments in which working women enjoyed an ability to behave like men – in their occupation of tavern space and their public consumption of drink.[28]

But it may also be that these were simply women behaving as women, yet in ways and cultural forms that our historical analyses are only now capturing. Roach's accounts hint that these working women encountered each other and paused together to share a treat or a mutual drink (see Figure 12). Mrs. McDonald and Mrs. Mallowry both called in and drank on 3 December 1855. Mrs. McDonald came in again on the 14th, the same day as Mrs. Harrison, and Harrison came back on the 27th, along with Mrs. Henry. Both women had their accounts debited for drink. Mrs. Walsh and Mrs. Gregory may well have met up at Roach's on 23 June 1858 and left with the quart of whiskey that Gregory bought. And Mrs. Mathes and Mrs. Barber were both in on 20 September that year. Mathes charged enough liquor (half a pint of brandy) to treat. One April day in 1859 Mrs. Smith bought three glasses and a pint of whiskey and a quart of beer. This was more than enough to share, and the purchases suggest that treating transitioned into drinking

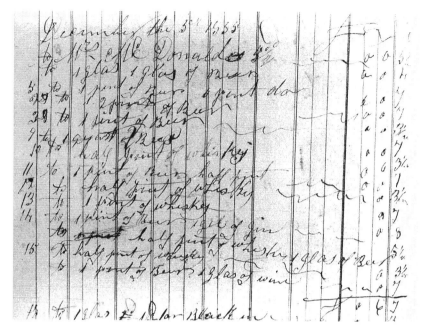

Figure 12   The excerpt, in Patrick Roach's hand, is part of Mrs. McDonald's running tab for drinks in his tavern. There are entries for glasses and pints of beer, half-pints and pints of whiskey (the latter an amount either to treat with or carry home) as well as for a gill of gin and a glass of wine.

Toronto Tavern keeper Daybook [1855-59] | Archives of Ontario (F 4296 #1)

at home. Finally, Mary Haron charged twelve glasses of liquor to her account in September 1855, debiting it by a full 2s. (or 2d. a glass). We do not know whom Haron was treating, but the amount of liquor purchased is too much even for a spree drinker, which suggests she bought liquor for others as well.

It is not clear that these women drank together, but some of them surely knew each other. The quick amounts they typically consumed, and the nature of the work that is indicated by their non-drink purchases, suggests that Roach's female patrons probably lived or worked within easy walking distance of the tavern. By linking the names in Roach's account book to the city directory – which is a tentative enterprise at best – I have provisionally identified three women. For instance, the "Mrs Harrison" on the books may be Isabella Harrison, a washerwoman, who lived on Douro Street, near Tecumseh, on the same intersection as the tavern itself. "Mrs Cummins" could be Mrs. C. Cummins, a widow and dressmaker, from King Street West, which was located a short block to the north. And if "Mrs McDonald" was Mary McDonald, she kept a boarding house at Bathurst and Front, two blocks to the south.

It would actually be more surprising if these women did not go to the tavern together.

The nature of the account book limits the conclusions that can be drawn from it, although some things are certain. We know women frequented Roach's and that some were regulars. They ordered both by small measure, to consume on the premises, and by larger amounts, to carry home. Women combined tavern going and public drinking with the demands of working lives. It is more likely than not that they treated together (and with men). Twenty-three of the patrons on Roach's books were women. So, while women were never present in sufficient numbers to threaten the male dominance of the space, Roach's tavern was, nevertheless, a local public house that women used quite freely. In part this was facilitated by the tavern's provision of household sundries. Calling in for a loaf or some vinegar shifted naturally into having a drink in public, be it the mixed public of the barroom or a female public apart from it. It requires only a small act of imagination to visualize Roach's female clientele using tavern rooms in ways that supported their mutual identification as working women.[29]

Roach's tavern supported female sociability in another way. Roach's female patrons clearly carried liquor away for home consumption. This is evident in Mrs. Gregory's and Mrs. Barber's quart of whiskey each. The colonial tavern played the same supportive role in women's (and men's) at-home drinking as public houses did elsewhere. In New York City drinking enabled female sociability not so much in taverns but in gatherings on stoops, on the flat roofs of tenements, or in kitchens. Women were bound to their houses, and they needed to integrate domestic responsibilities with social time – hence the need to "rush the growler" (to buy buckets of beer at the tavern to take home and share). We glimpse the same custom in 1836 in Hamilton, where Ann Lindly "bought considerable liquor from" Thomas Wilson. He "never saw her intoxicated." Lindly regularly came in to Wilson's substantial tavern, "bought some," and took it away. We know that Lindly headed her household and mothered two young children; tavern time must have been out of the question.[30]

While account books clearly document women's participation in the culture of drink and hint of its gendered nuances, they reveal little about the cultural and social meanings that colonists may have given to women's public consumption. The almost certainly contested nature of the relationship between feminine respectability and tavern drinking remains inaccessible. For Harry Jones and his bourgeois cronies, tavern drinking, as a pastime, tested the limits of the more freely realized masculine version of respectability. And of the plethora of women I discovered in the taverns, Mary Strickland was the only lady that closely and purposefully associated with alcohol, and she did not share in the quart of whisky with which she treated. Was there room for ladies – as there was for gentlemen and, it seems, working women – to situate public drinking within the bounds of respectability?

Margaret Home Lizars was a lady. She grew up in Edinburgh, and, according to family chroniclers, her father was a magistrate and her mother was a bishop's daughter. Home's parents died when she was seventeen and left her with a substantial inheritance, which was in "the trust" of Daniel Lizars, a publisher and engraver. Home married Lizars and had at least eight children before Daniel's death in 1812. One daughter wed Sir William Jardine of Apple-girth and became Lady Jane. A son, John Lizars, became a medical author and professor of surgery at the Royal College of Surgeons, Edinburgh. And William Home Lizars became an engraver and artist whose work still hangs in the National Gallery of Scotland. Margaret Lizars immigrated to Upper Canada when she was in her sixties, joining children and grandchildren who had already settled there.[31] Harry Jones met her in 1837 at Lawson's Tavern: "Met an old lady at Lawson's named Lizars, the mother of the famous Edin-burgh professor of that name, she has several other sons, one equally famous as an engraver, two or 3 are in the country – She is very Scotchy, and has one great failing, that of getting drunk – dead drunk after dinner – queer habit – Mrs Lawson who is notorious in that line herself was very severe on her."[32]

As a lady, albeit one raised well before ladies troubled with such niceties as private spheres and their constraints, Margaret Lizars saw no dissonance between her gendered identity and tavern going in a mixed company. She also drank to excess, incurring a written version of raised eyebrows from a gentleman and the open (if hypocritical) criticism of a tavern-keeper. This suggests one "old lady's" willingness to play around with the boundaries of feminine respectability or a freedom, born of mature years, to ignore them at will.

Another lady, who was much younger and married, felt no such freedom. When a pregnant Catharine Parr Traill arrived, wet and cold, at a wayside tavern, the landlady and "her damsels" roused the fire, gave her a warm footbath, and "provided a warm potation, which, I really believe, strange and unusual to my lips as it was, did me good." This gentlewoman found it expedient to pretend to her readers that she had no idea she was drinking what must have been a hot toddy (which was laced with spirits by definition) or a hot whisky punch.[33]

The sheer range of women's public activities in itself reveals much about the nature of tavern space. Whatever the men were up to, women used tav-erns to warm babies by the fire and feed and wash their children, whom they worried about sleeping in "nasty beds." They also drank and socialized in the tavern's public space, albeit working women had greater freedom of movement in this regard than ladies – Margaret Lizars in her cups aside. Without undermining male precedence in public life and space, the evidence for colonial taverns does spoil the separate spheres party by complicating the paradigm's tendency to gender the tavern male. Nor was the tavern public anti-domestic. Looking at the taverns through the prism of women's mid-nineteenth-century experience means seeing them, and the public life that cohered within, as utterly dependent on female skills and women's domestic labour. Public and domestic were inextricably linked in taverns, but to what extent was tavern keeping a female trade and tavern work women's work, particularly in the minor houses?

In 1850 a traveller wrote the following account of Andrews' Inn, which was located near Mallory's Town on the highroad to Kingston: "Arriving late, and leaving early, we saw nothing of the men; but the womenkind were tall, goodlooking, and barely civil. I learnt the very characteristic names of two of the daughters, as I was dressing in the dark, between five and six next morning ... 'Irene,' says one of them, 'you have not washed up the dishes yet.' 'No, Aurely,' replied the other, 'neither have you scoured the kitchen floor.'"[34] It was not male voices that dominated tavern discourse early in the morning at Andrews' Inn, because the very domesticity of most tavern work made it women's work. But male names do dominate tavern-licensing records in the mid-nineteenth century. It would be another generation before married women came to enjoy the right to an independent legal existence and gained the ability to enter into a legal obligation, like taking out a tavern licence. So taverns were licensed to husbands. Ninety-six percent of the tavern licences issued in the colony belonged to men.[35] In the principal taverns and the new hotels, male tavern-keepers maintained a high profile, especially in the barroom and the stable and in the management of arrivals and staff. And "showily dressed male attendants" served behind hotel bars, performing "the mysteries appertaining to their office." But in the minor houses, as at Andrews', many of the men were simply not around much; instead, they worked as farmers, merchants, artisans, and professionals while their wives kept tavern. Though husbands participated when able, or as needed, it is difficult to imagine that either the American ironmonger, "just starting a furnace for casting" on York Road, or James Watson, the proprietor of the Rising Sun Tavern on Newgate Street in Toronto and a tinsmith, had much time to spend inside the bar or serving meals. Nor did Ben Diffen, who operated a cooperage that adjoined the family tavern in Pelham in the 1840s and '50s. Nor did Henry Lawson, a physician licensed to keep tavern in the Western District. When Harry Jones reached Lawson's, he found "the doctor not at home, but Mrs Lawson and her fair daughter" looked after him.[36]

License inspectors certainly factored women's work into account when they reported on the state of the taverns under their authority. The Uxbridge inspectors reported in 1852 that "with reference to Leonard Long we have no complaint ... & we believe himself & wife are well & suitably adapted to keeping an inn."[37] And landlords attested to women's prominence in the trade. In 1843 in Chinguacousy Township, Thomas Burrell initially refused to rent his farm and house to Mr. and Mrs. Samuel Reid, "knowing" that Samuel "was not a good farmer." Burrell wrote that he "had no objection to them as Tavernkeepers – Mrs Reid is an active person and manages the business of the tavern."[38]

Patrons sometimes used the wife's name as the tavern's name. John Prince, for example, referred to Mrs. Freeman's tavern in Chatham as a good house with bad whiskey. We know that Mr. Freeman was alive and well and held the licence. At Guelph, Samuel Strickland "drove up to the only tavern in the place ... kept by one Philip Jones, an Englishman – or, rather, by his wife – a buxom, bustling body, who was, undoubtedly, the head of the establishment."[39] Far more often, though, the appellation "Mrs." indicated a widow's tavern. As the only women to be licensed in their own right, widows held the remaining 4 percent of the colony's licences.[40] Many of these widows had been married to tavern-keepers. In the Western District, for example, Veronique Charon took over her husband Jacques' licence in 1833. Mary Middleton took over from her husband, George, in 1839. Mrs. T. Mary Moore wrote to the magistrates in 1838 to say, "As the widow of the late Wm. Moore, deceased, ... it is my wish and intention to continue the tavern lately kept by my husband." The transition to sole proprietorship was a logical one as the work had been women's already.[41]

When William Hawkins died in 1832, his widow, Honor, took over the licence and continued in the trade for at least ten years. She ran a principal house in Sandwich that was patronized by the neighbourhood elite and a setting for community events. John Prince "attended a public dinner given to [him] by [his] constituents at Mrs. Hawkins' Western Hotel. Upwards of 40 sat down." Like Honor Hawkins, other widowed tavern-keepers did not run the poorest public houses: fully a third of them paid the highest licence rates in their districts, either £7 10s. or £10 annually, which indicates they ran well-located taverns in town. Women's representation was equal to men's at these rates, and the ability to pay indicated a level of economic stability, a real return from the tavern business, and an investment in the future. That women were proportionally equally represented in this high end of the fee scale is telling. It means that in Upper Canada tavern licences were not necessarily the possession of poor widows in need of relief, as they apparently were in the colonial United States. Though there were surely widows who kept poor houses, the fact that most widows (like men) paid either £3 or £5 for their licences simply reflects a rural location in a predominantly rural colony. Mrs. Aldego's tavern in the Longwoods, for example, was "the most comfortable ... in this part of the country," and she paid only £3 annually for the licence.[42]

Overall, widowed tavern-keepers showed a slightly higher propensity for stability than the average tavern-keeper. Elizabeth Lyttle kept tavern for more than a decade in the Western District, as did Maria Pierce and Catharine

McDonnell in the Eastern District and Margaret Terriberry in Gore. In 1824, Mrs. C. Anderson "kept the oldest [tavern] upon the road" into Grimsby. Her sign of "a deer, a huntsman, a hound, a double-barrelled rifle, and a green tree" had been up for some "twenty or thirty years." In Chapter 1, I noted that two thirds of Upper Canadian tavern-keepers spent less than five years in the trade. Only 15 percent spent a decade at it, and widows' persistence rate over ten years stood at 18.5 percent. This still high rate of turnover probably reflects the onerous addition to women's domestic labour that tavern keeping required, a work load that women, widows as much as married women keeping taverns licensed to their husbands, were not reluctant to set aside, when possible.[43]

Nevertheless, women's experiences with tavern keeping were diverse. There are success stories that contrast with the far more typical story of short tenures. Jane Marion Jordan, for example, spent twenty years in the trade. Three times wed, she kept tavern twice as a wife, twice as a widow. Her second husband, Paul Marion, died in 1808, and the magistrates of the Town of York "duly assigned" his tavern licence to his widow. Marion's tavern stood in the rear of John Jordan's York Hotel, and Jane and John soon married. Jordan's was a principal house where members of the House of Assembly boarded and entertained, where the courts and the House sat during the War of 1812 (because the government buildings burned), where large groups of militia officers "dined ... all very agreeable," where the stage office was on the York to Kingston line from 1820, and where patrons found newspapers. When John died in 1821, Jane inherited "forever" his real estate, goods, and "all sums of money that may be owing or due him." (This meant she could do with the property as she saw fit. Many widows only had use of a property for the rest of their lives, meaning they could not, for instance, leave it to whom they wanted.) As John's "beloved wife Jane Jordan, formerly widow of the late ... Paul Marion of the Town of York," she became a solo tavern-keeper. The will is a clear testament to the couple's partnership; the continuation of the prominent hotel is a testament to Jane's experience in the trade.[44]

Individual success stories like Jane Jordan's remained part of women's tavern-keeping history in the 1830s, the 1840s, and beyond. Although only a fortunate few realized it, the trade offered one of the very few available routes to female economic success. Blanche Westlake is one example. A new immigrant and a very recent widow, Westlake took out a tavern licence in the London District in 1833 at the urging, according to historian J.K. Johnson, of the lieutenant-governor. Westlake invested sufficient capital to erect a spacious frame building and called it the Royal Adelaide Inn. This was no primitive backwoods tavern but rather one that offered solid standards of accommodation. Travellers complained that it was cold and that Westlake talked too much; nevertheless, she succeeded and later, together with a brother-in-law, bought up adjacent lots and operated a blacksmith shop on her premises. Westlake became locally celebrated as "perhaps the most really useful settler" around.[45]

In Kingston Eliza Grimason made herself wealthy in the trade. For decades, from 1856, she kept tavern, first with her husband and later as a widow, in a prominent Princess Street location. She built an estimated fortune of $50,000. Grimason's was both a farmer's tavern and a site of Tory politics. Though she could not vote, Grimason actively campaigned for her lawyer and local member of provincial Parliament, John A. Macdonald. Grimason and her house are featured in older, political biographies of Macdonald. E.B. Biggar writes that it was said that Grimason "could control a hundred votes." Donald Swainson notes that her tavern was Macdonald's local election headquarters, and he "loved the barroom, effectively using conviviality as a political tool." Grimason hosted open houses for the Tories and lent her van to transport the party faithful. She attended the electoral strategy meetings at her hotel; according to Biggar, she was often the only female present.[46]

More than one historian has read women's tavern keeping and domestic labour in the taverns' public spaces as a breach of the public world itself. In this analysis the trade emerges as a tantalizing escape hatch from the private sphere.[47] Eliza Grimason's tavern, with its connections to political debate and prominent men, was exactly the kind of place these historians have in mind. Grimason's history certainly points to the unusually close links that the trade could support between individual interested women and the public sphere. But as the keeper of a central, prominent house, Grimason did not necessarily have the same experiences as the bulk of women who kept minor houses. Additionally, a historiographical analysis that equates the public with the political unnecessarily limits the scope of enquiry. A much fuller case can be made for women's inclusive participation in the everyday public of informal tavern life with which this book is concerned. (After all, many men were not politically engaged either, but they lived, theoretically and actually, "in public.")

The work female tavern-keepers did was the same domestic labour that women performed in other families, even though the value derived from it translated more easily into a recognizable economically productive role. When one traveller reached McDougall's tavern in the Western District, he expressed his gratitude that "Mrs McDougall was kind enough to mend my unfortunate breeches which before had set common decency at defiance."[48] Domestic labour – like mending – did not become less domestic or private when it was performed for patrons in public houses; nor did women become more public by performing labour in public houses. The categories of public and private are simply not interpretively useful. The evidence from the colonial taverns lays bare the fiction of separate spheres in the lives of working women, not the fluky chance that a select few dodged its dictates by picking the right trade.

Domestic work, the traditional province of women, sustained the minor houses. And it was "work": hard, labour-intensive, and important. On Lake Simcoe, overnight lodgers awoke to "busy sounds ... the mistress was up, the maid, and the children and each had something or other to do." The "clever, managing wife" at one early tavern made "excellent cheese and butter among other things." One boy hauled water every day from the river to his parents' Eagle Tavern. A "comely young woman" cooked and served a meal to a party of military travellers in a tavern at the Grand River in 1829. Jane Goodfellow worked in the kitchen of her brother's tavern. It was Charlotte Brown, not her licensed husband, who noticed that a "table spread, a quilt, and a sheet" were missing from the upstairs rooms. Mrs. Drakes kept tavern in 1833 in Amherstburg, where she promised two new arrivals she would "slay a fowl 'right off'" for their supper. In 1834, Eliza Galbraith "entered the service of Mrs. Welch, a widow lady, who then kept public house." In 1835 "Margaret" worked at Cartier's in Chatham where her duties included rousing sleepers intent on travel in the wee hours. At Mourhale's in Cornwall in 1837 Catherine McRory served drinks to men upstairs. Caroline Rosa worked at LeDuc's in Sandwich in the early 1840s, and in 1841 Elizabeth Boyle worked as a servant at Alexander Watson's tavern on Kingston Road. When a man came "rapping on the front door" about midnight, "Mrs. Watson went ... & enquired who was there." At Carmino's in Kingston, a "dark-eyed little Venus, with a child in her arms" greeted patrons at the front door and organized their rooms. The woman who worked at Taylor's Commercial Hotel in Chatham in 1843 caught a thief red-handed when she went down to fetch stores from the cellar. Margaret Graham and her daughter lived at Stinson's in Niagara in 1845; both "attended bar at that time." Sarah Armstrong, whose brother held a tavern licence, kept a similarly close eye on doings in the barroom, especially on the till behind the bar. Bridgett Higgins "was servant maid" in George Platt's tavern in 1849. She lived on the premises and her jobs included cleaning the "upper story." Near Guelph, a tavern-keeper's daughter, "a simple and good natured girl," collected patrons' payments. Thomas Lambert's little boy ran to get his father when he found "a very sick man in the barroom." Mary Marcey, "a young girl," lived and worked at Robert Zimmerman's tavern in 1852. And it was Zimmerman's sister, a young woman "a good deal sought after by young men," who actually "kept house" until he married. Keeping house included being "frequently in the barroom ... behind the counter," dealing with the "old ostler," and running the house in her brother's absence. Patrick Roach hired Margrit Kahel at his Railway Inn in August 1854 for board and £1 a month.[49]

The domestic identity of tavern work is underlined not only by the content of this list (dairying, cooking, linen care, cleaning, looking to children's chores, looking after others' needs) but also by its household setting. There are brothers and sisters, husbands and wives, daughters and sons, and live-in household help. It was the household setting that enabled women's participation in the trade. Women could earn money without neglecting their primary responsibilities to children and husbands.

It was just as important that women could draw on the contributions of children and husbands. For instance, married women sent their husbands to the Quarter Sessions every January to get the tavern licence. They gladly sought men's help if trouble or weirdness erupted. One female keep was behind the bar at the Travellers' House in the Longwoods when a bizarre man came in, "clothed in a suit of sheepskins with the wool on from head to toe, with a ram's head ... perfectly preserved, the horns being well set up, and two glaring glass eyes the size of a silver dollar" (see Figure 13). She hurried to the stable for her husband, who came running, pitchfork in hand.[50] The willingness of husbands to sponsor women's tavern keeping attests to its economic significance in household economies. This underlines the crucial importance of domestic labourers in tavern-keeping households and those

"WHO, AND WHAT THE DEVIL ARE YOU?"

Figure 13　Women's work in colonial taverns brought them into public life differently than female tavern-goers. Keeping a minor house was a predominantly female trade because of the domestic, or household, labour involved. Still, women did not hesitate to ask for male help when necessary. Here, according to the artwork of a prominent settler, William L. Bâby, a weirdo's arrival in the barroom impels a female tavern-keeper to dash to the barn for her husband. It simultaneously locates her at work in the tavern's public space.

households where women's work stretched wages and "mitigated the dangers of relying entirely" on them, where women's work freed capital and allowed its accumulation for reinvestment or status display (such as farm, artisanal, and, indeed, bourgeois households).[51] Uniquely, in a tavern household women's domestic labour became tangibly productive – that is, it produced measurable income. Debits to customers' accounts predominantly reflected the debts they owed to female labour – for linens supplied, services rendered, and drinks and meals prepared and served. Tavern families profited directly from women's public deployment of the feminine skills that were tradition-ally employed in the household to replenish and conserve its resources and succour its members.

Keeping tavern meshed very well, especially for mothers, with the demands of child rearing. Children who grew up in taverns contributed their labour to household economies and responded to parental expectations that some of their activities, namely chores, support the family's economic needs. This was a common childhood experience in pre-industrial and industrializing economies, where, from at least the age of eight, children's work – whether hauling water, minding patrons, running errands, or keeping an eye on the barroom – stretched resources by freeing adults for productive and repro-ductive tasks.[52]

The domestic identity of tavern work is most evident in cookery, in the endless rounds of meal provision engaged in by female tavern-keepers, as it was by all colonial housewives.[53] When a stagecoach party of nine made an unscheduled call for breakfast (due to the unseasonable cold) near dawn at a small wayside tavern near Prescott, a gentlewoman in the company de-scribed in detail the domestic kafuffle that ensued. She revealed the discrete tasks involved in food preparation, the helpful participation of a man in this most female-associated of realms, and the fact that women performed the actual work of cookery. A "half-clothed, red-haired Irish servant, was upon her knees, kindling up the fire" in readiness for cooking. The mistress of the house, identified only as Almira, was also still "dressing as fast as she could" and itemizing her larder in consultation with Joe, an "old, white-headed man" who also lived there. As Almira bemoaned the "bit of beef [that] will be nothing cut into steaks for nine," Joe suggested "eggs and ham, summat of that dried venison, and pumpkin pie." As he went to "lay out the table," Almira was "seizing a frying pan from the wall and preparing it for the reception of the eggs and ham." The passengers waited impatiently in the parlour while "she prepared from her scanty materials a very substan-tial breakfast." The meal, in the end, was fried steak and eggs and ham, dried venison – which was probably served as was the custom "cut in thin shav-ings, as a relish, with bread and butter" – pumpkin pie, and tea or coffee to drink, perhaps with a shot of spirits against the cold. Despite the emphasis on scantiness and confusion in this description, it implies that a great deal of earlier, orderly provisioning had taken place: purchasing or butchering and preserving beef, pork, and venison; looking after the poultry yard and collecting eggs; harvesting pumpkin, paring it, rendering it down, passing it "through a hair sieve or colander," mixing it with "new milk and two or three eggs well-beaten, with grated ginger, as much sugar as will make it sweet enough to be pleasant," and baking it in a pastry shell, all the while carefully managing the fire. The description also reveals that, while it was common knowledge that cookery and the specific skills associated with it were feminine, men were not absent from domestic labour. Recent work, in fact, suggests men's deep engagement with the most intimate workings of their homes, from being present at childbirth, to nursing their wives and children, to writing anxious letters about family matters when away. Like these men, Joe played a domestic role. He knew what was in the larder, and he set the table. His behaviour enhances our sense of the inutility of the separate spheres paradigm for describing real life.[54]

Women also routinely attended the public tables, where they brought food and poured tea and coffee for patrons in taverns far more substantial than Almira's. At the Farmer's Inn, a very comfortable country tavern, "a bevy of smiling damsels had everything about the house perfectly neat and clean." They served tea, "not without some regard to display; cakes of various kinds, capital cold apple pie and many a nice etcetera besides, with one of the fair daughters to do the honours of the board – an office she performed with singular propriety and ease." This overblown language celebrates domestic work and female skills, especially the sense of comfort provided by women's cleaning, baking, table service, and display. Far from challenging the norms of appropriate feminine behaviour, the tavern labour of these young women affirmed their propriety.[55] Women's work in taverns was a legitimate public presence, which was encoded as respectable by its very domestic nature.

Yet there is also a hint of male appraisal of female sexuality in more than one of these depictions of women's work. Words and phrases like *buxom, comely, dark-eyed Venus, much sought after,* and, even, *bevy* (of damsels) and *the fair daughter* suggest more than an appreciation of the products of female labour. Sometimes men's sexualized appraisal of tavern-keeping women was explicit. Engineer Walter Shanley wrote to his brother in 1851 about the women at Gilman's Hotel in Prescott. He could not get anywhere near "those sisters-in-law of Gilman's ... really very fine girls – but so 'severely proper' you can scarcely approach them ... Mrs Gilman who is as fine a looking woman as I ever saw keeps strict watch & ward over them."[56] Despite his prurience, Shanley conceded the evident respectability of Mrs. Gilman and her sisters, as is encoded in their "proper" deportment. (Perhaps they emphasized it for the benefit of this particularly penetrating male gaze.)

Cultural historian Peter Bailey has argued that by 1830 the barmaids' sex appeal was part of the trade in England, where these female labourers were seen as "a further item of allurement" among increasingly posh public house interiors. Diane Kirkby has persuasively argued that when barmaids (or female tavern-keepers, chambermaids, and other domestic helps) are imaged in sexualized terms, they are rendered invisible as workers. Moreover, the focus on women's heterosexual attractions suppresses the possibilities of homoerotic interaction between barmen – such as the showily dressed male attendants noted above – and male patrons. Mythologizing women's domestic labour in taverns as mere sexual allure is part of a masculinist historical narrative that discounts the ways in which women's work crucially enabled the trade.[57]

Tavern-goers' comments also raise the issue of respectability in its sexualized sense. For women, respectability had much to do with sexual behaviour. This is the subtext to Miss Leslie's advice about appropriate deportment in public. When male patrons appraised female tavern workers, whether mildly or explicitly, at least part of their appraisal was based on the possibility of sexual availability. Yet women's domestic work in colonial taverns did not include sex work. It is, for instance, disappointingly difficult to find evidence that prostitutes either traded on-site or sought out customers in the taverns (which does not mean it did not happen). The insidious association between prostitution and taverns, which is still present in popular culture, means one might expect a history of public houses to include a history of the most public of public women. Rose Ann Finnegan worked in the colonial sex trade in Kingston's French Village. In 1853 she invited Jacob Gibson into a house "where some other women were downstairs," asked him to treat her to a beer, and took him upstairs for fifteen minutes. Gibson claimed that he had declined sex and that she stole his money. In the words of a policeman, this was not a tavern, it was a "house of ill fame." Had it been a tavern, this eruption of disorder would have meant the end of the licence. Prostitutes certainly worked in Upper Canada, and their trade certainly involved liquor, but their primary place of business seems to have been the houses of ill fame (brothels) that purveyed free liquor or sold it illegally.

The absence of prostitution from the taverns is both expected and unexpected. The strong presumption toward good order that was encoded in the licensing system, and in tavern-goers' and tavern-keepers' own preferences, meant that prostitution, which is disorderly by definition, would be unwelcome and resisted in many of these public spaces. And what we now know of female tavern-keepers, their daughters, and their helps certainly indicates that the taverns in the colony were likewise governed by a presumption of feminine respectability, by the presumption that women in the tavern trade were not in the sex trade. But I will stereotype male sexuality to make a point: Surely sex must have been available in some of the taverns that catered to sailors and soldiers and other men alone and on the move? Judith Fingard's work on Halifax shows that this was the case in the taverns down by the docks; clearly we need a history of colonial prostitution in order to situate discussions such as this in a firmer historiographical context.

The evidence does reveal that illicit sexual activity, which might have been prostitution, took place in one tavern in Upper Canada. Adonijah Edwards held a licence near Kingston in 1833. His house was neither reputable nor orderly, nor was it suffered in its community for long. The Edwards family got into a great deal of trouble with the local magistrates when a neighbour complained about rowdiness and the behaviour of the patrons. Very quickly, the character of the women frequenting the place became a matter of grave concern to the justices. They took testimony from various men. One said, "He can't say ye women are bad – from what he saw [he] did not consider them good." Another could not "say the character of the women." F.W. Meyer had "danced with some of them"; Thomas Rutherfield thought them "loose characters." J. Woolstencraft and John Baker crystallized the magistrates' suspicions when they plainly stated that there were "women of bad fame" and "women of ill fame" who patronized Edwards'. Though he was not convicted of keeping a disorderly house, Edwards later lost his licence. Colonists and the local authorities suspected this tavern of supporting illegitimate sexual behaviour, if not prostitution. They shut it down.[58]

In contrast, taverns housed expressions of socially legitimated sexual activity. At Lawson's in 1834, for example, "a new married couple" behaved with such warmth in the sitting room that another patron "felt [he] was decidedly *de trop* and in danger of combustion." When lawyer Larratt Smith married Eliza Thom in 1845, they spent their wedding night at Hastwell's substantial country tavern on the way to Kingston. Its architectural arrangements probably allowed for the kind of privacy they were seeking. And it was not only newlyweds that sought this type of privacy. In the late 1840s Christina Grant Keefer spent a night with her husband, Jacob, who was a school inspector, at Press' Hotel in St. Catharines. Her husband reminisced in his diary that they "had a very good supper, had a good bedroom with 2 single beds, only used one of them."[59]

Despite its inherent respectability in all senses, and its recognized centrality, women's domestic work did not make tavern space entirely their own.[60] In tavern households, as elsewhere, women lived with the immutable fact of male property rights and legal authority and the insidious, sometimes hurtful, ways these translated into cultural assumptions and practices of male precedence. Thus, the nasty side of gendered power relations certainly played out in tavern households. A traveller tells us that Kingston hotel keeper Segro Carmino assaulted his wife, "having taken it into his head to be jealous" of her. He then rang the dinner bell until "a goodly assemblage of his boarders" gathered, "accused some of them, and abused others," "dealt his daughter a blow with a trayful of tea-cups," and "laid waste to the breakfast table." Later, "his wife and daughter endeavoured to restore the house to order, and excited our sympathy as they went sobbing about the house."[61] Though crucial to their household's trade, the domestic labour of the Carmino women failed to secure them any position of authority within it.

Similarly, local young women hired as domestic helps by tavern-keepers proved as vulnerable to sexual exploitation as those in other households. For example, in 1853 at Garrisons' tavern near Kingston, Mary Jane Burnett, "not quite 15," was the "only servant girl" to the tavern and household of five children. In his wife's absence, Garrison went to Burnett's room after she was asleep and "went into her bed – undressed." She "was frightened – tried to make him go away – he had connection with" her "that night and afterwards." She had a baby as a result and her father brought suit for seduction. No defence was attempted. The judge, taking note that Burnett "appears very respectable" and "deeply sensible of ... disgrace," awarded an immense £400 settlement. Burnett's domestic work placed her in the way of enormous harm, and as the amount for damages shows, its tavern location did nothing to call her feminine respectability into question.[62]

On the whole, taverns were no more likely to be sites of sexual danger for women than were their own houses, rural roadways, or the fields and bushes where they picked berries. Indeed, taverns may have been less so, given their inherent publicness. Existing records, whether they are newspaper stories, court documents, or petitions for mercy after a guilty verdict, document 104 reported sexual assaults in the colony between 1791 and 1850. These numbers are changing with current research underway, and must, like today's statistics, massively underestimate the actual incidence of sexual assault. Still, of these known cases, only four occurred in taverns. Eleven-year-old Margaret Kearney stopped at a tavern with her father, survived a sexual attack, and escaped rape when her father heard enough from the bar to know to run and rescue his daughter in the next room. Then, as now, more women survived sexual assaults in their homes than in public places. Fourteen-year-old Sarah O'Meary was one. She was about her daily domestic work at Gray's tavern (the home where she lived and laboured) in 1845 when a soldier raped her in the barn. Feminist scholars have argued that women were (and are) particularly vulnerable to sexualized insult and sexual assault when they moved beyond the boundaries that circumscribed legitimate female space. Such a breach could be metaphorical (as in challenging male authority at home or elsewhere) or literal (as in entering physical, most often public, spaces defined as male). Although, as historian Karen Dubinsky discusses, the *fear* of rape in public space, which today exerts such a powerful influence on female autonomy, may be a more recent phenomenon, the spatial analysis may explain the low incidence of known attacks in colonial taverns.

Taverns were legitimate female space. Without arguing that the occupation of legitimate space was any guarantee of personal security (or that it would be a just guarantee if so), colonial women had no reason to identify the taverns as sites of specific danger. Consequently, ladies, working women, female tavern-keepers, and other domestic labourers, armoured with the accoutrements of their different versions of respectability in the era of separate spheres, engaged in a variety of public activities within tavern walls.[63]

The material setting provided by all but the meanest backwoods taverns enabled female tavern-going through the provision of lady-specific spaces, entrances, and parlours and through the observation of cultural rituals (like wives and husbands going to taverns together) that both entitled women's patronage and contained it. Whether women retreated to female-only zones or claimed them forthrightly over privately expressed male objections (as at the Niagara Falls hotels), these tavern spaces gave women the ability to live out gendered rituals of belonging within them, much as the male bourgeois lived out theirs in tavern space. Drinking rituals, including women treating with each other, expressed common knowledge of the power of drink to forge and maintain social bonds, and it testified to women's continued willingness to engage, as they could, in the public culture of drink as it cohered in the colonial taverns. The extraordinary prevalence of women as tavern-keepers in the minor houses (the massive majority of taverns in the colony) meant that sometimes female travellers and patrons found truly kind and responsive treatment within, especially for their gender-specific needs. If today a hot whiskey punch is not the first thing handed to a cold, tired, pregnant, and socially privileged woman, in the era of separate spheres it nonetheless represented a female-centred service and a female-centred sense of right in the tavern's public space. All of this challenges the received historiography of drink, taverns, and women by developing an alternative set of narratives. The evidence of female relationships with the colonial taverns makes women (ladies included) subjects rather than objects in public space, and it makes them participants in everyday public life within the social and cultural parameters that are always beyond individual control.

Afterword

When Eileen O'Malley "allowed herself to be guided over the threshold" of the Seaman's Inn at Port Hope by her brother, Liam, "into a riot of male dancing," she entered a tavern world created by Canadian novelist Jane Urquhart. It is fiction, well spun, and shows the ability of the literary imagination to make a place and time so real that, were they able to read it, the tavern-goers and tavern-keepers in this book would find themselves nodding along in recognition. They would recognize the distance drawn between "Port Hope's brick hotels with dining rooms and shining cutlery" and the Seaman's down at the harbour, with its bare pine floors, "lake fish and potatoes" for dinner, and porous walls and ceilings that let the sounds from the barroom below into the bedrooms above. They would recognize the quiet of the mornings and the swell of noise and activity as afternoons drew into late nights of dance and politics, and they would recognize the charisma and special status that the other men accorded to Aidan Lanighan because of his skills as a dancer and the depth of his commitments. They would recognize the impulse of the tavern-keepers to give the O'Malleys the room adjoining the upstairs veranda, "because of the lady." They would recognize Eileen first sitting "primly on a high wooden stool near her brother" in the barroom, as if to assert her respectability, but then, as she warmed to the place and became familiar within it, embroidering in the bar with the room "full of Irish lake sailors" "swimming in the currents of conversation that flowed among the men." Eileen fell in love with Aidan and danced with him among the sailors and the "grinning" tavern-keepers as her brother's "shocked face slid by." And, like Sophia Beman in early York, under her father's watchful eye, Eileen found it difficult to escape the male vigilance of her brother in the tavern long enough to meet with her lover. But the couple found moments of secluded space in a nighttime hallway and up in the attic. A storyteller by trade, in *Away* Urquhart crafts a tavern world uniquely consonant with the themes in this book, and the novel is as real in its feel as those in the myriad stories told by colonial tavern-goers and tavern-keepers in their own time.[1]

Through stories, tavern-goers and tavern-keepers created an enduring set of narratives about colonial public houses as sites of everyday public life. They spoke of the possibilities for realizing public life that the setting enabled, in material and interpersonal ways, and of the parameters that limited its expression, especially for some. They did not tell one story, and they did not agree among themselves about what was most important. They tell us that colonists, as much as the First Nations peoples whom they displaced, found reason to think about, debate, and fight over the society and culture that was emerging in the colony and the forms in which it might publicly cohere.

Tavern stories resonate with three important reinterpretations of colonial Canadian tavern history. They provide, first, an alternative history of the taverns, a new tavern history for Canada, one that links to a growing literature on public drinking houses in other places and times. Taverns emerge as often inviting and overwhelmingly orderly material settings that supported public life in many guises and affirmed its value in colonial society and culture. In this new history, taverns stand as public space, as spaces that posed no incipient or inevitable threats to democracy, to ideals of development and progress, or even to families and women themselves. Tavern stories provide, then, an alternative history of women and gender relations. They put women and households at the forefront of tavern worlds, albeit in ways that differed in the early settlement period and the era of separate spheres. Tavern stories challenge the all too comfortable notion that pervades the historiography: that male precedence equated with female absence from public space, and that male precedence somehow ruled out the belonging of men and women alike in everyday public life. Tavern stories tell us that gender in public space was more complicated than this and that it changed between the early and mid-nineteenth century, especially for ladies. Tavern stories ask us to develop an analytic chronology that is attentive to the terms that governed female inclusion in and differential access to public life. They also underline women's economic roles and the enormous extent to which the tavern trade, and the public services and sociability it supported, literally depended on women's domestic labour for its success. Tavern stories provide, finally, an alternative history of colonial public space. In mixed company, the colony's different peoples negotiated, from unequal footings, the ways in which they belonged, or wanted to belong, to the public itself. That the outcomes of these negotiations were not always predictable attests to the willingness of some, at different times or places, to suspend the apparent certainties of race, class, and gender. This suggests the concurrent need to historically reflect on the wider meanings of such incertitude and flux in the public encounters of everyday life in spaces beyond taverns.

As places where material culture defined an orderly and balanced use of space, the material history of the tavern is about such issues of integration and separation. Decisions about building design, furniture placement, the accoutrements of the parlour, and the provisioning of beds, bars, and larders were decisions about the deployment and use of space. In the symmetry of the Georgian taverns, in their careful organization of façade and interior, was a representation of the ideal patterning of behaviour that ought to take place within them. Ideally, public life ought to pattern itself in similar equilibrium. The hundreds of minor houses that almost always provided satisfactory and sometimes excellent standards of accommodation, as well as the larger, better-endowed principal taverns and hotels, inherited and realized to varying degrees the primary legacy of Georgian design – balance and equilibrium. Hence the shocking awfulness of the frontier taverns from patrons' perspectives. In the promiscuity of their spatial arrangements, and in the necessary promiscuity of the company kept within, nobody could find room – literally or figuratively – to represent their desired forms of public life. When colonists and travellers complained about all that backwoods taverns were not – about the absence of a defined sense of space and the egregious disappointments they experienced – they were simply expressing common knowledge and common expectations about what a colonial tavern should be.

By peopling tavern space with household members, neighbours, and diverse patrons, Ely Playter's early York journal made the tavern visible as a site that blended public life and household life, a site where each was shaped by the close, daily proximity of the other. Playter's taverns gave room to throngs in the bar. They provided room apart for those who either desired it or were shunted into it. They housed domesticity. And they granted relatively privileged women (at times, together with gentlemen) a conditional scope to craft a genteel culture of polite sociability, enacted both in opposition to and at the mercy of the culture of the bar. This sometimes off-kilter balancing of women and men, household space and public space, the self-consciously polite and the unselfconscious throng, defined the early taverns, and paradoxically illustrates both the power that accrued to those who possessed seemingly undisputed social precedence (men, for example) and the willingness of others to contest and subvert the cultural control that those with power held over their lives (women who engaged in genteel sociability beside barrooms, for example).

Despite the presence of the household, taverns were public spaces, defined as such by their round-the-clock openness to callers intent on accessing essential services and those bent on drink and sociability from dawn to dusk. The colonial taverns must be read as public space in the first instance because they facilitated changing modes of travel and transport, shifting forms of economic exchange, and the everyday kinds of negotiation and conversation that lent coherence to political and community life. Despite a clear chronology of waning significance in some areas (such as long-distance travel) at mid-century, taverns still functioned as we, today, think good public space should – as spaces that connected colonists to each other and to the world around them.

The tavern was a particular public space, <u>structured by the rituals of drink</u> <u>and sociability that represented social bonds,</u> that made promises of inclusion and belonging. That these promises were betrayed in practice for some (like blacks, Natives, and women in the era of separate spheres) much of the time, and for almost all at least some of the time (like the American hotel keeper whose pro-British neighbours trashed his bar on the 4th of July) is by now a familiar subtext to the tavern tales. Yet, weighing against such failures are the positive assertions of distinctive identities made in tavern spaces, by ladies in the ladies' parlour or on the hotel balcony, by working women treating together at a tavern in industrializing Toronto, by blacks claiming public membership as fellow Englishmen under the renowned British Constitution, or, even, by middle-class men self-consciously enacting a gentlemanly identity with the support of the substantial houses but under no illusions about their relative power in numbers compared to the more "disreputable" types from whom they sought distance. As tavern-goers and -keepers articulated their understandings of place, membership, and the desirability of social heterogeneity itself, their differing vantage points and perspectives were affected by their possession of white privilege, or not, of male privilege, or not, and of class, or cultural, privilege, or not. Yet they rarely did so in predictable ways. In mixed company, tavern-goers and -keepers both enacted and contested the ranking hierarchies of their colonial society, recognized their power, and found moments to subvert it, if only fleetingly, in practice.

Sometimes by design, more often by circumstance or accident, instances of "heterogenous assemblage" – as Benjamin Lundy put it in Brantford in 1832 – genuinely transpired in tavern space. These mixed companies might even have displaced the casual and callous exclusions more routinely practised. But, unlike today, heterogeneity was rarely articulated as a social ideal, as a positive public good, as the best desired function of public space. An early exception here was the goal of integration voiced by some anti-racism activists. This absence of heterogeneity as an ideal of a mixed society distances "us" from "them," and makes "them" different. This suggests that, as the ideal public in Canada has changed before, it can, and will, change again, in ways that redefine terms of access, inclusion, and membership. One of the most compelling messages in tavern history is that the informal, everyday, public life of a mixed society has a history, one that is visible when differently identified peoples encounter each other in public space and reflect from their different perspectives on the meanings and feelings of such encounters.

All tavern stories in the colonial society of Upper Canada are about the complexities of public life and issues of public belonging. When tavern-keepers and tavern-goers told their tales of inclusion or exclusion, or expressed their desires for distance, they told us about issues that still matter. Surely one of modern scholarship's greatest insights is that constructions such as class, race, and gender do not explain everything. For all their force in setting the parameters of social experience, small zones of exchange and interaction (where ambiguity was more evident than determinacy) resided beneath them. These "categories" of identity were, and are, important, and noting the difference they made is important. Still, it is how people responded to their categorization, how they felt or thought about it, how it did or did not fit the situation at hand, and what they did in response that matters. Nowhere was this process more apparent than in the taverns of early Canada. There, difference met difference. The encounter and the negotiation it entailed became defining features of public life. When frequenting the bar, dining at the public table, taking a night's lodging, or simply looking for a newspaper, companions and travellers could be prejudiced and discriminatory on any number of grounds. At the same time, they struggled to learn the ways of tolerance in everyday life.

Notes

Preface
1 Arthur Conan Doyle, "The Copper Beeches," *Sherlock Holmes: The Complete Short Stories* (London: John Murray, 1953), 276.

Introduction
1 Jacob Lindley, "Jacob Lindley's Account of an Expedition to Detroit, 1793," *Historical Collections: Michigan Pioneer and Historical Society* 17 (1892): 603 [Shawnee]; William Renwick Riddell, *Michigan under British Rule: Law and Law Courts, 1760-1796* (Lansing, MI: Michigan Historical Commission, 1926), 345 [labourers]; United Church Archives, William Case Journal, 20 June 1805 [dancing]; Alexander Fraser, ed., "Minutes of the Court of General Quarter Sessions of the Peace for the Home District, 13 March 1800 to 28 December 1811," *Twenty-First Report of the Department of Public Records and Archives of Ontario, 1932* (Toronto: Herbert H. Ball, 1933), 128 [licence]; University of Toronto, Thomas Fischer Rare Book Room, Charles Fothergill Collection, Fothergill, "A Few Notes Made on a Journey from Montreal through the Province of Upper Canada in February 1817," 18 [brandy]; *Kingston Chronicle*, 14 May 1816 [Sanford]; Library and Archives Canada (LAC), RG 5 A1, Upper Canada Sundries Civil and Provincial Secretary's correspondence, Upper Canada and Canada West, volume 49, petition of Patrick Nolan, Township of Beckwith, 23 September 1820, p. 24428; *Canadian Emigrant* [Sandwich], 26 July 1834 [Schaeffer's]; Archives of Ontario (AO), Prince (Col.), John, Papers, Diaries, Hiram Walker Historical Museum Collection, 8 September 1837; Lambton County Archives (LCA), Henry John Jones diary, 30 January 1843 [Armour]; AO, Municipal Records, Township of Uxbridge, Council Minutes, 1850-80, Report of the Inspectors of Houses of Public Entertainment, 1852.
2 AO, RG 22-390, 20-3, Supreme Court of Ontario (SCO), Judges' Benchbooks, Robinson, Western/London Districts, *Rex v. John Ward* (1830).
3 The situation differed from England, for example, where each term had a specific legal meaning. See Peter Clark, *The English Alehouse: A Social History, 1200-1830* (London: Longman, 1983), 6, 12, 14; *Stratford Beacon and Perth County Intelligencer*, 2 March 1855 [ad].
4 *Rex v. John Ward* (1830). There were also licensed houses of entertainment that provided food and accommodation but could not sell liquor (some included it in the price of a meal): Julia Roberts, "Taverns and Tavern-goers in Upper Canada, the 1790s to the 1850s" (PhD diss., University of Toronto, 1999), 74-77; William Conway Keele, *A Brief View of the Township Laws Up To the Present Time: With a Treatise on the Law and Office of Constable, the Law Relative to Landlord and Tenant, Distress for Rent, Innkeepers &c.* (Toronto: W.J. Coates, 1835), 47 [quote]; "Regulations for Innkeepers, 1818, District of Newcastle," reproduced in *The Valley of the Trent*, Edwin C. Guillet (Toronto: Champlain Society, 1957), 293 [travellers]; AO, SCO, RG 22-390, 9-5, Macaulay, Home District, *Q. v. Bartholomew Ralph* (1848) ["up early"].
5 Peter Thompson, *Rum Punch and Revolution: Taverngoing and Public Life in Eighteenth-Century Philadelphia*, Early American Studies (Philadelphia: University of Pennsylvania Press, 1999);

David Conroy, *In Public Houses: Drink and the Revolution of Authority in Colonial Massachusetts* (Chapel Hill: University of North Carolina Press for Institute of Early American History and Culture, 1995); Daniel B. Thorpe, "Doing Business in the Backcountry: Retail Trade in Colonial Rowan County, North Carolina," *William and Mary Quarterly*, 3rd ser., 48, 3 (1991): 387-408, and "Taverns and Tavern Culture on the Southern Colonial Frontier: Rowan County, North Carolina, 1753-1776," *Journal of Southern History* 62, 4 (1996): 661-87.

On the public houses of Europe, see Clark, *The English Alehouse*; Thomas Brennan, *Public Drinking and Popular Culture in Eighteenth-Century Paris* (Princeton, NJ: Princeton University Press, 1988); W. Scott Haine, *The World of the Paris Café: Sociability among the French Working Class, 1789-1914* (Baltimore, MD: Johns Hopkins University Press, 1999); B. Ann Tlusty, *Bacchus and Civic Order: The Culture of Drink in Early Modern Germany* (Charlottesville: University Press of Virginia, 2001); Beat Kümin and B. Ann Tlusty, eds., *World of the Tavern: Public Houses in Early Modern Europe* (Aldershot, UK: Ashgate Publishing, 2002); Adam Smyth, ed., *A Pleasing Sinne: Drink and Conviviality in Seventeenth-Century England* (New York: Boydell and Brewer, 2004). For the medieval period, see Barbara A. Hanawalt, *"Of Good and Ill Repute": Gender and Social Control in Medieval England* (New York: Oxford University Press, 1998).

For recent Canadian studies, see Craig Heron, *Booze: A Distilled History* (Toronto: Between the Lines, 2003), and "The Boys and Their Booze: Masculinities and Public Drinking in Working-Class Hamilton, 1890-1946," *Canadian Historical Review* 86, 3 (September 2005): 411-52.

6 Robertson Davies, "Books: Tales of Our Wayside Inns," *Saturday Night*, 4 January 1958: 22-23; Edwin C. Guillet, *Pioneer Inns and Taverns* (Toronto: Edwin C. Guillet, 1954-62). See also Margaret McBurney and Mary Byers, *Tavern in the Town: Early Inns and Taverns of Ontario* (Toronto: University of Toronto Press, 1987).

7 William Lyon Mackenzie, *Sketches of Canada and the United States* (London: E. Wilson, 1833), 89.

8 Jeffrey L. McNairn, *The Capacity to Judge: Public Opinion and Deliberative Democracy in Upper Canada, 1791-1854* (Toronto: University of Toronto Press, 2000); Bonnie Huskins, "The Ceremonial Space of Women: Public Processions in Victorian Saint John and Halifax," in *Separate Spheres: Women's Worlds in the Nineteenth-Century Maritimes*, ed. Janet Guildford and Suzanne Morton (Fredericton, NB: Acadiensis Press, 1994), 145-60; David A. Sutherland, "Race Relations in Halifax, Nova Scotia, during the Mid-Victorian Quest for Reform," *Journal of the Canadian Historical Association*, new series, 7: 35-54, especially 50-51.

9 Peter DeLottinville, "Joe Beef of Montreal: Working-Class Culture and the Tavern, 1869-1889," *Labour/Le Travail* 8/9 (Autumn 1981/Spring 1982): 9-40; Robert A. Campbell, *Sit Down and Drink Your Beer: Regulating Vancouver's Beer Parlours, 1925-1954* (Toronto: University of Toronto Press, 2001); Heron, *Booze*, 17-30. On temperance, see F. Laurie Barron, "Alcoholism, Indians, and the Anti-Drink Cause in the Protestant Indian Missions of Upper Canada, 1822-1850," in *As Long as the Sun Shines and the Water Flows: A Reader in Canadian Native Studies*, ed. Ian A.L. Getty and Antoine Lussier (Vancouver: UBC Press, 1983), 191-202; Sharon Ann Cook, *"Through Sunshine and Shadow": The Woman's Christian Temperance Union, Evangelicalism, and Reform in Ontario, 1874-1930* (Montreal and Kingston: McGill-Queen's University Press, 1995); Graeme Decarie, "The Prohibition Movement in Ontario, 1894-1916" (PhD diss., Queen's University, 1972) and his review of *Booze: A Distilled History*, by Craig Heron, *Canadian Historical Review* 86, 1 (2005): 136-38; M.A. Garland and J.J. Talman, "Pioneer Drinking Habits and the Rise of Temperance Agitation in Upper Canada Prior to 1840," *Ontario Historical Society Papers and Records* 27 (1931): 341-62; Gerald Hallowell, *Prohibition in Ontario, 1919-1923* (Ottawa: Ontario Historical Society, 1972); Glenn Lockwood, "Temperance in Upper Canada as Ethnic Subterfuge," in *Drink in Canada: Historical Essays*, ed. Cheryl Krasnick-Warsh (Montreal and Kingston: McGill-Queen's University Press, 1993), 43-91; Jan Noel, *Canada Dry: Temperance Crusades before Confederation* (Toronto: University of Toronto Press, 1995).

10 See note 8 and Douglas McCalla, *Planting the Province: The Economic History of Upper Canada, 1784-1870*, Ontario Historical Studies Series (Toronto: University of Toronto Press, 1993); Bruce S. Elliott, "Irish Migrants in the Canadas: A New Approach," McGill-Queen's Studies in Ethnic History 1 (Montreal and Kingston/Belfast: McGill-Queen's University

Press/Belfast Institute of Irish Studies, 1987); David Gagan, *Hopeful Travellers: Families, Land, and Social Change in Mid-Victorian Peel County, Canada West,* Ontario Historical Studies Series (Toronto: University of Toronto Press, 1981); Elizabeth Jane Errington, *Wives and Mothers, Schoolmistresses and Scullery Maids: Working Women in Upper Canada, 1790-1840* (Montreal and Kingston: McGill-Queen's University Press, 1995); Cecilia Morgan, *Public Men and Virtuous Women: The Gendered Languages of Religion and Politics, 1791-1850,* Studies in Gender and History (Toronto: University of Toronto Press, 1996); Lynne Marks "No Double Standard? Leisure, Sex, and Sin in Upper Canadian Church Discipline Records, 1800-1860," in *Gendered Pasts: Historical Essays in Femininity and Masculinity in Canada,* ed. Kathryn McPherson, Cecilia Morgan, and Nancy M. Forestall (Toronto: Oxford University Press, 1999), 48-64; Paul Craven, ed., *Labouring Lives: Work and Workers in Nineteenth-Century Ontario,* Ontario Historical Studies Series (Toronto: University of Toronto Press, 1995).

11 Noel, *Canada Dry,* 217, 289; AO, [Ely] Playter diary, 22 February 1802; Roberts, "Taverns and Tavern-goers," 74-77.

12 AO, RG 22-113, Court of General Quarter Sessions of the Peace, tavern- and shop-licensing records, Essex County, Windsor, 25 April 1838, p. 5478.

13 This brief sketch of Upper Canada relies on McCalla's *Planting the Province* for population figures and the story of economic development: see especially 28, 84-85, 220; see also Michael Wayne, "The Black Population of Canada West on the Eve of the American Civil War: A Reassessment Based on the Manuscript Census of 1861," *Histoire sociale/Social History* 28, 56 (1995): 465-85; for tavern numbers, see Chapter 3 of this volume.

14 Fothergill, "A Few Notes Made on a Journey from Montreal through the Province of Upper Canada in 1817," p. 41.

Chapter 1: Architecture, Design, and Material Settings

1 Donaldson's army rank indicates plebeian origins. Archives of Ontario (AO), RG 22-311, Surrogate Court Records, Estate Files, Essex County, 1801, file 20, James Donaldson; Milo M. Quaife, ed., *The John Askin Papers,* Burton Historical Collection (Detroit: Detroit Library Commission, 1928), 2:291 [Coates' tavern]; "Return of Stores," *Pioneer Collections,* 2nd ed., vol. 10 (Lansing: Pioneer Society of the State of Michigan, 1908), 459 [rank, 1781]; "Discharged Rangers and Loyalists," *Michigan Historical Collections* 24 (1895): 177 [rank and occupation, 1791].

2 AO, RG 22-311 [will]; Quaife, ed., *John Askin Papers,* 598-602 [Askwith's bill].

3 Hugh Morrison, *Early American Architecture: From the First Colonial Settlements to the National Period* (New York: Oxford University Press, 1952), 273-74, 278-93.

4 Fiske Kimball, *American Architecture* (1928; repr., New York: AMS Press, 1970), 47.

5 For petitions to keep government houses, see, for example, Library and Archives Canada (LAC), RG 5 A1, Upper Canada Sundries, Civil Secretary's correspondence, Upper Canada and Canada West, volume 11, memorial of James Odell Roch, 26 May 1810, p. 4880; RG 1 E3, Executive Council Office of the Province of Upper Canada fonds, volume 12, petition of George Cutter, 16 May 1815, pp. 240-41.

6 Mary Quayle Innis, ed., *Mrs. Simcoe's Diary; with Illustrations from the Original Manuscript* (Toronto: Macmillan, 1965), 182. Interestingly, Ross' sketch bears little resemblance to those extant under the same title at the Archives of Ontario.

7 Archives of Ontario (AO), [Ely] Playter diary, 30 August 1805 (hereafter EP); *Dictionary of Canadian Biography,* vol. 5, s.v. "Weekes, William," by C.H. Patterson.

8 Innis, *Mrs. Simcoe's Diary,* 182.

9 Peter Clark, *The English Alehouse: A Social History, 1200-1830* (London: Longman, 1983), 286; David Conroy, *In Public Houses: Drink and the Revolution of Authority in Colonial Massachusetts* (Chapel Hill: University of North Carolina Press for the Institute of Early American History and Culture, 1995), 89-95; Peter Thompson, *Rum Punch and Revolution: Taverngoing and Public Life in Eighteenth-Century Philadelphia,* Early American Studies (Philadelphia: University of Pennsylvania Press, 1999), 106-10.

10 Julia Roberts, "Taverns and Tavern-goers in Upper Canada, the 1790s to the 1850s" (PhD diss., University of Toronto, 1999), 61-66.

11 *Upper Canada Gazette,* 7 March 1801; 4 December 1802.

12 EP, 18 June 1802 and 1 August 1802 and 24 March 1803 [deals, arbitration]; *Upper Canada Gazette,* 14 March 1801 and 27 November 1802 and 4 December 1802 [inquest, ads].

13 The plan itself is undated. The notation "1847" appears on the back, along with another drawing, to which the date may well refer. According to architectural historian Anthony Adamson, the plan was found among other of Howard's papers dating 1835-45. See Upper Canada Village Archives, Anthony Adamson to Jeanne Minhinnick and Peter Stokes, Ontario – St. Lawrence Development Commission, Morrisburg, ON, 12 October 1960. See also *Dictionary of Canadian Biography,* vol. 11, s.v. "Howard, John George," by Edith G. Firth. The Baldwin Room, Toronto Public Library, Toronto Reference Library, holds a large collection of John Howard's later work.

14 Toronto Public Library, Toronto Reference Library, Baldwin Room (BR), Powell Papers, 1783-1830, Circuit Papers, L16 B85, Fredricksburgh, 25 November 1805, loose leaf insert at p. 66.

15 Catherine Parr Traill, *The Backwoods of Canada: Being Letters from the Wife of an Emigrant Officer, Illustrative of the Domestic Economy of British America* (London: M.A. Natali, 1849), 72-73.

16 Samuel Strickland, *Twenty-Seven Years in Canada West: Or, The Experiences of an Early Settler,* ed. Agnes Strickland (London: Richard Bentley, 1853), 56; *William Pope's Journal: March 28, 1834-March 11, 1835,* ed. M.A. Garland, *Western Ontario History Nuggets* 16, pt. 2 (London, ON: Lawson Memorial Library, University of Western Ontario, 1952), 39; Edward Allen Talbot, *Five Years' Residence in the Canadas: Including a Tour Through Part of the United States of America In the Year 1823* (London: Longman, Hurst, Rees, Orme, Brown and Green, 1824), 2:262-67.

17 Clark, *The English Alehouse,* 195-99; Conroy, *In Public Houses,* 89-95; Thompson, *Rum Punch and Revolution,* 106-10.

18 Charles B. Fergusson, ed., *Diary of Simeon Perkins, 1797-1803,* Publications of the Champlain Society (Toronto: Champlain Society, 1967), 14, 279, 330, 331-33, 347-48, 351, 511 [eastern taverns]; Jean M. Murray, ed., *Newfoundland Journal of Aaron Thomas, Able Seaman in HMS Boston* (Don Mills, ON: Longmans Canada, 1968), 110 [Ferryland].

19 As late as 1863, for example, in the backwoods north of the Trent Lakes, "as many as sixty people in a single night" apparently crowded into McCauley's tavern, a one and a half storey log cabin. See Edwin C. Guillet, *Pioneer Inns and Taverns,* vol. 4, *Continuing the Detailed Coverage of Ontario with a Concluding Estimate of the Position of the Innkeeper in Community Life* (Toronto: Edwin Guillet, 1954-62), 101. Similarly, in the 1890s, on the US end of the Rocky Mountains, very crude structures of canvas, posts, and log foundations served as the first taverns in new mining districts: see Elliot West, *The Saloon on the Rocky Mountain Mining Frontier* (Lincoln: University of Nebraska Press, 1979), 30-38.

20 Adam Fergusson, *Practical Notes Made During a Tour In Canada and a Portion of the United States in 1831: Second Edition to Which Are Now Added Notes Made During a Second Visit to Canada in 1833* (Edinburgh: William Blackwood, 1834), 90.

21 Patrick Shirreff, *A Tour Through North America: Together with a Comprehensive View of the Canadas and the United States as Adapted for Agricultural Emigration* (Edinburgh: Oliver and Boyd, 1835), 179.

22 John Howison, *Sketches of Upper Canada: Domestic, Local and Characteristic to which are added Practical Details for the Information of Emigrants of Every Class; and some Recollections of the United States of America* (Edinburgh: Oliver and Boyd, 1821), 119.

23 William "Tiger" Dunlop, *Statistical Sketches of Upper Canada: For the Use of Emigrants,* 2nd ed. (London: John Murray, 1832): 55-57.

24 Clark, *The English Alehouse,* 6, 12, 14; Richard L. Bushman, *The Refinement of America: Persons, Houses, Cities* (New York: Alfred A. Knopf, 1992), 162-64.

25 A.D.P. Van Buren, "Pioneer Annals," *Pioneer Collections: Report of the Pioneer Society of the State of Michigan* 5 (1884): 241 [quote]; Upper Canada Village Archives, Thomas Robinson account book, 1843-58, supper for William Ambrose, September 1844, p. 46; Pope, Journal, pt. 2, 39, 46, pt. 3, 62; Thomas Need, *Six Years in the Bush: Or, Extracts from the Journal of a Settler in Upper Canada, 1832-1838* (London: Simpkin, Marshall, 1838), 15-16; George Head, *Forest Scenes and Incidents in the Wilds of North America: Being a Diary of a Winter's Route from*

Halifax to the Canadas during Four Month's Residence in the Woods on the Borders of Lakes Huron and Simcoe (London: John Murray, 1829), 277; Basil Hall, *Travels in North America in the Years 1827 and 1828* (Philadelphia: Carey, Lea and Carey 1829), 1:126-27. See also Jeanne Hughes, "Inns and Taverns," in *Consuming Passions: Eating and Drinking Traditions in Ontario*, papers presented at the 101st Annual Conference of the Ontario Historical Society, May 1989, Ottawa, Ontario (Willowdale, ON: Ontario Historical Society, 1989), 93-112.

26   University of Toronto, Thomas Fischer Rare Book Room, Charles Fothergill Collection, Fothergill, "A Few Notes Made on a Journey from Montreal through the Province of Upper Canada in February 1817," p. 54 [plums]; Howison, *Sketches of Upper Canada*, 165 [venison]; Strickland, *Twenty-Seven Years in Canada West*, 1:66 [ducks and bass]; Fergusson, *Practical Notes Made During a Tour*, 125-26 [trout]; Lambton County Archives (LCA), Henry (Harry) John Jones diary, 1831-83 (hereafter HJ), 20 November 1834 [turkey] and 8 February 1843 and 22 May 1856 [cooking game]; Shirreff, *A Tour Through North America*, 177, 189 [stew and cooking game].

27   James Alexander, *L'Acadie: Or, Seven Years' Explorations in British America* (London: Henry Colburn, 1849), 1:187-88 [privacy]; John Bigsby, *The Shoe and Canoe: Or, Pictures of Travel in the Canadas Illustrative of their Scenery and Colonial Life; With Facts and Opinions on Emigration, State Policy and Other Points of Public Interest* (London: Chapman and Hall, 1850) 2:72 [privacy]; Talbot, *Five Years' Residence*, 2:263 [linsy-woolsy]; Howison, *Sketches of Upper Canada*, 209 [French houses]; AO, RG 22-390, 47-5, Supreme Court of Ontario (SCO), Judges' Benchbooks, Draper, Home District, *Q. v. Alfred Tomlinson et al.* (1854) [Clyde Inn].

28   William Chambers, *Things As They Are in America* (London and Edinburgh: William and Robert Chambers, 1854), 123-25.

29   BR, Abner Miles account book, 1 September 1795-15 December 1796, accounts of a general store and tavern, 19 March 1796; LAC, R3747-0-8-E, James Philips fonds, Daybook of James Philips, 1828-30, pp. 25 and 30; Thomas Robinson account book, p. 46.

30   On wages, see Douglas McCalla, *Planting the Province: The Economic History of Upper Canada, 1784-1870*, Ontario Historical Studies Series (Toronto: University of Toronto Press, 1993), 114-15; Susanna Moodie, *Roughing It in the Bush, Or Life in Canada* (London: Richard Bentley, 1852), 252-53; Pope, Journal, *Western Ontario History Nuggets*, pt. 2, 32 [men and couples]. On charges, see, for example, A.W.H. Rose, *Canada in 1849: Pictures of Canadian Life, Or, The Emigrant Churchman, by a Pioneer of the Wilderness* (London: Richard Bentley, 1850), 1:62 [Toronto charges]; Alexander, *L'Acadie*, 148 [boarder's rates]. Alexander may have his conversion wrong here – the amounts he gives indicate York currency, not British sterling.

31   For example, James Philips charged Artemus Warren only 2s. 3d. for "2 glasses of whiskey and 2 dinners for himself & boy." This may also indicate a lesser charge for the boy's (probably smaller) meal. Daybook of James Philips, 26 September 1829.

32   This and the following five paragraphs draw exclusively on the following estate inventories: AO, RG 22-311, Surrogate Court Records, Estate Files, Essex County, 1832, file 356, John Casavan; AO, RG 22-311, Surrogate Court Records, Estate Files, Essex County, 1842, file 569, Cecilia Dauphin; AO, RG 22-311, Surrogate Court Records, Estate Files, Essex County, 1842, file 574, Elias Dauphin; AO, RG 22-311, Surrogate Court Records, Estate Files, Essex County, 1844, file 617, Gregoire LeDuc; AO, RG 22-311, Surrogate Court Records, Estate Files, Essex County, 1846, file 590, Claude Gouin; AO, RG 22-311, Surrogate Court Records, Estate Files, Essex County, 1846, file 642, William Hall [also spelled Hale]; AO, RG 22-311, Surrogate Court Records, Estate Files, Essex County, 1848, file 696, Benjamin Cheeseman; AO, RG 22-155, Court of Probate, Estate Files, St. Thomas, 5 May 1847, John Wilson, Innkeeper; AO, RG 22-155, Court of Probate, Estate Files, Pickering Township, 25 October 1853, John Symes, Tavern Keeper.

   Many more tavern-keepers left wills but not inventories. Tavern-keeper John Bradley's executors merely wrote "Tavern Stand ... £650," for example. AO, RG 22-205, Wentworth County Surrogate Court, Estate Files, 1841, file 456, John Bradley.

33   Japan trays were serving trays with a hard, black, glossy varnish.

34   AO, RG 22-179, Leeds and Grenville United Counties Surrogate Court, Estate Files, 1842, James Phillips [in other records, the same man's surname is spelled "Philips," as it is

throughout this book]. Surrogate Court Records, Estate Files, Brockville (Leeds and Grenville), 1842, James Philips; *Historical Atlas of Leeds and Grenville, Ontario, Illustrated* (Kingston, Canada West: Putnam and Walling, 1861-62; repr., Belleville, ON: Mika, 1973): "Map of Bastard Township," 72-73.

35 Philips was tried for murder because of an electioneering riot at his tavern, and the newspaper account provided many details about the tavern: *Brockville Recorder*, 11 September 1835 [barkeeper, shoemaker, blacksmith]; LAC, R3747-0-8-E, James Philips fonds, Copy of a Petition, Salomé Brown to the Lieutenant-Governor, Yonge [township], 15 August 1842 [Browns, potashery, tannery]; Daybook of James Philips, 25 November 1828, 16 and 17 September 1829.

36 AO, District of Johnston fonds, Johnstown District Census and Assessment, 1828, Bastard Township [neighbours]; *Brockville Recorder*, 11 September 1835 [Loucks]; LAC, Daybook of James Philips, 10 November 1829 [sling]; 18 September 1829 [gin]; 26 September 1829 [tobacco]; 29 May 1829 [bed]; 10 November 1829 ["bed, breakfast, and bitters, is 9d"].

37 *Canadian Freeman*, 1 December 1825, 6 December 1827 [ads]; Joseph Pickering, *Inquiries of an Emigrant: Being the Narrative of an English Farmer from the Years 1824 to 1830* (London: Effingham Wilson, 1831), 83 [obliging person]; Fergusson, *Practical Notes*, 119 [business]; Anna Jameson, *Winter Studies and Summer Rambles in Canada* (London: Saunders and Otley, 1838), 1:68-71 [*Don Juan*]; Hazel Chisholm Mathews discusses the Oakville House Hotel in *Oakville and the Sixteen: The History of an Ontario Port* (Toronto: University of Toronto Press, 1953), 71-75.

38 J. Armstrong, ed., *Rowsell's City of Toronto and County of York Directory, for 1850-1* (Toronto: Henry Rowsell, 1850), 34.

39 See, for instance, *Upper Canada Gazette*, 30 June 1798; John Goldie, *Diary of a Journey: Through Upper Canada and Some of the New England States 1819* (Toronto: William Tyrell, 1897), 20; Shirreff, *A Tour Through North America*, 89, 102-3, 146, 147, 179, 161-62, 170, 189-90, uses the word *hotel* exclusively for public houses in towns; *Canadian Emigrant*, 22 March 1834.

40 *Niagara Spectator*, 2 August 1817.

41 Head, *Forest Scenes*, 170; Morleigh, *Life in the West: Backwood Leaves and Prairie Flowers; Rough Sketches on the Borders of the Picturesque, the Sublime and the Ridiculous. Extracts from the Note Book of Morleigh in Search of an Estate* (London: Saunders and Otley, 1842), 196; Moodie, *Roughing it in the Bush*, 1: 252; Bigsby, *Shoe and Canoe*, 2:4-5; Charles Mackay, *Life and Liberty in America, Or, Sketches of a Tour in the United States and Canada, 1857-8* (New York: Harper and Brothers, 1859), 380 [adjectives]; *Chatham Journal*, 9 October 1841 [Eberts]; *Stratford and Perth County Intelligencer*, 2 March 1855 [Albion].

42 *Colonial Advocate*, 6 January 1831; *The Globe*, 14 October 1845; *The Globe*, 31 March 1849; *Correspondent and Advocate*, 14 June 1837; *The Globe*, 9 July 1844; *Kingston Chronicle*, 23 January 1830 [adjectives]; *The Globe*, 15 September 1847 [Yonge and Front]; *Patriot and Farmers' Monitor*, 2 September 1836 [McDonald's]; *Colonial Advocate*, 9 October 1828 [heart].

43 Thomas Fowler, *The Journal of a Tour Through British America to the Falls of Niagara* (Aberdeen, Scotland: Lewis Smith, 1832), 214; Bigsby, *Shoe and Canoe*, 4-9; Strickland, *Twenty-Seven Years*, 2:249; Shirreff, *Tour Through North America*, 89-90; for neighbours' views, see LAC, RG 5 A1, volume 106, William Wright, Petition to the Lieutenant-Governor, Stamford, Niagara Falls, 8 March 1831, pp. 60010-16.

44 *Correspondent and Advocate*, 11 January 1837; HJ, 28 November 1842; *Stratford Beacon and Perth County Intelligencer*, 2 November 1855; *Canadian Freeman*, 2 December 1830; *Kingston Chronicle*, 1 January 1831.

45 *Kingston Chronicle and Gazette*, 14 January 1837; Morleigh, *Life in the West*, 156-57.

46 *Niagara Chronicle*, 2 July 1845, 15 January 1847; *Toronto Examiner*, 11 January 1843; *Niagara Spectator*, 2 November 1820; *Canadian Emigrant*, 26 September 1834.

47 Fothergill, "A Few Notes Made on a Journey," 31; HJ, 3 July 1841.

48 *Chatham Journal*, 9 October 1841 [billiard room]; HJ, 2 July 1841.

49 Pickering, *Inquiries of an Emigrant*, 92-93 [list]; Samuel Phillips Day, *English America: Pictures of Canadian Places and People* (London: T. Cautley Newby, 1864), 2:222-24 [male pop.]; Rose, *Canada in 1849*, 1:68 [derogatory].

50 Quoted in Guillet, *Pioneer Inns and Taverns,* 1:121-23.
51 There is a large literature on taverns and the working class: Perry Duis, *The Saloon: Public Drinking in Chicago and Boston, 1880-1920* (Urbana: University of Illinois Press, 1983); Michael Kaplan, "New York City Tavern Violence and the Creation of a Working-Class Male Identity," *Journal of the Early Republic* 15 (Winter 1995): 591-617; James S. Roberts, *Drink, Temperance, and the Working Class in Nineteenth-Century Germany* (Boston, MA: Allen and Unwin, 1984); Roy Rosenzweig, *Eight Hours for What We Will: Workers and Leisure in an Industrializing City, 1870-1970,* Interdisciplinary Perspectives on Modern History (Cambridge: Cambridge University Press, 1983). For Canada see Craig Heron, "The Boys and Their Booze: Masculinities and Public Drinking in Working-Class Hamilton, 1890-1946," *Canadian Historical Review* 86, 3 (September 2005): 411-52; Peter DeLottinville, "Joe Beef of Montreal: Working-Class Culture and the Tavern, 1869-1889," *Labour/Le Travail* 8/9 (Autumn 1981/Spring 1982): 9-40.
52 AO, Toronto tavern keeper daybook, 1855-59, F 4296 #1. Although this source is unattributed, it was produced by Roach. The entry for 1 January 1859, for example, reads: "James Flinn has boughted my house at £100 from the 1st Feb. Rec'd from James Flinn up to this date £100. Patrick Roach." His name also appears all over the back cover, and there is another signature that reads "P. Roach" on the entry for 22 September.

Nearly forty of Roach's other customers, identified by full names in the accounts, appear in *Brown's Toronto General Street Directory for 1856* (Toronto: W.R. Brown for Maclear, 1856) or in *Canada Directory for 1857-58* (Montreal: John Lovell, 1857), "Toronto" section. Both list addresses and, frequently, occupations.

Chapter 2: Households and Public Life in a Tavern-Keeper's Journal

1 Archives of Ontario (AO), [Ely] Playter diary, 1801-43, 19 February 1802 (hereafter EP); for his licence, see Alexander Fraser, ed., "Minutes of the Court of General Quarter Sessions of the Peace for the Home District, 13 March 1800 to 28 December 1811," *Twenty-First Report of the Department of Public Records and Archives of Ontario, 1932* (Toronto: Herbert H. Ball, 1933), 16-17.
2 See Peter Thompson, *Rum Punch and Revolution: Taverngoing and Public Life in Eighteenth-Century Philadelphia,* Early American Studies (Philadelphia: University of Pennsylvania Press, 1999), 15 (and on female patrons generally, 75, 79, 85, 89, 98-99); Daniel B. Thorpe, "Taverns and Tavern Culture on the Southern Colonial Frontier: Rowan County, North Carolina, 1753-1776," *Journal of Southern History* 62, 4 (1996): 680-82. On the public houses of Europe, see Peter Clark, *The English Alehouse: A Social History 1200-1830* (London: Longman, 1983), 225, 235-36, 287-88, 311-12, 320-22, 341; Thomas Brennan, *Public Drinking and Popular Culture in Eighteenth-Century Paris* (Princeton, NJ: Princeton University Press, 1988), 146-51, 222, 225, 260, 275.
3 David Conroy, *In Public Houses: Drink and the Revolution of Authority in Colonial Massachusetts* (Chapel Hill: University of North Carolina Press for Institute of Early American History and Culture, 1995), 99-100, 109, 111-12, 119-22, 131-39, 146-47; Thompson, *Rum Punch and Revolution,* 32, 43-46, 64-67; Cynthia A. Kierner, *Beyond the Household: Women's Place in the Early South, 1700-1835* (Ithaca, NY: Cornell University Press, 1998), 19-20, 22-25, 119; Thorpe, "Taverns and Tavern Culture on the Southern Colonial Frontier," 680.
4 See also Barbara A. Hanawalt, *"Of Good and Ill Repute": Gender and Social Control in Medieval England* (New York: Oxford University Press, 1998), especially 104-23; W. Scott Haine, *The World of the Paris Café: Sociability among the French Working Class, 1789-1914,* Johns Hopkins University Studies in Historical and Political Science (Baltimore: Johns Hopkins University Press, 1996); B. Ann Tlusty, *Bacchus and Civic Disorder: The Culture of Drink in Early Modern Germany* (Charlottesville: University Press of Virginia, 2001), 138-45. There is also a concise discussion of female patronage in Beat Kümin, "Public Houses and Their Patrons in Early Modern Europe," in *The World of the Tavern: Public Houses in Early Modern Europe,* ed. Beat Kümin and B. Ann Tlusty (Aldershot, UK: Ashgate, 2002), 44-62.
5 EP, 10 July 1802.
6 Ibid., 16 September 1802. See 10 July 1802 for Ward's political difficulties getting called to the Bar. He became a prominent barrister under whom William Henry Draper, a prime

minister during the Union period (1841-67), articled. See George Metcalfe, "William Henry Draper," in *Pre-Confederation Premiers: Ontario Government Leaders, 1841-1867*, ed. J.M.S. Careless, Ontario Historical Studies Series (Toronto: University of Toronto Press, 1980), 33.

7   Henri-François de la Solle, *Memoirs of a Man of Pleasure, or, the Adventures of Versorand*, trans. John Hill, 5th ed. (London: T. Osborn, 1751). The novelist (d. 1761) is obscure, meriting only the briefest of entries in the *Dictionnaire des Lettres Françaises XVIVe Siècle*, vol. 4 (Paris: Librairie Arthème Fayard, 1960), 46; EP, 14 February 1802.

8   See *Solitude: Written Originally by J.G. Zimmerman to which Are Added Notes Historical and Explanatory ...*, 2 vols. (London: Thomas Maiden for Vernor and Hood/J. Cuthell, J. Walker, et al., 1804-05). The book was available in English translation from 1796 under various titles. The first American edition was *Solitude Considered, with Respect to its Influence on the Mind and Heart*, written originally in German by M.[onsieur] Zimmermann; translated from the French of J.B. Mercier (New York: Mott & Lyon for Evert Duyckinck, 1796), v-vii. Amanda Vickery, in *The Gentleman's Daughter: Women's Lives in Georgian England* (New Haven: Yale University Press, 1998), remarks that "the most overdrawn dualism drawn on in discussions of leisure and culture was that of fashionable worldliness versus philosophical retirement" (282).

9   R. Cole Harris, ed., *Historical Atlas of Canada*, vol. 1, *From the Beginning to 1800* (Toronto: University of Toronto Press, 1987), plate 35, "The Great Lakes Basin, 1600-1653"; Harold A. Innis, *The Fur Trade in Canada: An Introduction to Canadian Economic History*, rev. ed. (Toronto: University of Toronto Press, 1956), 89; John Bennett to John Neilson, York, Upper Canada, 18 September 1801, in Edith G. Firth, ed., *The Town of York, 1793-1815: A Collection of Documents of Early Toronto*, Ontario Series 5 (Toronto: Champlain Society, 1962), 242. Bennett was the king's printer in Upper Canada.

10   Firth, *Town of York, 1793-1815*, xxxiii-xlvi.

11   "Abstract of the Home District [the administrative district in which York was located] for the Year commencing 7th March 1802," in John Ross Robertson, *Robertson's Landmarks of Toronto* (1896; repr., Belleville, ON: Mika Publishing, 1987), 2:994; Firth, *Town of York, 1793-1815*, 242.

12   Playter, as the elected town clerk, enumerated the population as part of the duties of his office. His count is in Firth, *Town of York, 1793-1815*, "Population of York, 1797-1814," lxxvii, and it is published in Christine Mosser, ed. *York, Upper Canada: Minutes of Town Meetings, Lists of Inhabitants, 1793-1823* (Toronto: Metropolitan Library Board, 1984), 32-37.

13   "Report of the State of Public Works and Buildings at the Several Military Posts in Upper Canada, 12 Sept. 1802," in Firth, *Town of York, 1792-1815*, 71. The 41st Regiment replaced the Queen's Rangers in September 1802.

14   EP, 29 May 1802.

15   Histories of early York typically note that the "social life of the town was dominated by the handful of appointed, highly paid officials ... in positions of power": Frederick H. Armstrong, *Toronto: A Place of Meeting* (Burlington, ON: Ontario Historical Society and Windsor Publications, 1983), 38. Theirs was a different social sphere than Playter's; for its workings, see Katherine M.J. McKenna, *A Life of Propriety: Anne Murray Powell and Her Family, 1775-1849* (Montreal and Kingston: McGill-Queen's University Press, 1994).

16   Sam Bass Warner Jr., *The Private City: Philadelphia in Three Periods of its Growth* (Philadelphia: University of Pennsylvania Press, 1968); Gerald M. Craig, *Upper Canada: The Formative Years, 1784-1841*, Canadian Centenary Series 7 (Toronto: McClelland and Stewart, 1963), 42-49. See John Webster Grant, *A Profusion of Spires: Religion in Nineteenth-Century Ontario* (Toronto: University of Toronto Press, 1988), for the religious traditions of the colony. See also Daniel G. Hill, "Negroes in Toronto, 1793-1865," *Ontario History* 55, 2 (June 1963): 73-91, and on the Mississauga, see Robert J. Surtees, "Land Sessions, 1763-1830," in *Aboriginal Ontario: Historical Perspectives on the First Nations*, ed. Edward S. Rogers and Donald B. Smith, Ontario Historical Studies Series (Toronto: Dundurn Press, 1994), 101-4, 109-12.

17   EP, 22 and 27 February 1802 [bar and barroom]; 23 February, 1 and 11 March [parlour]; 2 April and 30 June [upstairs]; 15 September [Ely's room]; 25 February [south chamber]; 21 March [kitchen]; 6 July [cellar]. About seven people, plus guests, slept in the tavern most nights: Playter, Miss T., Abner, Mercy and Bettsey Miles, Betty Johnson, and P. White

(possibly a servant). See, for instance, EP, 26 February, 7 March, 10 and 23 April, 4 and 18 March 1802.

18   Ibid., 6 July 1802.
19   Ibid., 7 April 1802.
20   Ibid., 27 February, 4 April, 1802 [Quakers and soldiers]; 8 and 17 March 1802 [fur trading]; 3 and 10 April 1802 [schooner captains]; 26 and 27 Februrary, 9 April 1802 [Archibald Cameron, Samuel Heron merchants, and Erastus Dean, merchant clerk]; see Firth, *Town of York, 1793-1815*, 68, 13, 245; Stephen Heward was a government clerk at Peter Russell's office (the receiver-general and former acting governor): see Firth, *Town of York, 1793-1815*, 81, 107, 265, 268; Fraser, ed., "Minutes of the Court of General Quarter Sessions," 172; Thomas Ward was a lawyer: see Firth, *Town of York, 1793-1815*, 90; Thomas Stoyells was a physician: EP, 19 March 1802 and Firth, *Town of York, 1793-1815*, 130. It is difficult to distinguish between Angus and Alexander Mcdonnell in the journal. Angus was a lawyer, the treasurer of the Law Society, a member of the Legislative Assembly, and a Justice of the Peace. Alexander was sheriff of the Home District, a member of the Legislative Assembly, and also a JP: see Firth, *Town of York, 1793-1815*, 41; Fraser, ed., "Minutes of the Court of General Quarter Sessions," 2, 3, 20, 33, 100; Mosser, ed., *York, Upper Canada*, 13.
21   Toronto Public Library, Toronto Reference Library, Baldwin Room (BR), Abner Miles account book, accounts of a general store and tavern, 1, 3, 15, 16, and 23 September 1795; 28 June and 5 September 1796. To ensure that the individuals were tavern, not store, customers, I have included only those who had small-measure drink purchases on their accounts.
22   These seven are William Bond, Archibald Cameron, Samuel Heron, John and Joseph Kendrick, Captain Sillich, and Benjamin Cozens. Bond was a freeholder on Yonge Street, a hatter, a grand juror, a financial contributor for a bridge in York, and the representative sent to England in 1806 by the Agricultural and Commercial Society of York: see AO, RG 22-134, Court of Queen's Bench, Assize Minute Books, 1800, 1803; Fraser, ed., "Minutes of the Court of General Quarter Sessions," 29, 33, 35; Firth, *Town of York, 1793-1815*, 41. Cameron was a small merchant in York who had landed in Etobicoke, was elected collector, had been with the Queen's Rangers and was a lieutenant in the York Militia, and was a grand juror: see Firth, *Town of York, 1793-1815*, 68, 70; Fraser, ed., "Minutes of the Court of General Quarter Sessions," 5, 66, 68. Heron was a larger merchant who later ran a milling and distilling complex, a militia lieutenant, a grand juror, and the holder of various town offices: see Firth, *Town of York, 1793-1815*, 13; Mosser, ed., *York, Upper Canada*, 3, 9, 31; AO, RG 22-134, 1798, 1800. There were four Kendrick brothers with adjoining Yonge Street lots. Joseph was the schooner captain and owner and a grand juror. John was a house carpenter and high constable from 1800 to 1803: see Firth, *Town of York, 1793-1815*, 42, 224; Fraser, ed., "Minutes of the Court of General Quarter Sessions," 48, 65. Sillich does not appear in local records. Benjamin Cozens was the brother of J.D. and Shivers. All held local office at different times, served as grand jurors, and speculated in land. Benjamin was a tailor. J.D. was listed as a "gentleman" in the Court of Queen's Bench, Assize Minute Books, AO, RG 22-134, 1798: see also Firth, *Town of York, 1793-1815*, 11; Fraser, ed., "Minutes of the Court of General Quarter Sessions," 21, 31.
23   BR, Abner Miles account book, 23 September 1796; Fraser, ed., "Minutes of the Court of General Quarter Sessions," 32, 44, 84; EP, 26 February 1802.
24   BR, Abner Miles account book, 1, 3, 15, 16, and 23 September 1795 and 28 June and 5 September 1796.
25   EP, 13 July 1802. The only "Lester" on the list of inhabitants in 1802 was Lester Stuard, whose name came under the heading "Blacks in York." Mosser, ed., *York, Upper Canada*, 36.
26   EP, 25 February 1802. For further discussion of racialized relations in tavern space, see Julia Roberts, "'A Mixed Assemblage of Persons': Race and Tavern Space in Upper Canada," *Canadian Historical Review* 83, 1 (March 2002): 1-28.
27   EP, 4 June 1802.
28   Playter actually mentions fifty-two women by name in this period, but three lived along the route to Niagara and one was his sister in Pennsylvania. The quotes are EP, 21 and 23 March [Carpenter], 10 July [Rea], 10 April [Dutch family], 7 April [Dunkards], 21 April [Hatters], and 27 June [man and wife] 1802.

29 "Marriage Registers of St. James Church," 6 December 1802, in *Robertson's Landmarks of Toronto*, 3:396; EP, 18 February [Bettsey Miles in residence], 25 July [at Everson's], and 26 May [at Beman's] 1802.
30 EP, 25 July and 7 and 24 September 1802. See also 13 and 20 January 1806.
31 Ibid., 22 August 1804.
32 Ibid., 27 October 1805.
33 Ibid., 5 September 1805 [Niagara].
34 Ibid., 24 September 1802 and 14 November 1805.
35 Women did use the taverns alone when travelling, as in the example of Mrs. Carpenter. For a discussion of this exception to the rule, see Julia Roberts, "Taverns and Tavern-goers in Upper Canada, the 1790s to the 1850s" (PhD diss., University of Toronto, 1999), 273-80; Hanawalt, *"Of Good and Ill Repute,"* 73; B. Ann Tlusty, "Drinking, Family Relations, and Authority in Early Modern Germany," *Journal of Family History* 29, 3 (July 2004): 253-73, especially 263.
36 For my favourite example, see Mary Beth Norton, *Founding Mothers and Fathers: Gendered Power and the Forming of American Society* (New York: Knopf, 1996).
37 University of Toronto, Thomas Fischer Rare Book Room, Charles Fothergill Collection, Fothergill, "A Few Notes Made on a Journey from Montreal through the Province of Upper Canada in February 1817," 41.
38 Brennan, *Public Drinking*, 147-50; Clark, *The English Alehouse*, 225; Laurel Thatcher Ulrich, *A Midwife's Tale: The Life of Martha Ballard, Based on her Diary, 1785-1812* (New York: Random House, 1991), 144-45, 147.
39 On the geography of women's space in early modern Europe, see Martine Segalen, *Historical Anthropology of the Family*, trans. J.C. Whitehouse and Sarah Matthews (Cambridge: Cambridge University Press, 1986); Daphne Spain, *Gendered Spaces* (Chapel Hill: University of North Carolina Press, 1992); and, of course, Hanawalt, *"Of Good and Ill Repute."*
40 EP, 4 and 19 March and 1 April 1802.
41 Ibid., 20, 22, and 24 March 1802.
42 Ibid., 7 September [supper], 9 September, and 22 September 1802. Sophia Beman worked in the store attached to the family's tavern. Playter fails to note her work in the tavern itself. EP, 30 October 1802.
43 Ibid., 2 May and 29 September 1802.
44 Ibid., 6 March 1802.
45 There is an entry in Elizabeth Russell's diary (Elizabeth was Peter Russell's sister) about Thompson ironing at the Russell house (see Firth, *Town of York, 1793-1815*, "Extracts from Elizabeth Russell's Diary," 262). There is personal correspondence between Mary's husband, John Scarlett, and Elizabeth Russell referring to Mary being "chagrined that she has not been able to complete her job for you" (AO, William Baldwin family fonds, J. Scarlett to E. Russell, Humber, 19 December 1810). And there is a letter from Mary's uncle David regarding his wife's work dyeing some worsted cloth for Russell (AO, William Baldwin family fonds, David Thompson to E. Russell, Scarborough, 17 February 1811). Together, they hint that Mary Thompson may have stayed at Playter's tavern in order to pursue her trade, perhaps one shared by the women of her family.
46 EP, 11 January 1806.
47 Ibid., 15 January 1804 and 24 December 1805. See also 19 November 1802. George Washington Post kept tavern in Scarborough; earlier he had worked as a barkeep at Playter's tavern. See EP, 3 August 1802.
48 Ibid., 30 December 1802. Playter accompanies his mother to her daughter's first lying-in, sixty miles from York. They paid "Capt. Bates 2[s.] 6[d.] for [their] entertainment."
49 Ibid., 12 and 27 April, 28 May, and 6 and 31 July 1802.
50 Hanawalt, *"Of Good and Ill Repute,"* 105.
51 EP, 10 March and 28 February 1802.
52 Ibid., 8 April 1802; Fraser, ed., "Minutes of the Court of General Quarter Sessions," 30, 34.
53 Leonore Davidoff and Catherine Hall, *Family Fortunes: Men and Women of the English Middle Class, 1780-1850*, Women in Culture and Society (Chicago: University of Chicago Press,

1987), 428; Brennan, *Public Drinking and Popular Culture,* 147-49, makes the same argument regarding eighteenth-century Parisian wine shops.

54 EP, 22 September 1802. See also 4 August and 1 September 1802.

55 Ibid., 27 August 1802.

56 Ibid., 25 April 1802.

57 Ibid., 27 April 1802.

58 Ibid., 7 October 1802.

59 Ibid., 6 June, 21 and 22 July, 29 August, and 28 September 1802. Mrs. Beman was formerly Esther Sayre Robinson, the widow of Christopher Robinson, member of the governing elite. She married Elisha Beman on 5 September 1802 (EP, 9 September 1802). The first Mrs. Beman's death notice was published precisely a year earlier in the *Upper Canada Gazette,* 5 Sept. 1801.

60 Haine, *World of the Paris Café,* 181, 200, 185.

61 EP, 6 June 1802.

62 Ibid., 10 June 1802.

63 Davidoff and Hall, *Family Fortunes,* 367.

64 EP, 15 April 1802: "Mrs Clinger being in Miss B's bedroom called me in and detained me some time. I took the opportunity of recommending to Miss B to go down the lake with my sister & me about a fortnight hence."

65 For a philosophical discussion of the ways behaviour can indicate implied resistance to oppressive norms, see Iris Marion Young, *Justice and the Politics of Difference* (Princeton, NJ: Princeton University Press, 1990), 171-73.

66 Sophia was definitely under sixteen. The only female listed as a member of Elisha Beman's household in 1802 was listed under "children," which meant under the age of sixteen. See *York, Upper Canada,* 32. In addition, unable to find a conventional record of Beman's age and sensing her youth, I turned to www.ancestry.com, which lists her birth date as 15 January 1788, in Massachusetts. That would make Sophia eighteen years old the year she married Playter. See "Marriage Registers of St. James Church," 27 November 1806, in *Robertson's Landmarks of Toronto,* 3:399.

67 EP, 20 July 1802. The "occurrences" were definitely in the parlour, because that is where EP writes that they were meeting. There is an immediately preceding reference to company upstairs: EP, 28 and 30 August 1802. Peter Ward, "Courtship and Social Space in Nineteenth-Century English Canada," *Canadian Historical Review* 68, 1 (1987): 35-62, discusses the Beman-Playter courtship without noting its tavern location.

68 Vickery, *The Gentleman's Daughter,* 241-42; see also Richard L. Bushman, *The Refinement of America: Persons, Houses, Cities* (New York: Alfred A. Knopf, 1992), 87-90.

69 EP, 4 June 1802.

70 David Scobey, "Anatomy of the Promenade: The Politics of Bourgeois Sociability in Nineteenth-Century New York," *Social History* 17, 2 (1992): 221.

71 Vickery, *The Gentleman's Daughter,* 213.

72 Kierner, *Beyond the Household,* 1, 37-44.

73 EP, 6 May 1803.

74 *Dictionary of Canadian Biography,* vol. 6, s.v. "Beman, Elisha," by Robert E. Saunders; Mosser, ed., *York, Upper Canada,* 56, 8, 146. Ridout is almost certainly Samuel Street Ridout (son of the surveyor general of 1810, who was employed in his father's office as a clerk and appointed sheriff of the Home District in 1815): see, for instance, EP, 19 and 22 March 1804, Firth, ed., *Town of York: 1793-1815,* 17, and *Town of York 1815-1834: A Further Collection of Documents of Early Toronto,* Ontario Series 8 (Toronto: Champlain Society, 1966), 6. Charles Willcocks was the only son of William, who was himself a cousin to Peter Russell, the former president of the Executive Council and an extensive land speculator: see Firth, *Town of York: 1793-1815,* 14. On Small, see EP, 13 February 1804; for his work as a lawyer and link to the Ridout family, see AO, Ridout Papers, letters from J.R.S. Small to Samuel Ridout, 12 June 1805; 28 June, 12 September, 12 October, and 2 December 1808; 28 May and 4 August 1809. For Pudney, Dean, and "the Ladys," see EP, 21 November and 3 December 1802; Firth, *Town of York: 1793-1815,* 90, 99, 245.

75 EP, 24, 25, and 27 February, 26 April, and 19 August 1802 [all opening quotes]. On literacy rates, see Harvey J. Graff, *The Legacies of Literacy: Continuities and Contradictions in Western Culture and Society* (Bloomington: Indiana University Press, 1987), 249, and "Literacy and Social Structure in Elgin County, Canada West: 1861," *Histoire sociale/Social History* 6, 11 (April 1973): 25-48. Leo A. Johnson, *History of the County of Ontario, 1615-1875* (Whitby, ON: County of Ontario, 1973), 63; Linda K. Kerber, *Toward an Intellectual History of Women: Essays*, Gender and American Culture (Chapel Hill: University of North Carolina Press, 1997), 236-37. On barroom reading see, for example, Robert M. Weir, "The Role of the Newspaper Press in the Southern Colonies on the Eve of the Revolution: An Interpretation," in *The Press and the American Revolution*, ed. Bernard Bailyn and John B. Hench (Worcester, MA: American Antiquarian Society, 1980), 99-150 [little "serious reading"]. On American gentlemen in taverns, see David S. Shields, *Civil Tongues and Polite Letters in British America* (Chapel Hill: University of North Carolina Press for the Institute of Early American History and Culture, 1997), 65-88 [literacy as pleasure].

76 Karen Haltunnen, cited in Cecilia Morgan, *Public Men and Virtuous Women: The Gendered Languages of Religion and Politics in Upper Canada, 1791-1850*, Studies in Gender and History (Toronto: University of Toronto Press, 1996), 204; Bushman, *The Refinement of America*, 121; EP, 17 August 1802. For tea drinking, see also 29 June, 31 July, and 27 August 1802. For card tables, see EP, 11 March and 15 September 1802 and 24 December 1805. For wine at Beman's, see EP, 1 March, 5 April, and 7 June 1802; EP, 13 July 1802 [punch].

77 EP 18 December ["Spent the evening marking some music and writing some songs"], 8 April [flute], 1 July, and 30 August [music books] 1802. Joseph B. Abbot, music master at York, noted the elegance of flute playing in the *York Gazette*, 14 February 1810, in Firth, ed., *Town of York 1793-1815*, 208-9.

78 Vickery, *Gentleman's Daughter*, 195-224; Bushman, *Refinement of America*, 262-80; McKenna, *A Life of Propriety*, 61-90, Baldwin quoted at 75; Firth, ed., *Town of York 1793-1815*, "Extract from Alexander Mcdonnell's Diary," 226-29.

79 EP, 2 March 1802, and see Vickery, *Gentleman's Daughter*, 212-13, 223.

80 Scobey, "Anatomy of the Promenade," 221.

81 EP, 4 June 1802.

Chapter 3: Public Houses as Colonial Public Space

1 Roy Rosenzweig and Elizabeth Blackmar, *The Park and the People: A History of Central Park* (Ithaca, NY: Cornell University Press, 1992). On early Canada, see the work of Mary Anne Poutanen, for example, "The Homeless, the Whore, the Drunkard, and the Disorderly: Contours of Female Vagrancy in the Montreal Courts, 1810-1842," in *Gendered Pasts: Historical Essays in Femininity and Masculinity in Canada*, ed. Kathryn McPherson, Cecilia Morgan, Nancy Forestell (Toronto: Oxford University Press, 1999), 29-47. Current practitioners include Stephen Carr, Mark Francis, Leanne G. Rivlin, and Andrew M. Stone, *Public Space*, Cambridge Series in Environment and Behavior (Cambridge: University of Cambridge Press, 1992), 91. See also Benjamin R. Barber, "Malled, Mauled, and Overhauled: Arresting Suburban Sprawl by Transforming Suburban Malls into Usable Civic Space," in *Public Space and Democracy*, ed. Marcel Hénaff and Tracy B. Strong (Minneapolis: University of Minnesota Press, 2001), 201-20.

2 For me, the clearest explanation of these views is still found in Iris Marion Young, *Justice and the Politics of Difference* (Princeton, NJ: Princeton University Press, 1990).

3 Mary P. Ryan, *Civic Wars: Democracy and Public Life in the American City during the Nineteenth Century* (Berkeley: University of California Press, 1997); Patricia Cline Cohen, "Women at Large: Travel in Antebellum America," *History Today* 44, 12 (1994): 44-51. Later work in Canada includes Donald F. Davis and Barbara Lorenzkowski, "A Platform for Gender Tensions: Women Working and Riding on Canadian Urban Public Transit in the 1940s," *Canadian Historical Review* 79, 3 (September 1998): 431-65; Mary Louise Adams, "Almost Anything can Happen: A Search for Sexual Discourse in the Urban Spaces of 1940s Toronto," special issue on moral regulation, *Canadian Journal of Sociology* 19, 2 (1994): 217-32.

4 Ryan, *Civic Wars*, 7.

5 William Pope, *William Pope's Journal,* 28 March 1834-11 March 1835, ed. M.A. Garland, *Western Ontario History Nuggets* 16, pt. 2 (London, ON: Lawson Memorial Library, University of Western Ontario, 1952), 45.

6 Jan Noel, *Canada Dry: Temperance Crusades before Confederation* (Toronto: University of Toronto Press, 1995), 217, 289; Craig Heron, *Booze: A Distilled History* (Toronto: Between the Lines, 2003), 60, 54 [minority].

7 *Canada Temperance Advocate* 8, 2 (May 1842): 26.

8 Brian K. Harrison, *Drink and the Victorians: The Temperance Question in England, 1815-1872* (London: Faber and Faber, 1971), Table 7, "Persons per on-license in England and Wales, 1831-1966," 313; Thomas Brennan, *Public Drinking and Popular Culture in Eighteenth-Century Paris* (Princeton, NJ: Princeton University Press, 1988), 76; James S. Roberts, *Drink, Temperance, and the Working Class in Nineteenth-Century Germany* (Boston, MA: Allen and Unwin, 1984), 50; Perry Duis, *The Saloon: Public Drinking in Chicago and Boston, 1880-1920* (Urbana: University of Illinois Press, 1983), 28-29; Sam Bass Warner Jr., *The Private City: Philadelphia in Three Periods of Its Growth* (Philadelphia: University of Pennsylvania Press, 1968), 19.

9 Government houses were licensed much the same as any other tavern. For petitions (applications) to run government houses at Burlington Bay and Credit River, see Library and Archives Canada (LAC), RG 5 A1, Upper Canada Sundries, Civil Secretary's correspondence, Upper Canada and Canada West, volume 11, petition of James Odell Roach, 26 May 1820, p. 4880, and Executive Council Office of the Province of Upper Canada Papers, RG 1 E3, petition on George Roach, York, 16 May 1815, volume 12, pp. 240-42.

Elizabeth Simcoe, quoted in John Ross Robertson, *History of Freemasonry in Canada: From its Introduction in 1749* (Toronto: Hunter Rose, 1899), 1:626.

10 Quoted in Gerald M. Craig, *Upper Canada: The Formative Years, 1784-1841,* Canadian Centenary Series 7 (Toronto: McClelland and Stewart, 1963), 35, emphasis in original.

11 Alan Everitt, "The English Urban Inn, 1560-1760," in *Perspectives in English Urban History,* ed. Alan Everitt, Problems in Focus Series (London: Macmillan, 1973), 91-137; J.A. Chartres, "The Capital's Provincial Eyes: London's Inns in the Early Eighteenth Century," *London Journal* 3, 1 (1977): 24-39; Duis, *The Saloon,* 158; "Regulations for Innkeepers, 1818, District of Newcastle," reproduced in *Valley of the Trent,* Edwin C. Guillet (Toronto: Champlain Society, 1957), 293 [quote].

12 Lambton County Archives, Wyoming, Ontario, Henry (Harry) John Jones diary, 20-24 January 1837 (hereafter HJ). On this trip Jones also named Mosier's tavern at the Credit River, another in Oakville, Rousseau's (past Hamilton), one in Burford, and another in Delaware.

13 William Chambers, *Things as They Are in America* (London and Edinburgh: William and Robert Chambers, 1854), 135.

14 J.J. Talman, "Travel in Ontario before the Coming of the Railway," Ontario Historical Society *Papers and Records* 29 (1933): 85-102; *Niagara Herald,* 28 May 1818 [ad]; Richard D. Merritt, "Early Inns and Taverns: Accommodation, Fellowship, and Good Cheer," in *Capital Years: Niagara-on-the-Lake, 1792-1796,* ed. Richard Meritt, Nancy Butler, and Michael Power (Toronto: Dundurn Press for the Niagara Historical Society, 1991), 213; *Kingston Chronicle,* 14 January 1820 [Brown]; *The Globe,* 21 January 1851 [City Hotel]; *Canada Directory for 1857-8: Containing the Names of Professional and Business Men* (Montreal: John Lovell, 1857), 107-8, 126-27, 285, 448-49, 456, 542 [livery stables]); *Chatham Journal,* 17 December 1842 [Eberts]; HJ, 30 October 1837 [Jerry].

15 Douglas McCalla, *Planting the Province: The Economic History of Upper Canada, 1784-1870,* Ontario Historical Studies Series (Toronto: University of Toronto Press, 1993), 136; Archives of Ontario (AO), [Ely] Playter diary, 26 February 1802 (hereafter EP); "Huron District: Rules and Regulations for Innkeepers," 1849, Canadian Institute of Historical Microreproductions, Microfiche Series, no. 52535. See also, Thomas F. McIlwraith, "Transportation in the Landscape of Early Upper Canada," in *Perspectives on Landscape and Settlement in Nineteenth-Century Ontario,* ed. J. David Wood, Carleton Library Series 91 (Toronto: McClelland and Stewart, 1975), 51-63.

16 *Canadian Freeman,* 2 December 1830.

17 *Niagara Herald,* 4 April 1801 [Raymond]; *Upper Canada Gazette,* 1 March 1797 [table] and 10 January 1807 [clothing]; *The Globe,* 9 January 1854 [Chancery sale].

18 Chatham-Kent Museum Archives (CKMA), Chatham, Ontario, Matthew Dolsen journal, 4, 8, 12, and 15 December 1797; 12, 16, and 31 January, 2 March, 24 April, 13 May, 19 July, and 17 October 1798; Toronto Public Library, Toronto Reference Library, Baldwin Room (BR), Abner Miles account book, accounts of a general store and tavern, 1 September, 16 November, and 9 December 1795; LAC, R3747-0-8-E, James Philips fonds, Daybook of James Philips, 1828-30, 4 May, 6 and 9 October, and 1 November 1829; Upper Canada Village Archives (UCVA), Thomas Robinson account book, pp. 22, 26, 171, 193, 201, 226-27; J. Armstrong, ed., *Rowsell's City of Toronto and County of York Directory, for 1850-1* (Toronto: Henry Rowsell, 1850), 90.
19 Everitt, "The English Urban Inn, 1560-1760," 105.
20 LAC, RG 5 A1, J.B. Robinson to George Powell, 27 August 1833, volume 132, p. 72822 [cow and calf]; AO, RG 22-390, 9-5, Supreme Court of Ontario (SCO), Judges' Benchbooks, Macaulay, Home District, *Q. v. Michael Moran* (1848) [dress] [McBride]; *Colonial Advocate*, 8 July 1824 [business]; EP, 24 March 1803 [Mr. Terry]; CKMA, Matthew Dolsen journal, 11 and 17 February, 12 September, 14 and 17 October 1798; BR, Abner Miles account book, 16 September 1795; LAC, Daybook of James Philips, 20 January, 5 March, and 9 December 1829; UCVA, Thomas Robinson account book, 26 July and 1 August 1843.
21 *The Globe*, 5 January 1854.
22 *Upper Canada Gazette*, 6 and 26 September 1807 [physicians]; Robert L. Fraser, ed. *Provincial Justice: Upper Canadian Portraits from the Dictionary of Canadian Biography* (Toronto: University of Toronto Press for the Osgoode Society, 1992), xlv [lawyers]; *Kingston Chronicle and Gazette*, 16 October 1844 [Kahn]; *Upper Canada Gazette*, 5 and 19 April 1800; *Niagara Herald*, 9 May 1801 and 17 January 1839; *York Gazette*, 22 April 1815; Toronto *Examiner*, 12 April 1843 [examples of others].
23 *Upper Canada Gazette*, 14 March and 25 April 1822; David G. Burley, *A Particular Condition in Life: Self-Employment and Social Mobility in Mid-Victorian Brantford* (Montreal and Kingston: McGill-Queen's University Press, 1994), 23 [navigation company]; AO, Prince (Col.), John, Papers, Diaries, Hiram Walker Collection, 20 September 1836.
24 Christine Mosser, ed., *York, Upper Canada: Minutes of Town Meetings, Lists of Inhabitants, 1793-1823* (Toronto: Metropolitan Toronto Library Board 1984) [township meetings]; EP, 22 July 1802 [Ross]; McMaster University Archives, Mills Memorial Library, Hamilton Police Village Minutes, 2 April 1839 [police board], 11 August 1834 [Tolliver]; *Niagara Spectator*, 28 May 1818 [trustees]; *Chatham Journal*, 17 December 1842 and AO, RG 22-390, 47-5, Draper, Toronto, 1854. *Wilson v. O'Neil* [candidate selection].
25 Edith G. Firth, ed., *The Town of York 1793-1815: A Collection of Documents of Early Toronto*, Ontario Series, 5 (Toronto: Champlain Society 1962), 248, quoting EP, 4 March 1804; United Church Archives, William Case Journal, 6 August 1806.
26 The classic statement is Douglas Hay, *Albion's Fatal Tree: Crime and Society in Eighteenth-Century England* (London: Allen Lane 1975); The Toronto Police Court, a lesser court, has been studied. Paul Craven, "Law and Ideology: The Toronto Police Court 1850-80," in David H. Flaherty, ed., *Essays in the History of Canadian Law*, Vol. 2 (Toronto: University of Toronto Press, 1983), 248-307; see also, David R. Murray, *Colonial Justice: Justice, Morality and Crime in the Niagara District 1791-1849*, Osgoode Society for Canadian Legal History (Toronto: Published for the Osgoode Society for Canadian Legal History by the University of Toronto Press, 2002); Bibliothèque et Archives nationales du Québec, Cahier de dépenses de membres d'un grand jury [Loucks MS], P1000-S3-D1321; *Toronto Star*, 14 March 1846 [coroner].
27 See Jeffrey L. McNairn, *The Capacity to Judge: Public Opinion and Deliberative Democracy in Upper Canada, 1791-1854* (Toronto: University of Toronto Press, 2000); *Niagara Spectator*, 15 March 1816 ["What we hear"]; LAC, RG 5 A1, volume 16, deposition of George Cutler, 16 August 1815, p. 6548, and information of Robert Laquey, 21 August 1813, p. 6624 [1812].
28 Robert Gourlay, "Township Reports," in *Statistical Account of Upper Canada*, vol. 1, *Canadiana before 1867* (1822; repr., Wakefield, UK: S.R. Publishers, 1966), 257-583; David Conroy, *In Public Houses: Drink and the Revolution of Authority in Colonial Massachusetts* (Chapel Hill: University of North Carolina Press for the Institute of Early American History and Culture, 1995); W. Scott Haine, *The World of the Paris Café: Sociability among the French Working Class*,

1789-1914, Johns Hopkins University Studies in Historical and Political Science (Baltimore, MD: Johns Hopkins University Press, 1996), 211.

29 John C. Geikie, ed., *George Stanley: Or, Life in the Woods; A Boy's Narrative of the Adventures of a Settler's Family in Canada* (London: Routledge, Warner, and Routledge, 1864), 151-53 [speeches]; UCVA, Thomas Robinson account book, 27 November 1857 [bet]; HJ, 22 September 1836 [Head]; *Chatham Journal,* 30 August 1841 [Tecumseh]; HJ, 18 May 1836 [Constitutional Society].

30 J.M.S. Careless, *The Union of the Canadas: The Growth of Canadian Institutions, 1841-1857,* Canadian Centenary Series 10 (Toronto: McClelland and Stewart, 1967), 43.

31 United Province of Canada, Appendix S,"Report of the Commissioners appointed to investigate certain Proceedings at Toronto, connected with the Election for that City ... 3 Aug. 1841, *Legislative Assembly Journals,* 1941, (unpaginated), see third page of introductory remarks, emphasis in original.

32 LAC, RG 1 E3, Executive Council Papers, Draft of a Letter Addressed to the Chairmen of the Quarter Sessions of every District ... Relating to Tavern Licenses, 24 December 1838, volume 38a, p. 188; LAC, RG 5 A1, volume 179, Memorandum Regarding an Assembled Meeting, Home District, p. 98908.

33 *Western Herald and Farmers' Magazine,* 1, 48 (1838): 342 [poem]; HJ, 14 December 1837 [barroom politicians].

34 Gregory S. Kealey, "Orangemen and the Corporation: The Politics of Class during the Union of the Canadas," in *Forging a Consensus: Historical Essays on Toronto,* ed. Victor L. Russell (Toronto: University of Toronto Press, 1984), 41-86.

35 The population that year was 9,654, meaning one tavern per 116 residents. By 1841 the population had risen to 14,262, or one tavern per 120 residents. The number of taverns actually decreased marginally per capita in the intervening years and despite the change in political control: George Walton, *City of Toronto and the Home District Commercial Directory and Register with Almanack and Calendar for 1837* (Toronto: T. Dalton and W.J. Coates, 1837); Frederick H. Armstrong, *Handbook of Upper Canadian Chronology,* 2nd ed., Dundurn Historical Document Series 3 (Toronto: Dundurn Press, 1985), Table 3, 275.

36 "Report of the Commissioners," testimony nos. 10, 14, 29, 31, and 32.

37 *City of Toronto Poll Book Exhibiting a Classified List of Voters at the Late Great Contest for Responsible Government* (Toronto: Lesslie Brothers, 1841).

38 "A list of persons who have taken out licenses in the City of Toronto for the year 1842," *Toronto Patriot and Farmers' Monitor,* 1 March 1842; Francis Lewis, *Toronto Directory and Street Guide for 1843-4* (Toronto: H. and W. Roswell, 1843).

39 HJ, 1 March 1840.

40 McNairn, *Capacity to Judge,* 148-51.

41 Ibid., 149 [Mackenzie's paper]; UCVA, Robinson account book, pp. 45, 80, 98, 196; Susanna Moodie, *Roughing It in the Bush: Or, Life in Canada* (London: Richard Bentley, 1852), 1:74; *Canadian Emigrant,* 24 January 1835; *Patriot and Farmers' Market,* 14 June 1836; *Correspondent and Advocate,* 11 January 1837 [ads for papers in taverns].

42 Robert M. Weir, "The Role of the Newspaper Press in the Southern Colonies on the Eve of the Revolution: An Interpretation," in *The Press and the American Revolution,* ed. Bernard Bailyn and John B. Hench (Worcester, MA: American Antiquarian Society, 1980), 99-150; Morleigh, *Life in the West: Backwood Leaves and Prairie Flowers; Rough Sketches on the Borders of the Picturesque, the Sublime and the Ridiculous. Extracts from the Note Book of Morleigh in Search of an Estate* (London: Saunders and Otley, 1842), 203, 227 [quote]; AO, RG 22-390, 10-1, Macaulay, Sandwich District, *Larwill v. O'Rielly* (1849) [Flanagan].

43 *Upper Canada Gazette,* 10 January 1807 [Moore's]; *Chatham Journal,* 18 March 1843 [Kent Society]; John Ross Robertson, *The History of Freemasonry in Canada: From its Introduction in 1749* (Toronto: Hunter, Rose, 1899); *Kingston Chronicle,* 28 April 1820 [Hibernians]; Dennis Carter-Edwards, "Cobourg: A Nineteenth-Century Response to the Worthy Poor," in *Victorian Cobourg: A Nineteenth-Century Profile,* ed. J. Petryshyn (Belleville, ON: Mika Publishing Co., 1976), 168 [relief society]; Frederick Coyne Hamil, *Lake Erie Baron: The Story of Colonel Thomas Talbot* (Toronto: Macmillan, 1955), 190-91 [vigilance companies]; Bryan D. Palmer,

Working-Class Experience: Rethinking the History of Canadian Labour, 1800-1991, 2nd ed. (Toronto: McClelland and Stewart, 1992), 58-59 [stonecutters].

44   United Church Archives, William Case Journal, 20 June 1809, pp. 37-38; John MacTaggart, *Three Years in Canada: An Account of the Actual State of the Country in 1826-7-8* (London: Henry Colburn, 1829), 2:218; James Alexander, *L'Acadie: Or, Seven Years' Explorations in British America* (London: Henry Colburn, 1849), 1:203.

45   Henry A. Giroux, *Public Spaces, Private Lives: Beyond the Culture of Cynicism* (Lanham, UK: Rowman and Littlefield, 2001).

46   "Trial of William Townsend, alias Robt. J. McHenry, at Merrittsville, Canada West," 1854, published originally in the *Hamilton Spectator,* Canadian Institute of Historical Microreproductions, Microfiche series no. 63556 [Haw's]; AO, RG 22-390, 27-5, Robinson, Sandwich District, *Joseph Bertrand dit Coté v. Felix Lafferty* (1848) [Fluete]; RG 22-390, 20-3, Robinson, Western/London districts, *Luke Teeple v. Enock Moore* (1830).

Chapter 4: Regulation and Ritual in Everyday Public Life

1   Peter Thompson, however, does not see this sociability as being so self-evident: see his introduction in *Rum Punch and Revolution: Taverngoing and Public Life in Eighteenth-Century Philadelphia,* Early American Studies (Philadelphia: University of Pennsylvania Press, 1999).

2   Richard A. Preston, ed., *Kingston Before the War of 1812: A Collection of Documents* (Toronto: University of Toronto Press for the Champlain Society, 1959), 345; for Matthew Dolsen's similar recognizance in 1792 Detroit, see Milo M. Quaife, ed., *The John Askin Papers,* Burton Historical Collection (Detroit: Detroit Public Library, 1928), 1:396.

3   Robert E. Popham, *Working Papers on the Tavern 2: Legislative History of the Ontario Tavern, 1774-1974,* Substudy 809 (Toronto: Addiction Research Foundation, 1976); William Conway Keele, *A Brief View of the Township Laws Up to the Present Time: With a Treatise on the Law and Office of Constable, the Law Relative to Landlord and Tenant, Distress for Rent, Inn-Keepers &c.* (Toronto: W.J. Coates, 1835). Historians have pointed to a generalized expansion of the Canadian state in the 1840s, of which the growth of an inspectorate was part: see Allan Greer and Ian Radforth, eds., *Colonial Leviathan: State Formation in Mid-Nineteenth-Century Canada* (Toronto: University of Toronto Press, 1992) and on the inspectorate, Bruce Curtis, *True Government by Choice Men? Inspection, Education, and State Formation in Canada West,* State and Economic Life Series 17 (Toronto: University of Toronto Press, 1992).

4   The Chatham Temperance Society published its report in the *Chatham Journal* 1, 6 (1841).

5   Library and Archives Canada (LAC), RG 5 C1, Upper Canada Sundries, Provincial Secretary's Office, correspondence, Canada West, volume 270, file 1515, J.B. Robinson to Secretary Harrison, 8 May 1843.

6   LAC, RG 5 A1, volume 130, Whitby, Excerpts from an enquiry into charges against P. McDonald, Esq., June 1833, pp. 71576-82.

7   Archives of Ontario (AO), [Ely] Playter diary, 6 July 1802 (hereafter EP); AO, RG 22-390, 3-3, Supreme Court of Ontario (SCO), Judges' Benchbooks, Macaulay, Western/Gore Districts, *K. v. John Wallington* (1835); Lambton County Archives (LCA), Henry (Harry) John Jones diary, 6 December 1841 (hereafter HJ).

8   EP, 7 July 1802; James Alexander, *L'Acadie: Or, Seven Years' Explorations in British North America* (London: Henry Colburn, 1849), 1:196-97; William Pope, *William Pope's Journal,* ed. M.A. Garland, *Western Ontario History Nuggets* 16, part 2 (London, ON: Lawson Memorial Library, University of Western Ontario, 1952), 46; HJ, 12 November 1834.

9   Edward Allen Talbot, *Five Years' Residence in the Canadas: Including a Tour Through Part of the United States of America in the Year 1823* (London: Longman, Hurst, Rees, Orme, Brown and Green, 1824), 2:20-21.

10   Morleigh, *Life in the West: Backwoods Leaves and Prairie Flowers; Rough Sketches on the Borders of the Picturesque, the Sublime, and the Ridiculous. Extracts from the Note Book of Morleigh in Search of an Estate* (London: Saunders and Otley, 1842): 228-29.

11   HJ, 21 August 1837.

12   Abel Stevens, *Life and Times of Nathan Bangs* (New York: Carlton and Porter, 1863), 143 [quote]; EP, 23 December 1805 [quote]; Talbot, *Five Years' Residence,* 28 [quote]; LAC, RG

22-390, 4-1, Macaulay, Niagara District, *Q. v. James Stevenson and John Milton* (1837) [quote]; HJ, 28 and 29 August 1841 [quote]; Upper Canada Village Archives (UCVA), Thomas Robinson account book, 1843-58, p. 110.

13 British legislation dating from the reign of George II (30 George II, c. 24) was in force in Upper Canada within a piece of colonial legislation referred to as the *Tavern Act, 1818* (U.K.) 59 Geo. III, c. 2. It banned in any house "licensed to sell any sorts of liquors ... any gaming with cards, dice, draughts, shuffle boards, mississippi or billiard tables, skittles, nine pins."

14 For example, "Huron District: Rules and Regulations for Inkeepers," 1849, Canadian Institute for Historical Microreproductions, Microfiche series, no. 52535.

15 LAC, RG 5 A1, volume 74, petition of Daniel Haskell, n.d., inserted with September-October 1825, pp. 39488-90.

16 LAC, RG 5 A1, volume 141, W.L. Mackenzie, Mayor's Office, Toronto, 5 May 1834, quote at p. 76925.

17 Robert Cellem, *Visit of His Royal Highness, The Prince of Wales, to the British North American Provinces and United States in the Year 1860* (Toronto: H. Roswell, 1861), 231. Thanks to Ian Radforth for this reference.

18 UCVA, Thomas Robinson account book, pp. 69, 106, 144, 148, 189, 224.

19 AO, RG 22-390, 21-1, Robinson, Home District, *Waugh v. Cooper* (1832) and *Underhill v. Cooper et al.* (1832); EP, 19 February and 29 June 1802.

20 Robert W. Malcolmson, *Popular Recreations in English Society, 1700-1850* (Cambridge: Cambridge University Press, 1973), 40-50, 46.

21 AO, RG 22-390, 1-8, Macaulay, Midland District, *K. v. William O'Brien, Hugh Alynne, Patrick Killette, Hanrington* (1830).

22 Peter DeLottinville, "Joe Beef of Montreal: Working-Class Culture and the Tavern, 1869-89," *Labour/Le Travail* 8/9 (Autumn 1981/Spring 1982): 9-40; HJ, 11 July 1834.

23 Joseph Pickering, *Enquiries of an Emigrant: Being the Narrative of an English Farmer from the Years 1824 to 1830* (London: Effingham Wilson, 1831), 99.

24 EP, 2 September 1805; *Niagara Herald*, 18 July 1801; Talbot, *Five Years' Residence*, 28; David Kennedy Jr., *Kennedy's Colonial Travel: A Narrative of Four Years' Tour through Australia, New Zealand, Canada, &c.* (London: Simpkin, Marshall, 1876), 386-87.

25 Edwin E. Horsey, *Kingston: A Century Ago* (Kingston, ON: Kingston Historical Society, 1938), 11, 12 [circus]; *Kingston Chronicle*, 29 September 1829 [Rowley]; *Canadian Freeman*, 19 June 1828 [caravan and musics machine]; *William Pope's Journal*, 45 [mountebank]; HJ, 24 July 1834 [O'Neill's]; *Canadian Emigrant*, 27 July 1833 [twins]; Alexander, *L'Acadie*, 196-97 [wax]; HJ, 6 August 1834 [heroes]; Pickering, *Enquiries of an Emigrant*, 45 [Yankee show]; Mary Larrat Smith, ed., *Young Mr. Smith in Upper Canada* (Toronto: University of Toronto Press, 1980), 40 [City Hotel]; "Trial of William Townsend, alias, Robt. J. McHenry, at Merrittsville, Canada West," 1854, published originally in the *Hamilton Spectator*, Canadian Institute of Historical Microreproductions, Microfiche series no. 63556, pp. 8, 16, 19 [blackface].

26 See Ann Saddlemeyer, ed., *Early Stages: Theatre in Ontario, 1800-1914*, Ontario Historical Studies Series (Toronto: University of Toronto Press, 1990), 14, 114, 176, 181-83, 297.

27 Marcel Mauss, *The Gift: Forms and Functions of Exchange in Archaic Societies*, trans. Ian Cunnison (London: Cohen and West, 1970), 41; Marianna Adler, "From Symbolic Exchange to Commodity Consumption: Anthropological Notes on Drinking as Symbolic Practice," in *Drinking: Behaviour and Belief in Modern History*, ed. Susanna Barrows and Robin Room (Berkeley: University of California Press, 1991), 376-95.

28 *Niagara Herald*, 1 August 1801. For an analysis that contextualizes the competitive aspects of treating, see B. Ann Tlusty, *Bacchus and Civic Order: The Culture of Drink in Early Modern Germany* (Charlottesville: University Press of Virginia, 2001), 123-26.

29 John Howison, *Sketches of Upper Canada: Domestic, Local and Characteristic* (Edinburgh: Oliver and Boyd, 1821), 114-15.

30 Peter Blau, *Exchange and Power in Social Life* (New York: John Wiley and Sons, 1964), 89.

31 Ibid., 111.

32 EP, 7 December 1802 and 9 July 1803; AO, RG 22-390, 3-3, Macaulay, Western/Gore District, *K. v. Robert Bird* (1835); Susanna Moodie, *Roughing It in the Bush: Or, Life in Canada* (London: Richard Bentley, 1852), 1:254.

33 Blau, *Exchange and Power,* 107.
34 University of Toronto, Thomas Fischer Rare Book Room, Charles Fothergill Collection, Fothergill, "A Few Notes Made on a Journey from Montreal through the Province of Upper Canada in February 1817," 18; AO, RG 22-390, 4-3, Macaulay, Home District, *Q. v. Bertrand Garland and Michael Murry* (1838).
35 Roy Rosenzweig, "The Rise of the Saloon," in *Rethinking Popular Culture: Contemporary Perspectives in Cultural Studies,* ed. Chandra Mukerji and Michael Schudson (Berkeley: University of California Press, 1991), 145; Craig Heron addresses the theme in *Booze: A Distilled History* (Toronto: Between the Lines, 2003), 118-19.
36 Anna Clark, *The Struggle for the Breeches: Gender and the Making of the British Working Class* (Berkeley: University of California Press, 1995), 79-82 and [quote]; Tlusty, *Bacchus and Civic Order,* 135-36.
37 HJ, 20 September, 14 February, and 17 and 31 May 1837; Craig Heron has presented similar findings regarding twentieth-century public drinking in "The Boys and Their Booze: Masculinities and Public Drinking in Working-class Hamilton, 1890-1946," *Canadian Historical Review* 86, 3 (September 2005): 424-25 and 429-30.
38 *Q. v. Bernard Garland and Michael Murry* (1838); HJ, 20 May and 16 April 1837; *John Waugh v. George Cooper* (1832) and *George Underhill v. George Cooper et al.* (1832).
39 Jan Noel, *Canada Dry: Temperance Crusades before Confederation* (Toronto: University of Toronto Press, 1995), Appendix A, "US Consumption of Spirits, 1780-1970," 227 [includes quote]; see also Reginald G. Smart and Alan C. Ogborne, *Northern Spirits: Drinking in Canada, Then and Now* (Toronto: Addiction Research Foundation, 1986), 8-16. Smart and Ogborne note that tavern numbers were "very large" prior to the temperance movement (one tavern per 478 persons), that they "promoted heavy drinking," and that licences were readily granted. On Canada, see also F.L. Barron, "The Genesis of Temperance in Ontario" (PhD diss., University of Guelph, 1976), 125. For US statistics, see W.J. Rorabaugh, *The Alcoholic Republic: An American Tradition* (New York: Oxford University Press, 1979), 15, Appendix 1 (230-31), and Table A1; George B. Wilson, *Alcohol and the Nation: A Contribution to the Study of the Liquor Problem in the United Kingdom from 1800-1935* (London: Nicholson and Nicholson, 1940), Appendix F, "Liquor Consumption in the UK," 331-33; Thomas Brennan, *Public Drinking and Popular Culture in Eighteenth-Century Paris* (Princeton, NJ: Princeton University Press, 1988), 189-91; James S. Roberts, *Drink, Temperance, and the Working Class in Nineteenth-Century Germany* (Boston, MA: Allen and Unwin, 1984), 16.
40 Heartfelt thanks to Dr. Judy Eaton, Psychology and Contemporary Studies, Wilfrid Laurier University, Brantford, for help with the formula. See Douglas McCalla, *Planting the Province: The Economic History of Upper Canada, 1784-1870,* Ontario Historical Studies Series (Toronto: University of Toronto Press, 1993), Table 12.1, "Composition of the Provincial Population ... 1825-81," 319.
41 Douglas McCalla, *Consumption Stories: Customer Purchases of Alcohol at an Upper Canadian County Store in 1808-1809 and 1828-1829* (Quebec: Centre interuniversitaire d'études québécoises, 1999); Quaife, ed., *The John Askin Papers,* 1:92; LAC, RG 5 A1, volume 17, letter, "Supplies to the Militia, " Kingston, 12 June 1813, p. 7377; Heron, *Booze,* 32; AO, Prince (Col.), John, Diary, Hiram Walker Collection, margin note, 14 April 1837.
42 AO, RG 22-390, 9-5, Macaulay, Home District, *Q. v. Bartholomew Ralph* (1848). James Logan, *Notes of a Journey (1838)* in Edwin C. Guillet, *Pioneer Inns and Taverns,* combined edition (Toronto: Ontario Publishing Co., 1954-62), 3:241. James Roberts makes this point about patterns of daily drinking in *Drink, Temperance, and the Working Class,* 16-17.
43 AO, RG 22-390, 20-3, Robinson, Western/London District, *Rex v. Ward* (1830); 47-1, Draper, Sandwich District, *Robert Elliot v. Woodbridge* (1849); 9-5, Macaulay, Home District, *Q. v. James Wilson* (1848); 47-5, Draper, Toronto District, *Q. v. Alfred Tomlinson, Horatio S. Levins, Joseph Tomlinson, Cicero Tomlinson* (1854).
44 *Stratford Beacon and Perth County Intelligencer,* 4 April 1846 [Sebach]; *Q. v. James Wilson* (1848) [Woon]; AO, Municipal records, Township of Uxbridge, Council Minutes, Report of the Inspectors of Houses of Public Entertainment, 1852 [inspectors]; and *John Waugh v. George Cooper* (1832) and *George Underhill v. George Cooper et al.* (1832) [Waugh's].

45 Toronto Public Library, Toronto Reference Library (BR), Baldwin Room, Powell Papers, L 16, "Legal Notes," *K. v. Samuel Connor* [Presentier's]; *Q. v. Alfred Tomlinson et al.* (1854) [Arnett's]; *Q. v. James Stevenson and John Milton* (1837) [Stull]; *Q. v. James Wilson* (1848) [Woon's]. On the invention of the alcoholic, see Mariana Valverde,"'Slavery from Within': The Invention of Alcoholism and the Question of Free Will," *Social History* 22, 3 (October 1997): 251-68. On the Dunkin Act, see Popham, *Working Papers,* 23-24; Whitby Archives, letter, John Vandal Ham to Jacob Byron, Whitby, 10 July 1852 (rewritten as "10 August"). My thanks to archivist Brian Winter for this information.
46 *Q. v. Bernard Garland and Michael Murry* (1838); *John Waugh v. George Cooper* (1832) and *George Underhill v. George Cooper et al.* (1832); AO, RG 22-390, 23-3, Robinson, Cornwall District, *R. v. Henry York* (1837); 20-3, Robinson, Western/London Districts, *Luke Teeple v. Enock Moore* (1830).
47 HJ, 20 January 1837; LAC, RG 5 A1, volume 130, Re Charges against Peter McDonald, Esq., with Excerpts from Minutes of Disclosure from a Court of Enquiry, Whitby, June 1833, pp. 71576-82; on binges, see Heron, *Booze,* 40-45.
48 AO, RG 22-390, 1-9, Macaulay, Midland District, *King v. John and Jane Wright* (1830); *Robert Elliot v. Woodbridge* (1849); *John Waugh v. George Cooper* (1832) and *George Underhill v. George Cooper et al.* (1832); AO, RG 22-390, 47-5, Draper, Western District (Port Sarnia), *Q. v. Michael Clancy* (1854).
49 Kevin Wamsley and Robert Kossuth, "Fighting It Out in Nineteenth-Century Upper Canada/Canada West: Masculinities and Physical Challenges in the Tavern," *Journal of Sport History* 27, 3 (Fall 2000): 405-30; Rhys Isaac, *The Transformation of Virginia, 1740-1790* (Chapel Hill: University of North Carolina Press for the Institute of Early American History and Culture, 1982), 95, 98; Brennan, *Public Drinking and Popular Culture,* 24, 74; Michael Kaplan, "New York City Tavern Violence and the Creation of a Working-Class Male Identity," *Journal of the Early Republic* 15 (Winter 1995): 591-617.
50 Isaac, *Transformation of Virginia,* 94-98. Tlusty, *Bacchus and Civic Order,* provides a more nuanced interpretation that, like mine, emphasizes the forces of order: see particularly 126-33.
51 Brennan, *Public Drinking and Popular Culture,* 24, 74.
52 Cecilia Morgan, "In Search of the Phantom Misnamed Honour: Duelling in Upper Canada," *Canadian Historical Review* 76, 4 (1995): 529-62.
53 AO, RG 22-390, 9-5, Macaulay, Home District, *Q. v. Michael Moran* (1848); *K. v. John Wallington* (1835); *Q. v. James Wilson* (1848).
54 *Q. v. Michael Moran;* AO, RG 22-390, 47-5, Draper, Toronto District, *Wilson v. O'Neil* (1854); *Q. v. James Wilson* (1848).
55 *Rex v. John Ward* (1830).
56 *Wilson v. O'Neil* (1854); *K. v. John Wallington* (1835).
57 *John Waugh v. George Cooper* (1832) and *George Underhill v. George Cooper et al.* (1832).
58 *Q. v. James Wilson* (1843).
59 *Q. v. Michael Clancy* (1854); Brennan, *Public Drinking and Popular Culture,* 24, 74.
60 Wamsley and Kossuth, "Fighting it Out in Nineteenth-Century Upper Canada/Canada West," 419, 424.
61 Craig Heron provides a useful counterpoint to the above. He locates later public drinking by working men as a practice that simultaneously exercised male privilege and sought warm male bonds to compensate for life's indignities: see "The Boys and Their Booze," 411-52.

Chapter 5: Race and Space
1 For introductory surveys of racialized relations in North America, see Olive Dickason, *Canada's First Nations: A History of Founding Peoples from Earliest Times,* 2nd ed. (Toronto: McClelland and Stewart, 1997); Robin W. Winks, *The Blacks in Canada: A History,* 2nd ed. (Montreal and Kingston: McGill-Queen's University Press, 1997). See also Jason H. Silverman, "The American Fugitive Slave in Canada: Myths and Realities," *Southern Studies: An Interdisciplinary Journal of the South* 19, 3 (1980): 215-27.
2 James W. St. George Walker, *The Black Loyalists: The Search for a Promised Land in Nova Scotia and Sierra Leone, 1783-1870,* Dalhousie African Studies Series (New York/Halifax: Africana Publishing Company/Dalhousie University Press, 1976), 85.

3 W. Jeffrey Bolster, "'To Feel Like a Man': Black Seamen in the Northern States, 1800-1860,' *Journal of American History* 76, 4 (1990): 1197.

4 Archives of Ontario (AO), [Ely] Playter diary, 25 February 1802 (hereafter EP); University of Toronto, Thomas Fischer Rare Book Room, Charles Fothergill Collection, Fothergill, "A Few Notes Made on a Journey from Montreal through the Province of Upper Canada in February 1817," 30.

5 Tony Hall, "Native Limited Identities and Newcomer Metropolitanism in Upper Canada, 1814-1867," in *Old Ontario: Essays in Honour of J.M.S. Careless,* ed. David Keane and Colin Read (Toronto: Dundurn Press, 1990), 149.

6 John Howison, *Sketches of Upper Canada* (Edinburgh: Oliver and Boyd, 1821), 180-81, 192, 165.

7 Peggy Brock, "Building Bridges: Politics and Religion in a First Nations Community," *Canadian Historical Review* 81, 1 (2000): 67-96, especially 68-70.

8 Douglas McCalla, *Planting the Province: The Economic History of Upper Canada, 1784-1870,* Ontario Historical Studies Series (Toronto: University of Toronto Press, 1993), 28, 84-85.

9 John Webster Grant, *Moon of Wintertime: Missionaries and the Indians of Canada in Encounter since 1534* (Toronto: University of Toronto Press, 1984), 86-95; Janet Chute, "A Unifying Vision: Shingwaukonse's Plan for the Future of the Great Lakes Ojibwa," *Journal of the Canadian Historical Association,* new series, 7 (1996): 55-80, especially 63-64.

10 John L. Tobias, "Protection, Civilization, Assimilation: An Outline History of Canada's Indian Policy," in *Sweet Promises: A Reader on Indian-White Relations in Canada,* ed. J.R. Miller (Toronto: University of Toronto Press, 1992), 128-30; John S. Milloy, "The Early Indian Acts: Developmental Strategy and Constitutional Change," in *Sweet Promises,* 145-54; Sally M. Weaver, "The Iroquois: The Consolidation of the Grand River Reserve in the Mid-Nineteenth Century, 1847-1875," in *Aboriginal Ontario: Historical Perspectives on the First Nations,* ed. Edward S. Rogers and Donald B. Smith, Ontario Historical Studies Series (Toronto: Dundurn Press, 1994), 182-212, especially 185, 189, 199-201; Chute, "A Unifying Vision," 55-80.

11 Sidney L. Harring, *White Man's Law: Native People in Nineteenth-Century Canadian Jurisprudence,* Osgoode Society for Canadian Legal History (Toronto: University of Toronto Press, 1998), 99-105. Chute also points to 1853 colonial legislation that denied Native access to legal counsel: "Unifying Vision," 76-77.

12 Peter C. Mancall, *Deadly Medicine: Indians and Alcohol in Early America* (Ithaca: Cornell University Press, 1995), 11-28. For contemporaries' usage of this image, see F. Laurie Barron, "Alcoholism, Indians, and the Anti-Drink Cause in the Protestant Indian Missions of Upper Canada, 1822-1850," in *As Long as the Sun Shines and Water Flows: A Reader in Canadian Native Studies,* ed. Ian A.L. Getty and Antoine S. Lussier (Vancouver: UBC Press, 1983), 191.

13 Barron, "Alcoholism, Indians, and the Anti-Drink Cause," 196-98; Mancall, *Deadly Medicine,* 103, 140.

14 Morleigh, *Life in the West: Backwood Leaves and Prairie Flowers; Rough Sketches on the Borders of the Picturesque, the Sublime and the Ridiculous. Extracts from the Note Book of Morleigh in Search of an Estate* (London: Saunders and Otley, 1842), 217.

15 Joseph Moore, "Joseph Moore's Journal: Of a Tour to Detroit, in Order to Attend a Treaty, Proposed to be Held with the Indians at Sandusky [1793]," *Historical Collections: Michigan Pioneer and Historical Society* 17 (1892): 639.

16 Jacob Lindley, "Jacob Lindley's Account of an Expedition to Detroit, 1793," *Historical Collections: Michigan Pioneer and Historical Society* 17 (1892): 566-668.

17 Ibid., 592.

18 Ibid., 591; Mary Louise Pratt, *Imperial Eyes: Travel Writing and Transculturation* (London: Routledge, 1992), 6.

19 Richard White, *The Middle Ground: Indians, Empires, and Republics in the Great Lakes Region, 1650-1815,* Cambridge Studies in North American Indian History (Cambridge: Cambridge University Press, 1991); Bruce G. Trigger, *Natives and Newcomers: Canada's "Heroic Age" Reconsidered* (Montreal and Kingston: McGill-Queen's University Press, 1985), 186, 193, 198.

20 Toronto Public Library, Toronto Reference Library, Baldwin Room (BR), Powell Papers, circuit papers, Fredricksburgh, 25 November 1805, loose leaf insert at p. 66; Adam Fergusson,

Practical Notes Made During A Tour in Canada (Edinburgh: William Blackwood, 1834), 120; Fothergill, "A Few Notes," 59.

21 Joseph Pickering, *Inquiries of an Emigrant: Being the Narrative of an English Farmer from the Years 1824 to 1830* (London: Effingham Wilson, 1831), 48; Library and Archives Canada (LAC), R3747-0-8-E, James Philips fonds, Daybook of James Philips, 1828-30 [whiskey prices]. The report of the number of deer killed seems reasonable. Missionary Peter Jones wrote in the 1840s: "I have known some good hunters in one day kill ten or fifteen deer, and have heard of others killing as many as twenty": quoted in Edward S. Rogers, "Algonquian Farmers of Southern Ontario, 1830-1945," in *Aboriginal Ontario,* ed. Rogers and Smith, 131.

22 Chatham-Kent Museum Archives, Chatham, Ontario, Matthew Dolsen journal, 2 March 1798. The account book confirms Native access to credit: see Weaver, "The Iroquois," 186-88, and McCalla, *Planting the Province,* 86. On Dolsen, see Frederick Coyne Hamil, *The Valley of the Lower Thames, 1640-1850* (Toronto: University of Toronto Press, 1951), 60-64. David Zeisberger's occasional presence among the Delaware confirms their presence. He was a Moravian missionary to the Delaware at the Thames: Grant, *Moon of Wintertime,* 73.

23 Matthew Dolsen journal, 17 October 1798; 4, 8, 12, and 15 December 1797; 12, 16, and 31 January and 13 May 1798; 24 April and 19 July 1798 [Zeisberger]. Compare entries for John Dolsen, Indian, 8 May 1799, to Innis and company purchases, 10 May 1799.

24 Matthew Dolsen journal, 4 and 28 December 1797, 17 October 1798, and 8 and 9 May 1799.

25 Kenneth Coates, "Writing First Nations into Canadian History: A Review of Recent Scholarly Works," *Canadian Historical Review* 81, 1 (2000): 112; Mancall's *Deadly Medicine* focuses on First Nations adaptations to alcohol; Robert A. Campbell, "'A Fantastic Rigmarole': Deregulating Aboriginal Drinking in British Columbia, 1945-62," *BC Studies* 141 (Spring 2004): 81-105.

26 Patrick Campbell, *Travels in the Interior Parts of North America* (Edinburgh: John Guthrie, 1793), 157. The Coffee House was a tavern that drew, through its name, on the cachet of London and Philadelphia coffee house society.

27 Mancall, *Deadly Medicine,* 72 [King George]; Lindley, "Account," 600 [Shawnee]; Mary Sophia Gapper O'Brien, *The Journals of Mary O'Brien, 1828-1838,* ed. Audrey Saunders Miller (Toronto: Macmillan of Canada, 1968), 162 [Brant]; Alan Taylor, "Captain Hendrick Aupaumut: The Dilemmas of an Intercultural Broker," *Ethnohistory,* 43, 3 (1996): 433.

28 AO, RG 22-390, 12-2, Macaulay, Western District (Chatham), *Q. v. Francis Levare* (1852).

29 Hall, "Native Limited Identities," 152; Grant, *Moon of Wintertime,* 92.

30 Patricia Jasen, *Wild Things: Nature, Culture, and Tourism in Ontario, 1790-1914* (Toronto: University of Toronto Press, 1995), 16-20, 88.

31 Michael Wayne, "The Black Population of Canada West on the Eve of the American Civil War: A Reassessment Based on the Manuscript Census of 1861," *Histoire sociale/Social History* 28, 56 (1995): 465-85.

32 Colonial legislation in 1793 gradually eliminated slavery in Upper Canada. It did not free adult slaves or their existing children. The Imperial Act of 1 August 1834 emancipated all slaves in the British Empire.

33 Daniel G. Hill, "Negroes in Toronto, 1793-1865," *Ontario History* 55, 2 (1963): 74; Claudette Knight, "Black Parents Speak: Education in Mid-Nineteenth-Century Canada West," *Ontario History* 89, 4 (1997): 277; Fred Landon, "Social Conditions among the Negroes in Upper Canada before 1865," Ontario Historical Society *Papers and Records* 22 (1925): 147-48, quoting *Voice of the Fugitive,* 21 October 1852.

34 *Canadian Emigrant* (Sandwich), 26 July 1836, emphasis in original.

35 Ibid.

36 Ibid. The *Upper Canada Albion* is non-extant.

37 On the twentieth-century and the Supreme Court's failure to uphold blacks' rights to public accommodation, see James W. St. George Walker, *"Race," Rights and the Law in the Supreme Court of Canada: Historical Case Studies,* Osgoode Society for Canadian Legal History (Waterloo, ON: Wilfrid Laurier University Press, 1992), 122-81.

38 Peter Gallego to Thomas Rolph, 1 November 1841, in C. Peter Ripley, ed., *The Black Abolitionist Papers,* vol. 2, *Canada, 1830-1865* (Chapel Hill: University of North Carolina Press,

1986): 88-89; Michael Ondaatje, *Anil's Ghost* (Toronto: McClelland and Stewart, 2000), 156 ["dirty little acts"].

39 Gallego went to the magistrates to charge Hewitt with assault. Instead, they charged Gallego, convicted him, and sentenced him to thirty days in jail because he could not pay the £5 fine. Gallego was released three days later through the intervention of a district court judge. Gallego to Rolph, 1 November 1841.

40 James Oliver Horton, *Free People of Color: Inside the African American Community* (Washington, DC: Smithsonian Institution Press, 1993), 14.

41 Walker, *Black Loyalists*, 339-42.

42 BR, Abner Miles account book, accounts of a general store and tavern, 15 and 16 September 1795 and 11 September 1796; Christine Mosser, ed., *York, Upper Canada: Minutes of Town Meetings, Lists of Inhabitants, 1793-1823* (Toronto: Metropolitan Library Board, 1984), 3, 30; Matthew Dolsen journal, 21 January, 12 March, and 14 May 1798.

43 *Canadian Emigrant*, 26 July 1834; LAC, RG 5 C1, Upper Canada Sundries, volume 270, file 1515, J.B. Robinson to the Lieutenant-Governor, Woodstock, 4 May 1843, re *Q. v. Henry van Patton;* AO, RG 22-390, 47-5, Draper, Niagara District, *Q. v. Jacobs and Burke* (1854), and 39-1, Hagerman, Western District (Sandwich), *Q. v. William Murdoch* (1843-44). According to Ernest Green, "Upper Canada's Black Defenders," Ontario Historical Society *Papers and Records,* 27 (1931): 365-91, there was no black unit barracked in Sandwich in 1841.

44 AO, RG 22-311, Surrogate Court Records, Estate Files, Essex County, 1844, file 617, Gregoire LeDuc; Michael Doucet and John C. Weaver, "Town Fathers and Urban Continuity: The Roots of Community Power and Physical Form in Hamilton, Upper Canada, in the 1830s," in *Historical Essays on Upper Canada: New Perspectives,* ed., J.K. Johnson and Bruce G. Wilson, Carleton Library Series, 146 (Ottawa: Carleton University Press, 1991), 446. AO, RG 22-113, Court of General Quarter Sessions of the Peace, tavern- and shop-licensing records, Essex County, Windsor, 1841, p. 5515 [soldiers] (hereafter cited as Windsor licensing records); *Q. v. William Murdoch* (1843-44) [black patrons]; Howison, *Sketches of Upper Canada,* 209 [French taverns].

45 *Q. v. William Murdoch* (1843-44).

46 Windsor licensing records, 1841, p. 5515; 1835, p. 5677.

47 Ibid., p. 5515.

48 Jane Rhodes, *Mary Ann Shadd Cary: The Black Press and Protest in the Nineteenth Century* (Bloomington: Indiana University Press, 1998): 103-4.

49 Bolster, "To Feel Like a Man," 1179.

50 Windsor licensing records, 1842, p. 5532.

51 In Upper Canada, one of every seven married black men had a white wife: Wayne, "The Black Population of Canada West," 479. See also Gary Collison, "'Loyal and Dutiful Subjects of Her Glorious Majesty, Queen Victoria': Fugitive Slaves in Montreal, 1850-66," *Quebec Studies* 19 (1995): 63.

52 AO, RG 22-390, 38-2, Hagerman, Niagara District, *Q. v. Henry Byron and Farrel Foy* (1841). Two members of the charivari were tried for murder and acquitted. There is confusion in the court record about the name of the dead man – he appears as both James Ferinson and William Bruce – the two men were brothers-in-law.

53 Michael Kaplan, "New York City Tavern Violence and the Creation of a Working-Class Male Identity," *Journal of the Early Republic* 15 (Winter 1995): 591-617. Stinson's tavern figured prominently in a race riot in 1852: see *St. Catharines Journal*, 1, 8 July 1852; Landon, "Social Conditions," 148; James W. St. George Walker, *A History of Blacks in Canada: A Study Guide for Teachers and Students* (Hull, QC: Minister of State for Multiculturalism, 1980), 88.

54 See Scott W. See, *Riots in New Brunswick: Orange Nativism and Social Violence in the 1840s* (Toronto: University of Toronto Press, 1993).

55 AO, RG 22-390, 1-8, Macaulay, Midland District, *K. v. William O'Brien, Hugh Alynne, Patrick Killete, Hanrington* (1830).

56 See, for example, Ruth Bleasedale, "Class Conflict in the Canals of Upper Canada in the 1840s," in *Pre-Industrial Canada, 1760-1849: Readings in Canadian Social History,* vol. 2, ed. Michael S. Cross and Gregory S. Kealey (Toronto: McClelland and Stewart, 1982), 100-41; Michael S. Cross, "The Shiners' War: Social Violence in the Ottawa Valley in the 1830s,"

Canadian Historical Review 54 (March 1973): 1-26; Peter Way, *Common Labour: Workers and the Digging of North American Canals, 1780-1860* (Cambridge: Cambridge University Press, 1993), 178-81, 193-97.

57   United Province of Canada, Appendix S, "Report of the Commissioners appointed to investigate certain Proceedings at Toronto, connected with the Election for that City ... 3 Aug. 1841, *Legislative Assembly Journals*, 1941.

58   Stratford-Perth County Archives, W.F. McCulloch to John Longworth, Stratford, 10 January 1845, "Riots at Stratford" file, typescript.

59   LAC, RG 5 A1, volume 81, Captain Matthews to the Lieutenant-Governor, Lobo, 4 August 1821, pp. 43840-43.

60   *Farmers' Journal and Welland Canal Intelligencer*, 11 July 1833.

61   Upper Canada Village Archives (UCVA), Thomas Robinson account book; Province of Canada, Board of Registration and Statistics, Census of Canada West, 1851-52, Library and Archives Canada, Ontario census returns reels, Grenville County, Town of Prescott.

62   David R. Roediger, *The Wages of Whiteness: Race and the Making of the American Working Class*, Haymarket Series in North American Politics and Culture (London/New York: Verso, 1991), 103; Walker, *Black Loyalists*, 72-77; Winks, *Blacks in Canada*, 335; Wayne, "The Black Population of Canada West," 480.

63   Petition of Nero Lyons, Windsor licensing records, 1840, p. 5490. His petition was granted. Iris Marion Young, *Justice and the Politics of Difference* (Princeton, NJ: Princeton University Press, 1990), 170-73; Fred Landon, "The Buxton Settlement in Canada," *Journal of Negro History* 3, 4 (1918): 365; Hill, "Negroes in Toronto," 80; and see Shirley J. Yee, "Gender Ideology and Black Women as Community-Builders in Ontario, 1850-70," *Canadian Historical Review* 75, 1 (1994): 53-73.

64   AO, RG 22-311, Surrogate Court Records, Estate Files, Essex County, 1801, file 20, James Donaldson; [Ely] Playter diary, 28 February and 4 and 19 March 1802; William Pope, *William Pope's Journal, 28 March 1834-11 March 1835*, ed. M.A. Garland, *Western Ontario History Nuggets* 16, part 2 (London, ON: Lawson Memorial Library, University of Western Ontario, 1952), 46; James Alexander, *L'Acadie: Or, Seven Years' Explorations in British America* (London: Henry Colburn, 1849), 135, 204; A.W.H. Rose, *Canada in 1849: Pictures of Canadian Life, Or, The Emigrant Churchman* (London: Richard Bentley, 1850), 1:136; Patrick Shirreff, *A Tour Through North America: Together with a Comprehensive View of Canada and the United States* (Edinburgh: Oliver and Boyd, 1835), 90; Edwin C. Guillet, *Pioneer Inns and Taverns*, combined edition (Toronto: Ontario Publishing Co., 1954-62), 1:194, quoting Mrs. Edward Copleston, *Canada: Why We Live in It and Why We Like It* (London: Parker and Bourn, 1861). The waiters at the Montreal House in Montreal were also black. See Collison, "Loyal and Dutiful Subjects," 60.

Chapter 6: Harry Jones, his Cronies, and the Haunts of Respectable Men

1   For example, Lynne Marks, "Religion, Leisure and Working-Class Identity," in *Labouring Lives: Work and Workers in Nineteenth-Century Ontario*, ed. Paul Craven, Ontario Historical Studies Series (Toronto: University of Toronto Press, 1995), 278-334.

2   John Webster Grant, *A Profusion of Spires: Religion in Nineteenth-Century Ontario*, Ontario Historical Studies Series (Toronto: University of Toronto Press, 1988).

3   Lambton County Archives (LCA), Henry (Harry) John Jones diary, dates quoted (hereafter HJ).

4   HJ, opening remarks, n.d. July 1841.

5   Ibid., 14 December 1842.

6   Paul Romney, "The Ordeal of William Higgins," *Ontario History* 58 (June 1975): 73.

7   *Dictionary of Canadian Biography (DCB)*, vol. 8, s.v. "Sullivan, Robert Baldwin," by Victor Loring Russell, Robert Lochiel Fraser, and Michael S. Cross.

8   HJ, 14 November 1841; See James A. Roy, *Kingston: The King's Town* (Toronto: McClelland and Stewart, 1952), 245-49.

Dr. Stewart did not keep Stewart's tavern; W.L. Stewart held the licence. See Archives of Ontario (AO), RG 22-54, Midland District Court of General Quarter Sessions of the Peace minutes, volume 8, Kingston (Frontenac), minutes (1800-49), tavern licences (1841-42), and adjourned sessions (1835-49).

9 HJ, 3 March 1840 and 10 October 1842. See also W. Stewart Wallace ed., *Macmillan Dictionary of Canadian Biography,* 4th ed. (Toronto: Macmillan of Canada, 1978), 287.

10 For the language of class, see R.D. Gidney and W.P.J. Millar, *Professional Gentlemen: The Professions in Nineteenth-Century Ontario,* Ontario Historical Studies Series (Toronto: University of Toronto Press, 1994), 203-4; Cecilia Morgan, *Public Men and Virtuous Women: The Gendered Languages of Religion and Politics in Upper Canada, 1791-1850,* Studies in Gender and History (Toronto: University of Toronto Press 1996), 19-20; David Burley, *A Particular Condition in Life: Self-Employment and Social Mobility in Mid-Victorian Brantford, Ontario* (Montreal and Kingston: McGill-Queen's University Press, 1994), 6-12; J.I. Little, *The Child Letters: Public and Private Life in a Canadian Merchant-Politician's Family, 1841-1845* (Montreal and Kingston: McGill-Queen's University Press, 1995), 5, 9, 12, 30. On the "respectable," see Peter A. Russell, *Attitudes to Social Structure and Mobility in Upper Canada, 1815-1840: "Here We Are Laird Ourselves,"* Canadian Studies 6 (Lewiston, ME: Edward Mellon Press, 1990), 77-80.

11 HJ, 15 January 1837; 5 and 9 January, 20 and 21 February, and 20 March 1840; 1 July 1841; 2 and 4 November and 12 December 1842; 5 and 6 October 1834 [the electors].

12 Both T.W. Acheson, *Saint John: The Making of a Colonial Urban Community* (Toronto: University of Toronto Press, 1985), 69, and Bryan D. Palmer, *Working-Class Experience: Rethinking the History of Canadian Labour, 1800-1991,* 2nd ed. (Toronto: McClelland and Stewart, 1992), 55, note the ban on apprentices in taverns. On student teachers, see Susan E. Houston and Alison Prentice, *Schooling and Scholars in Nineteenth-Century Ontario,* Ontario Historical Studies Series (Toronto: University of Toronto Press, 1988), 167.

13 Little, *Child Letters,* 57, 59, 76-77, 83, 108; Richard White, *Gentlemen Engineers: The Working Lives of Walter and Frank Shanley* (Toronto: University of Toronto Press, 1999), 42, 63.

14 Helen Burrowes, *Maxwell – and Henry Jones: Lambton's Communal Settlement* (Lambton County Historical Society, 1986), 6; *DCB,* vol. 8, s.v. "Jones, Henry," by George Woodcock, p. 437.

15 Because Jones read every day and began and ended most journal entries with descriptions of his reading material and his reactions to it, I have not given precise references. For everything else, see examples at HJ, 3 February 1842 [newsroom subscription in Kingston], 12 March and 19 May 1843 [Hamilton School], 16 January 1837 [Orange Order]; 18 May 1836 and 8 and 10 November 1842 [Constitutional Society]. Political observations are also frequent. For focused remarks on the dangers of republicanism, see 8 February 1842 and on Tories and Reformers, see 14 and 19 January and 13 March 1840; 26 to 29 April 1837 [duties as a Justice of the Peace]; 11 May, 14 and 18 July, and 27 September 1837 [land and house]; 9 January 1840 [room]; Church of England services are noted almost every Sunday: for Mass, see 10 July 1842; 6 March and 17 April 1842 [mixed sociability in family parlours]; 25 October 1842 [prints]; 3 June 1842 [thermometer]; 5 August 1842 [fishing]; 15 September 1841 [hunting]; 18 May 1837 [ornithology]; 28 March 1838 [taxidermy].

16 Burrowes, *Maxwell,* 2; *DCB,* vol. 8, s.v. "Henry Jones," 437; HJ, 1 January 1837.

17 HJ, 6 June, 11 November, and 7 September 1834.

18 LCA, Jones family papers, letter, H. Jones [Sr.] to Lord Seaton, 18 February 1843.

19 AO, RG 1 19-0-4, Commissioner of Crown Lands Statement Books, "List of Officers and Clerks in the Department of Crown Lands for the Year ending 31 December 1861."

20 HJ, opening remarks (n.d.) and 20 July 1841. Millwrights and bricklayers, the highest paid artisans, could earn £90 annually. See Douglas McCalla, *Planting the Province: The Economic History of Upper Canada, 1784-1870,* Ontario Historical Studies Series (Toronto: University of Toronto Press, 1993), 115.

21 P.G. Wodehouse, *A Few Quick Ones* (London: Herbert Jenkins, 1959), 112.

22 HJ, opening remarks (n.d.) July 1841. On income and respectability see Russell, *Attitudes to Social Structure,* 81.

23 AO, RG 22-54, Midland District Court of General Quarter Sessions of the Peace minutes, Kingston (Frontenac), volume 8, tavern licences (1841-42) and adjourned sessions (1835-49); *Kingston Chronicle and Gazette,* 5 December 1840.

24 Edwin C. Guillet, *Pioneer Inns and Taverns,* combined editon (Toronto: Ontario Publishing Co., 1954-62), 3:68-76; Roy, *Kingston,* 192-93, 204, 206, 226-27.

25 See the discussions below for Jones' patronage of these places. For advertisements, see *Kingston Chronicle and Gazette,* 23 September 1843 [Smith's]; 23 June 1841 [Belanger's]; 7 August 1841 [Caledonia Springs Spa]; 28 June 1843 [Bamford's].

26　HJ, 3 July 1841.
27　Margaret Angus, *The Old Stones of Kingston: Its Buildings Before 1867* (Toronto: University of Toronto Press, 1966), 78-79.
28　HJ, 1 July 1841.
29　Ibid., 15 July 1841.
30　Little, *Child Letters*, 76-77.
31　Brian S. Osborne and Donald Swainson, *Kingston: Building on the Past* (Westport, ON: Butternut Press, 1988), 113-43. The "working-classes" quote, which is from the Kingston *Daily British Whig* (28 May 1850) is at p. 119; the number of emigrants is at p. 140.
32　Adele Perry, *On the Edge of Empire: Gender, Race, and the Making of British Columbia, 1849-1871* (Toronto: University of Toronto Press, 2001), 79-96.
33　HJ, 19 January and 8 February 1840 and 8 July 1841; *DCB*, vol. 8, "Small, James Edward," by Frederick H. Armstrong, pp. 725-26.
34　HJ, 1 January 1837; Wallace, ed., *Macmillan Dictionary of Canadian Biography*, 674.
35　HJ, 1 July 1841; Hitchings' first name was Edward, according to the "Barrister's Roll of the Law Society of Upper Canada," in Frederick H. Armstrong, *Handbook of Upper Canadian Chronology*, 2nd ed., Dundurn Canadian Historical Document Series 3 (Toronto: Dundurn Press, 1985), 131.
36　HJ, 17 February 1840.
37　HJ, 4 July 1841; *DCB*, vol. 10, "Aylwin, Thomas Cushing," by André Garon.
38　HJ, 3 July 1841; in the Western District, see HJ, 29 May 1835; *DCB*, vol. 7, "Dunlop, William," by Gary Draper and Roger Hall, pp. 260-64.
39　HJ, 31 March 1840; *DCB*, vol. 11, "Hincks, Sir Francis," by William G. Ormsby, pp. 406-16.
40　HJ, 1 July 1841; for Western District, see HJ, 17 and 20 April 1837.
41　J. Keith Johnson, *Becoming Prominent: Regional Leadership in Upper Canada, 1791-1841* (Montreal and Kingston: McGill-Queen's University Press, 1989).
42　HJ, 1 and 3 July 1842; 16 August 1841; 29 November 1842.
43　Ibid., 12 May 1842.
44　Amanda Vickery, *The Gentleman's Daughter: Women's Lives in Georgian England* (New Haven: Yale University Press, 1998), 195-98, 207; Margaret Visser, *Much Depends on Dinner: The Extraordinary History and Mythology, Allure and Obsessions, Perils and Taboos, of an Ordinary Meal* (New York: Grove Press, 1987).
45　James B. Brown, *Views of Canada and the Colonists* (Edinburgh: Adam and Charles Black, 1844), 45-46.
46　HJ, 2 January 1837.
47　Upper Canada, House of Assembly, "Report of Select Committee on the Subject of Losses Sustained by Sundry Persons in Consequence of the Rebellion," Appendix 1 to 4. *Appendix to the Journal of the House of Assembly of Upper Canada*, 3rd sess., 13th Parl., 1837-38. It is possible that Linfoot inflated his claim, but it must have been believable for a good tavern at the time.
48　Jeanne Minhinnick, *At Home in Upper Canada* (Toronto: Clarke, Irwin, 1970), 200-1.
49　Peter Thompson, *Rum Punch and Revolution: Taverngoing and Public Life in Eighteenth-Century Philadelphia* (Philadelphia: University of Pennsylvania Press, 1999) is structured around the idea of tavern space as shared space.
50　HJ, 11 July 1841. I have been unable to identify Steers. There were several Steers brothers known to Jones from the Western District. For example, see HJ, 24 November 1841.
51　Ibid., 29 November 1837; 2 August and 2 July 1841.
52　Library and Archives Canada (LAC), R3747-0-8-E, James Philips fonds, Daybook of James Philips, [liquor prices]; HJ, 12 May 1842, 4 February 1843, 11 November 1842, 4 June 1843.
53　HJ, 31 July and 1 and 2 August 1841 and 18 September 1842.
54　Kingston *Chronicle* and *Gazette*, 25 January 1842; HJ, 24 January 1842. This is the same place as Stewart's tavern and billiard room. In 1842 Alex Smith (of the Royal Pavilion) transferred his tavern and billiards licences to W.L. Stewart. See AO, RG 22-54, volume 8, Kingston (Frontenac), tavern licences, 1842, no. 288.
55　HJ, 12 December 1842.

56 This was not the case when Jones lived in the Western District. He socialized regularly with both country merchants and gentlemen farmers. In Kingston, as in Toronto, he circulated among a much more occupationally defined circle, which was probably a result of critical mass rather than any conscious decision to exclude retail proprietors. Catharine Parr Traill, British gentlewoman and author, certainly counted storekeepers among the locally prominent in Peterborough, Upper Canada. See Traill, *The Backwoods of Canada: Being Letters from the Wife of an Emigrant Officer* (London: C. Knight, 1836), 81.

57 Patrick Shirreff, *A Tour Through North America* (Edinburgh: Oliver and Boyd, 1835), 161-2; Kingston *Chronicle and Gazette*, 3 July 1841; HJ, 6 March 1842; Little, *Child Letters*, 76-77.

58 HJ, 15 December 1841; 21 January 1843.

59 Ibid., 5 February 1842.

60 On the women in Western District taverns, see HJ, 20 November 1834; 1 June, 16 July, 2 and 27 September, and 27 November 1837; 9 May 1838. On Cockburn, see HJ, 26 March 1840, and George Walton, *City of Toronto and the Home District Commercial Directory and Register with Almanack for 1836-7* (Toronto: T. Dalton and W.J. Coates, 1837), 10; Kingston references are HJ, 31 October 1842, 2 September 1841, and 30 January 1843.

61 HJ, 6 and 13 November 1842; for the rakes quotes, see Morgan, *Public Men and Virtuous Women*, 168, 217.

62 HJ, 20 and 21 February 1840.

63 Janet Guildford, "Creating the Ideal Man: Middle-Class Women's Constructions of Masculinity in Nova Scotia, 1840-1880," *Acadiensis* 24, 2 (Spring 1995): 5-23. Two useful Canadian collections trace gender and its meanings in history: Joy Parr and Mark Rosenfeld, eds., *Gender and History in Canada* (Toronto: Copp Clark, 1996), and Kathryn McPherson, Cecilia Morgan, and Nancy M. Forestall, eds., *Gendered Pasts: Historical Essays in Femininity and Masculinity in Canada* (Toronto: Oxford University Press, 1999). There is an extensive literature on the formation of the middle class: major texts include Stuart M. Blumin, *The Emergence of the Middle Class: Social Experience in the American City, 1760-1900* (Cambridge: Cambridge University Press, 1989); Leonore Davidoff and Catharine Hall, *Family Fortunes: Men and Women of the English Middle Class, 1780-1850* (Chicago: University of Chicago Press, 1987); Mary P. Ryan, *Cradle of the Middle Class: The Family in Oneida County, New York, 1790-1865* (New York: Cambridge University Press, 1981). On masculinity and its middle-class forms, see Anthony E. Rotundo, *American Manhood: Transformations in Masculinity from the Revolution to the Modern Era* (New York: Basic Books, 1993), and his "Romantic Friendship: Male Intimacy and Middle-Class Youth in the Northern United States, 1800-1900," *Journal of Social History* 23 (Fall 1989): 1-25; Michael Kimmel, *Manhood in America: A Cultural History* (New York: New Press, 1996); R.W. Connell, *Masculinities* (Berkeley: University of California Press, 1995).

64 Susanna Moodie, *Life in the Clearings versus the Bush* (London: Richard Bentley, 1853).

65 HJ, 2 January 1843.

66 Craig Heron, *Booze: A Distilled History* (Toronto: Between the Lines, 2003), Preface and 6-15.

67 HJ, 19 May 1843 and 20 January 1837. On temperance, see M.A. Garland and J.J. Talman, "Pioneer Drinking Habits and the Rise of Temperance Agitation in Upper Canada Prior to 1840," Ontario Historical Society *Papers and Records* 27 (1931): 341-62; Gerald Hallowell, *Prohibition in Ontario, 1919-1923* (Ottawa: Ontario Historical Society, 1972); Glenn Lockwood, "Temperance in Upper Canada as Ethnic Subterfuge," in *Drink in Canada: Historical Essays*, ed. Cheryl Krasnick-Warsh (Montreal and Kingston: McGill-Queen's University Press, 1993), 43-91; Jan Noel, *Canada Dry: Temperance Crusades before Confederation* (Toronto: University of Toronto Press, 1995); Darren Ferry, "'To the Interests and Conscience of the Great Mass of the Community': The Evolution of Temperance Societies in Nineteenth-Century Central Canada," *Journal of the Canadian Historical Association* 14 (2003): 137-63.

68 HJ, 5 August 1842.

69 For a full and engaging analysis of this theme, see Mike Huggins and J.A. Mangan, *Disreputable Pleasures: Less Virtuous Victorians at Play* (London: Routledge, 2004).

70 LCA, Jones family papers, copy of the marriage certificate of Henry (Harry) John Jones and Harriet Robinson Hall; see also HJ, 25 September 1860.

71 For a discussion that includes consideration of working-class men's later freedoms, see Craig Heron, "The Boys and Their Booze: Masculinities and Public Drinking in Working-Class Hamilton, 1890-1946," *Canadian Historical Review* 86, 3 (September 2005): 411-52.

Chapter 7: Public Life for Women in the Era of Separate Spheres

1   Fred Landon, ed., "The Diary of Benjamin Lundy: Written During His Journey through Upper Canada, January 1832," Ontario Historical Society *Papers and Records* 19 (1922): 127-28. The emphasis is mine.

2   Lambton County Archives (LCA), Henry (Harry) John Jones diary, 24 July 1834 (hereafter HJ).

3   Christine Stansell, in *City of Women: Sex and Class in New York City* (New York: Knopf, 1986), more so than Jones, has sympathetically portrayed the proclivity for display in dress among New York City's young working women as part pleasure, part sociability, and part a claim to independence.

4   Paisley Harris, "Gatekeeping and Remaking: The Politics of Respectability in African American Women's History and Black Feminism," *Journal of Women's History* 15, 1 (Spring 2003): 212-20; Shirley J. Yee, "Gender Ideology and Black Women as Community-Builders in Ontario, 1850-70," *Canadian Historical Review* 75, 1 (1994): 59 [Mrs. Little].

5   The classic analysis is Leonore Davidoff and Catherine Hall, *Family Fortunes: Men and Women of the English Middle Class, 1780-1850,* Women in Culture and Society (Chicago: University of Chicago Press, 1987).

6   J.M. Bumsted, *Peoples of Canada: A Pre-Confederation History,* 2nd ed. (Don Mills, ON: Oxford University Press, 2003), 322; R. Douglas Francis, Richard Jones, Donald B. Smith, *Origins: Canadian History to Confederation,* 5th ed. (Scarborough, ON: Thomson Nelson, 2004), 282; Margaret Conrad and Alvin Finkel, *History of the Canadian Peoples: Beginnings to 1867,* 4th ed. (Toronto: Pearson Longman, 2006), 383.

7   Kathy Lee Peiss, "Going Public: Women in Nineteenth-Century Cultural History," *American Literary History* 3, 4 (1991): 817. In Upper Canada, see the introductions to Cecilia Morgan, *Public Men and Virtuous Women: The Gendered Languages of Religion and Politics in Upper Canada, 1791-1850* (Toronto: University of Toronto Press, 1996), and Elizabeth Jane Errington, *Wives and Mothers, Schoolmistresses and Scullery Maids: Working Women in Upper Canada, 1790-1840* (Montreal and Kingston: McGill-Queen's Unversity Press, 1995).

Julie Roy Jeffrey, "Permeable Boundaries: Abolitionist Women and Separate Spheres," *Journal of the Early Republic* 21, 1 (Spring 2001): 80, 88, 92; Mary Kelley, "Beyond the Boundaries," *Journal of the Early Republic* 21, 1 (Spring 2001): 75, 78; Sarah Wilson, "Melville and the Architecture of Antebellum Masculinity," *American Literature* 76, 1 (2004): 60, 80; Laura McCall and Donald Yacavone, "Introduction," in *Shared Experience: Men, Women, and the History of Gender,* ed. McCall and Yacavone (New York: New York University Press, 1998), 1-2; Carol Lasser, "Beyond Separate Spheres: The Power of Public Opinion," *Journal of the Early Republic* 21, 1 (Spring 2001): 116, 121. See also Mary Louise Roberts, "True Womanhood Revisited," *Journal of Women's History* 14, 1 (2002): 150-55.

8   Toronto *Globe*, 20 February 1854; and see Madelon Powers, "Women and Public Drinking, 1890-1920 (Women in the New World)" *History Today* 45, 2 (February 1995): 46-52.

9   W. Scott Haine, *The World of the Paris Café: Sociability among the French Working Class, 1789-1914,* Johns Hopkins University Studies in Historical and Political Science (Baltimore, MD: Johns Hopkins University Press, 1996), 181, 185; Diane Kirkby, *Barmaids: A History of Women's Work in Pubs* (Cambridge: Cambridge University Press, 1997), 117; A.D.P. Van Buren, "Pioneer Annals," *Pioneer Collections: Report of the Pioneer Society of the State of Michigan* 5 (1884): 241-42 [Dow's].

10 See also Sarah Hand Meacham, "Keeping the Trade: The Persistence of Tavernkeeping among Middling Women in Colonial Virginia," *Early American Studies: An Interdisciplinary Journal* 3, 1 (Spring 2005): 140-63.

11 The following two paragraphs and all primary quotes are based on Archives of Ontario (AO), RG 22-390, 58-2, Supreme Court of Ontario (SCO), Judges' Benchbooks, Burns, Kingston [Midland District], *Shuman v. Hearn* (1853); Julia Roberts, "Taverns and Tavern-goers in Upper Canada, the 1790s to the 1850s" (PhD diss., University of Toronto, 1999), 128-31.

12 Barbara Bardes and Suzanne Gossett, *Declarations of Independence: Women and Political Power in Nineteenth-Century American Fiction* (New Brunswick, NJ: Rutgers University Press, 1990), 69, quoted in Peiss, "Going Public," 822.

13 *Canadian Emigrant,* 26 September 1834.

14 James E. Alexander, *L'Acadie, Or, Seven Years' Explorations in British America* (London: H. Colburn, 1849), 1:197.

15 Alexander, *L'Acadie,* 187-88 [robes]; Samuel Strickland, *Twenty-Seven Years in Canada West: Or, The Experiences of an Early Settler,* ed. Agnes Strickland (London: Richard Bentley, 1853), 1:142-43 [bedroom].

16 Eliza Leslie, *Miss Leslie's Behaviour Book: A Guide and Manual for Ladies* (1853; repr., Philadelphia, PA: T.B. Peterson and Brothers, 1859).

17 Leslie, *Miss Leslie's Behaviour Book,* 94 [gloves], 97 [evidently respectable], 99 [painted face, etc.], 100 [deportment], 103 [salt fish], 108 [books], 141 [reading room]; John F. Kasson, *Rudeness and Civility: Manners in Nineteenth-Century Urban America* (New York: Hill and Wang, 1990), 117-32.

18 Leslie, *Miss Leslie's Behaviour Book,* 97 [ladies' parlour]. On ladies and the meanings of their public space, see Abigail A. van Slyck, "The Lady and the Library Loafer: Gender and Public Space in Victorian America," Gendered Spaces and Aesthetics, *Winterthur Portfolio* 31, 4 (Winter 1996): 221-42.

19 Morleigh, *Life in the West: Backwood Leaves and Prairie Flowers; Rough Sketches on the Borders of the Picturesque, the Sublime and the Ridiculous. Extracts from the Note Book of Morleigh in Search of an Estate* (London: Saunders and Otley, 1842), 181 [Cataract House at Niagara Falls]; letter, 27 August 1840, extracted in G. Poulett Scrope, *Memoir of the Life of the Rights Honourable Charles Lord Sydenham* (London: J. Murray, 1843), 192-93 [Clifton]; HJ, 10 October 1841 [Chartres'].

20 Wilson, "Melville," 79.

21 Craig Heron, *Booze: A Distilled History* (Toronto: Between the Lines, 2003), 36; Bryan D. Palmer, *Working-Class Experience: Rethinking the History of Canadian Labour, 1800-1991,* 2nd ed. (Toronto: McClelland and Stewart, 1992), 102; Cheryl Krasnick-Warsh, "Introduction," *Drink in Canada: Historical Essays,* ed. Krasnick-Warsh (Montreal and Kingston: McGill-Queen's University Press, 1993), 5, 8, 12.

22 Susanna Moodie, *Roughing It in the Bush: Or, Life in Canada* (London: Richard Bentley, 1852), 1:44 [warming child]; Patrick Shirreff, *A Tour Through North America* (Edinburgh: Oliver and Boyd, 1835), 181-82 [nasty beds]; AO, Prince (Col.), John, Papers, Diaries, Hiram Walker Collection, 6 November 1836 [Mary Anne]; "Trial of William Townsend, alias, Robt. J. McHenry, at Merrittsville, Canada West," 1854, published originally in the *Hamilton Spectator,* Canadian Institute of Historical Microreproductions, Microfiche series, no. 63556 [Fleming and Grant]; Strickland, *Twenty-Seven Years,* 268-69 [Fryfogle's].

23 As examples, see Jan Noel, *Canada Dry: Temperance Crusades before Confederation* (Toronto: University of Toronto Press, 1995), 97-102 [on the temperance movement and women's participation]; Heron, *Booze,* 36, 121-28 [on conflicts with male drinking]; Krasnick-Warsh, "'Oh Lord Pour a Cordial on Her Wounded Heart': The Drinking Woman in Victorian and Edwardian Canada," in *Drink in Canada,* ed. Krasnick-Warsh, 70-91 [secret drinking]; Mary Anne Poutanen, "The Homeless, the Whore, the Drunkard, and the Disorderly: Contours of Female Vagrancy in the Montreal Courts, 1810-1842," in *Gendered Pasts: Historical Essays in Femininity and Masculinity in Canada,* ed. Kathryn McPherson, Cecilia Morgan, Nancy Forestell (Toronto: Oxford University Press, 1999), 29-47 [women's disorderly consumption].

24 Niagara Historical Society and Museum, Niagara-on-the-Lake, *Susan Raynor v. Mrs. Mellon,* Tavern-keeper, informations and complaints, no. 482.54, local legal 2, 1855C. For an analysis of similar behaviour by women in public space, see Katherine M.J. McKenna "Women's Agency in Upper Canada: Prescott's Board of Police Record, 1834-1850," *Histoire sociale/Social History* 36, 72 (November 2003): 347-70.

25 See especially, Anna Clark, *The Struggle for the Breeches: Gender and the Making of the British Working Class* (Berkeley: University of California Press, 1995), 13-87.

26 Susan Lewthwaite, "Violence, the Law, and Community in Rural Upper Canada," in *Essays in the History of Canadian Law,* vol. 5, *Crime and Criminal Justice,* ed. Jim Phillips, Tina Loo,

and Susan Lewthwaite (Toronto: University of Toronto Press for the Osgoode Society, 1991), 351 [Crudens]; AO, RG 22-390, 7-3, Macaulay, Western District, *Q. v. Peter Stover* (1843). On drink and the affirmation of familial and marital bonds, see B. Ann Tlusty, "Drinking, Family Relations, and Authority in Early Modern Germany," *Journal of Family History* 29, 3 (July 2004): 253-73.

27 Lynne Marks, "Religion, Leisure and Working-Cass Identity," in *Labouring Lives: Work and Workers in Nineteenth-Century Ontario,* ed. Paul Craven, Ontario Historical Studies Series (Toronto: University of Toronto Press, 1991), 288 [Hillas]; Library and Archives Canada (LAC), R3747-0-8-E, James Philips fonds, Daybook of James Philips, 5 March 1829; Carl Benn and Bev Hykel, *Thomas Montgomery: Portrait of a Nineteenth-Century Businessman* (Etobicoke, ON: Etobicoke Historical Board, 1980), 39, and, for more female patrons, see "Appendix O" [Grahme and Campbell]; Upper Canada Village Archives (UCVA), Thomas Robinson account book, 15 August 1844, 18 August 1847, and 31 October-16 November 1847; Peter Clark, *The English Alehouse: A Social History, 1200-1830* (London: Longman, 1983), 225, 235-36, 287-88, 311-12, 320-22, 341 [women treating]; Powers, "Women and Public Drinking," 47.

28 AO, F 4296 #1, Toronto Tavern keeper's Daybook, [1855-59]. Roach was a poor record keeper. This account book is disorganized and unpaginated. The dates suggest an ease of use that does not exist in the document; consequently, I have also supplied page locations, counting from the front: September 1858 (n.d.) (Scott on p. 175); 10 September 1858 (Cane on p. 179); 3 April 1857 (Hardin on p. 124); 13 April 1857 (Mrs. Hayden on p. 127); 20 September 1858 (Mathes on p. 176); 1 January 1856 (McDonald on p. 66); Diane Kirkby, *Barmaids,* 55 [quote] The image of Mrs. McDonald's bill at Roach's is at p. 61.

29 AO, F 4296 #1, Toronto Tavern keeper's Daybook, 3 December 1855 (McDonald and Mallowry on p. 61 and 47, respectively); 14 December 1855 (McDonald and Harrison on p. 61 and 64, respectively); 27 December 1855 (Harrison and Henry on p. 55 and 63, respectively); 23 June 1858 (Walsh and Gregory, p. 168); 20 September 1858 (Mathes and Barber p. 176 and 178, respectively); 3 April 1859 (Sinet on p. 185); 12 September 1855 (Haron on p. 31).

Also see *Canada Directory For 1857-8, Containing Names of Professional and Business Men, And the Principal Inhabitants of the Cities, Towns and Villages Throughout the Province* (Montreal: John Lovell, 1857), 761-856.

The nature of Roach's account book makes it very difficult to estimate female patronage as a percentage of the total: it is far easier to count women (with one exception, they are referred to as "Mrs.") than it is to count men. It is often impossible to know, for example, if the John Laye on one page is the same John Lackey mentioned several pages later, or whether Dave the Engineer is one of the several Daves mentioned elsewhere.

30 AO, F 4296 #1, Toronto Tavern keeper's Daybook, 2 August 1858 (Barber on p. 171); Stansell, *City of Women,* 56, 80, 95; Kathy Lee Peiss, *Cheap Amusements: Working Women and Leisure in New York City, 1880-1920* (Philadelphia, PA: Temple University Press, 1986), 28; McMaster University Archives, Mills Memorial Library, Marjorie Freeman Campbell Collection, Hamilton Police Village Minutes, 19 December 1836 [Lindly].

31 *Oxford Dictionary of National Biography,* "Lizars, William Home," by Jennifer Melville, http://www.oxforddnb.com; *Oxford Dictionary,* "Lizars, John," by Malcolm Nicolson; Roberta and Katherine MacFarlane Lizars, *In the Days of the Canada Company: The Story of the Settlement of the Huron Tract and a View of the Social Life of the Period, 1825-1850* (1896; repr., Belleville, ON: Mika Publishing, 1973), 222-26.

32 HJ, 2 September 1837.

33 Catharine Par Traill, *The Backwoods of Canada: Being Letters from the Wife of an Emigrant Officer, Illustrative of the Domestic Economy of British America* (London: M.A. Natali, 1849), 79.

34 John Bigsby, *The Shoe and Canoe: Or, Pictures of Travel in the Canadas Illustrative of their Scenery and Colonial Life; With Facts and Opinions on Emigration, State Policy and Other Points of Public Interest* (London: Chapman and Hall, 1850), 2:50-51.

35 Roberts, "Taverns and Tavern-goers," 67-72.

36 Samuel Phillips Day, *English America: Or Pictures of Canadian Places and People* (London: T. Newby, 1864), 223 [showy men]; Joseph Pickering, *Inquiries of an Emigrant: Being the Narrative of an English Farmer from the Years 1824 to 1830* (London: Effingham Wilson, 1831), 76

[ironmonger]; George Watson, *The City of Toronto and the Home District Commercial Directory and Register with Almanack and Calendar for 1836-7*, "City of Toronto Commercial Directory for 1836-7: An Alphabetical List of the Inhabitants," (Toronto: T. Dalton and W.J. Coates, 1837), 48 [tinsmith]; "Trial of William Townsend," [cooperage]; HJ, 5 June 1834 [Lawson].

37 AO, Municipal Records, Township of Uxbridge, Council Minutes, 1850-1880, n.p. Report of the Inspectors of Houses of Public Entertainment, 1852.

38 AO, RG 22-390, 39-1, Hagerman, Home District, *Samuel Reid v. John Macdonald* (1843).

39 AO, Colonel John Prince Diary, 4 April 1836, p. 96. Harry Jones lived at Freeman's at this time; therefore, for the husband, see HJ, 3 April 1837. Strickland, *Twenty-Seven Years*, 204.

40 Bruce Kercher, *Debt, Seduction, and Other Disasters: The Birth of Civil Law in Convict New South Wales* (Sydney, Australia: Federation Press, 1996), 72-73, argues that in early New South Wales married women were given tavern licences in their own names, in defiance of the doctrine of marital unity. His evidence is for 1814 and earlier. While widows were the majority of licensed women in Upper Canada, it is possible married or single women were sometimes licensed. License applications usually reveal women's marital status, but very few are extant. The Western District is an exception. There, some male and female applicants have the same surnames, and not all female names list "widow," which raises the possibility that some were, in fact, granted to married or single women, perhaps because the family kept more than one tavern. In this case, it may be that the JPs wished to know who was in charge of which tavern, but this needs further study.

41 See respective years, AO, RG 22-113, Court of General Quarter Sessions of the Peace (QS), tavern- and shop-licensing records, Essex County, Windsor.

42 AO, Prince (Col.), John, Diary, 29 March 1836 [Hawken's Hotel]. On differential licensing rates, see, for example, AO, RG 22-113, QS, tavern- and shop-licensing records, Essex County, Windsor, 1835, p. 5677; Shirreff, *A Tour Through North America*, 189-90 [Mrs. Aldego]. For Aldego/Aldego's fee, see *Appendix to the Journal of the House of Assembly of Upper Canada* (1835) (Toronto: Legislative Assembly 1836).

43 The data for the summary statements regarding widows' persistence as tavern-keepers is scattered throughout the applicable years of the *Appendix to the Journal of the Legislative Assembly of Upper Canada* and the *Appendix to the Journal of the Legislative Assembly of the Province of Canada* in the public accounts section under the heading "Tavern Licenses." For full references to these appendices, see Roberts, "Taverns and Tavern-goers," 61-72; "The Irish Hostess," *Colonial Advocate and Journal of Agriculture, Manufactures, and Commerce*, 1 July 1824 [Anderson].

44 AO, RG 22-305, Surrogate Court Records, Estate Files, York County, 1807, Paul Marraw [Marion]. For licensing details, see "Minutes of the Court of General Quarter Sessions of the Peace for the Home District, 13 March 1800 to 28 December 1811," in *Twenty-First Report of the Department of Public Records and Archives for the Province of Ontario*, ed. Alexander Fraser (Toronto, Herbert H. Ball, 1932), 64, 78, 115, 121; John Ross Robertson, *History of Freemasonry in Canada: From its Introduction in 1749, Embracing a General History of the Craft and its Origin* (Toronto: Hunter Rose, 1899), 1:77 [location]; Edith G. Firth, ed., *The Town of York 1793-1815: A Collection of Documents of Early Toronto*, Ontario Series 5 (Toronto: Champlain Society, 1962), 140, 186, 252, 281; Edith G. Firth, ed., *Town of York, 1815-1834: A Further Collection of Documents of Early Toronto*, Ontario Series 8 (Toronto: Champlain Society, 1966), xviii [uses of hotel]; *Kingston Chronicle*, 14 January 1820 [stage house].

    Jane Jordan appears in Elizabeth Jane Errington, *Wives and Mothers, Schoolmistresses and Scullery Maids: Working Women in Upper Canada, 1790-1840* (Montreal and Kingston: McGill-Queen's University Press, 1995), 192-97.

    AO, RG-305, Surrogate Court Records, Estate Files, York County, 1819, John Jordan; *Upper Canada Gazette*, 14 January 1822 [Jordan's advertisement].

45 J.K. Johnson, "Gerald Craig's *Upper Canada: The Formative Years* and the Writing of Upper Canadian History," *Ontario History* 90, 2 (Autumn 1998): 127; see HJ, 3 May 1834: "Mrs Westlake nearly talked us to death in the evening – very nearly frozen as usual – the stove would not burn – it is my belief that this is the coldest house in the world."

46 Lena Newman, *The John A. Macdonald Album* (Montreal: Tundra Books, 1974), 52-56; James A. Roy, *Kingston: The King's Town* (Toronto: McClelland and Stewart, 1952), 193; Donald

Swainson, *John A. Macdonald: The Man and the Politician* (Toronto: Oxford University Press, 1971), 41; E.B. Biggar, *Anecdotal Life of Sir John Macdonald* (Montreal: J. Lovell, 1891), 237-38.

47 For instance, Cynthia Kierner argues of the early southern United States that "when patrons gathered to read newspapers and pamphlets, to toast the king, or later to conspire against his government, businesswomen could learn from such discussions and, like poor or middling men, be politicized by them." Cynthia A. Kierner, *Beyond the Household: Women's Place in the Early South, 1700-1835* (Ithaca, NY: Cornell University Press, 1998), 19-20, 25.

48 HJ, 15 June 1834.

49 George Head, *Forest Scenes and Incidents in the Wilds of North America: Being a Diary of a Winter's Route from Halifax to the Canadas* (London: John Murray, 1829), 278 [Lake Simcoe]; University of Toronto, Thomas Fischer Rare Book Room, Charles Fothergill Collection, Fothergill, "A Few Notes Made on a Journey from Montreal through the Province of Upper Canada in February 1817," 57 [butter and cheese]; Joseph Busby, "Recollections," *Pioneer Collections: Report of the Pioneer and Historical Society of the State of Michigan*, 9 (1886): 121 [water boy]; Basil Hall, *Travels in North America in the Years 1827 and 1828* (Philadelphia, PA: Carey, Lea and Carey, 1829), 1:127 [Grand River]; AO, RG 22-390, 2-10, Macaulay, Niagara District, *King v. Charles Frier* (1834) [Goodfellow] and 42-1, Jones, Western District, *Queen v. William Vincent* (1846) [Brown]; HJ, 15 September 1833 [Drakes]; *Canadian Emigrant*, 27 (20 September 1834) [Galbraith]; HJ, 23 October 1835 [Margaret]; AO, RG 22-390, 23-3, Robinson, Cornwall District *Regina v. Henry York* (1837) [McRory]; AO, RG 22-390, 39-1, Hagerman, Western District (Sandwich), *Q. v. William Murdoch* (1843-44) [Rosa]; "Report of the Commissioners Appointed to Investigate Certain Proceedings at Toronto, Connected with the Election of that City ... 3 August, 1841," *Journal of the Legislative Assembly of the Province of Canada*, First Session, First Parliament, Appendix S (Toronto: Legislative Assembly), n.p. [Boyle and Watson]; Morleigh, *Life in the West*, 156 [Carmino's]; *Chatham Journal*, 9 December 1843 [cellar]; AO, RG 22-390, 43-5, Sullivan, Niagara District, *John Stinson v. Thomas Stinson, admin of Joseph Stinson* (1850) [Stinson's], 43-1; Sullivan, Home District *Queen v. James Eagle* (1848) [Armstrong], 47-1; Draper, Home District, *R. v. John Dolan* 1849 [Higgins]; William Chambers, *Things As They Are in America* (London and Edinburgh: William and Robert Chambers, 1854), 125 [Guelph]; AO, RG 22-1895, Essex County Coroner inquest files 1845-55, deposition of witness in relation to death of William Barclay, 14 September 1850. Formerly part of Hiram Walker Collection [little boy]; AO, RG 22-390, 47-3, Draper, Western District (Chatham) *Zimmerman v. Sexton* (1852) [Zimmerman's]; AO, Toronto Tavern keeper's Daybook, August 1854, n.d., n.p. [Kahel].

50 W.L. Bâby, *Souvenirs of the Past, with Illustrations: An instructive and amusing work, giving a correct account of the customs and habits of the pioneers of Canada* (Windsor, ON, 1896), 146-77, illustration is opposite 147.

51 Bettina Bradbury, "The Home as Workplace," in *Labouring Lives*, 429-30, 459 [quote]; Marjorie Griffen Cohen, *Women's Work: Markets and Economic Development in Nineteenth-Century Ontario*, The State and Economic Life Series 11 (Toronto: University of Toronto Press, 1988); Janet Guildford, "'Whate'er the Duty of the Hour Demands': The Work of Middle-Class Women in Halifax, 1840-1880, *Histoire sociale/Social History* 30, 59: 1-20.

52 David Gagan, "'The Prose of Life': Literary Reflections on the Family, Individual Experience, and Social Structure in Nineteenth-Century Canada," in *Interpreting Canada's Past: Before Confederation*, vol. 1, ed. J.M. Bumsted (Toronto: Oxford University Press, 1986), 308-20; John Bullen, "Hidden Workers: Child Labour and the Family Economy in Late Nineteenth-Century Urban Ontario," in *Canadian Family History: Selected Readings*, ed. Bettina Bradbury (Toronto: Copp Clark Pitman, 1992), 199-219; Bradbury, "The Home as Workplace," 429-30.

53 For a description see Errington, *Wives and Mothers*, 90-96, and *Women and Their Work in Upper Canada*, Historical Booklet 64 (Ottawa: Canadian Historical Association, 2006), 10-14.

54 Susanna Moodie, *Roughing It in the Bush*, 1: 43-44; Catharine Parr Traill, *Canadian Emigrant Housekeeper's Guide* (Montreal: J. Lovell, 1861), 92-96, 96 [quote]. On men and domesticity, see J.I. Little, *The Child Letters: Public and Private Life in a Canadian Merchant-Politician's*

Family, 1841-1845 (Montreal and Kingston: McGill-Queen's University Press, 1995), esp. 30-38; Françoise Noël, *Family Life and Sociability in Upper and Lower Canada, 1780-1870: A View from Diaries and Family Correspondence* (Montreal and Kingston: McGill-Queen's University Press, 2003).

55 Adam Fergusson, *Practical Notes Made During a Tour In Canada and a Portion of the United States in 1831: Second Edition to Which Are Now Added Notes Made During a Second Visit to Canada in 1833* (Edinburgh: William Blackwood, 1834), 118-19.

56 Shanley, quoted in McKenna, "Women's Agency in Upper Canada," 360.

57 Peter Bailey, "Parasexuality and Glamour: The Victorian Barmaid as Cultural Prototype," *Gender and History* 2 (Summer 1990): 150; Kirkby, *Barmaids,* 50 and 64.

58 Judith Fingard, *The Dark Side of Life in Victorian Halifax* (Porters Lake, NS: Pottersfield Press, 1989), 65; AO, RG 22-390, 29-5, Robinson, Kingston District, *Q. v. Rose Ann Finnegan* (1853) and 2-6, Macaulay, Kingston District, *K. v. Adonijah Edwards* (1833).

59 HJ, 20 November 1834; Mary Larratt Smith, ed., *Young Mr. Smith in Upper Canada* (Toronto: University of Toronto Press, 1980), 98; Bruce Curtis, "Mapping the Social: Notes from Jacob Keefer's Educational Tours, 1845," *Journal of Canadian Studies* 28, 2 (Summer 1993): 59.

60 On the geographies of gendered power, see, for example, Daphne Spain, *Gendered Spaces* (Chapel Hill: University of North Carolina Press, 1992); Martine Segalen, *Historical Anthropology of the Family,* trans. J.C. Whitehouse and Sarah Matthews (Cambridge: Cambridge University Press, 1986).

61 Morleigh, *Life in the West,* 165-66.

62 AO, RG 22-390, 29-5, Robinson, Kingston District, *Burnett v. Garrison* (1853).

63 Patrick J. Connor, "'The Law Should Be Her Protector': The Criminal Prosecution of Rape in Upper Canada," in *Sex Without Consent: Rape and Sexual Coercion in America,* ed. Merril D. Smith (New York: New York University Press, 2001), 113-14, 122 [stats and examples]. Since publishing this article, Connor has found evidence of ninety-four more rape cases, but he notes that these cases do not change his original conclusion. He writes that "women could be raped anywhere, and the tavern was just one of the many places in which Upper Canadian women were to be found": private communication by email, 2 January 2004; Karen Dubinsky, *Improper Advances: Rape and Heterosexual Conflict in Ontario, 1880-1929* (Chicago: University of Chicago Press, 1993), 14-16, 40. See also Constance Backhouse, *Petticoats and Prejudice: Women and Law in Nineteenth-Century Canada* (Toronto: Women's Press for the Osgoode Society, 1991), 40-111.

Afterword

1 Jane Urquhart, *Away* (Toronto: McClelland and Stewart, 1993), 240-67.

Bibliography

Archival and Library Collections

Archives of Ontario
Baldwin Papers.
Commissioner of Crown Lands Statement Books. "List of Officers and Clerks in the Department of Crown Lands for the Year ending 31 December 1861," RG 1 19-0-4.
Court Records.
–. Court of General Quarter Sessions of the Peace. Tavern- and shop-licensing records, Essex County, Windsor (formerly within Hiram Walker Collection), MS 205 Reel 6.
–. Court of Probate estate files, RG 22-155.
–. Court of Queen's Bench, Assize Minute Books, 1792-1848, RG 22-134.
–. Essex County Coroner inquest files, 1845-55, RG 22-1895.
–. Essex County Surrogate Court estate files, RG 22-311.
–. Leeds and Grenville United Counties Surrogate Court estate files, RG 22-179.
–. Midland District Court of General Quarter Sessions of the Peace Minutes, RG 22-54.
–. Supreme Court of Ontario, Judges' Benchbooks, RG 22-390.
–. Wentworth County Surrogate Court estate files, RG 22-205.
[Ely] Playter diary, 1801-53, Ely Playter fonds F 556.
Municipal Records.
–. District of Johnstown fonds. Johnstown District Census and Assessment, 1828, Bastard Township, F1721.
–. Township of Uxbridge. Council Minutes, 1850-80. Report of the Inspectors of Houses of Public Entertainment, 1852.
Prince, Colonel John. Papers. Diaries. Hiram Walker Collection, MS 656, Reel 1.
Thomas Ridout family fonds, F43.
Toronto Tavern keeper's Daybook, 1855-59, F 4296.
William Baldwin family fonds, F17.

Bibliothèque et archives nationales du Québec
Cahier de dépenses de membres d'un grand jury [Loucks ms], P1000-S3-D1321, 1797.

Chatham-Kent Museum Archives, Chatham, Ontario
Matthew Dolsen journal, 1797-99.

Lambton County Archives, Wyoming, Ontario
Henry (Harry) John Jones diary.
Jones family papers, Henry (Harry) John Jones Diary.

Library and Archives Canada, Ottawa, Ontario
James Philips fonds. Daybook of James Philips, 1828-30, R3747-0-8-E.
RG 1 E3, Executive Council Office of the Province of Upper Canada fonds.

RG 5 A1, Upper Canada Sundries, Civil Secretary's correspondence, Upper Canada and Canada West.
RG 5 C1, Provincial Secretary's Office correspondence, Canada West.

McMaster University Archives, Mills Memorial Library, Hamilton, Ontario
Marjorie Freeman Campbell Collection. Hamilton Police Village Minutes.

Niagara Historical Society and Museum, Niagara-on-the-Lake, Ontario
Legal 2, 1855C, legal information and complaints.

Stratford-Perth County Archives, Stratford, Ontario
"Riots at Stratford" file.

Thomas Fischer Rare Book Room, University of Toronto, Ontario
Charles Fothergill Collection, Papers, MS Coll. 140.

Toronto Public Library, Toronto Reference Library, Baldwin Room
Powell Papers, circuit papers, 1783-1830, L16 B85.
Abner Miles account book, daybook B, 1 September-15 December 1796. Accounts of a general store and tavern.
John G. Howard manuscript collection.

United Church Archives, Toronto, Ontario
William Case journal, 1803-9.

Upper Canada Village Archives, Upper Canada Village, Morrisburg, Ontario
Thomas Robinson account book, 1843-58.

Whitby Archives, Whitby, Ontario
Letter, John Vandal Ham to Jacob Byron, Whitby, 10 July 1852.

Newspapers

Kingston and Region
Brockville Recorder, 1830-37
Kingston Chronicle, 1819-32
Kingston *Chronicle and Gazette* and *Kingston Commercial Advertiser*, 1833-46
Kingston Gazette, 1810-19

Niagara and Region
Farmers' Journal and Welland Canal Intelligencer, 1826-35
Niagara Chronicle, 1839-54
Niagara Gleaner, 1820-37
Niagara Herald, 1801-3
Niagara Spectator, 1817-19
St. Catharines Journal, 1835-50
Upper Canada Gazette, or *American Oracle*, 1793-98

Western Region
Canadian Emigrant, 1831-37 (Sandwich)
Chatham Journal, 1841-44
Stratford Beacon and *Perth County Intelligencer*, 1855-58 (Stratford)
Western Herald and *Farmers' Magazine*, 1838-42 (Amherstburg and Sandwich)

York, Toronto, and Region
Canada Temperance Advocate, 1842
Canadian Freeman, 1825-33

Colonial Advocate and Journal of Agriculture, Manufactures, and Commerce, 1824-34
Correspondent and Advocate, 1835-37
Examiner, 1843
The Globe, 1844-55
Patriot and Farmers' Monitor, 1832-34
Upper Canada Gazette, or *American Oracle,* and *York Gazette,* 1798-1819

Other Sources

Acheson, T.W. *Saint John: The Making of a Colonial Urban Community.* Toronto: University of Toronto Press, 1985.

Adams, Mary Louise. "Almost Anything Can Happen: A Search for Sexual Discourse in the Urban Spaces of 1940s Toronto." Special issue on moral regulation, *Canadian Journal of Sociology* 19, 2 (1994): 217-32.

Adler, Marianna. "From Symbolic Exchange to Commodity Consumption: Anthropological Notes on Drinking as a Symbolic Practice." In *Drinking: Behaviour and Belief in Modern History,* edited by Susanna Barrows and Robin Room, 376-98. Berkeley and Los Angeles: University of California Press, 1991.

Alexander, James. *L'Acadie: Or, Seven Years' Explorations in British America.* 2 vols. London: Henry Colburn, 1849.

Angus, Margaret. *The Old Stones of Kingston: Its Buildings Before 1867.* Toronto: University of Toronto Press, 1966.

Armstrong, Frederick. *Handbook of Upper Canadian Chronology.* 2nd ed. Dundurn Canadian Historical Document Series 3. Toronto: Dundurn Press, 1985.

–. *Toronto: A Place of Meeting.* Burlington, ON: Ontario Historical Society and Windsor Publications, 1983.

Armstrong, J., ed. *Rowsell's City of Toronto and County of York Directory, for 1850-1.* Toronto: Henry Rowsell, 1850.

Bâby, William L. *Souvenirs of the Past, With Illustrations: An Instructive and Amusing Work Giving a Correct Account of the Customs & Habits of the Pioneers of Canada and the Surrounding Country.* Windsor, ON, 1896.

Backhouse, Constance. *Petticoats and Prejudice: Women and Law in Nineteenth-Century Canada.* Toronto: Women's Press for the Osgoode Society, 1991.

Bailey, Peter. "Parasexuality and Glamour: The Victorian Barmaid as Cultural Prototype." *Gender and History* 2, 2 (Summer 1990): 148-72.

Barber, Benjamin R. "Malled, Mauled, and Overhauled: Arresting Suburban Sprawl by Transforming Suburban Malls into Usable Civic Space." In *Public Space and Democracy,* edited by Marcel Hénaff and Tracy B. Strong, 201-20. Minneapolis: University of Minnesota Press, 2001.

Bardes, Barbara, and Suzanne Gossett. *Declarations of Independence: Women and Political Power in Nineteenth-Century American Fiction.* New Brunswick, NJ: Rutgers University Press 1990.

Barron, F. Laurie. "Alcoholism, Indians, and the Anti-Drink Cause in the Protestant Indian Missions of Upper Canada, 1822-1850." In *As Long as the Sun Shines and Water Flows: A Reader in Canadian Native Studies,* edited by Ian A.L. Getty and Antoine S. Lussier, 191-202. Vancouver: UBC Press, 1983.

–. "The Genesis of Temperance in Ontario." PhD diss., University of Guelph, 1976.

Barrows, Susanna, and Robin Room, eds. *Drinking: Behaviour and Belief in Modern History.* Berkeley and Los Angeles: University of California Press, 1991.

Bell, William. *Hints to Emigrants: In a Series of Letters from Upper Canada.* Edinburgh: Waugh and Innes, 1824.

Benn, Carl, and Bev Hykel. *Thomas Montgomery: Portrait of a Nineteenth-Century Businessman.* Etobicoke, ON: Etobicoke Historical Board, 1980.

Biggar, E.B. *Anecdotal Life of Sir John Macdonald.* Montreal: J. Lovell, 1891.

Bigsby, John. *The Shoe and Canoe: Or, Pictures of Travel in the Canadas Illustrative of their Scenery and Colonial Life; With Facts and Opinions on Emigration, State Policy and Other Points of Public Interest.* 2 vols. London: Chapman and Hall, 1850.

Blau, Peter. *Exchange and Power in Social Life*. New York: John Wiley and Sons, 1964.

Bleasedale, Ruth. "Class Conflict in the Canals of Upper Canada in the 1840s." In *Pre-Industrial Canada 1760-1849: Readings in Canadian Social History*, Vol. 2, edited by Michael S. Cross and Gregory S. Kealey, 100-41. Toronto: McClelland and Stewart, 1982.

Blocker, Jack S., and Cheryl Krasnick-Warsh, eds. "Social History of Alcohol." Special issue *Histoire sociale/Social History* 27, 54 (November 1994).

Blumin, Stuart M. *The Emergence of the Middle Class: Social Experience in the American City, 1760-1900*. Interdisciplinary Perspectives on Modern History. Cambridge: Cambridge University Press, 1989.

Bolster, W. Jeffrey. "'To Feel Like a Man': Black Seamen in the Northern States, 1800-1860." *Journal of American History* 76, 4 (1990): 1173-99.

Bradbury, Bettina, ed. *Canadian Family History: Selected Readings*. New Canadian Readings. Toronto: Copp Clark Pitman, 1992.

–. "The Home as Workplace." In *Labouring Lives: Work and Workers in Nineteenth-Century Ontario*, edited by Paul Craven, 412-78. Ontario Historical Studies Series. Toronto: University of Toronto Press, 1995.

Brennan, Thomas. *Public Drinking and Popular Culture in Eighteenth-Century Paris*. Princeton, NJ: Princeton University Press, 1988.

Brock, Peggy. "Building Bridges: Politics and Religion in a First Nations Community." *Canadian Historical Review* 81, 1 (2000): 67-96.

Brown, James B. *Views of Canada and the Colonists: Embracing the Experience of a Residence; Views of the Present State, Progress, and Prospects of the Colony; With Detailed and Practical Information for Intending Emigrants*. Edinburgh: Adam and Charles Black, 1844.

Brown's Toronto General Street Directory for 1856. Toronto: W.R. Brown for Maclear, 1856.

Buckingham, James Silk. *Canada, Nova Scotia, New Brunswick and the other British Provinces in North America: With a Plan of National Colonization*. London and Paris: Fisher, 1843.

Bullen, John. "Hidden Workers: Child Labour and the Family Economy in Late Nineteenth-Century Urban Ontario." In *Canadian Family History: Selected Readings*, edited by Bettina Bradbury, 199-219. New Canadian Readings. Toronto: Copp Clark Pitman, 1992.

Bumsted, J.M. *Peoples of Canada: A Pre-Confederation History*. 2nd ed. Don Mills, ON: Oxford University Press, 2003.

Burley, David G. *A Particular Condition in Life: Self-Employment and Social Mobility in Mid-Victorian Brantford, Ontario*. Montreal and Kingston: McGill-Queen's University Press, 1994.

Burrowes, Helen. *Maxwell – and Henry Jones: Lambton's Communal Settlement*. Lambton County Historical Society, 1986.

Busby, Joseph. "Recollections." *Pioneer Collections: Report of the Pioneer and Historical Society of the State of Michigan* 9 (1886): 121.

Bushman, Richard L. *The Refinement of America: Persons, Houses, Cities*. New York: Alfred A. Knopf, 1992.

Campbell, Patrick. *Travels in the Interior Inhabited Parts of North America in the Years 1791 and 1792*. Edinburgh: John Guthrie, 1793.

Campbell, Robert A. "'A Fantastic Rigmarole': Deregulating Aboriginal Drinking in British Columbia, 1945-62." *BC Studies* 141 (Spring 2004): 81-105.

–. *Sit Down and Drink Your Beer: Regulating Vancouver's Beer Parlours, 1925-1954*. Toronto: University of Toronto Press, 2001.

Canada Directory For 1857-8: Containing Names of Professional and Business Men, and the Principal Inhabitants In the Cities, Towns and Villages Throughout the Province. Montreal: John Lovell, 1857.

Careless, J.M.S. *The Union of the Canadas: The Growth of Canadian Institutions, 1841-1857*. Canadian Centenary Series 10. Toronto: McClelland and Stewart, 1967.

Carr, Stephen, Mark Francis, Leanne G. Rivlin, Andrew M. Stone. *Public Space*. Cambridge Series in Environment and Behavior. Cambridge: University of Cambridge Press, 1992.

Carter-Edwards, Dennis. "Cobourg: A Nineteenth-Century Response to the Worthy Poor." In *Victorian Cobourg: A Nineteenth-Century Profile*, edited by I. Petryshyn, 167-81. Belleville, ON: Mika Publishing Co., 1976.

Cavan, Sherri. *Liquor Licence: An Ethnography of Bar Behaviour*. Observations. Chicago: Aldine, 1966.

Cellem, Robert. *Visit of His Royal Highness, The Prince of Wales, to the British North American Provinces and United States in the Year 1860*. Toronto: H. Roswell, 1861.

Chambers, William. *Things As They Are in America*. London and Edinburgh: William and Robert Chambers, 1854.

Chartres, J.A. "The Capital's Provincial Eyes: London's Inns in the Early Eighteenth Century." *The London Journal* 3, 1 (1977): 24-39.

Chute, Janet. "A Unifying Vision: Shingwaukonse's Plan for the Future of the Great Lakes Ojibwa." *Journal of the Canadian Historical Association*, new series, 7 (1996): 55-80.

City of Toronto Poll Book Exhibiting a Classified List of Voters at the Late Great Contest for Responsible Government. Toronto: Lesslie Brothers, 1841.

Clark, Anna. *The Struggle for the Breeches: Gender and the Making of the British Working Class*. Berkeley: University of California Press, 1995.

Clark, Peter. *The English Alehouse: A Social History, 1200-1830*. London: Longman, 1983.

Coates, Kenneth. "Writing First Nations into Canadian History: A Review of Recent Scholarly Works." *Canadian Historical Review* 81, 1 (2000): 99-114.

Cohen, Marjorie Griffen. *Women's Work: Markets and Economic Development in Nineteenth-Century Ontario*. The State and Economic Life Series 11. Toronto: University of Toronto Press, 1988.

Cohen, Patricia Cline. "Women at Large: Travel in Antebellum America." *History Today* 44, 12 (1994): 44-51.

Collison, Gary. "'Loyal and Dutiful Subjects of Her Glorious Majesty, Queen Victoria': Fugitive Slaves in Montreal, 1850-66." *Quebec Studies* 19 (1995): 59-70.

Connell, R.W. *Masculinities*. Berkeley: University of California Press, 1995.

Connor, Patrick J. "'The Law Should Be Her Protector': The Criminal Prosecution of Rape in Upper Canada." In *Sex without Consent: Rape and Sexual Coercion in America*, edited by Merril D. Smith, 103-35. New York: New York University Press, 2001.

Conrad, Margaret, and Alvin Finkel. *History of the Canadian Peoples: Beginnings to 1867*. 4th ed. Toronto: Pearson Longman, 2006.

Conroy, David. *In Public Houses: Drink and the Revolution of Authority in Colonial Massachusetts*. Chapel Hill: University of North Carolina Press for the Institute of Early American History and Culture, 1995.

Cook, Sharon Ann. *"Through Sunshine and Shadow": The Woman's Christian Temperance Union, Evangelicalism, and Reform in Ontario, 1874-1930*. Montreal and Kingston: McGill-Queen's University Press, 1995.

Copleston, Mrs. Edward. *Canada: Why We Live in It and Why We Like It*. London: Parker and Bourn, 1861.

Craig, Gerald M. *Upper Canada: The Formative Years, 1784-1841*. Canadian Centenary Series 7. Toronto: McClelland and Stewart, 1991.

Craven, Paul, ed. *Labouring Lives: Work and Workers in Nineteenth-Century Ontario*. Ontario Historical Studies Series. Toronto: University of Toronto Press, 1995.

–. "Law and Ideology: The Toronto Police Court, 1850-80." In *Essays in the History of Canadian Law*, Vol. 2, edited by David H. Flaherty, 248-307. Toronto: University of Toronto Press, 1983.

Curtis, Bruce. "Mapping the Social: Notes from Jacob Keefer's Educational Tours, 1845," *Journal of Canadian Studies* 28, 2 (Summer 1993): 51-68.

–. *True Government by Choice Men? Inspection, Education, and State Formation in Canada West*. State and Economic Life Series 17. Toronto: University of Toronto Press, 1992.

Davidoff, Leonore, and Catherine Hall. *Family Fortunes: Men and Women of the English Middle Class, 1780-1850*. Women in Culture and Society. Chicago: University of Chicago Press, 1987.

Davies, Robertson. "Books: Tales of Our Wayside Inns." *Saturday Night* (4 January 1958): 22-23.

Davis, Donald F., and Barbara Lorenzkowski. "A Platform for Gender Tensions: Women Working and Riding on Canadian Urban Public Transit in the 1940s." *Canadian Historical Review* 79, 3 (September 1998): 431-65.

Day, Samuel Phillips. *English America: Pictures of Canadian Places and People.* 2 vols. London: T. Cautley Newby, 1864.

Decarie, Graeme. "The Prohibition Movement in Ontario, 1894-1916." PhD diss., Queen's University, 1972.

–. Review of *Booze: A Distilled History,* by Craig Heron. *Canadian Historical Review* 86, 1 (2005): 136-38.

de la Solle, Henri-François. *Memoirs of a Man of Pleasure, or, the Adventures of Versorand.* Translated by John Hill. 5th ed. London: T. Osborn, 1751.

DeLottinville, Peter. "Joe Beef of Montreal: Working-Class Culture and the Tavern, 1869-1889." *Labour/Le Travail* 8/9 (Autumn 1981/Spring 1982): 9-40.

Dickason, Olive. *Canada's First Nations: A History of Founding Peoples from Earliest Times.* 2nd ed. Toronto: McClelland and Stewart, 1997.

Dictionary of Canadian Biography. Toronto: University of Toronto Press, 1966-.

Dictionnaire des Lettres Françaises XVIVe Siècle. Vol. 4, part 2. Paris: Librairie Arthème Fayard, 1960.

"Discharged Rangers and Loyalists." *Michigan Historical Collections* 24 (1895): 177.

Doucet, Michael, and John Weaver. "Town Fathers and Urban Continuity: The Roots of Community Power and Physical Form in Hamilton, Upper Canada, in the 1830s." In *Historical Essays on Upper Canada: New Perspectives,* edited by J.K. Johnson and Bruce G. Wilson, 425-60. Carleton Library Series. Ottawa: Carleton University Press, 1991.

Drummond, Ian M. *Progress without Planning: The Economic History of Ontario from Confederation to the Second World War.* Ontario Historical Studies Series. Toronto: University of Toronto Press, 1987.

Dubinsky, Karen. *Improper Advances: Rape and Heterosexual Conflict in Ontario, 1880-1929.* Chicago: University of Chicago Press, 1993.

Duis, Perry. *The Saloon: Public Drinking in Chicago and Boston, 1880-1920.* Urbana: University of Illinois Press, 1983.

Dunlop, William "Tiger." *Statistical Sketches of Upper Canada: For the Use of Emigrants.* 2nd ed. London: John Murray, 1832.

Elliott, Bruce S. *Irish Migrants in the Canadas: A New Approach.* McGill-Queen's Studies in Ethnic History 1. Montreal and Kingston/Belfast: McGill-Queen's University Press/Belfast Institute of Irish Studies, 1987.

Errington, Elizabeth Jane. *Wives and Mothers, Schoolmistresses and Scullery Maids: Working Women in Upper Canada, 1790-1840.* Montreal and Kingston: McGill-Queen's University Press, 1995.

–. *Women and Their Work in Upper Canada,* Historical Booklet 64. Ottawa: Canadian Historical Association, 2006.

Everitt, Alan. "The English Urban Inn 1560-1760." In *Perspectives in English Urban History,* edited by Alan Everitt, 91-137. Problems in Focus Series. London: Macmillan Press, 1973.

Ex-Settler. *Canada in the Years 1832, 1833, and 1834: Containing Information and Instructions to Persons Intending to Emigrate Thither in 1835.* Dublin: Phillip Dixon Hardy, 1835.

Fergusson, Adam. *Practical Notes Made During a Tour in Canada and a Portion of the United States in 1831; Second Edition to Which Are Now Added Notes Made During a Second Visit to Canada in 1833.* Edinburgh: William Blackwood, 1834.

Fergusson, Charles B., ed. *Diary of Simeon Perkins, 1797-1803.* Publications of the Champlain Society. Toronto: Champlain Society, 1967.

Ferry, Darren. "'To the Interests and Conscience of the Great Mass of the Community': The Evolution of Temperance Societies in Nineteenth-Century Central Canada." *Journal of the Canadian Historical Association* 14 (2003): 137-63.

Fingard, Judith. *The Dark Side of Life in Victorian Halifax.* Porters Lake, NS: Pottersfield Press, 1991.

–. *Jack in Port: Sailortowns of Eastern Canada.* Social History of Canada 36. Toronto: University of Toronto Press, 1982.

Firth, Edith G., ed. *The Town of York, 1793-1815: A Collection of Documents of Early Toronto.* Ontario Series 5. Toronto: Champlain Society, 1962.

–, ed. *The Town of York, 1815-1834: A Further Collection of Documents of Early Toronto.* Ontario Series 8. Toronto: Champlain Society, 1966.

Fowler, Thomas. *The Journal of a Tour Through British America to the Falls of Niagara: Containing an Account of the Cities, Towns and Villages along the Route with Descriptions of the Country and of the Manners and Customs of the Inhabitants, &c. &c.* Aberdeen, Scotland: Lewis Smith, 1832.

Francis, R. Douglas, Richard Jones, and Donald B. Smith, *Origins: Canadian History to Confederation.* 5th ed. Scarborough, ON: Thomson Nelson, 2004.

Fraser, Alexander, ed., *Eleventh Report of the Bureau of Archives for the Province of Ontario.* Toronto: Wilgress, 1915.

–, ed. "Minutes of the Court of General Quarter Sessions of the Peace for the Home District, 13 March 1800 to 28 December 1811." In *Twenty-First Report of the Department of Public Records and Archives of Ontario, 1932,* 1-205. Toronto: Herbert H. Ball, 1932.

–, ed. "Tavern and Shop Licenses." In *Eleventh Report of the Bureau of Archives for the Province of Ontario,* 749-58, 774-75. Toronto: A.T. Wilgress, 1915.

–, ed. "Tavern and Shop Licenses." In *Tenth Report of the Bureau of Archives for the Province of Ontario,* 291-301. Toronto: L.K. Cameron, 1913.

–, ed. *Tenth Report of the Bureau of Archives for the Province of Ontario.* Toronto: L.K. Cameron, 1913.

Fraser, Robert L., ed. *Provincial Justice: Upper Canadian Portraits from the Dictionary of Canadian Biography.* Toronto: University of Toronto Press for the Osgoode Society, 1992.

Frisby, David, and Mike Featherstone, eds. *Simmel on Culture: Selected Writings.* Theory Culture and Society Series. London: Sage, 1997.

Gagan, David. *Hopeful Travellers: Families, Land, and Social Change in Mid-Victorian Peel County, Canada West.* Ontario Historical Studies Series. Toronto: University of Toronto Press, 1981.

–. "'The Prose of Life': Literary Reflections on the Family, Individual Experience, and Social Structure in Nineteenth-Century Canada." In *Interpreting Canada's Past: Before Confederation,* Vol.1, edited by J.M. Bumsted, 308-20. Toronto: Oxford University Press, 1986.

Garland, M.A., and J.J. Talman. "Pioneer Drinking Habits and the Rise of Temperance Agitation in Upper Canada Prior to 1840." *Ontario Historical Society Papers and Records* 27 (1931): 341-62.

Geikie, John C., ed. *George Stanley: Or, Life in the Woods; A Boy's Narrative of the Adventures of a Settler's Family in Canada.* London: Routledge, Warner, and Routledge, 1864.

Gidney, R.D., and W.P.J. Millar. *Professional Gentlemen: The Professions in Nineteenth-Century Ontario.* Ontario Historical Studies Series. Toronto: University of Toronto Press, 1994.

Giroux, Henry A. *Public Spaces, Private Lives: Beyond the Culture of Cynicism.* Lanham, UK: Rowman and Littlefield, 2001.

Given, Robert A. *A Story of Etobicoke: Centennial Year, 1850-1950.* N.p.: [1950?].

Goldie, John. *Diary of a Journey Through Upper Canada and Some of the New England States, 1819.* Toronto: William Tyrell, 1897.

Goldman, Lawrence, ed. *Oxford Dictionary of National Biography* [electronic resource]. Oxford: Oxford University Press, 2004.

Gourlay, Robert. *Statistical Account of Upper Canada.* Vol. 1, *Canadiana Before 1867.* 1822. Reprint, Wakefield, UK: S.R. Publishers, 1966.

Graff, Harvey J. *The Legacies of Literacy: Continuities and Contradictions in Western Culture and Society.* Bloomington: Indiana University Press, 1987.

–. "Literacy and Social Structure in Elgin County, Canada West: 1861." *Histoire sociale/Social History* 6, 11 (April 1973): 25-48.

Grant, John Webster. *Moon of Wintertime: Missionaries and the Indians of Canada in Encounter since 1534.* Toronto: University of Toronto Press, 1984.

–. *A Profusion of Spires: Religion in Nineteenth-Century Ontario.* Ontario Historical Studies Series. Toronto: University of Toronto Press, 1988.

Green, Earnest. "Upper Canada's Black Defenders." *Ontario Historical Society Papers and Records* 27 (1931): 365-91.

Greer, Allan, and Ian Radforth, eds. *Colonial Leviathan: State Formation in Mid-Nineteenth-Century Canada.* Toronto: University of Toronto Press, 1992.

Guildford, Janet. "Creating the Ideal Man: Middle-Class Women's Constructions of Masculinity in Nova Scotia, 1840-1880." *Acadiensis* 24, 2 (Spring 1995): 5-23.

–. "'Whate'er the Duty of the Hour Demands': The Work of Middle- Class Women in Halifax, 1840-1880. *Histoire sociale/Social History* 30, 59: 1-20.

Guillet, Edwin C. *Pioneer Inns and Taverns.* 5 vols. Vol. 1, *Ontario: With Detailed Reference to Metropolitan Toronto and Yonge Street.* Vol. 2, *The Province of Quebec, the Ottawa Valley and American Inns.* Vol. 3, *Quebec to Detroit.* Vol. 4, *Continuing the Detailed Coverage of Ontario with a Concluding Estimate of the Position of the Innkeeper in Community Life.* Vol. 5, *The Origin of Tavern Names and Signs in Great Britain and America.* Toronto: Edwin Guillet, 1954-62.

–. *Pioneer Inns and Taverns.* Combined edition. Toronto: Ontario Publishing Co., 1954-62.

Haine, W. Scott. *The World of the Paris Café: Sociability among the French Working Class, 1789-1914,* Johns Hopkins University Studies in Historical and Political Science. Baltimore, MD: Johns Hopkins University Press, 1996.

Hall, Basil. *Travels in North America in the Years 1827 and 1828.* 2 vols. Philadelphia, PA: Carey, Lea and Carey, 1829.

Hall, Francis. *Travels in Canada and the United States 1816 and 1817.* London: Longman, Hurst, Rees, Orme and Brown, 1818.

Hall, Tony. "Native Limited Identities and Newcomer Metropolitanism in Upper Canada, 1814-1867." In *Old Ontario: Essays in Honour of J.M.S. Careless,* edited by David Keane and Colin Read, 148-73. Toronto: Dundurn Press, 1990.

Hallowell, Gerald. *Prohibition in Ontario, 1919-1923.* Ottawa: Ontario Historical Society, 1972.

Hamil, Frederick Coyne. *Lake Erie Baron: The Story of Colonel Thomas Talbot.* Toronto: Macmillen, 1955.

Hanawalt, Barbara A. *"Of Good and Ill Repute": Gender and Social Control in Medieval England.* New York: Oxford University Press 1998.

Hand Meacham, Sarah. "Keeping the Trade: The Persistence of Tavernkeeping among Middling Women in Colonial Virginia." *Early American Studies: An Interdisciplinary Journal* 3, 1 (Spring 2005): 140-63.

Harring, Sidney L. *White Man's Law: Native People in Nineteenth-Century Canadian Jurisprudence.* Osgoode Society for Canadian Legal History. Toronto: University of Toronto Press, 1998.

Harris, Paisley. "Gatekeeping and Remaking: The Politics of Respectability in African American Women's History and Black Feminism." *Journal of Women's History* 15, 1 (Spring 2003): 212-20.

Harris, R. Cole, ed. *Historical Atlas of Canada.* Vol. 1, *From the Beginning to 1800.* Toronto: University of Toronto Press, 1987.

Harrison, Brian K. *Drink and the Victorians: The Temperance Question in England, 1815-1872.* London: Faber and Faber, 1971.

Hay, Douglas, ed. *Albion's Fatal Tree: Crime and Society in Eighteenth-Century England.* London: Allen Lane, 1975.

Head, George. *Forest Scenes and Incidents in the Wilds of North America: Being a Diary of a Winter's Route from Halifax to the Canadas during Four Month's Residence in the Woods on the Borders of Lakes Huron and Simcoe.* London: John Murray, 1829.

Heron, Craig. *Booze: A Distilled History.* Toronto: Between the Lines, 2003.

–. "The Boys and Their Booze: Masculinities and Public Drinking in Working-Class Hamilton, 1890-1946," *Canadian Historical Review* 86, 3 (September 2005): 411-52.

Hey, Valerie. *Patriarchy and Pub Culture.* Social Science Paperbacks 323. London: Tavistock Publications, 1986.

Hill, Daniel G. "Negroes in Toronto, 1793-1865." *Ontario History* 55, 2 (June 1963): 73-91.

Hinds, Anne Leone. *Pioneer Inns and Taverns of Guelph.* Waterloo-Wellington Series 2. Cheltenham, ON: Boston Mills Press, 1977.

Historical Atlas of Leeds and Grenville, Ontario, Illustrated. Kingston, Canada West: Putnam and Walling, 1861-62. Reprint, Belleville, ON: Mika, 1973.

Horsey, Edwin E. *Kingston a Century Ago*. Kingston, ON: Kingston Historical Society, 1938.

Horton, James Oliver. *Free People of Color: Inside the African American Community*. Washington, DC: Smithsonian Institution Press, 1993.

Houston, Susan E., and Alison Prentice. *Schooling and Scholars in Nineteenth-Century Ontario*. Ontario Historical Studies Series. Toronto: University of Toronto Press, 1988.

Howison, John. *Sketches of Upper Canada: Domestic, Local and Characteristic to Which Are Added Practical Details for the Information of Emigrants of Every Class; and Some Recollections of the United States of America*. Edinburgh: Oliver and Boyd, 1821.

Huggins, Mike, and J.A. Mangan. *Disreputable Pleasures: Less Virtuous Victorians at Play*. London: Routledge, 2004.

Hughes, Jeanne. "Inns and Taverns." In *Consuming Passions: Eating and Drinking Traditions in Ontario*, 93-112. Papers presented at the 101st Annual Conference of the Ontario Historical Society, May 1989, Ottawa, Ontario. Willowdale, ON: Ontario Historical Society, 1989.

"Huron District: Rules and Regulations for Innkeepers." 1849. Canadian Institute of Historical Microreproductions. Microfiche Series, no. 52535.

Huskins, Bonnie. "The Ceremonial Space of Women: Public Processions in Victorian Saint John and Halifax." In *Separate Spheres: Women's Worlds in the Nineteenth-Century Maritimes*, edited by Janet Guildford and Suzanne Morton, 145-60. Fredericton, NB: Acadiensis Press, 1994.

Innis, Harold A. *The Fur Trade in Canada: An Introduction to Canadian Economic History*. Rev. ed. Toronto: University of Toronto Press, 1956.

Innis, Mary Quayle, ed. *Mrs. Simcoe's Diary; with Illustrations from the Original Manuscript*. Toronto: Macmillan, 1965.

Isaac, Rhys. *The Transformation of Virginia, 1740-1790*. Chapel Hill: University of North Carolina Press for the Institute of Early American History and Culture, 1982.

Jameson, Anna. *Winter Studies and Summer Rambles in Canada*. 2 vols. London: Saunders and Otley, 1838.

Jasen, Patricia. *Wild Things: Nature, Culture, and Tourism in Ontario, 1790-1914*. Toronto: University of Toronto Press, 1995.

Jeffrey, Julie Roy. "Permeable Boundaries: Abolitionist Women and Separate Spheres." *Journal of the Early Republic* 21, 1 (Spring 2001): 79-93.

Johnson, J. Keith. *Becoming Prominent: Regional Leadership in Upper Canada, 1791-1841*. Montreal and Kingston: McGill-Queen's University Press, 1989.

–. "Gerald Craig's *Upper Canada: The Formative Years* and the Writing of Upper Canadian History." *Ontario History* 90, 2 (Autumn 1998): 117-133.

Johnson, Leo A. *History of the County of Ontario, 1615-1875*. Whitby, ON: County of Ontario, 1973.

Kaplan, Michael. "New York City Tavern Violence and the Creation of a Working-Class Male Identity." *Journal of the Early Republic* 15 (Winter 1995): 591-617.

Kasson, John F. *Rudeness and Civility: Manners in Nineteenth-Century Urban America*. New York: Hill and Wang, 1990.

Kealey, Gregory S. "Orangemen and the Corporation: The Politics of Class during the Union of the Canadas." In *Forging a Consensus: Historical Essays on Toronto*, edited by Victor L. Russell, 41-86. Toronto: University of Toronto Press for the Toronto Sesquicentennial Board, 1984.

Keele, William Conway. *A Brief View of the Township Laws Up To the Present Time: With a Treatise on the Law and Office of Constable, the Law Relative to Landlord and Tenant, Distress for Rent, Innkeepers &c.* Toronto: W.J. Coates, 1835.

–. *The Provincial Justice or Magistrate's Manual: Being A Complete Digest of the Criminal Law and a Compendium and General View of the Provincial Law; With Practical Forms for the Use of the Magistracy of Upper Canada*. Toronto: Upper Canada Gazette Office, 1835.

Kelley, Mary. "Beyond the Boundaries." *Journal of the Early Republic* 21, 1 (Spring 2001): 73-78.

Kennedy, David, Jr. *Kennedy's Colonial Travel: A Narrative of a Four Years' Tour through Australia, New Zealand, Canada, &c.* London: Simpkin, Marshall, 1876.

Kerber, Linda K. *Towards an Intellectual History of Women: Essays*. Gender and American Culture. Chapel Hill: University of North Carolina Press, 1997.

Kercher, Bruce. *Debt, Seduction, and Other Disasters: The Birth of Civil Law in Convict New South Wales*. Sydney, Australia: Federation Press, 1996.

Kierner, Cynthia A. *Beyond the Household: Women's Place in the Early South, 1700-1835*. Ithaca, NY: Cornell University Press, 1998.

Kimball, Fiske. *American Architecture*. 1928. Reprint, New York: AMS Press, 1970.

Kimmel, Michael. *Manhood in America: A Cultural History*. New York: New Press, 1996.

Kirkby, Diane. *Barmaids: A History of Women's Work in Pubs*. Cambridge: Cambridge University Press, 1997.

Knight, Claudette. "Black Parents Speak: Education in Mid-Nineteenth-Century Canada West." *Ontario History* 89, 4 (1997): 269-84.

Krasnick-Warsh, Cheryl, ed. *Drink in Canada: Historical Essays*. Montreal and Kingston: McGill-Queen's University Press, 1993.

–. "'Oh Lord Pour a Cordial on Her Wounded Heart': The Drinking Woman in Victorian and Edwardian Canada." In *Drink in Canada*, edited by Cheryl Krasnick-Warsh, 70-91.

Kümin, Beat. "Public Houses and Their Patrons in Early Modern Europe." In *The World of the Tavern: Public Houses in Early Modern Europe*, edited by Beat Kümin and B. Ann Tlusty, 44-62. Aldershot, UK: Ashgate Publishing, 2002.

Kümin, Beat, and B. Ann Tlusty, eds. *The World of the Tavern: Public Houses in Early Modern Europe*. Aldershot, UK: Ashgate Publishing, 2002.

Landon, Fred. "The Buxton Settlement in Canada." *Journal of Negro History* 3, 4 (1918): 360-67.

–. "Social Conditions among the Negroes in Upper Canada before 1865." Ontario Historical Society *Papers and Records* 22 (1925): 144-61.

Landon, Fred, ed. "The Diary of Benjamin Lundy: Written During His Journey Through Upper Canada, January 1832." Ontario Historical Society *Papers and Records* 19 (1922): 110-33.

Lasser, Carol. "Beyond Separate Spheres: The Power of Public Opinion." *Journal of the Early Republic* 21, 1 (Spring 2001): 115-23.

Leslie, Eliza. *Miss Leslie's Behaviour Book: A Guide and Manual for Ladies*. 1853. Reprint, Philadelphia, PA: T.B. Peterson and Brothers, 1859.

Lewis, Francis. *Toronto Directory and Street Guide for 1843-4*. Toronto: H. and W. Roswell, 1843.

Lewthwaite, Susan. "Violence, the Law, and Community in Rural Upper Canada." In *Essays in the History of Canadian Law*. Vol. 5, *Crime and Criminal Justice*, edited by Jim Phillips, Tina Loo, and Susan Lewthwaite, 353-86. Toronto: University of Toronto Press for the Osgoode Society, 1991.

Lindley, Jacob. "Jacob Lindley's Account of an Expedition to Detroit, 1793." *Historical Collections: Michigan Pioneer and Historical Society* 17 (1892): 566-68.

Little, J.I. *The Child Letters: Public and Private Life in a Canadian Merchant-Politician's Family, 1841-1845*. Montreal and Kingston: McGill-Queen's University Press, 1995.

Lizars, Robina, and Katherine MacFarlane Lizars. *In the Days of the Canada Company: The Story of the Settlement of the Huron Tract and a View of the Social Life of the Period, 1825-1850*. 1896. Reprint, Belleville, ON: Mika Publishing, 1973.

Lockwood, Glenn. "Temperance in Upper Canada as Ethnic Subterfuge?" In *Drink in Canada: Historical Essays*, edited by Cheryl Krasnick-Warsh, 43-91. Montreal and Kingston: McGill-Queen's University Press, 1993.

MacAndrew, Craig, and Robert B. Edgerton. *Drunken Comportment: A Social Explanation*. Chicago, IL: Aldine Publishing, 1969.

Mackay, Charles. *Life and Liberty in America: Or, Sketches of a Tour in the United States and Canada in 1857-8*. New York: Harper and Brothers, 1859.

Mackenzie, William Lyon. *Sketches of Canada and the United States*. London: E. Wilson, 1833.

MacTaggart, John. *Three Years in Canada: An Account of the Actual State of the Country in 1826-7-8; Comprehending its Resources, Productions, Improvements and Capabilities and*

Including Sketches of the State of Society, Advice to Emigrants, &c. 2 vols. London: Henry Colburn, 1829.

Malcolmson, Robert W. *Popular Recreations in English Society, 1700-1850.* Cambridge: Cambridge University Press, 1973.

Mancall, Peter C. *Deadly Medicine: Indians and Alcohol in Early America.* Ithaca: Cornell University Press, 1995.

Manning, Mary E. *The Inns and Hotels of Streetsville, 1824-1924.* Mississauga, ON: Streetsville Historical Society, 1977.

Marks, Lynne. "No Double Standard? Leisure, Sex, and Sin in Upper Canadian Church Discipline Records, 1800-1860." In *Gendered Pasts: Historical Essays in Femininity and Masculinity in Canada,* edited by Kathryn McPherson, Cecilia Morgan, and Nancy M. Forestall, 48-64. Toronto: Oxford University Press, 1999.

–. "Religion, Leisure and Working-Class Identity." In *Labouring Lives: Work and Workers in Nineteenth-Century Ontario,* edited by Paul Craven, 278-334. Ontario Historical Studies Series. Toronto: University of Toronto Press, 1995.

Marrus, Michael R. "Social Drinking in the Belle Époque." *Journal of Social History* 7, 2 (Winter 1974): 115-41.

Mathews, Hazel Chisholm. *Oakville and the Sixteen: The History of an Ontario Port.* Toronto: University of Toronto Press, 1953.

Mauss, Marcel. *The Gift: Forms and Functions of Exchange in Archaic Societies.* Translated by Ian Cunnison, with an introduction by E.E. Evans-Pritchard. London: Cohen and West, 1970.

McBurney, Margaret, and Mary Byers. *Tavern in the Town: Early Inns and Taverns of Ontario.* Toronto: University of Toronto Press, 1987.

McCall, Laura, and Donald Yacavone, "Introduction." In *Shared Experience: Men, Women, and the History of Gender,* edited by Laura McCall and Donald Yacavone, 1-18. New York: New York University Press, 1998.

McCalla, Douglas. *Consumption Stories: Customer Purchases of Alcohol at an Upper Canadian County Store in 1808-1809 and 1828-1829.* Quebec: Centre interuniversitaire d'études québécoises, 1999.

–. *Planting the Province: The Economic History of Upper Canada, 1784-1870.* Ontario Historical Studies Series. Toronto: University of Toronto Press, 1993.

McIlwraith, Thomas F. "Transportation in the Landscape of Early Upper Canada." In *Perspectives on Landscape and Settlement in Nineteenth Century Ontario,* edited by J. David Wood, 51-63. Carleton Library Series 91. Toronto: McClelland and Stewart/Institute of Canadian Studies, Carleton University, 1975.

McKenna, Katherine M.J. *A Life of Propriety: Anne Murray Powell and Her Family, 1775-1849.* Montreal and Kingston: McGill-Queen's University Press, 1994.

–. "Women's Agency in Upper Canada: Prescott's Board of Police Record, 1834-1850." *Histoire sociale/Social History* 36, 72 (November 2003): 347-70.

McNairn, Jeffrey L. *The Capacity to Judge: Public Opinion and Deliberative Democracy in Upper Canada, 1791-1854.* Toronto: University of Toronto Press, 2000.

McPherson, Kathryn, Cecilia Morgan, and Nancy M. Forestall, eds. *Gendered Pasts: Historical Essays in Femininity and Masculinity in Canada.* Toronto: Oxford University Press, 1999.

Merritt, Richard D. "Early Inns and Taverns: Accommodation, Fellowship, and Good Cheer." In *Capital Years: Niagara-on-the-Lake, 1792-1796,* edited by Richard Merritt, Nancy Butler, and Michael Power, 187-222. Toronto: Dundurn Press for the Niagara Historical Society, 1992.

Mika, Nick, and Helma Mika. *Splendid Heritage: Historical Buildings of Ontario.* Belleville, ON: Mika Publishing, 1992.

Miller, J.R., ed. *Sweet Promises: A Reader on Indian-White Relations in Canada.* Toronto: University of Toronto Press, 1991.

Milloy, John S. "The Early Indian Acts: Developmental Strategy and Constitutional Change." In *Sweet Promises: A Reader on Indian-White Relations in Canada,* edited by J.R. Miller, 145-54. Toronto: University of Toronto Press, 1991.

Minhinnick, Jeanne. *At Home in Upper Canada.* Toronto: Clarke, Irwin, 1970.

Moodie, Susanna. *Life in the Clearings versus the Bush.* London: Richard Bentley, 1853.

–. *Roughing It in the Bush: Or, Life in Canada.* 2 vols. London: Richard Bentley, 1852.

Moore, Joseph. "Joseph Moore's Journal: Of a Tour to Detroit, in Order to Attend a Treaty, Proposed to be Held with the Indians at Sandusky," [1793] *Historical Collections: Michigan Pioneer and Historical Society* 17 (1892): 639.

Morgan, Cecilia. *Public Men and Virtuous Women: The Gendered Languages of Religion and Politics in Upper Canada, 1791-1850.* Studies in Gender and History. Toronto: University of Toronto Press, 1996.

–. "In Search of the Phantom Misnamed Honour: Duelling in Upper Canada." *Canadian Historical Review* 76, 4 (1995): 529-62.

Morleigh. *Life in the West: Backwood Leaves and Prairie Flowers; Rough Sketches on the Borders of the Picturesque, the Sublime, and the Ridiculous. Extracts from the Note Book of Morleigh in Search of an Estate.* London: Saunders and Otley, 1842.

Morrison, Hugh. *Early American Architecture: From the First Colonial Settlements to the National Period.* New York: Oxford University Press, 1952.

Mosser, Christine, ed. *York, Upper Canada: Minutes of Town Meetings, Lists of Inhabitants, 1793-1823.* Toronto: Metropolitan Library Board, 1984.

Murray, David R. *Colonial Justice: Justice, Morality and Crime in the Niagara District, 1791-1849.* Toronto: University of Toronto Press for the Osgoode Society for Canadian Legal History, 2002.

Murray, Jean M., ed. *Newfoundland Journal of Aaron Thomas, Able Seaman in HMS Boston.* Don Mills, ON: Longmans Canada, 1968.

Need, Thomas. *Six Years in the Bush: Or, Extracts from the Journal of a Settler in Upper Canada, 1832-1838.* London: Simpkin, Marshall, 1838.

Newman, Lena. *The John A. Macdonald Album.* Montreal: Tundra Books, 1974.

Noël, Françoise. *Family Life and Sociability in Upper and Lower Canada, 1780-1870: A View from Diaries and Family Correspondence.* Montreal and Kingston: McGill-Queen's University Press, 2003.

Noel, Jan. *Canada Dry: Temperance Crusades before Confederation.* Toronto: University of Toronto Press, 1995.

Norton, Mary Beth. *Founding Mothers and Fathers: Gendered Power and the Forming of American Society.* New York: Knopf, 1996.

O'Brien, Mary Sophia Gapper. *The Journals of Mary O'Brien, 1828-1838.* Edited by Audrey Saunders Miller. Toronto: Macmillan of Canada, 1968.

Ondaatje, Michael. *Anil's Ghost.* Toronto: McClelland and Stewart, 2000.

Osborne, Brian S., and Donald Swainson. *Kingston: Building on the Past.* Westport, ON: Butternut Press, 1988.

Palmer, Bryan D. *Working-Class Experience: Rethinking the History of Canadian Labour, 1800-1991.* 2nd ed. Toronto: McClelland and Stewart, 1992.

Parr, Joy, and Mark Rosenfeld, eds. *Gender and History in Canada.* Toronto: Copp Clark, 1996.

Parr Traill, Catharine. *The Backwoods of Canada: Being Letters from the Wife of an Emigrant Officer.* London: C. Knight, 1836.

–. *Canadian Emigrant Housekeeper's Guide.* Montreal: J. Lovell, 1861.

Peiss, Kathy Lee. *Cheap Amusements: Working Women and Leisure in New York City, 1880-1920.* Philadelphia, PA: Temple University Press, 1986.

–. "Going Public: Women in Nineteenth-Century Cultural History." *American Literary History* 3, 4 (1991): 817-28.

Perry, Adele. *On the Edge of Empire: Gender, Race, and the Making of British Columbia, 1849-1871.* Toronto: University of Toronto Press, 2001.

Pickering, Joseph. *Inquiries of an Emigrant: Being the Narrative of an English Farmer from the Years 1824 to 1830; During which Period He Traversed the United States of America amd the British Province of Canada, with a View to Settle as an Emigrant.* 2nd ed. London: Effingham Wilson, 1831.

Pope, William. *William Pope's Journal, 28 March 1834-11 March 1835,* ed. M.A. Garland. *Western Ontario History Nuggets* 16, Part 2. London, ON: Lawson Memorial Library, University of Western Ontario, 1952.

Popham, Robert. *Working Papers on the Tavern 2: Legislative History of the Ontario Tavern, 1774-1974.* Substudy 809. Toronto: Addiction Research Foundation, 1976.

Potter-MacKinnon, Janice. *While the Women Only Wept: Loyalist Refugee Women in Eastern Ontario.* Montreal and Kingston: McGill-Queen's University Press, 1993.

Poutanen, Mary Anne. "The Homeless, the Whore, the Drunkard, and the Disorderly: Contours of Female Vagrancy in the Montreal Courts, 1810-1842." In *Gendered Pasts: Historical Essays in Femininity and Masculinity in Canada,* edited by Kathryn McPherson, Cecilia Morgan, and Nancy Forestell, 29-47. Toronto: Oxford University Press, 1999.

Powers, Madelon. *Faces along the Bar: Lore and the Workingman's Saloon, 1870-1920.* Historical Studies of Urban America. Chicago: University of Chicago Press, 1998.

–. "Women and Public Drinking, 1890-1920 (Women in the New World)." *History Today* 45, 2 (February 1995): 46-52.

Pratt, Mary Louise. *Imperial Eyes: Travel Writing and Transculturation.* London: Routledge, 1992.

Preston, Richard A., ed. *Kingston before the War of 1812: A Collection of Documents.* Ontario Series 3. Toronto: University of Toronto Press for Champlain Society, 1959.

Province of Canada. Board of Registration and Statistics. Census of Canada West, 1851-1852: Lennox County. Grenville County. Canada Public Archives. Ontario census returns reel.

–. Legislative Assembly. *Appendices to the Journal of the Legislative Assembly of the Province of Canada.* Public Accounts. Toronto: Legislative Assembly, various years.

–. "Report of the Commissioners Appointed to Investigate Certain Proceedings at Toronto, Connected with the Election of that City Laid before the House by Message from His Excellency the Governor General, dated Kingston 3 August, 1841." *Journal of the Legislative Assembly of the Province of Canada 1841.* First Session, First Parliament. Appendix S.

Quaife, Milo M., ed. *The John Askin Papers.* 2 vols. Burton Historical Collection 1 and 2. Detroit: Detroit Library Commission, 1928-31.

Radforth, Ian. "The Shantymen." In *Labouring Lives: Work and Workers in Nineteenth-Century Ontario,* edited by Paul Craven, 204-77. Ontario Historical Studies Series. Toronto: University of Toronto Press, 1995.

"Regulations for Innkeepers, 1818, District of Newcastle." Reproduced in *The Valley of the Trent,* Edwin C. Guillet. Toronto: Champlain Society, 1957.

"Return of Stores." *Pioneer Collections.* 2nd ed., Vol. 10. Lansing: Pioneer Society of the State of Michigan, 1908.

Rhodes, Jane. *Mary Ann Shadd Cary: The Black Press and Protest in the Nineteenth Century.* Bloomington: Indiana University Press, 1998.

Rhys, Horton. *A Theatrical Trip on a Wager: Through Canada and the United States.* London: privately printed by Charles Dudley, 1861.

Riddell, William Renwick. *Michigan under British Rule: Law and Law Courts 1760-1796.* Lansing, MI: Michigan Historical Commission, 1926.

Ripley, C. Peter. "The Ancaster 'Bloody Assizes' of 1814." Ontario Historical Society *Papers and Records* 20 (1923): 107-25.

–, ed. *The Black Abolitionist Papers.* Vol. 2, *Canada, 1830-1865.* Chapel Hill: University of North Carolina Press, 1986.

Roberts, James S. *Drink, Temperance, and the Working Class in Nineteenth-Century Germany.* Boston, MA: Allen and Unwin, 1984.

–. "The Tavern and Politics in the German Labour Movement, c. 1870-1914." In *Drinking: Behaviour and Belief in Modern History,* edited by Susanna Barrows and Robin Room, 98-111. Berkeley and Los Angeles: University of California Press, 1991.

Roberts, Julia. "'A Mixed Assemblage of Persons': Race and Tavern Space in Upper Canada." *Canadian Historical Review* 83, 1 (March 2002): 1-28.

–. "Taverns and Tavern-goers in Upper Canada, the 1790s to the 1850s." PhD diss., University of Toronto, 1999.

Roberts, Mary Louise. "True Womanhood Revisited." *Journal of Women's History* 14, 1 (2002): 150-55.

Robertson, John Ross. *The History of Freemasonry in Canada: From its Introduction in 1749, Embracing a General History of the Craft and Its Origin but more Particularly a History of the Craft in the Province of Upper Canada.* 2 vols. Toronto: Hunter Rose, 1899.

–. *Robertson's Landmarks of Toronto*. Vol. 3. 1896. Reprint, Belleville, ON: Mika Publishing, 1987.

Roediger, David R. *The Wages of Whiteness: Race and the Making of the American Working Class*. The Haymarket Series in North American Politics and Culture. London/New York: Verso, 1991.

Rogers, Edward S. "Algonquian Farmers of Southern Ontario, 1830-1945." *Aboriginal Ontario: Historical Perspectives on the First Nations*, edited by Edward S. Rogers and Donald B. Smith, 122-66. Ontario Historical Studies Series. Toronto: Dundurn Press, 1994.

Romney, Paul. "The Ordeal of William Higgins." *Ontario History* 67, 2 (June 1975): 69-89.

Rorabaugh, W.J. *The Alcoholic Republic: An American Tradition*. New York: Oxford University Press, 1979.

Rose, A.W.H. *Canada in 1849: Pictures of Canadian Life, Or, The Emigrant Churchman, by a Pioneer of the Wilderness*. 2 vols. London: Richard Bentley, 1850.

Rosenzweig, Roy. *Eight Hours for What We Will: Workers and Leisure in an Industrializing City, 1870-1970*. Interdisciplinary Perspectives on Modern History. Cambridge: Cambridge University Press, 1983.

–. "The Rise of the Saloon." *Rethinking Popular Culture: Contemporary Perspectives in Cultural Studies*, edited by Chandra Mukerji and Michael Schudson, 121-56. Berkeley: University of California Press, 1991.

Rosenzweig, Roy, and Elizabeth Blackmar. *The Park and the People: A History of Central Park*. Ithaca, NY: Cornell University Press, 1992.

Roth, Rodris. "Tea Drinking in Eighteenth-Century America: Its Etiquette and Equipage." In *Material Life in America, 1600-1860*, edited by Robert Blair St. George, 439-62. Boston, MA: Northeastern University Press, 1987.

Rotundo, Anthony E. *American Manhood: Transformations in Masculinity from the Revolution to the Modern Era*. New York: Basic Books, 1993.

–. "Romantic Friendship: Male Intimacy and Middle-Class Youth in the Northern United States, 1800-1900." *Journal of Social History* 23 (Fall 1989): 1-25.

Roy, James A. *Kingston: The King's Town*. Toronto: McClelland and Stewart, 1952.

Russell, Peter A. *Attitudes to Social Structure and Mobility in Upper Canada, 1815-1840: "Here We Are Laird Ourselves."* Canadian Studies 6. Lewiston, ME: Edward Mellon Press, 1990.

Ryan, Mary P. *Civic Wars: Democracy and Public Life in the American City during the Nineteenth Century*. Berkeley: University of California Press, 1997.

–. *Cradle of the Middle Class: The Family in Oneida County, New York, 1790-1865*. Interdisciplinary Perspectives on Modern History. Cambridge: Cambridge University Press, 1981.

Saddlemeyer, Ann, ed. *Early Stages: Theatre in Ontario, 1800-1914*. Ontario Historical Studies Series. Toronto: University of Toronto Press, 1990.

Scobey, David. "Anatomy of the Promenade: The Politics of Bourgeois Sociability in Nineteenth-Century New York." *Social History* 17, 2 (1992): 203-27.

Scrope, G. Poulett. *Memoir of the Life of the Right Honourable Charles Lord Sydenham*. London: J. Murray, 1843.

See, Scott W. *Riots in New Brunswick: Orange Nativism and Social Violence in the 1840s*. Social History of Canada 48. Toronto: University of Toronto Press, 1993.

Segalen, Martine. *Historical Anthropology of the Family*. Translated by J.C. Whitehouse and Sarah Matthews. Cambridge: Cambridge University Press, 1986.

Shields, David S. *Civil Tongues and Polite Letters in British America*. Chapel Hill: University of North Carolina Press for the Institute of Early American History and Culture , 1997.

Shirreff, Patrick. *A Tour Through North America: Together with a Comprehensive View of Canada and the United States as Adapted for Agricultural Emigration*. Edinburgh: Oliver and Boyd, 1835.

Silverman, Jason H. "The American Fugitive Slave in Canada: Myths and Realities." *Southern Studies: An Interdisciplinary Journal of the South* 19, 3 (1980): 215-27.

Small, Nora Pat. "The Search for a New Rural Order: Farmhouses in Sutton Massachusetts, 1790-1830." *William and Mary Quarterly*, third series, 53, 1 (January 1996): 67-86.

Smart, Reginald G., and Alan C. Ogborne. *Northern Spirits: Drinking in Canada, Then and Now*. Toronto: Addiction Research Foundation, 1986.

Smith, Mary Larrat, ed. *Young Mr. Smith in Upper Canada*. Toronto: University of Toronto Press, 1980.

Smyth, Adam, ed. *A Pleasing Sinne: Drink and Conviviality in Seventeenth-Century England*. New York: Boydell and Brewer, 2004.

Spain, Daphne. *Gendered Spaces*. Chapel Hill: University of North Carolina Press, 1992.

Stansbury, Phillip. *A Pedestrian Tour: Of Two Thousand Three Hundred Miles in North America to the Lakes, the Canadas, and the New England States; Performed in the Autumn of 1821*. New York: J.D. Myers and W. Smith, 1822.

Stansell, Christine. *City of Women: Sex and Class in New York City*. New York: Knopf, 1986.

Stevens, Abel. *Life and Times of Nathan Bangs*. New York: Carlton and Porter, 1863.

Strickland, Samuel. *Twenty-Seven Years in Canada West: Or, The Experiences of an Early Settler*. Edited by Agnes Strickland. 2 vols. London: Richard Bentley, 1853.

Surtees, Robert J. "Land Sessions, 1763-1830." In *Aboriginal Ontario: Historical Perspectives on the First Nations,* edited by Edward S. Rogers and Donald B. Smith, 92-121. Ontario Historical Studies Series. Toronto: Dundurn Press, 1994.

Sutherland, David A. "Race Relations in Halifax, Nova Scotia, during the Mid-Victorian Quest for Reform." *Journal of the Canadian Historical Association,* new series, 7 (1996): 35-54.

Swainson, Donald. *John A. Macdonald: The Man and the Politician*. Toronto: Oxford University Press, 1971.

Sweeney, Kevin M. "Furniture and the Domestic Environment in Wethersfield, Connecticut, 1639-1800." In *Material Life in America, 1600-1860,* edited by Robert Blair St. George, 261-90. Boston, MA: Northeastern University Press, 1987.

–. "High-Style Vernacular: Lifestyles of the Colonial Elite." In *Of Consuming Interests: The Style of Life in the Eighteenth Century – Perspectives on the American Revolution,* edited by Cary Carson, Ronald Hoffman, and Peter J. Albert, 1-58. Charlottesville: The University Press of Virginia for the United States Capitol Historical Society, 1994.

Talbot, Charles K. *Justice in Early Ontario, 1791-1840: A Study of Crime, Courts and Prisons in Upper Canada; With a Description of 1300 Original Unpublished Letters Located at the Public Archives of Canada (Upper Canada Sundries)*. Ottawa: Crimcare, 1983.

Talbot, Edward Allen. *Five Years' Residence in the Canadas: Including a Tour through Part of the United States of America In the Year 1823*. 2 vols. London: Longman, Hurst, Rees, Orme, Brown and Green, 1824.

Talman, J.J. "Travel in Ontario before the Coming of the Railway." Ontario Historical Society *Papers and Records* 29 (1933): 85-102.

Taylor, Alan. "Captain Hendrick Aupaumut: The Dilemmas of an Intercultural Broker." *Ethnohistory* 43, 3 (1996): 431-57.

Thompson, E.P. *The Making of the English Working Class*. London: Penguin Books, 1980.

Thompson, Peter. *Rum Punch and Revolution: Taverngoing and Public Life in Eighteenth-Century Philadelphia*. Early American Studies. Philadelphia: University of Pennsylvania Press, 1999.

Thorpe, Daniel B. "Doing Business in the Backcountry: Retail Trade in Colonial Rowan County, North Carolina." *William and Mary Quarterly,* third series, 48, 3 (1991): 387-408.

–. "Taverns and Tavern Culture on the Southern Colonial Frontier: Rowan County, North Carolina, 1753-1776." *Journal of Southern History* 62, 4 (1996): 661-87.

Tlusty, B. Ann. *Bacchus and Civic Order: The Culture of Drink in Early Modern Germany*. Charlottesville: University Press of Virginia, 2001.

–. "Drinking, Family Relations, and Authority in Early Modern Germany." *Journal of Family History* 29, 3 (July 2004): 253-73.

–. "Gender and Alcohol Use in Early Modern Augsburg." *Histoire sociale/Social History* 27, 54 (November 1994): 241-60.

Tobias, John L. "Protection, Civilization, Assimilation: An Outline History of Canada's Indian Policy." In *Sweet Promises: A Reader on Indian-White Relations in Canada,* edited by J.R. Miller, 127-44. Toronto: University of Toronto Press, 1991.

"Trial of William Townsend, alias, Robt. J. McHenry, at Merrittsville, Canada West." 1854. Published originally in the *Hamilton Spectator*. Canadian Institute of Historical Micro-reproductions. Microfiche series, no. 63556.

Trigger, Bruce G. *Natives and Newcomers: Canada's "Heroic Age" Reconsidered.* Montreal and Kingston: McGill-Queen's University Press, 1985.

Ulrich, Laurel Thatcher. *A Midwife's Tale: The Life of Martha Ballard, Based on her Diary, 1785-1812.* New York: Random House, 1991.

Upper Canada. House of Assembly. *Appendix to the Journal of the House of Assembly of Upper Canada.* Public Accounts. Various Years.

–. "Report of Select Committee on the Subject of Losses Sustained by Sundry Persons in Consequence of the Rebellion." *Appendix to the Journal of the House of Assembly of Upper Canada.* 3rd sess., 13th Parl., 1837-38.

Urquhart, Jane. *Away.* Toronto: McClelland and Stewart, 1993.

Valverde, Mariana. "'Slavery from Within': The Invention of Alcoholism and the Question of Free Will." *Social History* 22, 3 (October 1997): 251-68.

Van Buren, A.D.P. "Pioneer Annals." *Pioneer Collections: Report of the Pioneer Society of the State of Michigan* 5 (1884): 241-42.

van Slyck, Abigail A. "The Lady and the Library Loafer: Gender and Public Space in Victorian America." Gendered Spaces and Aesthetics. *Winterthur Portfolio* 31, 4 (Winter 1996): 221-42.

Vickery, Amanda. *The Gentleman's Daughter: Women's Lives in Georgian England.* New Haven: Yale University Press, 1998.

Visser, Margaret. *Much Depends on Dinner: The Extraordinary History and Mythology, Allure and Obsessions, Perils and Taboos, of an Ordinary Meal.* New York: Grove Press, 1987.

Walker, James W. St. George. *The Black Loyalists: The Search for a Promised Land in Nova Scotia and Sierra Leone, 1783-1870.* Dalhousie African Studies Series. New York/Halifax: Africana Publishing Company/Dalhousie University Press, 1976.

–. *A History of Blacks in Canada: A Study Guide for Teachers and Students.* Hull, QC: Minister of State for Multiculturalism, 1980.

–. *"Race," Rights and the Law in the Supreme Court of Canada: Historical Case Studies.* Osgoode Society for Canadian Legal History. Waterloo, ON: Wilfrid Laurier University Press, 1992.

Wallace, W. Stewart, ed. *Macmillan Dictionary of Canadian Biography.* 4th ed. Toronto: Macmillan of Canada, 1978.

Walton, George. "City of Toronto Commercial Directory for 1836-: An Alphabetical List of the Inhabitants." In *The City of Toronto and the Home District Commercial Directory and Register with Almanack and Calendar for 1836-7.* Toronto: T. Dalton and W.J. Coates, 1837.

Wamsley, Kevin, and Robert Kossuth. "Fighting It Out in Nineteenth-Century Upper Canada/Canada West: Masculinities and Physical Challenges in the Tavern." *Journal of Sport History* 27, 3 (Fall 2000): 405-30.

Ward, Peter. "Courtship and Social Space in Nineteenth-Century English Canada." *Canadian Historical Review* 68, 1 (1987): 35-62.

Warner, Sam Bass Jr. *The Private City: Philadelphia in Three Periods of its Growth.* Philadelphia: University of Pennsylvania Press, 1968.

Way, Peter. *Common Labour: Workers and the Digging of North American Canals, 1780-1860.* Cambridge: Cambridge University Press, 1993.

Wayne, Michael. "The Black Population of Canada West on the Eve of the American Civil War: A Reassessment Based on the Manuscript Census of 1861," *Histoire sociale/Social History* 28, 56 (1995): 465-85.

Weaver, John C. *Crimes, Constables, and Courts: Order and Transgression in a Canadian City, 1816-1870.* Montreal and Kingston: McGill-Queen's University Press, 1995.

Weaver, Sally M. "The Iroquois: The Consolidation of the Grand River Reserve in the Mid-Nineteenth Century, 1847-1875." In *Aboriginal Ontario: Historical Perspectives on the First Nations,* edited by Edward S. Rogers and Donald B. Smith, 182-212. Ontario Historical Studies Series. Toronto: Dundurn Press, 1994.

Weir, Robert M. "The Role of the Newspaper Press in the Southern Colonies on the Eve of the Revolution: An Interpretation." In *The Press and the American Revolution,* edited by Bernard Bailyn and John B. Hench, 99-150. Worcester, MA: American Antiquarian Society, 1980.

Weld, Isaac. *Travels Through the States of North America and the Provinces of Lower and Upper Canada: During the Years 1795, 1796, and 1797.* 3rd ed. 2 vols. London: John Stockdale, 1800.

West, Elliot. *The Saloon on the Rocky Mountain Mining Frontier.* Lincoln: University of Nebraska Press, 1979.

White, Richard. *Gentlemen Engineers: The Working Lives of Walter and Frank Shanley.* Toronto: University of Toronto Press, 1999.

–. *The Middle Ground: Indians, Empires, and Republics in the Great Lakes Region, 1650-1815.* Cambridge Studies in North American Indian History. Cambridge: Cambridge University Press, 1991.

Wilson, George B. *Alcohol and the Nation: A Contribution to the Study of the Liquor Problem in the United Kingdom from 1800-1935.* London: Nicholson and Nicholson, 1940.

Winks, Robin W. *The Blacks in Canada: A History.* 2nd ed. Montreal and Kingston/New Haven: McGill-Queen's University Press/Yale University Press, 1997.

Wilson, Sarah. "Melville and the Architecture of Antebellum Masculinity." *American Literature* 76, 1 (2004): 59-87.

Wodehouse, P.G. *A Few Quick Ones.* London: Herbert Jenkins, 1959.

Wood, J. David. "Population Change on an Agricultural Frontier: Upper Canada 1796-1841." In *Patterns of the Past: Interpreting Ontario's History,* edited by Roger Hall, William Westfall, and Laurel Sefton MacDowell, 55-77. Toronto: Dundurn Press, 1988.

Wood, Sumner Gilbert. *Taverns and Turnpikes of Blandford, 1735-1833.* Blandford, MA: Sumner Gilbert Wood, 1908.

Wrightson, Keith. "Alehouses, Order, and Reformation in Rural England, 1590-1660." In *Popular Culture and Class Conflict 1590-1914: Explorations in the History of Labour and Leisure,* edited by Eileen Yeo and Stephen Yeo, 1-27. Brighton, UK: Harvester Press, 1981.

Yee, Shirley J. "Gender Ideology and Black Women as Community-Builders in Ontario, 1850-70." *Canadian Historical Review* 75, 1 (1994): 53-73.

Yoder, Paton. *Taverns and Travellers: Inns of the Early Midwest.* Bloomington: Indiana University Press, 1969.

Young, Iris Marion. *Justice and the Politics of Difference.* Princeton, NJ: Princeton University Press, 1990.

Zimmerman, Johann Georg. *Solitude: Written Originally by J.G. Zimmerman to Which Are Added Notes Historical and Explanatory ...* 2 vols. London: Thomas Maiden for Vernor and Hood, J. Cuthell, J. Walker et al., 1804-05.

Index